D1594462

The Politics of Justice
and Justice Reform
in Latin America

The Politics of Justice and Justice Reform in Latin America

The Peruvian Case in Comparative Perspective

Linn A. Hammergren

Westview Press
A Member of the Perseus Books Group

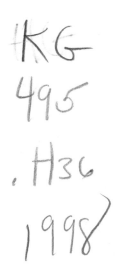

Copyright © 1998 by Westview Press, A Member of the Perseus Books Group

Published in 1998 in the United States of America by Westview Press, 5500 Central Avenue, Boulder, Colorado 80301-2877, and in the United Kingdom by Westview Press, 12 Hid's Copse Road, Cumnor Hill, Oxford OX2 9JJ

A CIP catalog record for this book is available from the Library of Congress.
ISBN 0-8133-3418-7

The paper used in this publication meets the requirements of the American National Standard for Permanence of Paper for Printed Library Materials Z39.48-1984.

10   9   8   7   6   5   4   3   2   1

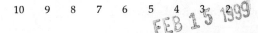

Contents

Acknowledgments

Parts of this book were researched and written over a period when I managed a series of USAID administration of justice projects in Latin America. The contract work developed my interest in and knowledge of the theme, and introduced me to many of the individuals who contributed to my further education in it. I would stress, however, that this is an independent product and in no way reflects the views of USAID. The final updating and revision coincides with a two-year fellowship from USAID's Global Center for Democracy and Governance. Although the book was not directly supported by the fellowship, it obviously benefited from the opportunity to revisit many countries and resume or initiate conversations with key informants. I am grateful to USAID and World Learning, which manages the fellowship, for this contribution, but again stress that they have no responsibility for the opinions and interpretations expressed herein. My special thanks go to World Learning staff members David Burgess, Jennifer McCaskill, and Sora Friedman, and to the center's Director and Deputy Director, Charles Costello and Jennifer Windsor.

The finished product draws on the suggestions, knowledge, and perspectives of a list of individuals too long to cite. They also are absolved of any responsibility for the use made of their contributions. At the risk of important omissions, I would like to thank specifically the following individuals. In Costa Rica, I owe a particular debt to Chief Justice Edgar Cervantes, Justices Luis Paulino Mora, Luis Fernando Solano, Daniel González, Mario Houed, Carlos Arguedas, Judges Fernando Cruz and Carmen Blanco, Alvaro Ferrandino, and Randall Quirós. In El Salvador, the list is also lengthy, but special mention goes to Sonia Delgado, Felipe Umaña, Albino Tinetti, and the nonSalvadoran members of the JRPII technical assistance team, Jorge Obando, Mark Williams, Aldo Espinoza, Gabriela Fernández, Luis Ospina, Robert Selk, Luis Chang, Ana Montes, and, again, Alvaro Ferrandino, Carmen Blanco, and Randall Quirós. All of them also provided invaluable information on other countries where they have worked. In Peru, the list is endless, but I owe a particular debt to Grimaldo Guipptons, who over the years has been a formidable guide to the changes in the judicial reform scene. Grimaldo and I obviously differ over the implications of Peru's current reform, but that is one of the fascinating aspects of the theme. I also thank Jeff Borns and Ana Sánchez, both of USAID, who facilitated my most recent trip to Peru and helped me locate old friends and make new ones. In Colombia, Lars Klassen, María Eugenia Valencia, and Madga Rocío Moreno of USAID helped identify key informants and set up interviews; Fernando Alvárez, Jaime Giraldo, Alvaro Umaña, and Oscar Flores were exceptionally generous with their time and suggestions, while from a distance, both Aldo Espinoza and Ana Montes contributed ideas. Aura Feraud and Samuel Chacón served as invaluable guides to the Panamanian situation as did Beth Hogan, Brian Tracey, Steve Uris and Tim Cornish in Guatemala, and Carl Cira, Gerardo Villalobos, Olga Larraín, and Lorena Fernández in Bolivia. I am also indebted to present and former promoters of USAID's AOJ efforts, especially James Michael, Norma Parker, Carl Cira, Fay Armstrong, and Debra McFarland. Absent their interest in the topic, and in my own potential contribution, this book would never have been written.

There is also a whole other group, some duplicating those mentioned above, who have been especially important in encouraging my enthusiasm, serving as sounding boards, and generally providing moral support when both the book and the reforms seemed to be lagging. Here I owe a special debt to friends Debra McFarland, Fay Armstrong, Carmen Blanco, Lisette Broillet, Robert Buergenthal, Erin Soto, Alfredo Cuellar, and Sharon Isralow. Finally, I thank Blair Rudes for the final editing and formatting of this manuscript, and my sister, Susan Adkins and her family for letting me occupy their guest room for weeks on end to work on the various drafts.

Linn A. Hammergren

PART ONE

Introduction

1

Justice in Latin America: Some Reflections on Its Problems and the Prospects for Reform

When Peruvian President Alberto Fujimori staged his *autogolpe* or institutional coup on April 5, 1992, closing the Congress and proposing an executive-military government by decree pending a new constitution and congressional elections, a major justification for this measure and a prime target for immediate action was the Peruvian judiciary. Charging that a Supreme Court justice could be bought for $20,000 to $50,000 and a lower level judge for as little as $5,000,[1] Fujimori depicted the court system as one of the most corrupt Peruvian institutions. He identified it as a major obstacle in his battle against terrorism and drug trafficking as well as to his efforts to implement basic socioeconomic reforms. Many observers continue to question Fujimori's motives[2] and his ability and resolve to work real changes in this or any of the institutions targeted for reform. His characterization of the Peruvian justice system, however, was apparently shared by a majority of Peruvians and had been for some time.[3] His attacks on the judiciary and his immediate dismissal of numerous key members, including most of the Supreme Court, recalled actions taken by the military government that ruled Peru from 1968 to 1980 and, if to a lesser extent, by the democratically elected government that followed. The sense of déjà vu added weight to Fujimori's accusations, but it did not bode well for the consequences of his actions. Instead, Peru's recent experience suggests that a reform strategy based only on replacing the incumbents with individuals more friendly to the administration in power will worsen rather than resolve the underlying problems. There are indications that the government itself may have reached this conclusion. Still, its subsequent entrance into more proactive reforms continues to demonstrate disturbing parallels with past efforts, and failures.

President Fujimori's criticisms and actions doubtlessly struck a sympathetic cord throughout Latin America. His methods were unusually drastic, but the situation he described to justify them would fit any number of countries. Stories of judicial corruption, or that of police, prosecutors, or private lawyers, have become commonplace in the region. Opinion polls routinely demonstrate that citizens have little expectation of fair treatment by their justice systems and that these institutions are among the least respected in the public or private sectors. Entire special vocabularies have evolved to describe the most common "irregular practices"—the Salvadoran *sacadores* or lawyers specializing in extricating their clients from legal problems by whatever means available; the Honduran Civil Code's "article 1,000" (the thousand *lempira* note, once the most common bribe); or the Venezuelan "legal tribes" (*tribus legales*), clans of judges and lawyers linked by their partisan identifications who can be expected to give special treatment to each other's cases. The complaints are not limited to corruption or to purely official misbehavior. Tales of official incompetence, ignorance, and prejudice abound—judges who make erroneous decisions, not out of malice but because they do not understand the substantive facts of a case, or even the laws they are supposed to apply; civil or criminal cases that are lost in the system or drag on forever, long after their resolution has become irrelevant; police who violate defendants' rights because they were unaware they had any. And while the public is the usual victim of these miscarriages of justice, its members have not been adverse to manipulating the system's flaws to their own ends, whether by offering bribes, convincing highly placed friends to apply pressure, or threatening legal action for its nuisance value. Given the inevitable and protracted delays, taking a case to court may be the best way of cutting ones losses. By the time a judgment is made, inflation may have rendered it worthless or the other party may not be available to collect. Even the relatively efficient Costa Rican Constitutional Chamber, the *Sala Cuarta* (fourth chamber), has inspired a new term, the *sala cuartalazo*, referring to a threatened request for a temporary injunction. Because the chamber grants the injunction almost automatically, a party who might lose an eventual law suit can use the threat to force a more favorable private settlement. In short, were one to hold a competition for the most corrupt, ineffectual, or discredited system, Peru might not have the dubious honor of carrying off the prize.

Peru might, however, figure as the country that has most repeatedly, if unsuccessfully attempted to rectify these problems, or used its attempts as a pretext for actions as drastic as those following the *autogolpe*. Not all of Peru's recent reform efforts have been this dramatic or this intrusive, but the repeated efforts, and failures, are indicative of the seriousness of the situation and the difficulties of its resolution. They also suggest that, while bad reforms can be worse than no reform at all, society's patience can run out. Measures like those enacted by Fujimori could become realistic alternatives for other countries. A number of recent reforms elsewhere in Latin America have produced more substantive change or less chaos. Still, the positive response to Fujimori's program, domestically and throughout the region, does raise the question of whether the reforms are aiming at the right targets or achieving them rapidly enough. The public's displeasure with their justice systems is evident. It is less clear whether the widespread complaints constitute a mandate and basis for reform, let alone for the conventional current efforts. A negative answer to either question does not invalidate the reformers' objectives. It will make their work more difficult and recommends a reexamination of their goals and the means they have selected to achieve them.

The present work explores these and other issues regarding justice sector reform in Latin America. Focusing on the Peruvian experience, it examines the nature of the problem, its origins, and the past and present efforts at reform. Peru's justice system, may be, as is argued here, one of the more difficult cases in the region. Its problems may be quantitatively and, to some extent, qualitatively different than those faced by most of its neighbors, but they are illustrative of regional trends. Although Peru's situation is nowhere near resolution, its example remains significant. Peru was one of earliest to undertake the kind of reforms now being introduced in a variety of countries, and its justice system has been the target of an unusual amount of domestic criticism and of the interventions of a series of very different administrations. Thus, its experience is useful in understanding the general phenomenon and as a source of lessons, some of them negative, as to what is likely to work and what results can be expected.

To make the applicability of these lessons more evident, the rest of the present chapter offers a general discussion of justice reform and an overview of Latin American justice systems. Considering the reaction initial versions provoked among partisans of one or another national institution or system, a few caveats are in order. First, although the argument here and throughout the work posits the existence of regional trends and tendencies, it is obvious that there are always exceptions. Even in the most compromised system, there are individuals and sometimes entire institutions that have escaped unscathed. While I am leery of one observer's contention[4] that Mexico's courts, apparently of all its criminal justice sector, pose no notable problem of corruption, this may be an example. On a more personal level, some of the most dedicated, honest, and talented judges and prosecutors I know I met in Peru during what may have been the nadir of their respective institution's fall into disrepute.

Second, these trends and tendencies encompass significant variations among and within nations. Some of these are so great as to suggest qualitative leaps. To return to the example noted above, Mexico's courts may not be impervious to systemic problems, but they probably are far less corrupt than its Procuraduría General and judicial police. Costa Rican, Chilean, Uruguayan, and Brazilian (federal and some state) courts do function far above the regional average for integrity, modernity, or professionalism. However, I have discarded the suggestion that they be excluded as exceptional cases that would also mean ignoring the more "typical" behavior of other national institutions and these same judiciaries' participation in a broader set of political issues transcending purely functional performance. Instead I have treated such "exceptions" as an alternative institutional response to a common set of pressures. This response is cause and result of their historically higher levels of "internal autonomy."[5] The trade-off has been some degree of self-imposed isolation from their sociopolitical environments. If they are currently regional models, the same cannot be said of the Chilean, Uruguayan, and Brazilian reaction to recent military dictatorships.

Finally, as this last comment suggests, the variations also extend across time. The "Latin American justice system," to the extent it can be generalized is a moving target. The problematic tendencies discussed here are still emerging in some countries, were deflected by alternative responses in others, and are already under reform in still a third set. The temporal aspect of the phenomena requires a corollary set of caveats. First, there is the danger of overstating the impact of new developments. The proliferation of human rights ombudsman, or Brazil's experiments with instruments to protect social rights have been touted as harbingers of a new era. However, anticipating an argument developed in later chapters, they too easily divert attention from more generalized practices and behaviors that are a far better indication of where things currently stand, and possibly of where they are heading.[6] Second, truth is usually not in the packaging and many new departures and reforms are just that, dramatic titles for more of the same. Third, although one of the arguments advanced involves the frequently unanticipated consequences of reform, there is a learning process at work. Over time it will invalidate a part of that thesis at least as regards the most common reform mechanisms. Preemptive reform, to prevent more drastic, often extra-sectoral change, has not been common in the past. However, participants have become more skillful in manipulating reform programs. Both the current Peruvian efforts and Mexico's recent constitutional amendments as they affect the justice sector[7] are two apparent departures that may be signs of still another emerging trend.

Latin American Justice: From Neglect to Rediscovery

It is conventional wisdom among Latin Americans that their judiciaries and indeed their entire justice systems are the orphan branch of government, underfinanced, bypassed by modernization, and politically dominated by the executive and legislature or by various governmental and nongovernmental elites. Until recently, this seemed to be the consensus among academic observers as well. In writing about the region, they expended little effort on the courts, prosecution, bar, or, except for their use in political repression, the police and prison systems. There is, of course, a well developed literature on the Law (*Derecho*) and legislation (*leyes*), written by Latin American and extraregional experts.[8] However, its focus is more theoretical and doctrinal than empirical and institutional. It most commonly uses legal theory or science (*Derecho*) to analyze the content of specific laws, or comments on changes in the latter for the benefit of practitioners. Efforts to describe or explain the de facto workings of the law and legal institutions have traditionally been rare, a situation that has only recently begun to change.[9]

Although empirical research remains scarce compared to that on other political institutions, the region's justice systems have begun to attract wider attention over the past decade, if only as the objects of more intense criticism. The various reasons for this interest are themselves important. They suggest a growing appreciation of the broader political implications of the sector's functional role. The return to democracy of the 1980s is one cause since it encouraged an examination of the use of sector institutions by prior authoritarian governments. While most attention has gone to the police (and in their sectoral role, the military), it has also focused on instances of judicial collaboration with state repression.[10] In this context, and as part of a wider concern about the region's marginalized populations, both regional and extraregional observers have examined the role of sector institutions in perpetuating discriminatory policies, either directly or indirectly.[11] Observers have also echoed the Kissinger Commission's[12] characterization of the justice sector as the "weak pillar" of Latin American democracy, suggesting its role in bolstering repressive rule and the fear that its generally negative performance might undermine future democratic stability. This fear appears born out by a series of recent events, including the Fujimori *autogolpe* in Peru and attempted coups in Venezuela and Guatemala. All sought justification and found popular support with their claims of widespread judicial corruption.

Similar concerns have been expressed about the sector's negative impact on socioeconomic development, both in its reenforcement or application of misguided policies, and in what it simply fails to do.[13] Complaints parallel those directed at criminal justice—undue delays in conducting trials, archaic legislation, judges' lack of training in finance and commerce, corruption, and failure to hold down common crime and civil violence. Rather surprisingly, but significantly, this theme has received least attention from reformers, politicians, academic observers, or, at least in public fora, economic elites. As regards the latter, one likely explanation is their greater success in manipulating or avoiding any involvement with the sector. Whatever the reason, the majority of contemporary reforms have focused on themes that appear peripheral to their interests and in some instances have advanced changes that seem to contradict them.[14] Whether in reaction to this last development or because their traditional strategy no longer works, these groups and the broader concern with economic impacts have begun to influence discussions of reform needs. However, they have so far failed to displace the earlier emphasis on political and social themes.

Beginning in the 1980s, these various considerations gave rise to a renewed interest in sector reform. This is not the first time such concerns have emerged within the region, but in their current form, they have produced the most broadly focused complaints and reform proposals. It is the first time these internal movements have been closely linked to the efforts of external groups. Internationally based human rights activists, private foundations, and economic assistance agencies have given political support to domestic efforts and in the case of the latter two, provided funding as well.[15] For all these groups and for domestic reformers, the results have been disappointing. This has not discouraged their increasing involvement, or, more recently, the willingness of Latin American governments to enter into loan agreements for more costly programs.[16] Still, what changes have occurred have been less than envisioned and, some would argue, have done little to produce real improvements. It could be contended that the disappointment stems from insufficient patience combined with overly ambitious goals. Change will come, but given the dimensions of the problems, far less rapidly than initially expected. Others have argued that the obstacle is less in overblown ambition than in faulty strategies, poorly conceived or misguided objectives, and an incomplete understanding of the problem, and that until this is resolved, not much more can be expected.

Why the Justice Sector?

If the justice sector is so difficult to reform, one logical question is "why bother?" As the orphan branch of government it is perhaps just as well left that way. Costa Rica and Uruguay, the countries with the least problematic justice sectors, have not been spared a number of additional developmental challenges. Nations with less reformed sectors have still managed to make headway in other areas. Peru's progress in the years following the Fujimori *autogolpe* is a case in point. Despite having reduced parts of its justice sector to near inactivity and circumventing the rest through the creation of special or parallel institutions, the Fujimori administration has almost overcome terrorism and advanced a program of economic recovery that had stymied other governments. The country's growth rate in 1994 was a record 12.9 percent and continues in the high range for the region; inflation was reduced from near 8,000 to 15 percent; the privatization of state enterprises is well underway; and foreign investment is returning. Progress has not only been economic. An elected Constituent Assembly drafted a new constitution that was subsequently approved in a national referendum. Despite complaints about antiterrorist policies and repressive police tactics, the country still enjoys relative freedom of the press and political expression, its political parties remain active if considerably discredited, and Fujimori's electoral victories appear to have been won fairly. When his candidates have not prevailed (as in the Lima mayoral elections of 1995), their opponents have been able to assume office. If not enjoying the extra backing accorded to one of the government's own, they still manage to go about their normal business.

To the extent any of this progress involves the justice sector, Peru's government removed potential obstacles by deactivating its most retrograde institutions and taking direct control over others. If it did not improve their performance, it reduced their negative impact. For most Latin American reformers, however, the tactic is inadequate and the progress illusory. Even when recognizing the short run accomplishments, they argue that over the longer term the measures have serious costs. In part their objections draw on ideological preferences, prescriptive models, and often unrealistic visions of how justice works elsewhere. They are based on such axiomatic principles as the absolute superiority of greater judicial independence or adversarial criminal justice systems. However, if equally untested, their position has increasingly been articulated as a theoretical argument linking justice reform to political stability and especially to the emergence of democratic government.

This argument rests on two fundamental assumptions, apparent in one form or another in most criticisms of the existing justice system in Peru and elsewhere. The first holds that there are certain basic functions performed by the sector—law determination,[17] social control, and conflict resolution—that are vital to socioeconomic development, political stability, and citizen welfare in general. Where these functions are not performed or not performed well, individuals' well being suffers, economic and social activity is stifled, and political stability is threatened. This part of the argument can be summarized as efficacy and efficiency or justice as an essential public service. Certainly in societies complex enough to distinguish between a public and private sector (or indeed to have institutions specialized in the administration of justice), nonpublic entities may perform some of these functions. However, "private justice," if more convenient, accessible, and congruent with elite and popular subcultures, generally lacks the broad-based authority of public institutions and so can complement but not replace them. This is hardly a new or strictly regional discovery. Dimitri Obolensky, one of the architects of Russia's 1864 legal reforms, wrote that "judicial authority preserving the personal and proprietary rights of citizens is the basis upon which the entire edifice of state administration rests."[18]

This public service function is essential to the stability of any government, not just democratic ones. The second part of the formula thus looks beyond functional performance to the values informing it, their conformity with societal notions of "justice," and their embodiment of such democratic principles as equal treatment, broad access, and respect for human rights. Here too, private or partial justice, while conceivably more congruent with the norms of subnational groups or communities, is limited in its integrative impact and its ability to embody the more egalitarian values that presumably are a pillar of any democratic system. In an inegalitarian, multicultural society where privilege reigns and democratically chosen values may not be democratic, the sector and the courts in particular face an unusually difficult dilemma. However, more than any other institution, their ability to combine societal definitions of justice with democratic principles is vital. Where courts fail on either count, and in Latin America they have often failed on both, they undermine the credibility of their own actions and obstruct the emergence of a broadly based democratic culture.

In summary, contemporary reformers identify two characteristics of the justice sector, efficacy in conflict resolution, social control, and law determination, and its furtherance of democratic values, as vital to the creation and maintenance of stable democracy. While elitists or authoritarians might pursue only efficacy, and social revolutionaries democratic values, the two together constitute the sector's essential and perhaps unique contribution. However valid the theory, the historical moment lent it great appeal. As Latin America emerged from years of predominantly authoritarian regimes, the sector's potential contribution to engendering and institutionalizing democratic outlooks and practices offered an interesting remedy to past and persisting ills. The fact that its institutions often accomplished just the opposite during the prior period may actually have enhanced the argument. It also provided a means to rectify the damage they had done to their own image in the process. Even the public service component was influenced by this perspective. The predominant concern expressed by those promoting reform was the impact of inefficiency, incompetence, and corruption on public confidence rather than on economic development or social control, except as the latter involved the elimination of state abuses.

This was not the first time Latin Americans had voiced these claims. Individually or jointly, they run through most of the past complaints about justice administration throughout the region. Their importance has rarely translated into the provision of ample resources to encourage better performance. Nor has it prevented efforts to influence the exercise of these functions, either by direct control of the institutions or by the creation of parallel or extra-official organizations to compensate for what the formal institutions fail to do. These informal mechanisms have been particularly important for populations with limited access to formal justice (the urban and rural poor) or, who for cultural reasons, do not accord it legitimacy.[19] They have also been used by elites who may find them more convenient. In many countries, recent years have witnessed an apparent resurgence of such parallel justice systems, ranging from private police and vigilante groups to officially sanctioned alternative dispute resolution mechanisms and special courts. Still, lingering complaints about the formal institutions suggest that the latter, however inadequately they fulfill it, retain an essential role. This is not only in the eyes of the political analyst but also for the populations they purportedly serve. This last consideration is one reason why governments, while seeking other means for carrying out their high priority policies, have avoided the most expedient measure of permanently eliminating the sector's core institution, the ordinary courts, and have downplayed their direct intervention in the others. The other reason, of course, is a concern for their international image. Arguably, this is a far more recent consideration and less useful in explaining a longer history of restrained interventions.

Latin American Justice Systems: An Overview

The following chapters treat the Peruvian institutions in some detail, noting where relevant their departures from the regional "norm." In preparation, the present section summarizes some common characteristics of the various Latin American systems. First, in speaking of the justice system, while a primary emphasis is usually on the courts, we are generally talking about a sector composed of a number of institutions, both governmental and private. Unlike the courts, many of these other institutions have substantial, occasionally primary, nonjustice functions. However partial their dedication to sector activities, their involvement in the latter cannot be ignored. On the criminal justice side the picture is most complex, including at a minimum not only the common courts and any military or special courts (a highly controversial innovation in Colombia, Peru, and Bolivia to handle terrorist or drug cases), but also prosecution (often, but not always a separate organization, most usually called the Public Ministry), legal defense (the least developed and sometimes comprising on the public sector side, only a few lawyers named by the court for indigent defendants[20]), the Ministry of Justice[21] (which usually but not always manages the prisons and in a few cases, also controls judicial appointments or administration), and one or more national police forces. In some countries, separate police forces operate at the state, departmental or municipal level. These secondary forces are usually not very important. The exceptions are the larger, federally organized countries (Argentina, Brazil, and Mexico[22]) where subnational police forces, as well as courts and other institutions, play a more important role.

For civil justice, the most important institutions are the courts and the bar. Although bar associations usually exist, they have limited powers and often function as little more than social or political clubs. Most countries formally require that judges, prosecutors, and public defenders be lawyers. For a number of reasons this is not always possible. Throughout Central America and in the poorest South American nations, it is common to find law students or lay officials at the lower ranges of the institutional hierarchies.

In addition to the common courts, there are often separate courts that handle administrative cases (fiscal, civil service, customs, etc) or that review purported administrative abuses (*contencioso-administrativo*). A few countries have retained an entirely separate administrative court system, following the French tradition. Colombia is the most extreme example, including a second supreme court (the *Concejo de Estado*) for administrative cases. It is worth mentioning that administrative law is generally not well developed anywhere in the region and that it, like these separate courts, is only beginning to attract attention. It is also an area where a mixture of civil and common law practices has caused the most confusion within national systems and the most variation among them.[23] The abuses they address, or sometimes encourage, may be quantitatively far more important than those in the criminal justice system. Efforts to improve the situation have been few, and current trends are hardly uniform. Since 1917, Mexico has gradually expanded its administrative court system, most recently adding a series of land reform courts in 1992.[24] Other countries (Ecuador, Nicaragua, Panama) have reincorporated their administrative courts into the ordinary system, although with little other impact on their operations.[25] There is also a tendency to create new entities or expand the powers of existing ones (usually the Public Ministry,[26] Procuraduría, or Ombudsman) to help citizens pursue their complaints against administrative offices or, occasionally to represent them in individual or collective legal actions. This is clearly an area where the need for remedy far exceeds what has been provided. Over time the arrangements for contesting administrative actions will undoubtedly require their own reform.

A complete catalogue of institutions relevant to the sector encompasses various other executive agencies, the legislature, the universities, and even the military, although obviously only as regards a very restricted portion of their broader roles. Several countries have added one or more institutional innovations. Recent examples include separate arbitration centers, constitutional courts, and judicial councils. The latter two are of particular interest as they are increasingly popular elements in contemporary reform programs. The councils are generally, but not always composed of representatives from several public and private institutions. Imitating European models, they have been introduced to participate in judicial appointments and very occasionally (Colombia, Mexico, Bolivia[27]), to control judicial budgets and administrative systems. The argument behind their introduction is that they offer a means to depoliticize the judiciary and its governance by taking these responsibilities out of the hands of the Supreme Court or various executive agencies.[28] Experience to date has not dealt well with this contention, although it so far has not discouraged interest in these mechanisms.

The constitutional courts are also patterned on earlier European experience. They are often combined with preexisting mechanisms for constitutional control that were influenced by the U.S. tradition of judicial review. Here, as in the case of administrative law, a tendency to mix the two legal traditions has produced considerable variety in the courts' organization, operations and impact. The underlying concerns with providing a check on executive and legislative abuses, protecting human and legal rights, and guaranteeing the primacy of the constitution as the supreme law of the land have not always been well served. The new entities have often not lived up to their proposed roles or have become the centers of unintended and unanticipated interinstitutional battles. Several countries have discarded the option of separate constitutional courts in favor of expanding powers of judicial review in the Supreme Court or a separate constitutional chamber. While eliminating at least one potential source of interinstitutional disputes, these alternatives have otherwise proved an equally potent source of conflicts.

Most complaints about sector performance and most reform efforts focus on courts, police, and occasionally prisons. It is generally conceded, however, that the problems are sectorwide and will require more global solutions. It should also be noted that the problems are not limited to the sector institutions. The wider political system, and society as a whole provide the environment in which they operate and contribute their own influences to their performance. Indeed, one of the basic questions confronting any reform effort is how much change can be produced within the justice sector, if extrasectoral behavior remains relatively untouched. This is often phrased as an issue of "political will." As such is usually limited to that of elites. The phenomenon, however, extends beyond the wishes of powerholders to the habits, aspirations, and expectations of a variety of groups, both within and outside the sector institutions.

Precise organizational arrangements and the interinstitutional distribution of functions and powers vary considerably from country to country. Although jurists and reformers have devoted much time to debating their relative merits, most of these variations of detail do not appear to have a major impact on the quality of performance. Performance seems more determined by common characteristics or, where differences do arise, by sociocultural, historical, or even such physical variables as the size of the country. There are obviously some alternatives the impact of which is uniformly negative, for example, those whereby a new Supreme Court and judiciary are selected with every change of administration. Even here the results are modified by culture and tradition. During the 1980s, when this practice was in effect in both Honduras and Ecuador, studies indicate that judicial turnover was far more extreme in the former country.[29]

The varying performance of judicial councils and constitutional courts is another case in point. The ability of the former to depoliticize judicial appointments and of the latter to protect constitutional rights depends in part on the details of their organization and composition. It also hinges on the nature of wider political competition and certain attitudinal characteristics of the judiciary. For example, in 1989 Costa Rica's Constitutional Chamber assumed powers of judicial review formerly held by individual judges and, in some cases, by the entire Supreme Court. Contrary to frequent arguments about the greater accessibility and thus efficacy of decentralized systems, the chamber has established an all time regional and national record in the number of cases it has decided and its willingness to override legislation and actions backed by the executive.[30] Almost half its workload and most of its extraordinary popularity come from the type of cases formerly assigned to lower level judges.[31] Within its first year, it was attending to over ten times the filings handled by the Court and individual judges under the previous system. It is also significant that the chamber's performance showed no variation regardless of the party in power, although most of its members had been selected by, and were presumed to identify with the National Liberation Party. Provisions increasing the ease of filing account for part of the difference in performance, but the outlook of the members of the chamber and their willingness to confront even their own party in the interest of protecting citizens' rights are clearly major determinants. Despite the overwhelming workload, the justices have resisted any effort to make access more difficult or to shift original jurisdiction for some cases back to lower level judges. Finally, Costa Rica's small size is obviously a factor. Both Brazil's Supreme Federal Tribunal and Colombia's Constitutional Court have amassed comparable workloads, but much of this is in last instance review.[32] It is hard to imagine Costa Rica's directly accessible, centralized system working in a country with a much larger and more dispersed population.

As to their more common characteristics, without exception, Latin American justice systems represent variations of the continental or civil code tradition.[33] They are based on written procedures as opposed to concentrated oral hearings, an almost exclusive reliance on statutory rather than customary or judge-made law, inquisitorial criminal practices (with judicial responsibility for investigation and sentencing and an underdeveloped or nonexistent role for separate public defenders and prosecutors) and, in civil proceedings, the notion that the parties rather than the judge will define the factual and legal issues and take the primary responsibility for moving the case ahead.[34] They also share in the tradition of the judge and, where they exist, public prosecutor and defender, as a career bureaucrat, expected to enter the profession after law school and remain thereafter. This tradition has been subject to extensive abuse. When combined with the absence of special selection or preparatory mechanisms typical of a majority of countries,[35] it has meant that from the beginning most Latin American judges enjoyed less professional recognition than many of their extraregional colleagues. This effect was less apparent in earlier years when judges, recruited from the elite or subelite, brought their personal prestige to office. More "democratic" recruitment has taken its toll on the profession's image. This is generally still more true of public prosecutors and defenders, as members of more recently developed institutions that lack the courts' illustrious if faded tradition.

Most Latin American nations are unitary rather than federal republics. Key sector institutions, most notably the courts, prosecutors and police, usually have a nationwide rather than locally based organization. This has not precluded an often substantial influence by local elites in the appointment of officials to "local" offices It has had several important consequences for institutional operations and efforts to make improvements. Most of these stem from the notion that unitary organization means standardized practices, regardless of differing local conditions. This principle discourages experimentation and innovation, which are often illegal unless adopted nationally. It also produces the consequent, if paradoxical emergence of still greater de facto variations from the norm than might have occurred with a more openly flexible system. Where local conditions make strict compliance with the law difficult or impossible, irregular practices may be the only alternative, at some point becoming so entrenched that no one recognizes the difference. The phenomenon is not limited to outlying districts. Studies of criminal trial court procedures in Lima in the late 1980s found that every chief clerk (*secretario*) had a slightly different notion of the steps to be taken for handling a case. Each believed that his or her version was legally mandated. These personalized systems were almost invariably more complicated than the actual legal requirements and often came as a surprise to the presiding judge when called to his or her attention.[36]

In almost all countries, the prosecution and defense have the narrowest geographic reach. As the newest and least developed functions, they are often hindered by poorly prepared personnel and equally poorly defined responsibilities and mandates. There are some important, if not always positive exceptions. They include the Panamanian Public Ministry and the Mexican Procuraduría General de la República, both of which have long played central, if very controversial roles in their countries' criminal justice systems.[37] For institutions like the courts, police, and prisons, quality of personnel, low budgets, and inadequate mandates are also a problem. However, it is the weight of institutional tradition, rather than the lack of a clear mission that complicates their present operations. For the police and prisons, institutional tradition is too strong a term for what is more accurately described as a historically circumscribed role that downplayed any kind of professionalism or did not provide the resources for cultivating it. For the courts, however, institutional culture and the peculiar nature of judicial professionalism have inhibited the ability to adapt to changing circumstances or even to recognize the need to do so.

The general organizing principles in themselves may provide the basis for an adequate justice system and, arguably, did so during the regions's earlier history. Obviously, measured against contemporary standards, adequacy can be questioned, but, in the past, sector performance rarely encountered the kind of complaints it faces today. As societal change has altered the nature and level of demand for system output, these underlying principles have increasingly been seen as the source of a series of dysfunctionalities and vices. For a minority of countries and a minority of institutions, the trend is less a qualitative worsening of performance than an inability to keep up with quantitative demand. To the extent quality is an issue, complaints focus on increasing formalism, bureaucratization, and elitism or social isolation and irrelevance. While frequently a response to external political threats, these tendencies have also been linked to traditional institutional culture and to a consequent intellectual rigidity in the face of any kind of external change.[38] To varying degrees such criticisms have been directed at courts in Costa Rica, Uruguay, Chile, Brazil, and Colombia. However, in the majority of cases and for most other institutions, the effects of new demands have been more pernicious.

Looking just at the judiciary, the following tendencies are often described. As caseloads grow, the emphasis on written procedures has allowed an increasing delegation of judicial powers to poorly trained and inadequately supervised paralegal or administrative staff who become responsible for the preparation of the written dossier (*expediente*) on the basis of which the judge decides a case. This delegation, while often illegal, allows nonjudicial personnel an enormous, frequently determining control over shaping the "facts" on which the judge will base his decision. The potential for abuse is further magnified when delegation is combined with the inquisitorial tradition (i.e. the judge or as often, his staff, determines whether criminal action is in order, develops the investigation and may also decide on the guilt or innocence of the subject). Low salaries, insecure tenure, and politicized appointment systems may turn abuse into out-and-out corruption or at least discourage efforts to counter external pressures. In such circumstances, the preeminence of statutory law and, thus, limited judicial discretion, looks advantageous. In practice, it encourages arbitrariness and a denial of judicial responsibility for the consequences of their decisions. These factors in turn discourage timely outcomes or any effort to make justice intelligible and accessible to marginalized groups. Finally, these marginalized groups often suffer because of the "national" character of the systems. While not adverse to violating centrally imposed rules when it serves their purposes, local officials apply them selectively to the further disadvantage of nonpreferred clients.

These reactions, whether in their minor or major variations, can only be partly explained by the basic architecture of these systems. Certainly the European experience suggests the possibility of successful reform within the continental tradition.[39] However, the Latin American systems have deviated considerably from the original and contemporary European models. Such considerations have not prevented a regionwide determination to modify the formal organizing principles, chiefly by revising basic legislation (procedural and substantive codes and organic laws). It does mean that to understand the problems and in turn to introduce real improvements one is advised to look beyond the formal legal tradition. Many of the additional explanations begin outside the justice system, in social, political, and economic traits that are themselves changing, but in ways that often exacerbate sector problems. Thus, economic growth and modernization, the diversification of social forces and interests, the integration and politicization of formerly marginalized groups, the emergence of more open and competitive polities and economies, the adoption of new values and a corresponding change in expectations as to the role of the state have dramatically altered the pressures on the sector. The latter rather than responding creatively and flexibly, has most often retreated into formalism, an exaggerated attachment to traditional practices, an effort to artificially limit responsibility and demand and, when all else fails, by caving in to external pressures. The latter at worst is corruption. At best, it further undermines institutional integrity.

This adaptive failure can also be traced to sectoral traits originating independently of the dominant legal tradition. One of the most important of these is the historically limited jurisdiction of formal justice institutions in these highly inegalitarian societies. As one Peruvian scholar has noted,[40] justice was never for the rich, who did not need it, nor for the poor who could not afford it. Thus, the recent and relatively sudden demands forthcoming, if for different reasons, from both groups have raised a series of problems ranging from inadequate capacity to an incompatible value structure. These new demands have had a qualitative as well as quantitative impact on jurisdiction, changing the nature of the problems seen by the sector in ways for which its institutions and individual members are often not prepared. This historically limited jurisdiction also explains a number of secondary traits that have become problems in their own right: the resource poverty of sector institutions, the inadequacy of substantive legislation, the declining quality of sector personnel (a result of financial constraints and diminished prestige), and the lack of mechanisms to facilitate access to nontraditional clientele, especially to the popular masses. Not all systems suffer from all problems, and many are already the targets of reforms. However, left unattended, these factors reinforce each other, leading to a further downward spiral.

The sector's lack of political independence is also a consequence of its traditional role. The situation is neither so clear cut nor so uniform as commonly portrayed. Conventional wisdom usually depicts the courts and other sector institutions as captives of the executive. A long history of extra-constitutional interventions is frequently cited as evidence.[41] In the case of the courts and, where they exist, defense and prosecution, the relationship has been more nuanced and variable over time and among different countries. In most instances, there is an expectation, supported by law, that the political party in power will make appointments of key officials, sometimes to the extent of naming an entire new Supreme Court and much of the lower level judiciary. In Central America, even ordinary police have frequently been patronage appointees, changing with each new administration. However, in many countries, the courts' traditionally higher prestige but lesser instrumental importance actually gave them a certain protection from the executive's exercise of its "right" to political intervention. Real turnover on the bench was less than might be expected and such qualities as vocation and personal background seemed to have been honored as much as political loyalty in the selection of candidates.[42]

In a minority of cases, this informal autonomy has been maintained or evolved into a de jure career system managed by the institution. The trade-off has usually been an institutional policy of nonintervention in politically sensitive issues. This often implicit understanding has only recently begun to be challenged, not always with positive results.[43] In most cases, however, within the last decades, three factors—the emergence of mass-based parties, increased and more open political competition, and an expanding jurisdiction for sector institutions (both in terms of what and whom they affected)—have combined to encourage new forms of politicization. Judgeships and other offices became both targets and *vehicles* of partisan battles. The effect on independence has been less uniform. In some instances, it has increased the subservience of judges to political elites (e.g. Peru since 1969). In others (e.g. El Salvador and possibly the rest of Central America), it has made court leadership political actors in their own right, unfortunately often with personal rather than institutional agendas. Thus, some of the most politicized judiciaries have in fact become the most independent; their members are simply politicians with a different power base.[44] Admittedly, this is not what is usually meant by judicial independence and, for these as well as the more subservient benches, the further consequences have been declines in prestige, internal morale, and professionalism. More generally, greater politicization has decreased the ability of individual institutions to control the behavior of their own members. Selected and protected by non-institutional elites and well aware of declining institutional prestige, they may no longer respond to traditional institutional values and see little reason to consider forging new ones.

Setting the Stage for Reform

In summary, Latin American justice systems may have at one time per-formed satisfactorily for their societies. At present, measured against the criteria of efficacy and democratic values, the sector as a whole and its individual institutions come up short on both counts. The negative assess-ment is not limited to external observers or a minority of concerned elites. Public opinion polls conducted in any number of countries have repeatedly demonstrated a lack of faith in sector institutions and a conviction as to their basic inefficacy, corruption, or inequitable treatment. This is true, if to a lesser degree, even of systems regarded as less problematic. More disturb-ingly, contact with sector institutions often worsens the evaluations.[45] Prisons crowded with unsentenced prisoners, growing case backlogs and average times for case resolution that double or quadruple the legal limits, rising levels of crime and social violence, a high incidence of police brutality and other irregular practices, and the recourse to parallel institutions by all social strata are frequently cited evidence of their inadequacies. To this can be added criticisms of arbitrariness, ineptitude, and submission to political pressures, bribes, and prejudice.

Beyond the concerns about collaboration with repressive governments or susceptibility to political pressures, the general complaints and more sys-tematic observations paint a picture of relatively passive, weak, antiquated, nonprofessional and penetrable institutions. This is true even of the police who, at most, figure as the poor relatives of a much stronger military.[46] The implications for reform are significant. They suggest a goal of institutional reorientation and *strengthening* in which the target organizations (if not all their members) are natural allies. For those attempting reforms in other sociohistorical contexts, it bears noting the different implications for programs that might require removing, rather than adding powers and resources. Of course, in a context of overall sectoral strengthening, there is still the issue of the optimal balance among the member institutions and the conflicts its resolution may generate. Institutions and their allies may not take kindly to a *relative* loss of power, even when it constitutes an *absolute* gain. Unfortunately, those best equipped to utilize new resources and opportunities may not be the preferred beneficiaries. Thus, absent measures to counteract this tendency, reforms to strengthen the sector's institutions can exacerbate existing imbalances and abuses of power within it. The principle is simple. Its application is more difficult—especially when it involves convincing police to accept supervision of their investigations by inexperienced prosecutors or encouraging members of a newly created public defender's office to appeal the decisions of well-connected judges.[47]

Several additional characteristics of the public's complaints deserve mention. They are universal and on certain points—corruption, formalism, inefficacy—coincide across social classes. In the early 1980s, as a consequence of the fall of a series of repressive governments, they tended to emphasize criminal justice, human rights, and the abuses perpetrated by the state itself. As a focus of broad support, these themes appear to be losing force, replaced by concerns with corruption, efficiency, or crime control. Still, the groups retaining an interest in the initial themes tend to do so intensely and have thus far managed to keep them on the reform agenda. Finally, in most cases even extreme dissatisfaction with the system did not appear to produce complete alienation from it. The complaints still appeared to be demands for improvement, not a threat to take their business elsewhere, for example to indigenous or private institutions.[48]

The problems identified and their presumed origins are so complex as to make it difficult to separate cause from effect or to determine where to begin to seek improvement. There are easier cases, but for every Uruguay or Costa Rica with their relatively limited problems, there are any number of countries where the police are perceived as bandits with badges, the judges know less law than first-year students from a good university (which may not matter anyway since their decisions are usually made by corrupt administrators), the laws themselves embody violations of human rights or just of good business practices, and the best way to deal with the justice system is to avoid it. Barring that recourse, the next best solution is to buy ones' way out, and many successful lawyers specialize in helping their clients do just that.

Given this situation, it's not surprising that justice reform has been adopted as an issue throughout Latin America. What is surprising is the form it has taken and the subset of demands and solutions it includes.[49] First, while this was a regionwide phenomenon with often strong cross-national linkages, it did not have much of a national base. Formed by groups of distinguished jurists and drawing much of its inspiration from slightly earlier European developments,[50] the initial movement neither sought nor gained support among a wider domestic public nor among nonpolitical elites. It addressed principles that few could really oppose (a respect for human and due process rights), but these were not themes that attracted a broad, permanent, *and* intensely involved constituency. The incipient movement also incorporated objectives that meant little to the lay person whatever his or her concern with limiting human rights abuses. Examples include the transformation from written, inquisitorial criminal procedures to oral, adversarial ones; the introduction of a variety of new constitutional rights and remedies to protest their violation; differentiated appeals systems; and the reconciliation of statutory law with major trends in doctrine.

Second, this was a lawyers' reform not only in its technical presentation, but also in its virtually exclusive focus on changing laws. The few apparent exceptions—higher budgets, new appointment systems for judges and other sector officials, the creation or strengthening of institutions like judicial councils or the Public Ministry—were also envisioned as essentially questions of rewriting legislation. There was little attention to other types of change and the content of the proposed laws often seemed chosen with more regard for style and doctrinal purity than for likely impact.

Finally, and perhaps most importantly, many of the issues that had been disturbing the public—corruption, inaccessibility, excessive formalism and failure to keep abreast of modern trends outside the legal arena—had been overlooked, when they were not explicitly rejected as an undesirable "popularization" of justice. In short, there existed a rather conspicuous disjuncture between the growing discontent with the justice system and the reform movement itself. This was not necessarily an oversight on the part of the reformers. They may have seen it as an advantage in getting legislation drafted and approved. Nevertheless, it did not bode well for their long term success in producing real as opposed to legal change.

Advances in Reform

Despite this disjuncture, the sectoral reform movement has gathered momentum over the past decade. By the early 1990s, it had produced visible results across the region. Many of these were quite similar in content if not always in purpose, even in the two countries—Mexico and Brazil—that were less direct participants in the regional movement.[51] Not surprisingly, most of the impact came as changes in legislation: constitutional amendments, new procedural and substantive codes, and other secondary laws. Both Colombia (1991) and Peru (1993) adopted new constitutions that introduced changes in judicial organization, criminal procedures, and judicial protection of constitutional rights. El Salvador in its 1983 Constitution and a series of amendments introduced in 1991 made similar modifications. Costa Rica revised its system of constitutional guarantees in 1989, consolidating judicial review functions in one chamber of the Supreme Court. Brazil strengthened and reorganized its judicial review functions in its 1988 Constitution. Ecuador, Bolivia, the Dominican Republic, and Mexico also made changes in this area. While Costa Rica's judicial council was introduced as part of the Judicial Organic Law, other countries (Argentina, Bolivia, the Dominican Republic, Ecuador, El Salvador, Mexico, Colombia and Peru) have used constitutional amendments or new constitutions to introduce or modify the powers of such bodies. Several countries (Peru, Costa Rica, El Salvador, Ecuador) adopted amendments earmarking a percentage of the national budget for the judicial branch, usually without considering how this would affect the distribution of powers within the sector. Such changes were not limited to individual institutions. They frequently mandated modified interinstitutional relationships, for example, giving the judiciary or Public Ministry control over police investigation of crimes, or removing the power to name judges or control the judicial budget from the Court, legislature or executive in favor of a judicial council.

By 1996 a number of countries were either considering (El Salvador, Honduras, Ecuador, Chile, Uruguay, Bolivia) or had adopted (Argentina, Brazil, Colombia, Guatemala, Costa Rica) new criminal or criminal procedures codes embodying many of the principles promoted by the reformers. Several were contemplating the Uruguayan example of a new civil procedures code as well.[52] The criminal justice legislation has usually required additional laws to create or strengthen the Public Ministry and Defense and to modify the judiciary's powers and organization. Judicial organic laws have also been modified to create new substantive jurisdictions (e.g. agrarian or family law), and occasionally to change the territorial or hierarchical organization of the courts. Finally, in a few countries (Bolivia, Guatemala, Colombia, and Peru), constitutional changes have allowed the recognition of indigenous legal systems or customary law within the communities where it traditionally has held force.

Most of this legislation has tended to focus on the judiciary and the related institutions of defense, prosecution, judicial councils, and constitutional courts or chambers; other institutions have received some attention. Several countries have reorganized the police forces or the laws controlling their operations. Legislation on prisons has also been under discussion, and very occasionally that controlling the wider legal profession. Some countries have also experimented with laws introducing or legalizing extrajudicial or court annexed mediation and arbitration.

This burst of legislative activity may seem inconsistent with the earlier comments on the narrow base of support. Here it was aided by several additional factors. First, it had been slowly gathering momentum since the late 1960s, on both a national and regional basis. The contact among the various national movements is evident in the similarity of many of the measures adopted. It has facilitated the process of convincing individual governments, at times leading to an almost competitive rush to see who could approve the most progressive legislation. The recent emergence of the region, and most of its nations from a period of authoritarian government also helped. Many of the new laws were characterized as progressive and humanistic and as such represented an opportunity to break with a repressive past. Additionally, even if this legislation did not deal with the most pressing public concerns, governments were certainly aware of growing discontent with their justice sectors. They thus were disposed to accept the proposals as a way of addressing an emerging problem. Given the absence of alternative ideas, it was either do this or do nothing. Finally, a legislative solution, however inadequate in the long run, is inexpensive and highly visible. What opposition emerged never focused on the potentially more serious problems of costs, displaced personnel, organizational capabilities, or, still more surprisingly, the broader political implications of a number of the measures. It instead remained at a fairly abstract level, couched in terms that were no more intelligible nor engaging than the proposals it criticized. This made it easy to defeat and produced still more opportunity for favorable publicity for the reformers' political allies.

If costs were to become an issue, there was another factor to consider, the interest of foreign donors and international financial institutions (IFIs) in assisting the process. Some countries, like Peru, Costa Rica, and Uruguay, made considerable headway on their legislative agenda before these external agencies appeared on the scene. Brazil and Mexico made their changes without any appreciable external technical or financial assistance. Nonetheless, it is probable that broader regional progress would not have occurred, or at least not so rapidly, without the promise of external funding. Increasingly, this has been more than a promise. Although through the mid-1990s only the U.S. government had invested in large programs,[53] other donors have provided technical assistance to reform groups, sponsoring conferences, trips, and visits by foreign experts to aid in drafting laws and reform plans. This has undoubtedly moved the legislative agenda along. The greatest impact in attracting wider domestic backing may have been the knowledge that additional foreign financing would be available to support the resulting programs. True, the external involvement has occasionally led to charges of foreign interference. However, given the burgeoning domestic complaints about the sector, most governments have seized the opportunity to resolve what had appeared to be an intractable problem.

External assistance agencies did not have their own reform agenda for the sector. They were aware of its shortcomings and had been sensitized by human rights groups to such issues as human rights abuses and the past collaboration of justice institutions with repressive governments. They thus were attracted by the promise of a progressive, humanistic reform that seemed to be backed by the right groups within the countries in question and within their own domestic constituencies. If the overriding themes were human rights and democracy, the promise of more modern and efficient

justice systems was also consistent with a number of other concerns, ranging from economic development to a more effective treatment of nonconventional criminality—terrorism, drug trafficking and environmental and
white collar crime. Over the longer run, the programs' ability to give satisfactory or at least equal attention to this collection of disparate goals would
be called into question. However, until proponents entered the details of
implementation and began evaluating results, they could remain oblivious
to the potential contradictions.

Translating these general concerns into specific assistance projects has not
been easy. Never having worked in this area, the external agencies lacked
both a program and the in-house expertise to design and implement
assistance packages. As the numerous false starts and abortive undertakings
suggest,[54] their past experience in other types of aid programs was not
readily transferable. The initial problems ranged from identifying the
appropriate institutional and individual contacts to working with local
counterparts who themselves had little or no comprehension of development projects or foreign assistance. The former was a major issue for donors
from a common law background who had some difficulties understanding
the roles of apparently familiar organizations in the Latin American context.
For this reason, the Ministry of Justice was often included in projects despite
its frequently minor role in sector operations. Not understanding what it
did, some U.S. program designers mistakenly equated it with the U.S.
Department of Justice. They also, understandably, found it easier to work
with a hierarchically organized executive institution than with a collegially
organized judicial body. Unfortunately, they overlooked the fact that in
countries like Peru, Argentina or Colombia, one goal of local reformers has
been to decrease the ministry's control over the judiciary.

Further challenges were those of identifying technical assistance skills
and individuals who possessed them and converting abstract goals into
concrete objectives and measures of progress. As they were to discover, at
this level there was far less agreement as to what constituted an improvement in justice than existed in conventional assistance areas like health,
education, or agriculture. Moreover, there was no functional equivalent of
child survival, vaccination, or literacy rates as an indicator of success. Often
what was presented as an achievement could be turned around by critics
to constitute a new problem. Early release programs and reduction of
pretrial detention put "criminals" on the streets. Speedier criminal trials or
higher conviction rates were signs of increased state repression. The introduction of alternative dispute resolution programs either created a second
class justice system for the poor or encouraged special treatment for the
economic elites, depending on the identity of the targeted clientele.

Agencies that arrived later in the process faced their own problems. Not
the least of these was how to coordinate with or work around existing U.S.

government programs. Their heralded entrance has spurred or maintained interest in reform programs in a number of countries and may have accelerated the passage of some legislation. It also dispersed local efforts in a number of new directions. In the process, the relatively single-minded thrust of the initial movement has been weakened, replaced by a more amorphous emphasis on modernization. This may not in itself be a negative development. It does beg the question as to what objectives and improvements are really being pursued. Also, while it has broadened the thematic content of the reform debate, it has not necessarily widened participation in it. The center has shifted from independent jurists to highly placed technocrats and sector officials. It still excludes the general public as well as special interest groups with a concrete stake in the proposed changes. If the first exclusion is not surprising, the second, especially as it regards economic and other elites, is puzzling. Their lack of involvement in the majority of countries has helped maintain the focus on "public interest issues" and may have discouraged the diversion of efforts to the furtherance of their more particular concerns. However, it also has costs. In the few instances where economic elites and interest groups have engaged in the process, they have contributed resources and pushed programs into real enactment.[55] Since their absence suggests they assign little importance to the undertakings, the most critical question is whether this is a function of their shortsightedness or a more accurate perception of the likely outcomes.

The Future of Reform

The last few years' progress in enacting reform legislation and attracting external support has removed some of the initial skepticism about the possibility of justice reform. It leaves a number of important questions unanswered. There is first a series of questions relating to the overall feasibility of the reforms as proposed. One fundamental issue is whether, even with substantial external funding, the legal changes can be implemented into reality. Often written in an apparent competition to produce the most progressive legislation on the books, the constitutional amendments, codes, and other laws presuppose a considerable amount of organizational and behavioral change, both within and among the affected institutions and within the wider public. Producing those changes will require financial investments, dedication, and technical skills that may well be beyond the immediate or medium-range capabilities of the national systems and their external allies.

A related issue concerns the technical quality of the laws themselves. Written and reviewed as abstract, desk exercises, they may in practice produce results quite different than those envisioned by their authors. Experience already indicates the probable need of further readjustments or changes in their content to avoid a host of bottlenecks and unintended consequences. The danger is that an accumulation of such problems could bring a decision to paralyze implementation or reverse the direction of change. The continued postponements of passage of El Salvador's new Criminal Procedures Code and of the implementation of the code approved by Peru in 1991 are illustrative. If partly motivated by other factors, the delays also seem to derive from a closer examination of the laws' content, something missing from the rather abstract discussions surrounding their initial introduction. In both cases, observation of the problems encountered by codes that had already entered into effect elsewhere (e.g. Guatemala in 1994) and in El Salvador,[56] its own experience with the new Family Code and Juvenile Offenders Law approved in 1994 created additional disincentives for more rapid movement forward.

Finally, there is the issue of whether these reforms are on the right track as regards resolving citizen discontent and improving the overall quality of justice in the region. It is not unusual, in fact is to be expected, that any reform delivers far less than it promises. This problem is aggravated when what is promised is not what is needed or desired. In this respect, reforms can be either irrelevant or counterproductive. While the current reform packages probably should not be characterized in either fashion, there are reasons for concern. Their authors and supporters, and thus their objectives, are not exactly representative of the respective national populations. The problems they identify are real, but one may ask whether their resolution will make much difference to the bulk of the citizenry. In cases where publicity surrounding reform has awakened wider popular discussion, it is already apparent that citizens often have different priorities.[57] This has occasionally forced additional modifications, or a different presentation of objectives. Where these responses are not sufficient, further progress may be jeopardized.

A related cause for concern and a second series of questions regard the technical thrust of reform proposals and their avoidance of the sector's political role. Although for different reasons, external supporters and national participants have shared an interest in downplaying or ignoring the extrasectoral implications of reform and, especially, its impact on the broader conduct of politics within the affected nations. One theme common to both groups has been the image of apolitical justice and especially an apolitical judiciary—one which is not only nonpartisan, but which leaves the determination of policy to the other branches of government. To the extent the reform movement has been fed by a reaction against the sector's capture by or collaboration with prior authoritarian governments this traditional goal has become part of its justification. True, this has also entailed an overtly partisan effort to remove individuals and factions associated with these past regimes, but always in the name of political neutrality. For the multilateral development banks, political involvement is expressly forbidden in their mandates. Bilateral donors are not equally constrained, but practical considerations may dictate a comparable stance as they shape their programs. Legal reforms often stress the recognition of the rights of certain groups, most usually, women, the poor, children, and indigenous populations. However, even where mechanisms transcend simple equality to special treatment, the underlying justification is greater rather than lesser political neutrality.

Ironically, this emphasis on apoliticism comes at a time when the sector and the judiciary are confronting a new level of political involvement. The phenomenon is not limited to Latin America; it is observable worldwide.[58] A contrast can be made here between the traditional concern with micro-politics—which parties or which individuals dominated institutions and so influenced specific decisions and actions—and macropolitics, having to do with structural biases and the balance of institutional powers within a political system. The historical fluctuations in the Latin American judiciary's political role has most often been at the micro level. For at least the last century, it has rarely been an active institutional player, but has either avoided macropolitical issues or been a pawn in conflicts among political and economic elites. While all the sector's institutions had built-in structural biases that worked to the disadvantage of politically and economically marginalized groups, changing these was not a part of the game. Instead, the usual objective was to use judicial and other sectoral positions to reward followers, ensure the outcomes of certain distributive decisions, and otherwise enhance the political advantage of one partisan faction or another.

There was considerable variation in the overtness and frequency with which this occurred. In some countries, political elites reached an earlier understanding to minimize the practice or its impact. According to one observer,[59] Chilean political elites as early as the 1920s agreed to keep politics out of the judiciary and the judiciary out of politics, thus giving the courts considerable "internal autonomy." Brazil's federal courts manage their career systems with virtually no political intervention, but even after the removal of various constitutional limitations (introduced by the military) continue to exercise self-imposed restraints on their judicial review powers.[60] In Colombia and Costa Rica, the agreement took the form of shared or alternating control of judicial appointments between the two major national parties, of course, cutting out all the others. In Colombia this was managed despite the unique arrangement whereby the judiciary appointed its own members, including those on the Supreme Court. Both countries have recently changed their appointment systems, with uncertain consequences for this gentlemen's agreement. More generally, however, unconditioned control of the judiciary and other sector institutions was one of the accepted fruits of political victory.

The traditional goal of judicial independence aims at eliminating partisan manipulation, usually by insulating judicial appointments and budgets from external control. This has been an aim of the judiciary itself, of the reformers, and increasingly of politicians. Although politicians were the chief beneficiaries of the traditional system, some have begun to regret the costs in corruption, incompetence, and unpredictability of outcomes. Unpredictability has become a particular problem as more competitive political systems wrest control away from any single party, dividing courts against themselves and carrying partisan conflicts into judicial chambers. Where the dominant party or coalition no longer "owns" all the justices, decisions are influenced not only by extrasectoral partisan negotiations but also by intrajudicial politics or such mundane factors as who is out sick on a given day.[61] The temptation of partisan intervention remains, but the increasing acceptance of new appointment mechanisms introduced to make it more difficult suggest a growing consensus on its undesirability. In a more cynical interpretation, and to the extent mass-based parties represent nonestablishment interests, the old guard may prefer a nonpartisan judiciary to one with a political coloration that threatens the status quo.

When couched as increased professionalism, the goal of micropolitical independence generally underestimates the potential for altering the judiciary's structural biases and completely overlooks that for enhancing its role as a political actor in its own right. It ignores the fact that judicial independence is not judicial neutrality, and that a more independent judiciary will inevitably promote some set of values, both in its traditional functions and in its interactions with the rest of government. These interactions have become particularly important with the return to democracy and the agreement to channel competition through constitutionally mandated mechanisms. One result has been a series of conflicts over institutional powers and, thus, more recourse to the normal judiciary and separate constitutional courts as arbiters. The interactions assumed more importance as these same judicial institutions received a broader role in protecting citizens' legal and constitutional rights against legislative and administrative abuses. These are not responsibilities the judiciary always accepted willingly. Where they did, the result has often come as a shock to political and other elites. Where reformers have promoted these developments, they usually focus only on the judiciary's application of more progressive or professional criteria in its normal decision making. Overlooked is the possibility that as the judiciary and other sectoral actors adopt new values, they may redefine their normal functions, producing unanticipated alterations in the balance and application of institutional powers.[62]

A third set of questions is to what end and for whose benefit these changes will be used. In a society with fewer existing and incipient conflicts, a more equitable access to resources, and higher levels of institutional stability in the surrounding political system, the possible answers are less varied and many lie within the realm of micropolitics. However, for most of Latin America the potential, if not the likely answers are far more diverse, with substantial macropolitical implications. A reformed, merit-based, technocratic and bureaucratic judiciary may simply do its traditional work better with only a minor impact on the status quo. Alternatively, it may go in directions of that have little to do with anyone else's values or interests, and produce changes that no one notices. It may, however, envision itself as a political activist, advancing its own institutional position or that of allied elites, attacking abuses of power elsewhere in government, or defending citizen rights or the interests of marginalized groups. If the latter options seem less likely than the former, they are not outside the realm of possibilities. Examples include recent conflicts between Costa Rica's Constitutional Chamber and the executive,[63] or the Colombian political elite's several decade battle with their Supreme Courts.[64] The actions of Courts less noted for their progressive characters, like those of Ecuador, Nicaragua, or Guatemala,[65] provide additional examples. Needless to say, and as illustrated by the second set of cases, in a country with a less democratic tradition and higher levels of political instability than Costa Rica or even Colombia, the resolution of such confrontations might not be so peaceful.

Two final questions are how far the process can go before reaction sets in and whether any reaction will reverse the changes already made. As noted above and further elaborated in subsequent chapters, the implications of the reforms reach far beyond the imagination of their backers, and beyond that of many political and nonpolitical elites. The reform proposals originated among groups with relatively little independent influence and were ostensibly for the general good or the benefit of the marginalized and powerless. As was inevitable, they have worked to the advantage of still other groups, many of them members of existing or new institutions. The results to date have worked a part of the promised improvements. They have also reconfigured the political landscape, shifting power among institutions and among political actors. Improved performance is hard to oppose; the alterations to the power structure are another issue. Peru's recent shift to a new "reform" model, one closely controlled by the government, certainly signals one potential reaction to this latter development and its unfortunate consequences for the more politically neutral reform components. Whether Peru is once more breaking new ground or only going off in an idiosyncratic direction remains to be seen. However, it is unlikely to be a unique case.

Conclusions

The answers to all these questions lie far beyond the Peruvian experience or indeed that of any of Latin America's present reform movements. The examples at most can indicate the nature of and reasons for concern and the likelihood of their being aggravated, resolved, or even addressed by the current set of programs. The purpose of the present treatment is less to provide solutions than to draw attention to the full scope of the problem posed by the Latin American justice sectors, a scope that extends considerably beyond its current definition. Reformers may cultivate a narrow vision in order to get on with their task. At some point, a wider view is essential if only to allow course corrections and stave off some of the less productive unintended consequences. Otherwise, the simplified interpretations on which reform is necessarily based may completely overtake reality, leading to imaginary solutions for nonexistent problems. Attempted reforms, in Peru and elsewhere, have generated a host of proposed remedies, the implantation of which occasionally threatens to supersede their original objectives. Code revision, judicial purges, constitutional courts and judicial councils, modified institutional mandates, and alternative dispute resolution have individually or simultaneously appeared as the keys to improved justice. As such they take on lives of their own, with their own cluster of dedicated proponents and a larger group of "associated" supporters who may be less interested in the innovation itself than in its potential for serving their individual ends. At the risk of excessive cynicism, it is well to remember that any established reform movement will attract a constellation of opportunistic backers. In the end these should not detract from reform's merit, but they likewise cannot serve as a evidence for its existence. As the fate of a number of these innovations has already demonstrated, they are in no sense immune to the very vices they were introduced to eliminate.

The larger point is that, however ambitious the scope of current reform proposals, it is both too narrow and too broad. On the one hand, the problems the reforms actually resolve will necessarily be far less then they pretend. On the other, the pattern of changes they begin may go far beyond that envisioned. Justice reform is partly about remedying a series of very discrete complaints deriving from conventional expectations about sectoral functions. Here, the principal challenge is to be sure reform programs aim at the problems that matter and that they do so in the most effective manner. The relatively small groups active in the diagnosis of sector shortcomings and the development of remedies give reason for concern on both counts. The danger is not only that they will work changes to serve an equally narrow set of interests. By failing to draw in wider participation and support, they risk undermining their own ability to act. This has been the case in Peru's past reforms and seems no better handled in its present one. It may be one of the most important lessons to be derived from Peru's experience. Saving an institution that has traditionally had so little relevance for the mass of the population requires either reversing that sense of irrelevance or developing support among small, but strategically located groups of allies. Peruvian reformers never attempted the first tactic. Where they have adopted the second, they have either erred on strategic location, or allied with groups whose own (usually partisan) agenda eventually subverted the reformers' objectives.

Justice reform also implies political change in its broadest sense—not just who controls the sectoral institutions, but what interests and values they represent, how they apply them, and to what ends. A more independent, efficient, and democratically principled court, prosecution or judicial council may lose some of its accustomed docility. In the process, it can initiate new conflicts with other institutional and political actors on the basis of all or any one of these new values. This evidently is not a risk the current Peruvian administration or most of its predecessors have been willing to take. In the past, and potentially in the present reform, it has preferred to sacrifice greater functional efficacy for more predictable behavior. That the risk has been taken in other countries may be a consequence of lesser political acumen on the part of their elites, or an expectation that they can use the results to their own advantage.

It is in this area of macropolitical change that sectoral reform has its most interesting and least predictable consequences. The implications of greater judicial dependence or independence were fairly evident in the prior authoritarian regimes. Greater judicial dependence meant support of or, at least, nonresistance to the party in power; greater judicial independence usually was short-lived and terminated by a reassertion of external control. However, in the current situation of greater political flux, institutional instability and occasional deadlock, and demands for increased participation by "civil society," the place of stronger, or at least differently strengthened justice institutions represents a political wild card, the value of which will only be known as it is played. In consequence, many of our expectations about the normal roles of justice institutions may require reexamination. An independent, active if not activist judiciary may not be a neutral arbiter, but rather another political actor the functional performance of which becomes less important than its ability to advance certain interests, be they partisan, social, or institutional, in the broader political arena. A dependent, passive one may so poorly perform its functions as to force the transfer of these functions to alternative and more radically disposed institutions. Although to a lesser extent, the same is also true of other sector institutions as they take their new roles or their new powers more seriously.[66] How society or groups within it will respond to and evaluate these changes is also far from certain. Among all these uncertainties, one thing seems clear. Over the short run, the sector's contribution to enhanced political stability and democratic values will be far less direct and far more conflictual than the reformers' theories indicate.

The Plan for the Book

The following pages explore these and related themes in the context of Peru's experience and that of its regional neighbors. The collapse of Peru's justice system is examined in greater detail, with specific attention to its historical and sociopolitical origins, current dimensions, prospects for change, and the lessons it offers to and may draw from other Latin American reforms. Chapter 2 reviews the wider historical setting of Peru's justice sector. Chapters 3 and 4 describe the sector's institutional composition and operations on the eve of the 1992 coup. Chapter 5 traces the origins and objectives of Peru's past thirty years of frustrated reform and their links to the current "Fujimori program" described in Chapter 6. The last three chapters address the comparative theme more directly: first, through an overview of reform efforts in three other countries and, then, through a reexamination of the general questions and issues raised in the initial discussion.

Notes

1. These figures were cited by President Fujimori in his speech of April 5, 1992, announcing the *autogolpe*.

2. It has been suggested that the coup was precipitated by a series of threatened investigations involving members of the president's family and close advisors. No one has claimed that any important revelations were likely, but the nuisance factor and the threat to his authority may have been sufficient to push the president over the brink. See *Caretas* (Lima), April 10, 1992, for speculation on this and other issues leading to the coup.

3. Polls taken shortly after the coup found as many as 95 percent of those surveyed in Lima in agreement with the measures taken against the judiciary and only 2 percent in opposition. In contrast, 75 percent registered general support for the *autogolpe* (*New York Times*, April 9, 1992, A3). While the figures were never this high, public opinion polls and surveys of members of the judiciary conducted over the prior two decades had uniformly registered significant discontent with the court system, police, and prisons, and a belief that all were inefficient and ridden with corruption. See, for example, Peru, Senate, Comisión Especial, 1989, pp. 323-324.

4. González Oropeza, 1996, p. 76.

5. The term is from Fruhling's (1993) analysis of the Chilean judiciary.

6. As de Lima Lopes, 1997, p. 15, notes of social rights litigation in Brazil, given its low incidence (in terms of overall caseload), its current effect is largely "symbolic" and "immaterial."

7. For a discussion of the Mexican example, see Finkel, 1997; Domingo, 1995; and González Oropeza, 1996. Finkel argues quite convincingly that the 1994 package was the PRI's means of protecting itself against a future electoral defeat. Anticipating a victory by opposition parties, it restructured the judiciary to prevent their using it to introduce more radical policy change.

8. Illustrative examples include those by Bartra, 1990; Cooper, 1968; González and Garita, 1990; Llobet, 1993; Monroy, 1967; and Navarro, 1992.

9. See Salas and Rico, 1989a, 1989b; Gamarra, 1989; and Solís and Wilson, 1991, as examples of descriptive overviews of various national systems. For slightly more analytic discussions of the role of the judiciary and the reform process, see de Belaúnde López de Romaña, 1984; and articles in Inter-American Bank, 1993. Rosenn, 1987, 1995, offers a comparative analysis of judicial independence and federalism. Barker, 1986, 1991; Brandt, 1987, 1990; Brumm, 1992; Cappalli, 1990; de Lima Lopes, 1995, 1997; Domingo, 1997; Finkel, 1997; Grynszpan, 1997; Howell, 1995; Murray, 1987; Pérez Perdomo, 1988; Revilla and Price, 1991; Schwank and Mayén, 1992; Shodt, 1991; Sierra, 1995; Stotzky, 1993; and Valenzuela, 1991, are also relevant. An abortive attempt at judicial reform in Peru in the 1970s, inspired in large part by the Law and Development movement (see Gardner, 1980) of that decade, produced some of the earliest efforts to analyze the sociopolitical role of the judiciary in that country. See Pásara, 1978, 1982, 1988. Works by Colombia's Instituto SER offer some of the best empirical studies of sector operations and were instrumental in drawing attention to the need for reform. See Giraldo, 1987a, 1987b. Analytic works on other sector institutions are still rarer; for one example on the Peruvian police, see Vega Torres, 1990.

10. See Constable and Valenzuela, 1991, pp. 115-139, and articles in Stotzky, 1993.

11. Among the organizations devoting most effort to such studies are Amnesty International and the Andean Commission of Jurists (see García-Sayán, 1987; Comisión Andina, 1988a, 1988b). For a discussion of indigenous legal traditions that also touches this theme, see Schwank and Mayén, 1992; articles in Stavenhagen and Iturralde, 1990; and Drzewieniecki, 1995.

12. Bipartisan National Commission, 1984.

13. While this potentially negative impact has been commented for some time, there is little published on it. Recent exceptions include works by World Bank consultants and staff. See Buscaglia and Domingo Villegas, 1995; Dakolias, 1995.

14. These include the extension of judicial protection of constitutional rights to private as well as public actions.

15. For early discussions of USAID's Administration of Justice Program, see Alvarez, 1992, and WOLA, 1990. A later, critical report is found in GAO, 1993.

16. As early as the mid-1980s, the Argentine government was negotiating a $2 million loan with the World Bank to finance modernization of its justice sector. The loan was never consolidated although some initial preparatory work was done. More recently, both the World Bank and the Inter-American Development Bank (IDB) have begun planning and in some cases, signed far more sizable loan agreements—amounts ranged from $500 million for a proposed World Bank project in Argentina to $30 million for its Venezuelan program and a $13 million loan in Ecuador. The IDB has consolidated a loan to Costa Rica for roughly the latter amount and a $23 million package for El Salvador.

17. "Law determination" is here used to encompass the sector and in particular, the judiciary's role in law making, law interpretation and decisions as to the applicability of laws. Although also a means for performing its other functions, law determination is important in and of itself, the judiciary's contribution to defining

34

the rules under which society will operate. Whether or not a judiciary is expected
to "make" law, how (and whether) it interprets and applies those created elsewhere
ultimately determines their force. If to a lesser extent, the function is also performed
by other sectoral institutions as a consequence of the discretion they formally or
informally exercise in carrying out their activities.

18. G. Smith, 1996, p. 16.

19. The field of legal anthropology in Latin America, whether in urban or rural
settings, still leaves many gaps, especially as regards the relationship of these systems or their practitioners to the formal legal system. For some of the few exceptions, see Brandt, 1987, 1990; Sierra, 1995; Stavenhagen and Iturralde, 1990; Nadar,
1990; and Ayala, 1992. Drzewieniecki, 1995, provides an apparently exhaustive
bibliography on relevant works on Peru. One problem, visible in many articles in
Ayala, 1992, and Stavenhagen and Iturralde, 1990, is that such studies often have
little empirical base and incorporate much romantic mythology about indigenous
practices. Nadar, 1990; Sierra, 1995; and Brandt, 1987, 1990, constitute important
exceptions.

20. Two other common variations are the use of law students, who represent
defendants or prepare work for presentation by graduated lawyers as part of their
degree requirements, and, less frequently, a separate public office with lawyers
(and occasionally law students) paid by the state to represent poor clients. Because
these separate offices are generally a recent innovation, one major problem has been
their placement. In Costa Rica they are part of the judiciary. In Bolivia they remain
in the new Ministry of Justice. In El Salvador they are part of a legal and social assistance office (Procuraduría General). Colombia's Procuraduría, although performing a very different primary function, houses both its Human Rights Ombudsman
and its Office of Public Defense. With the exception of Costa Rica and more recently,
Panama and Bolivia, none of the systems works very well. Low salaries and poor
working conditions make it hard to attract capable personnel and lead to such vices
as the charging of fees for supposedly free services and "full time" employees who
treat the position as a part time job. In Colombia, salaries are so low that defenders
are officially allowed to handle outside, for-pay cases.

21. Mexico, Nicaragua, and Uruguay do not have Ministries of Justice, dividing
the functions they perform elsewhere among other institutions. Bolivia's ministry,
created in 1993, has taken a prominent role in promoting sectoral reform. In Argentina and Colombia the ministries have been the strongest, until recently controlling
the judiciary's administrative systems and budget. In both countries, they promoted
reforms that eliminated some of their traditional powers.

22. See Rosenn, 1995, for a discussion of Latin American federalism as it relates
to the justice sector, and the judiciary in particular. Venezuela is also technically a
federal state, but as regards the justice sector this has little effect. It eliminated its
subnational judicial organization some time ago. In Brazil, most ordinary justice (i.e.
normal trials) is at the state level; federal trial courts did not exist between 1937 and
1970 (Howell, 1995; de Lima Lopes, 1997).

23. See Brumm, 1992, for a discussion of this situation, especially as it relates to
the emerging interest in constitutional law, which often appears to include issues
that might be handled by administrative courts. Brumm's argument for a return to

the civil law tradition of a separate administrative jurisdiction rests on at least one questionable assumption—his contention that civil servants enjoy relatively high prestige that they could transfer to their quasi-judicial rulings. This may be true in Chile, but in a majority of countries it is not the case.

24. González Oropeza, 1996, pp. 64-67.

25. Nicaragua and Ecuador are now drafting new legislation to regulate them. However, the efforts appear more motivated by a desire to standardize operations than by an exploration of the underlying problems.

26. Brazil's Public Ministry is one example. See articles by Fuks, 1995; de Lima Lopes, 1997; Grynszpan, 1997. Most countries seem to prefer a separate Ombudsman for this purpose.

27. A 1994 constitutional amendment created the Bolivian council, but as of early 1997, it still existed only on paper. The Mexican council is the product of the 1994 reforms in that country.

28. See Rico, 1993, for a summary of Latin American and European experience.

29. See FIU, 1987, p. 124, and ILANUD, 1991, pp. 10-16.

30. Through 1996, it was averaging about 7,000 filings a year and resolving most of them. About 40 percent of the cases it received were *amparos*, having to do with legal or constitutional rights allegedly violated. For a discussion of the chamber's formation and first years of operation, see Barker, 1991.

31. These were *amparos*; see note 30 above.

32. Details on the Colombian court are given in Chapter 7. For Brazil see de Lima Lopes, 1997.

33. See Merryman, 1985; Zweigert and Kotz, 1987, for general discussions. Works by Jacob et al., 1996; Thome, 1993; Cappalli, 1990; Brumm, 1992; and Salas and Rico, 1993, are also relevant.

34. Most commonly, if at least one of the parties does not take an active interest in moving the case forward, it will go nowhere. In some countries (El Salvador) this has encouraged the use of private prosecutors by wealthy parties with an interest in a criminal case.

35. In the continental tradition, the judge is always a civil servant, but may enjoy a relatively high status because of the rigorous examinations or special education required to enter the career. See articles in Jacob et al., 1996. This has rarely been the situation in Latin America, where the most important prerequisites have usually been personal contacts, a "credential" that has been significantly devalued as political ties have replaced those of family and bourgeois society. Important exceptions include Brazil (at both the state and federal levels) and more recently Costa Rica, where competitive entrance examinations (*concursos de oposición*) are used to screen candidates. The more frequent *concursos de méritos* are only comparisons of curricula vitae and are generally of little importance compared to recommendations and contacts.

36. The study was sponsored by USAID preparatory to a pilot project on simplifying courtroom procedures.

37. Panama's Public Ministry has recently undergone a substantial reform process. Mexico's Procuraduría and its judicial police are widely perceived as the cause and focus of corruption and abuses.

38. Such tendencies are often identified in judicial handling of everything from modern commercial practices to the complaints of marginalized groups. De Lima Lopes' (1997) discussion of the Brazilian Court's treatment of social rights litigation is illustrative. Here his concern is less the Court's inability to handle substance than a decision-making style that emphasizes zero-sum outcomes.

39. The relative merits of the civil and common law traditions, especially as regards their inquisitorial and accusatory (or adversarial) criminal procedures, has been the subject of extensive and continuing arguments. While writers from a common law tradition (e.g. Merryman, 1985) are more adamant about its intrinsic superiority, some have begun to question this position (e.g. Strier, 1994). See Jacob et al., 1996, and Fennell et al., 1995, for a discussion of recent trends in both traditions and of changes in continental criminal and constitutional law that influenced the Latin American reforms. Damaska's (1997) comparative treatment of the use of evidence is also relevant.

40. Luis Pásara, "Peru: Administración de justicia?" in de Belaúnde López de Romaña, 1984, p. 206.

41. See Rosenn, 1987.

42. This generalization is based largely on anecdotal evidence. Historical studies of judicial recruitment are virtually absent. There are some good contemporary studies, including Pásara, 1982, 1988; Pásara and Parodi, 1988; Giraldo, 1987b; Gutiérrez, 1979; and Mackinson and Goldstein, 1993, that all suggest more humble family origins than might be expected. The judiciary has undoubtedly had its share of villainous members, but there was apparently some effort to avoid placing notorious scoundrels in the more visible positions, a practice that is not as evident today. For a journalistic account of the public sins of the current Argentine judiciary, see Verbitsky, 1993.

43. Costa Rica's Constitutional Chamber, Colombia's Supreme Court and later its Constitutional Court are recent examples of these more proactive stance.

44. This is more typical of Central than South America. In the latter region it is usually unheard of for a Court president to have the national political aspirations harbored by several recent Central American chief justices. Ecuador is one exception; the interim president appointed after Bucaram's ouster had served, briefly, on the Supreme Court. The same is not true of other sector institutions. Colombia's *Fiscal General*, Alfonso Valdivieso, resigned to run for president in 1997. The Bolivian ex-Minister of Justice, René Blattman, was also, briefly, a presidential candidate. Although Mexico's judiciary is not noted for its independence, both it and the Procuraduría have become resting places for politicians "in transit" (González Oropeza, 1996, pp. 67-68).

45. Grynszpan, 1997, offers some interesting results from surveys in Rio de Janeiro indicating that, whereas contact produced slightly more positive evaluations of the labor courts, it worsened those of the ordinary courts. The negative rating rose from 35.5 to 52.7 percent in the latter case.

46. Costa Rica has been an exception for decades, ever since it eliminated its military. However, its police forces still leave much to be desired.

47. Both examples are drawn from the Salvadoran experience with initial revisions to its Criminal Procedures Code.

48. One recent example is the demand of various indigenous groups to have their legal traditions recognized within their own communities. Interestingly, this demand has usually not extended to giving such traditions equal status with the formal national system, let alone replacing it. Here, as in the case of the recent interest in alternative dispute resolution (especially for commercial cases), proposals tend to depict these as complementary to the formal state system and to still demand improvements in the latter. For example, a USAID financed pilot activity in Ecuador training indigenous leaders in conciliation produced a request for a legal assistance office to help the communities deal with conflicts that cannot be resolved internally. Interviews, Ecuador, 1995.

49. For a discussion of regional trends in criminal and civil law reform, see Llobet, 1993, and Maier et al., 1993.

50. These included the creation of specialized constitutional courts and judicial councils in a number of countries and the introduction of more accusatory criminal procedures in Germany, Spain, and Italy.

51. Brazil's lesser concern with judicial independence, which is not perceived as a problem, put a premium on protection of constitutional rights and introduced several novel mechanisms including an ombudsman-like role for the Public Ministry and the public civil suit (*ação pública civil*), which is used to protest both the violation and nonprovision of social rights. Although Latin American constitutions usually express a series of such rights, constitutional litigation has normally been limited to government violation of individual political rights.

52. Brazil introduced a new Civil Procedures Code in 1973. Although it incorporates elements now being considered elsewhere, it has had less regional attention than that of Uruguay. For a discussion of the code, see Rosenn, 1986.

53. The largest of its programs were financed by foreign assistance funds and implemented either by USAID or ICITAP, an office in the Department of Justice specifically created to do police training in conjunction with the USAID programs. The United States Information Service (USIS), the Drug Enforcement Agency (DEA), the FBI, and the State Department's Bureau of International Narcotics and Law Enforcement (INL) also participated in the effort as part of their broader programs. Their coordination with USAID, and even with ICITAP, was often minimal. More recently, the various Department of Justice agencies have entered into competition with USAID, claiming that they have a comparative advantage in this kind of assistance. See Alvarez, 1992; WOLA, 1990; and reports by the GAO for general discussions.

54. USAID has delayed for years in beginning a project in Nicaragua, abruptly terminated one in Guatemala and, after years of pilot efforts, finally ended its first Peruvian project in the early 1990s. Both the World Bank and the Inter-American Bank stepped back on several occasions from projects they were on the brink of initiating—most notably in Argentina, Chile, Venezuela and Peru. Although interested in the sector for almost a decade, as of late 1996, they had signed few agreements. Among the factors slowing their progress are fears of inadequate local management of loan funds, interinstitutional battles within the beneficiary countries, indecision as to implementation mechanisms (i.e. whether to let weak sector institutions manage their own projects and, if not, what mechanism to substitute)

and the banks' own uncertainty as to their overall sectoral strategy (as well as some internal conflicts over who will define and implement it).

55. Two examples are Colombia, where business groups in the town of Itaguí financed court modernization, and Uruguay, where the Chamber of Commerce was instrumental in pushing passage of the Civil Procedures Code. Whatever the disadvantages of elite involvement, they also contribute a technical expertise that the usual reformers often lack.

56. Guatemala's handling of its new Criminal Procedures Code is the classic case of a country that passes a law and then does nothing to prepare for implementation. (This also occurred in Nicaragua with a 1991 modification to its criminal code, reintroducing juries.) During the year between the code's passage and entrance into effect, no preparations were made. When the day for the transition finally came, it took everyone by surprise. El Salvador, with U.S. government urging, actually prepared for both the Family and Juvenile Offenders codes, postponing their respective entrance into effect by six months and one year. This still was not enough time. Two years later, it was evident that a more or less adequate implementation was long off. Furthermore, the Juvenile Offenders Law had raised concerns about its being soft on crime, and especially on juvenile gang activity. Therefore, in 1996, the Assembly passed an "Emergency Law" reversing some of the legislation's due process orientation. Both a reinstatement of the death penalty and the lowering of the age for trial as an adult to fourteen years were also under discussion.

57. In El Salvador, concern over violent crime and judicial corruption seems far more important to the public than the protection of defendants' rights or improved treatment of prisoners, two main thrusts of the reformers' proposals. This produced modifications to the content of the reform proposals. It has also forced individual institutions to take their own measures to respond to public complaints.

58. Increasingly described as the judicialization of politics, it is discussed in the articles in Tate and Vallinder, 1995.

59. Fruhling, 1993.

60. See Howell, 1995, for a discussion. De Lima Lopes' (1997) discussion of social rights litigation is also relevant.

61. In late 1995, El Salvador's governing party (ARENA) was surprised to find two critical articles of Law 471, reducing public sector employment, declared unconstitutional. The vice president of the Court, its key member in the Constitutional Chamber, was traveling when the decision was made.

62. Here the reformers might have benefitted from a consideration of how earlier efforts to professionalize the region's militaries sometimes encouraged more, rather than less political activism. This effect is now seen as contributing to the upsurge of military governments in the 1970s as the professionalized institutions came to see themselves as better qualified to govern than the traditional political class. Peru's Revolutionary Government of the 1970s is a prime example; others include the Chilean and Brazilian regimes of roughly the same period.

63. See Chapter 7 for an example.

64. See Chapter 7 for a discussion.

65. Ecuador's Supreme Court, the first selected under a new "less political" process, initiated its term with a series of high profile investigations threatening

cabinet-level officials. The first of these, in 1994, ended in the impeachment of the Court president and two justices. The second, in 1995, resulted in the flight into exile of the national vice president and at one point threatened to implicate the president. Both the Nicaraguan Supreme Court and the Guatemalan Constitutional Court have engaged in battles with the executive and legislature. While partisan sympathies have been held responsible in both cases, it also appears that Court members were motivated by a more serious consideration of their institutional mandates.

66. In 1994 the Costa Rican Public Defense Office filed a habeas corpus against the executive in connection with a notorious extradition case. El Salvador's Public Defense Office similarly challenged that country's "Emergency Law." (See note 56.) The Colombian Fiscalía's investigation of drug traffickers' financing of political campaigns is another example. Clearly an activist prosecutor's office could be a greater threat than the courts to other institutions and power holders.

PART TWO

The Peruvian Case

2

Historical Background[1]

If Peru's 1992 coup caught the national and the international communities by surprise, it was hardly inconsistent with the country's recent and not so recent history. As of 1992, Peru had been on the verge of breakdown for almost a decade, making imminent national collapse a near permanent condition. Almost two years into the Fujimori administration, the signs of improvement were few. The nation had had over eleven years of democratically elected government, a record at least since 1919. The Fujimori government had finally ended the raging hyperinflation inherited from its predecessor. And while, like hyperinflation, it would be a constant threat for the visible future, the cholera epidemic, which had killed over 3,000 and affected hundreds of thousands more, had been brought under control.

On the other hand, the country was in its twelfth year of near civil war. A victory by the terrorist forces seemed unlikely, but the losses in human lives, property, and productivity continued unabated. If hyperinflation had been temporarily controlled, it was virtually the only bright spot in the dismal economic scene. Real incomes and productivity had been stagnant or declining since the early 1970's, 60 percent of the population was below the poverty line, and only 10 percent of the economically active population was fully employed.[2] Although Peru was making efforts to repay or renegotiate its foreign debt, it remained one of the highest per capita in the region. The only constant growth industry was coca cultivation. Largely illegal,[3] it was estimated to represent from one-third to one-half of the country's export earnings. The chronic economic crisis, combined with terrorist and drug-trafficking activities, had pushed any preexisting social consensus to its limits. Violence had become a facet of everyday life from which no institution or individual was exempt. In this sense, the popular support for Fujimori's actions was less surprising, but more disturbing than the *autogolpe* itself as a vote of no confidence for democratic government. In the minds of many it also appeared vindicated by Fujimori's subsequent successes in areas where constitutional regimes had made no appreciable progress.

Peru's problems have been blamed on geopolitics, natural disasters, international economics and politics, and the developed world's drug habits, but they are all linked by its more fundamental crisis of institutional failure—a failure extending beyond poor performance to a more basic devaluation of institutional legitimacy. As demonstrated by similar, but less dramatic events elsewhere in the region, this institutional bankruptcy and many of its underlying causes are hardly unique to Peru. In a pattern that to varying degrees holds throughout Latin America, the nation's political, economic, and social institutions survived for centuries on an inegalitarian, exclusionary logic that protected the privileges of an elite few and either ignored, patronized or exploited the dispossessed masses. Despite their limited flexibility and absorptive powers these institutions were adequate to the demands placed on them until well into the present century. This was in large part because of the coexistence of a whole series of parallel informal structures,[4] including, on the political side, periodic recourse to de facto regimes when de jure governments reached an impasse. After the 1960s, the pressures on the formal institutions increased substantially, eroding their performance and discrediting them as the vehicles of further national integration. Ad hoc tinkering with the formal structures and a growing reliance on informal mechanisms prevented complete collapse, but only while further aggravating social conflict and undermining any consensus on the legitimate basis for its resolution.

Peru's justice system represents both an example and a consequence of this chronic national crisis. It is also an extreme example of a situation currently confronted by a number of its regional neighbors as they attempt to reform their own justice sectors and define their place within the broader political system. It is tempting to interpret Peru's latest crisis, in the justice sector and in society at large, as unique developments, the products of recent major threats posed by terrorism and drug trafficking. The argument is that both an understanding of and any long term solution to that crisis must address the more fundamental origins of a regionwide pattern of institutional breakdown. Like the cholera epidemic and hyperinflation, these two exceptional threats became so menacing as to require direct and immediate attention, but the wider set of problems that allowed them to take these proportions is the same one affecting the majority of Peru's neighbors. It is possible that many of the latter, facing few of Peru's additional obstacles, can avoid a remedy as drastic as that imposed by the Fujimori administration. However, the Peruvian case is also significant in demonstrating the dangers of delayed or opportunistic reforms and in suggesting that society's tolerance for a maintenance of the status quo will eventually reach its limits.

The Setting

Located on the Pacific Coast of South America, Peru is the continent's third largest country by area and fourth largest by population (estimated at 23 million in 1994). The population reflects the normal LDC profile, with the largest portion, 57 percent, under twenty-five years of age and 37 percent under fifteen. This youthful profile is in part a function of the high birth rate and in part of the life expectancy of sixty-three years.[5] Racial distinctions are no longer used in the official census; the last census (1940) to include them classified 46 percent of the population as Indian (largely Quechua and Aymara-speaking, with roughly two-thirds exclusively fluent in those languages) and another 53 percent of European or mixed Indian and European descent. The small remainder was composed of groups of African and Asian ancestry. Because in Peru, "Indianness" is as much a cultural as biological phenomenon, it is likely that the percentage self-defined or defined by others as Indian has diminished substantially since 1940, with a consequent increase in the mestizo and white categories. This shift can be indirectly inferred from the dramatic reduction in the proportion of monolingual Quecha or Aymara speakers.[6] It is a probable result of patterns of internal migration that have reduced the physical and cultural isolation of Indian communities. It is also the logical response of affected individuals to the long-standing second-class status of Indian peoples, a phenomenon once summed up in the brutal saying that "the Indian is the animal closest to man."

Peru's economy has traditionally depended on agriculture, mining, and other primary activities. By the early 1990s, industry accounted for 20 to 25 percent of the GNP and perhaps 20 percent of exports.[7] The latter in particular remain heavily dependent on the basic processing of raw materials. Throughout its history, Peru's economy has been characterized by a boom and bust development, as one principal export after another rises to importance and then either disappears or succumbs to declining international markets. This has also meant that the benefits of the booms have been narrowly distributed and have not contributed their full potential to overall economic development. What was true of guano and nitrates in the nineteenth century, has followed for rubber, copper, cotton, and fishmeal in the twentieth, and is equally true of the latest boom crop, coca, the developmental impact of which is further diminished by its largely illegal status. Another consequence is that, although Peru's per capita income (estimated at $2,070 in 1994) places it in the medium range of Latin American countries, it is extremely unequally distributed. In recent years, up to 90 percent of the economically active population (EAP) has been underemployed. An estimated 60 percent worked in the so-called informal sector, most often in undercapitalized small industries or service activities.[8] Similarly, although 34 percent of the EAP is employed in agriculture, much of this is at the subsistence or barely subsistence level. As a consequence agriculture represents less than 10 percent of the GDP.[9]

Peru's territory is divided into three major regions: an arid coastal strip with 11 percent of the nation's area and almost half of its population; the mountainous highlands and upland plains, the traditional center of population until well into the present century, with over 25 percent of the territory and 39 percent of the population; and the eastern high and low jungle area, over two-thirds of Peru's territory with only about 11 percent of its population. As of 1990, 70 percent of the population was classified as urban; as late as 1940, that figure was only 35 percent. Although rich in mineral resources, the country has a shortage of arable land, representing only about 15 percent of its total area. Its topography has made internal transportation and communication difficult and still poses obstacles to national integration and development.

The Pre and Early Independence Periods

The most serious obstacles are not physical, however, but originate in the country's history and patterns of development, beginning with the fifteenth and sixteenth-century consolidation of the Inca empire. At its height this extended from present day Colombia into northern Chile, with most of the population concentrated in the mountain highlands. The Spanish, arriving in 1532, took advantage of conflicts among the Incas to establish their own control of the conquered areas and peoples, and to create what was to be Spain's most valued viceroyalty in the New World. In founding their own empire, the Spaniards made a decision with enormous implications for Peru's further development. Rather than settling in the highland Inca capital, Cuzco, they based themselves on the relatively neglected coast, creating a new capital city, Lima. This decision facilitated contact with Spain and with other colonial administrative centers. It also dictated a weakening of the ties between Peru's capital and its hinterlands, and a reliance on a system of intermediaries, indirect controls, and parallel institutions to link the two. This fostered a situation in which Peruvian elites and other modern groups were said to have more contact with and knowledge of Europe and later, the United States, than they did with the majority of their own countrymen.

The Incas had interfered relatively little with the internal structure of the societies they conquered, imposing only their language, some aspects of their religion and a system to extract labor and tribute. The Spanish proved more difficult and disruptive masters. The Spaniards' first interests were the treasures of the Inca state. The already organized supply of indigenous labor soon became a more important asset, used to work mines and later for agriculture. The harsh working conditions, combined with the new diseases introduced by the colonists produced a dramatic decline in the indigenous population, from an estimated nine million in 1532 to two million by 1600.[10] Efforts by the Church and the Crown to curb mistreatment of the Indians were generally unsuccessful as were the Indians' attempts to flee colonial control or, when this failed, to stage periodic revolts. Setting a pattern visible to this day, Lima's direct penetration of the rest of the country remained limited. Effective control of the rural areas remained in the hands of local elites or, within the more isolated Indian communities, their own traditional leaders.

During the colonial period, further development did little to change the basic pattern of a small elite living comfortably off the labor of a large indigenous majority. Peru's value to Spain intensified the latter's efforts to enforce mercantilist policies, ensuring that local economic production did not compete with what Spain could sell to the colonists and prohibiting trading ties with third nations. The achievements here fell short of Spain's ambitions, but they had a longer term effect in distorting Peru's subsequent development. Although the colonists occasionally bridled at these controls, the overall benefits were substantial and, not surprisingly, Peru came to independence reluctantly.

Declared in 1821 and consolidated in 1825, independence was followed by several decades of economic stagnation, political chaos, and internal warfare as various military and civilian leaders (*caudillos*) attempted to gain control of the nation or subnational regions. Between 1826 and 1866, the country had thirty-four presidents, only seven of them civilians. Much of the nation's economic infrastructure had been destroyed during the independence wars and the continuing conflict gave little opportunity for rebuilding it. Isolated from its European markets and with its mines almost worked out, Peru's exports fell to half of their previous level in the last quarter of the eighteenth century. The political and economic disruptions had their strongest impacts on "modern" (i.e. coastal) Peru. The breakdown of national institutions and the generally adverse economic conditions actually encouraged the revival and strengthening of Indian culture and communities in the rural highlands, a trend that would not be reversed until the last quarter of the nineteenth century. Recent studies[11] refer to Peru's "Indianization" during the late colonial and post-independence era, reflected in a slight increase in the Indian proportion of the population (to roughly 60 percent) until the mid-century with the long term decline reinitiating only in the 1870s. This century long reversal of a trend visible from the earliest colonial days to the present—i.e. the steady reduction in the relative proportion of the biologically and culturally defined Indian population—is an important factor in explaining the persistence of a strong indigenous tradition even in contemporary Peru. Curiously, it has yet to produce a nationally based indigenous rights movement.

Overall economic and political conditions began to improve in the mid-century. This was first apparent on the coast and only later in the interior of the country. The guano boom (1840-1880) temporarily restored export earnings, but most of the profits went to pay off foreign and domestic debt.

They also served as collateral on new foreign loans, often used to import luxury items. In the 1860s the government took out more foreign loans to begin a massive program of railroad construction. This would bankrupt the country and eventually deliver what remained of the guano operations to foreign control. The temporary economic recovery did lead to the emergence of a new commercial class that began to invest in export agriculture, especially cotton and sugar. This new elite would represent an important political as well as economic force over the following decades.

The nation's first real political stability also came at mid-century, under the government of the "popular *caudillo*," General Ramón Castillo. In or out of office, Castillo dominated national politics for two decades, putting an end to conflicts among the lesser *caudillos*. However, it was not until 1872 that Peru had its first elected civilian president, Manuel Pardo, founder of the Civilista Party. As its name indicates, the party was created to end military rule. Unfortunately, Pardo chose to reduce military expenditures and the size of the army just as Peru was threatened by war with Chile. The Chileans declared war in 1880. In 1881, their armies occupied Lima, remaining for two years. The war cost Peru its portion of the nitrate-rich Atacama desert and further bankrupted a nation already heavily in foreign debt. However, the dramatic defeat may have eliminated any remaining taste for the old style *caudillo* rule, as well as ending the country's dependence on guano and nitrates.

The Aristocratic State

Once recuperated from the war's destruction, the country entered over twenty years (1895-1919) of relatively peaceful civilian rule accompanied by rapid and diversified economic growth and initial efforts to accommodate emerging social forces. This period saw the further consolidation of central government, the formation of the first real political parties and labor unions, and the expansion of political participation beyond a closed elite to a small but growing middle class. It also brought the consolidation of the coastally based agro-export oligarchy. In alliance with the highland landlords and the military, this new group would control national development for almost three-quarters of a century, and set the stage for the explosion to follow.

These years also produced the first serious criticism of Peruvian society, its domination by a small civilian and military oligarchy, its inadequate attention to the demands of a small but expanding urban middle and working class, and its total isolation of the Indian majority. In the 1920s these criticisms contributed to the formation of the country's first real leftist parties, the Socialist (later, Peruvian Communist) Party and, in 1924, the American Popular Revolutionary Alliance (APRA).[12] Despite its illegal or quasi-illegal status for most of its history, APRA remained Peru's most important political party with an enormous impact on the country's political development. By the time APRA finally came to power in 1985, its movement to the right, and the movement to the left of political discourse, placed it in the center of the political spectrum. However, in the 1920s, its anti-imperialist, anticapitalist, pro-land reform, and pronationalization platform made it a decidedly radical threat to the status quo.

The democratizing tendencies of the era ended abruptly with the eleven-year Leguía dictatorship (1919-1930). Augusto Leguía was elected amidst riots and strikes staged over price increases decreed by his predecessor. He used these events as a pretext for closing Congress and imposing what was first a mild civilian dictatorship. Over the following years he arranged for two reelections and for the complete acquiescence of the Court and the (re-opened) Congress. Despite the new liberal constitution of 1920 and some early populist tendencies, by 1925 Leguía's government had entered a fully repressive stage. He jailed or exiled opponents, placed curbs on the press, and closed the national university. His policies generally augmented the powers and centralizing character of the state, while also lining the pockets of his cronies. The 1920 Constitution also introduced a new mechanism for control of the judiciary—a system of judicial ratifications whereby the Supreme Court at five-year intervals was to confirm or separate from office all first and second-instance judges. The ratification system remained in the 1933 Constitution. Its exercise has often been a mere formality or a tool for the Court's control of its own judges, but on occasion it has been manipulated by the executive for political reasons.

On the socioeconomic front, Leguía's achievements were more positive although later critics have charged that they established patterns contrary to the long run interests of the nation's independent development. His regime actively encouraged foreign investment, especially in public utilities and financial institutions. He also promoted agro-industry, mining and the rationalization of the public administration. Unfortunately, his extensive public works and road building programs increased the public debt tenfold. Despite his government's repressive tendencies, Leguía promoted long neglected policies, including the expansion of the educational system and passage of a minimum wage and eight-hour workday. He also professed an interest in the welfare of the Indian majority. In the end, his heavy-handed style, his reliance on a small and increasingly corrupt inner circle, and the impact of the Great Depression brought his overthrow in 1930.

The Beginnings of Modernization

There followed a brief period of populist government under the head of the military junta, Luis Sánchez Cerro, who was elected president in 1931.

Two extremely important if very different events occurred during his administration, the framing of a new constitution (1933) and the Aprista rebellion in Trujillo, involving the massacre of some sixty troops and government officials. The 1933 Constitution remained in force until 1979 and shaped the modern political development of the country, although it in fact only confirmed trends already visible in the 1860 and 1920 Constitutions. The Trujillo rebellion occurred after the Apristas' defeat in the 1931 national elections. The ensuing massacre placed APRA outside the political pale for most of the period until the 1980s and earned it the undying hostility of a whole generation of military officials. Government reprisals also produced the summary executions of at least an equal number of Apristas, a fact conveniently forgotten by the anti-Aprista military. Despite its frequently illegal status, the party's platform and demands formed an important part of the national political dialogue over the following decades. Its bouts of illegality also strengthened its militant mass organization, still unequaled by any other Peruvian party. However, by the time APRA finally came to power most of its radical energy had been dissipated and much of what it had campaigned for had already been achieved by other governments or at least incorporated in the programs of other parties.

Sánchez Cerro was assassinated in 1933, allegedly by an Aprista. The Congress named General Oscar Raimundo Benavides to complete his term. The 1936 elections were declared invalid by the National Electoral Board, apparently because the APRA backed candidate had won. Although not a candidate, Benavides was named president. He governed under moderate dictatorial powers until 1939. Benavides' six-year presidency represented a reassertion of the military-elite alliance in its most enlightened form. While brooking no disorder, he encouraged the passage of various social programs aimed at undercutting APRA's support among the middle and lower middle class.

Benavides' consolidation of the old alliance guaranteed political continuity for the next thirty years. It had a different effect on social and economic conditions. Economic growth and development and especially the post World War II export boom and import substitution industrialization opened the economy still further to foreign investment while creating a wide variety of new economic groups and interests. Most of this economic activity was concentrated in Lima or on the Peruvian coast. It thus accentuated another tendency, the rural to urban and sierra to coastal migration that had begun in the 1920s. From 1935 to 1965 the country went from 35 to 65 percent urban, and Lima's population grew three times as fast as the national average. This altered the face of Lima and eventually of other major urban centers, and greatly accelerated the pace of change in the countryside by increasing outside contacts. Although the out migration reduced pressure over the short run, the situation in many parts of the highlands was fast approaching crisis proportions, generated by the scarcity of land and the introduction of modern, market-oriented agriculture. Beginning in the 1920's land-related litigation and more violent conflicts increased dramatically as "progressive" landholders attempted to oust their traditional tenants or expand their holdings by annexing lands farmed by peasant communities. The communities themselves also engaged in litigations with their own members and were not adverse to taking the initiative in boundary disputes with private holders.[13]

Peru's growth and development over these years paralleled wider regional trends. It was unusual for its resistance to state direction or planning. Until the end of the 1960s Peru's governments were adamantly noninterventionist. Economic policy was effectively decided by private actors, and then if necessary, officially sanctioned by the state. The size and role of the state remained so limited that even such basic functions as tax collection were left in private hands. This did not prevent government from becoming an important source of employment for the small urban middle class,[14] or an occasional generator of private fortunes (especially in conjunction with public works programs) or from being used by major economic actors to enhance their private efforts. Still, the concept of the state as planner and director of economic activities remained outside the lexicon of those in power.

Peru was also slow in expanding political participation, still effectively excluding the majority of the urban and rural masses. A major factor here was the literacy requirement for voting, only eliminated with the 1979 Constitution. The governments during this period did make some concessions to the urban populace, introducing limited social programs, holding down food prices, and giving some attention to the growing urban slums. The rural population, however, was largely ignored. This was especially true of the highland areas, the traditional home of the bulk of the Indian population.

Recent studies[15] have only begun to uncover the variety and fluctuating nature of the living situations and power relations in the "traditional" highlands. At the risk of oversimplifying, it is fair to say that in much of these areas, the large landowners or their representatives were the effective law. The situation was tolerated or simply ignored by the urban economic and political elites since it still did not conflict with their own interests. Also, at least for the bulk of the period, these arrangements offered the only effective way of controlling the hinterlands. Furthermore, the local landlords controlled the rural vote, and thus a good portion if not a majority of the Congress. They were also a decisive factor in presidential elections. However, if the rural landlords were critical to the ruling alliance, they were also its weakest link. The alliance's acceptability began to break down in the mid-fifties, as the landowners became a more noticeable drag on the economy, as the shortage of land and opportunities in the highlands led to vastly increased rates of rural to urban migration and rural violence, and as political parties began to find ways and reasons to seek support among the urban and rural masses. By 1970, when Lima already had a quarter of the national population, the rural problem had in effect been transposed from the rural areas to the doorsteps of the urban elites and middle class.

For most of the period from 1933 to 1962, the traditional political alliance produced a series of conservative governments of varying degrees of repressiveness. The one exception was the brief period from 1945 to 1948 when the Apristas entered government in coalition with the reformist president, José Luis Bustamante y Rivera. Bustamante y Rivera's liberal aims and the coalition proved impossible to maintain in the face of economic difficulties, civil disorders, and the military's continued distrust of APRA. The experience only served to convince the large anti-Aprista faction that the party was dangerous and should remain illegal, and eventually led to Bustamante's overthrow and replacement by the military dictator, Manuel Odría.[16]

Odría had himself elected president in 1950 and remained in power until the election of the civilian, Manuel Prado, in 1956. Odría's control of the country's principal political institutions included the Supreme Court. He habitually invited his candidates to the Court to a champagne toast the night before their "selection" by the Congress.[17] Although Odría exercised his dictatorial powers unapologetically, he retained admirers for decades after his departure from government. This was largely because his regime coincided with the economic recuperation and export boom of the 1950s and early 1960s. The favorable economy distracted attention from his repressive policies and also allowed certain popular and populist measures. These included a program of attention to urban slums (headed by his wife) and some of the earliest efforts to encourage economic development outside of Lima through the promotion of industrial expansion and a program of public works. By the 1950s the growing gap between Lima and certain parts of the coast (where most of the economic growth occurred and still more of the profits accrued) and the rest of the country could no longer be ignored. Efforts under Odría and subsequent governments to reverse these trends were largely unsuccessful, but over the short run, they undercut protests and discontent.

The attempted political reforms of the early 1930s and the mid-1940s were not repeated until the early 1960s. Following a short military government (1962-63), invited or encouraged by the political and economic elites to prevent a victory by the Aprista-Odriísta presidential candidate, the first administration of Fernando Belaúnde (1963-68) represents the final attempt by progressive civilian forces to work change within the old rules of the game. In his unsuccessful presidential bid of 1956, and in his first administration, Belaúnde emphasized many of the themes already raised by previous would-be reformers. These included the need to decentralize economic development and its benefits, land reform and attention to the poor urban and rural masses, community development, and popular participation. Belaúnde proposed to accomplish all this within the context of a fully democratic government where the emphasis would be less on redistribution than on promoting growth for the benefit of all. While he introduced a land reform, it is significant that he placed far greater emphasis on the development of the largely unclaimed and unsettled eastern lowlands and on large-scale irrigation projects that would make the desert bloom. However, the political system and, especially, the now conservatized APRA, which struck a parliamentary alliance with the ex-dictator Odría, conspired against him. The optimistic beginnings of Belaúnde's presidency soon ran aground on political inertia, corruption, economic decline, and mismanagement.

In the meantime, one of the key elements of the traditional alliance, the military, had undergone a radical change and was viewing Belaúnde's efforts critically. The new factions within the military had briefly held power between 1962 and 1963. They had become concerned about the need for faster and more fundamental socioeconomic change. Two factors in particular alienated their support. First was the government's inability to stem the growing rural violence and the military's consequent involvement in combating land invasions and rural guerilla movements. The second was a controversial agreement with the International Petroleum Company (IPC) that earned Belaúnde charges of *entreguismo* (selling out the country).[18] As the next elections neared and Belaúnde and his party rapidly lost popular support, an Aprista victory seemed imminent. Ironically, the new military feared this not because of APRA's leftist heritage, but rather because they now viewed the party as an opportunistic ally of traditional elites. Thus, preempting an Aprista victory, the military ousted Belaúnde on October 3, 1968, and declared the initiation of their "Revolutionary Government."

Military Rule, 1968-1980[19]

The military's self-proclaimed Revolutionary Government, whatever else it did or did not accomplish, effectively moved the country out of its five decade impasse. In the course of twelve years it worked a basic socioeconomic and political transformation. This included the introduction of a dramatically larger and interventionist role for the state; the termination of the political and economic domination by a closed oligarchy; the virtual elimination of the traditional landed elite; efforts to define a new role for foreign capital and investment; a series of nationalizations of basic industries and services; a massive land redistribution program; and a program of public works and public investment that quadrupled the government budget and the foreign debt. The military claimed to be following a "third way" between capitalism and communism; it was aggressively nationalistic, populistic and redistributive.

Most of this occurred in the "first phase" government under General Juan Velasco Alvarado. The growth in the size, functions, and internal organization of government is especially noteworthy. The changes were in line with general trends in the region, but differed in their dimensions and the speed with which they occurred. From the late 1960s to the mid-1970s, government expenditures as a portion of GNP rose from 6 to 25 percent. Total government employment rose from 270,000 in 1967 to over 1.2 million in 1979.[20] The number of ministries increased from twelve to eighteen. The state owned enterprises (the semi-autonomous sector) burgeoned from less than two dozen to over 170. More significantly, the semi-autonomous sector prior to 1968 was composed of relatively unimportant entities with a negligible economic impact. The enterprises added by the military gave the state direct control of a significant portion of the national economy—a majority of the banking industry, almost all mining, the entire industrial fishing sector (in 1972 the highest export earner), the telephone and electric service, and for a brief period, the major newspapers. The agricultural lands expropriated under the agrarian reform program were turned over to their workers. State control of agricultural production was maintained through the creation of a series of enterprises for the marketing, import, and export of basic commodities. Although much of the growth of government occurred in Lima, the military's interest in promoting decentralization and regionalization led to the creation of regional and zonal offices for individual ministries and ministerial level entities, and to the first systematic attempts at establishing departmental governments.[21] The decentralized bodies were still subject to strict central control. The decentralization was more physical than functional, but it did extend government's active presence further into the national territory.

State expansion reached its peak in the mid-1970s. The second phase, from 1975 to 1980, brought more conservative military leaders to power under General Francisco Morales Bermúdez, grandson of a previous president and representative of military ties with the older establishment. Starting in the late 1970s and continuing through the first civilian government, the number of ministries was reduced, offices were eliminated or scaled down, efforts were made, if not very successfully to cut back personnel, and the reprivatization of the state enterprises began.[22] However, while the Morales administration may have disagreed with the aims and intents of the more radical Velasco, it could only slow but not reverse the pattern of change. Thus, the 1979 Constitution specifically eliminated some of the military's innovations, but it incorporated many of their ideological goals.

Among these are the increased role of the state in social and economic life and its official commitment to such objectives as the eradication of illiteracy and the elimination of poverty.

If the Peru of 1980 faced most of the problems of the pre-1968 period, it was clear that solutions still possible in the pre-Velasco era would no longer work. Aside from the basic structural transformations of the first phase, many of its most important changes were attitudinal and behavioral. They can be summarized as the political awakening of the popular masses, especially the urban poor and a large portion of the rural peasant (Indian)[23] class, and the creation of a set of expectations about the role of government and its responsibility for directing socioeconomic development and assuring the equitable distribution of its benefits. The objective conditions of these groups did not improve markedly and, in fact, would decline drastically in the eventual economic collapse stemming in part from the military's mismanaged policies. The revolution, however, raised their expectations and their demands while giving them the organizational tools to make these heard. Subsequent studies[24] of the government's achievements suggest that even their most radical redistributive policies had a narrower impact than was intended or first thought. Actual redistribution of wealth is reported to have occurred only within the upper 25 percent of the income groups. Even the land reform fell short of its aims, affecting only 39 percent of agricultural land and benefitting only a quarter of the rural population, only about half of whom actually received land. The remaining beneficiaries, members of peasant communities, were made indirect associates of cooperative holdings awarded to their ex-tenants and workers.

Whether as direct beneficiaries of these policies, or only as observers, the dispossessed majority could not fail to appreciate the lessons they taught regarding the vulnerability of the oligarchy, the inequalities and injustices of the traditional system, and the role governmental institutions had played in perpetuating them. Aside from its direct actions, the military's rhetoric and its efforts at creating a base of organized popular support also contributed to this attitudinal change and to the dramatic expansion of the politically relevant population.

By late 1974, a significant portion of the military was dissatisfied with the continuing radicalization of the velasquistas and the signs that their policies were leading the country into social and economic disorder. In mid-1975, a more conservative military faction overthrew Velasco and his group, replacing them with the second phase government, under the leadership of Morales Bermúdez. The second phase leaders almost immediately began to make amends with prominent civilian leaders and foreign creditors, as a first step toward an announced return to civilian rule. While not entirely disavowing the aims and objectives of the first phase, the Morales administration was less ideological and more technocratic. In an attempt to reverse some of the less felicitous trends of the velasquistas, it promoted economic decentralization and austerity. Its policies included a drastic devaluation, import and wage controls, and increases in prices and taxes; foreign and private investment; and the divestiture of many of the state owned enterprises. In effect little reprivatization actually occurred, in part, because the military officers were reluctant to leave their positions as heads of the state companies. The government also announced an end to the land reform program, claiming its goals had been met, and began a plan to compensate foreign owners of nationalized enterprises.

In 1977, the second phase government announced a return to civilian rule, first calling a Constituent Assembly (1978) to replace the 1933 Constitution, never officially abrogated. The new constitution was promulgated in 1979, elections were held, and in 1980, Fernando Belaúnde assumed the presidency for the second time.

Redemocratization: 1980-1992

Belaúnde's policies in his second term were not that different from his first. The political environment was far less propitious. APRA again changed its political colors, this time to the left. Belaúnde, who once represented the reformist hope, was now portrayed as the ally of conservative, traditional forces. His regime's policies of economic readjustment, conciliation with its foreign creditors, and reprivatization of the state enterprises, although implemented inconsistently at best, were hardly suited to overcoming that image. A dramatic economic decline began in 1983, caused by a drop in export prices and a series of natural disasters. The strict monetarist policies followed by his new minister of economy increased discontent with his economic management. Real wages fell 20 percent in 1983, validating the minister's announcement that he was not there to reactivate the economy and producing a new wave of popular unrest and protests. Added to this were a series of political scandals and charges of corruption at the highest levels. The scandals never directly touched Belaúnde, but they further discredited his party. Thus by the end of his term, with his popularity at low ebb and no obvious successor, it was hardly surprising that the two main contenders in the national elections were the Apristas and a coalition of leftist parties.

Although not major issues in the 1985 elections, the period also saw the emergence to national attention of two phenomena, drug trafficking and internal terrorism. Both would assume much greater importance in the late 1980s and 1990s. Drug trafficking, principally the production of coca leaf and its derivative basic paste (*pasta básica*) for export and processing into cocaine, was the least noticed of the two since it largely occurred in the sparsely populated upper jungle regions. Because the trade was managed principally by foreign traffickers, the majority of Peruvian participants were the expanding group of small farmers[25] for whom this represented the only chance to escape abject poverty. The industry's physical location and the ease of access across Peru's jungle borders encouraged and required less direct involvement by Peruvian political and economic elites than has been the case in other countries. Peru has had more than its share of high level political and economic scandals over the past two decades. Considering the size of the drug economy, remarkably few have involved drug trafficking. This may indicate the greater efficiency of the traffickers in protecting their own, but it is equally a result of the lesser need for official "cooperation," except in the areas of production. Despite the lack of an immediate visible influence on or threat to the rest of the country, drug money was making its way into the larger economic, social and political circles where the sheer quantities involved could not help but have an effect.[26] Moreover, the industry was already disturbing relations with the United States as it began conditioning its economic and military assistance on Peruvian efforts to curb coca production, something that the Peruvians still termed "an American problem."[27]

Terrorism, and especially the actions of the Shining Path (Sendero Luminoso),[28] was another matter. It was also not perceived as the threat it later would become. Peru's history with militant subversive groups, whether the Apristas during their underground period, or various extreme leftist factions, had enured its population and leaders to a certain amount of political violence. This was generally in the form of strikes, protests, and similarly limited urban and rural uprisings, as well as the often equally violent reactions of the police and military. Peruvians were thus not prepared for the fanatical, nihilistic internal warfare waged by the Senderistas against virtually all of modern Peru. Thus, until well into the 1980s, they continued to see Sendero as just another guerrilla group, which furthermore focused most of its activities in the far removed provinces of the sierra. The fact that in those provinces, the Senderistas and the armed forces combating them were committing atrocities on the civilian population also came to light very slowly. Recognition of the danger posed by Sendero might have been further delayed had it not been for two phenomena of the mid-1980s—the rapidly increased migration of rural groups to Lima and other urban areas responding both to the depressed rural economy and the Senderista, and military, threat to their lives and livelihood, and Sendero's own change of strategy, taking its activities into the urban areas. In the meantime, Sendero's war had been complemented by that of a new, if more conventional terrorist group, the Túpac Amaru Revolutionary Movement (MRTA). Despite its name, that of a colonial Indian leader, MRTA had begun as an urban guerrilla movement. It eventually took its activities to the jungle areas as well, where it fought not only the state's forces, but those of Sendero.

The 1985 presidential and congressional elections were won by the Apristas with the United Left making a strong second place showing.[29] The new government was headed by Alán García, a relative newcomer to politics. García was the personally chosen successor of Víctor Haya de la Torre, APRA's founder and leader until his death in 1979. García's populistic, nationalistic platform, including his early promise to limit payments on the foreign debt to 10 percent of export earnings, won approval even from his most conservative opposition. However, his volatile personality and tendency to avoid consultations with his cabinet or party in favor of a small group of advisors (many not even Apristas) or direct appeals to the public quickly eroded his backing. The monies withheld from debt payment created an economic upturn for the first two years. By the second half of his term it was apparent that the government's "heterodox strategy" (which at one point was said to have contemplated the so-called Colombian strategy, the use of drug money to revitalize the economy[30]) was not working. The economy was once again on the verge of collapse. Added to this were increasing rumors of corruption at all levels, and rapidly escalating problems with terrorism and drug trafficking. By the time García left office in 1990, the government had lost control not only of the economic situation but also of a good portion of the national territory. At least half of the country was under emergency and, thus, military rule because of terrorist activities, drug trafficking, or the two combined. It was widely believed that a military coup had been avoided only because even the military could not see their way out of the chaotic situation. More Machiavellian observers claimed that the military rejected a coup to avoid giving García an honorable early exit from the disaster he had created.

The García administration, like that of Belaúnde, departed office at the low ebb of its popularity. In the 1990 elections, the two chief competitors were the newly formed Liberation Front headed by the novelist, Mario Vargas Llosa, and including elements from the traditional conservative parties, and the wholly unknown Change 90, headed by Alberto Fujimori.[31] Fujimori's surprisingly strong showing on the first round, and his overwhelming victory on the second, can only be interpreted as a sign of popular disillusionment with the old guard in any form, whether rightist or leftist, and with the institutions that supported them. Unfortunately, Fujimori's own electoral success did not translate to his hastily formed party that constituted a minority in both chambers of Congress. The disadvantage was temporarily offset by his informal alliance with the Apristas. By the second year of his administration, after his government's unsuccessful attempt to prosecute ex-President García on charges of illegal enrichment, the alliance fell apart. This produced a head-on collision between the executive and the Congress. Unable to get his programs through Congress, Fujimori increasingly relied on government by executive decree. He was further frustrated when the Congress moved to regulate even that constitutionally provided power.

Fujimori's most important accomplishment during his first year in office was the imposition of a radical economic stabilization program, popularly dubbed the "*Fujishock.*" Contrary to his campaign promises, he abandoned efforts to produce change gradually in favor of a more drastic package recommended by the IMF. The government abruptly cut back public sector expenditures and price subsidies, and introduced measures to increase tax revenues. In the program's first month, inflation actually rose to its highest historical rate, reducing real salaries by 37.9 percent and increasing underemployment by 20 percent.[32] In its first year, economic output fell by 10 percent.[33] Ironically, Fujimori's initial core supporters, owners of small and microbusinesses, were among the hardest hit by the downturn. Despite popular protests and criticisms from the political opposition, the government held firm and succeeded in halting the galloping hyperinflation it had inherited from the García administration.

Aside from his reliance on a cabinet composed of an unusual mixture of Apristas, ex-Accionpopulistas, and relative unknowns, and a somewhat schizophrenic policy-making style, Fujimori's first year in government failed to demonstrate any more substantial change in either form or content. In his approach to the various more enduring problems—the economic collapse, the moral and financial bankruptcy of government, drug trafficking, terrorism, and civil disorder—he was accused of indecisiveness, arbitrariness, oversimplification, and a simple lack of vision. As he entered his second year in office, Fujimori also came under attack for what was perceived as an increasingly autocratic style, especially as regards his anti-terrorist policies, and his dealings both with his own cabinet and with the legislature. By late 1991, although his standing in opinion polls was high, his relationship with almost every organized political and economic group, except the military, had deteriorated and rumors of a self- induced coup were already circulating. The rumors were realized on April 5, 1992.

Despite the evident obstacle posed by the opposition Congress and the widespread domestic and international acceptance of his argument that he had no other means to deal with Peru's three crises—terrorism, drug trafficking, and the economy—his critics[34] charged that Fujimori created his own political impasse. They characterized this as unintentional at first, a result of his inability to deal with democratic opposition. However, it later became a conscious means of justifying the projected *autogolpe.* Critics suggested for example, that given Peru's notoriously bad record on human rights violations, granting more power to the military to combat terrorism and drug trafficking was hardly justifiable. They noted that the president's failure to build an organized base of support exacerbated his problems with the Apristas and, thus, with the Congress. Even his attacks on the judiciary seem exaggerated, especially given his last minute reversal on its new organic law. This move added seven new members to the Supreme Court, all of whom he would select, albeit from lists provided by the National Magistrates' Council. In short, it was less the admittedly myriad failings of the institutional structure, than Fujimori's own lack of political skills that provoked his drastic move. Still, if his personality and political style precipitated events, his frustrations were evidently shared by a much broader public whose attachment to traditional institutions was visibly weaker than their demand for results the latter were not producing.

The Post-Coup Period

Fujimori's ability to produce some of those results in the simplified political environment he imposed following his coup reduced the pressures and created space for maneuver. As many have noted, his economic policies, even before 1992 and increasingly afterwards differed little from those promoted by Vargas Llosa and his neoliberal advisors. The results, however, have been impressive. It is worth noting his continued ability to hold down inflation to two digit figures (15 percent for 1994), to encourage economic growth that reached 6.4 percent in 1993 and 12.9 percent in 1994,[35] to attract foreign investment, and to move ahead rapidly with the privatization of state enterprises, the reduction of public sector expenditures and employment, and the growth of tax revenues. Although Peru's foreign debt remains high, foreign reserves are also at an all time peak. More recently a part of them have been invested in social works programs, and efforts to modernize public sector operations, including after 1994, its justice sector. These later moves also responded to external pressures and to Fujimori's preparations for the 1995 presidential elections. Overall his program has been criticized for its continued reliance on primary exports,[36] its inattention to the substantial commercial deficit, and its failure to reactivate local industry or to spread the benefits very widely. Economic growth while impressive, remains concentrated as do the new economic opportunities it has generated. Much of the foreign investment has gone into the purchase of state enterprises rather than the creation of new industries. Nonetheless, the progress made has given Peru's population a sense of optimism about the future it has not enjoyed in decades.

The optimism also drew on another accomplishment, the administration's near elimination of the terrorist threat. The capture in mid-1992 of Abimael Guzmán, the founder and leader of Sendero Luminoso, was conceivably the government's major coup. It is widely recognized that Guzmán's arrest like that of dozens of cadre and hundreds of other suspected terrorists was the result of years of footwork by the antiterrorist police. Fujimori himself was sufficiently removed from the loop so as to be absent from Lima when

Guzmán was finally apprehended. Nonetheless the near dismantling of the Senderista organization and that of the lesser, but still threatening MRTA, was widely interpreted as a vindication of the *autogolpe* and the prior and subsequent extraconstitutional measures taken to combat the terrorist movement. Terrorism has not been eliminated, but what remains is a mere shadow of what existed a few years earlier. Furthermore, as indicated by popular reactions to the seizure of the Japanese Embassy by a small MRTA band (conceivably all that was left in the country) in late 1996, it now inspires neither the fear nor the support it did earlier.

While Fujimori's popularity has declined over time, it would still be envied by most national leaders. He has also been remarkably successful in carrying out the major elements of his program of government, more or less on schedule and even when they depend on the cooperation of groups and forces outside his control. The privatization program and his other actions to reduce the size of the public sector have accelerated over time. A Constituent Assembly drafted a new constitution that was approved by referendum, and two municipal and one national election have been held. The vote on the 1993 Constitution and the fate of his congressional and mayoral candidates were less positive than the president might have hoped, but, his reelection for a second term left no doubt as to his public support. Clearly in his favor is the inability of the opposition forces, and especially the traditional political elites, to unite their efforts and more importantly to develop a realistic set of alternative policies. Over time, many of their members have in fact defected to Fujimori's ranks, or at least entered informal alliances. This process has allowed the administration to keep control of the new, unicameral Congress. When that fails, it has pushed through its programs using decree legislation or creative interpretations of existing laws. One of the latter, in fact, brought a suggestion that Fujimori might be eligible for a third term. This latter interpretation was struck down by the Constitutional Tribunal in 1997; the decision was surprisingly, but is unlikely to be the last word on the issue.

Those concerned with the country's political future are of course troubled by such irregular uses of its constitution and other legal framework. Still more perturbing is the continuing lack of transparency in the government's decision making, its domination by an inner circle of advisors whose entrance or occasional exit seems largely dictated by their relations with the president, and the consequent sense that the public will know what will happen as it occurs, but will have no chance to make its opinions known beforehand. This may be, as many have argued, the most convenient if not the only way for Peru to leave its developmental impasse. However, it certainly is not laying the ground work for the emergence of broadly based political institutions, capable of withstanding changes of leadership, policy failures, and the incorporation of dissenting viewpoints.

Notes

1. The historical discussion of this section does not pretend to add anything new to ground already well covered by historians and social scientists. The reader wishing more detail is directed to the following works and their more extensive bibliographies. For general background, see Astiz, 1969; Bourricaud, 1969; Chaplin, 1976; Nyrop, 1981; Reid, 1985; and Thorp, 1978. For the military period, see Lowenthal, 1975; McClintock and Lowenthal, 1983; and sections of Reid, 1985, and Thorp, 1978. Crabtree, 1992, covers the García period. One of the best overall treatments, unfortunately available only in Spanish, is Peru, Senate, Comisión Especial, 1989.

2. These are the most widely quoted estimates for 1991 and 1992. They are in part a result of Fujimori's economic shock program that did eliminate hyperinflation, but predictably aggravated an already depressed economic situation. Figures for the two preceding years look somewhat better, with only about 40 to 50 percent of the population below the poverty line and about 70 percent underemployed. See Webb and Baca, 1991, pp 304; *Quehacer* (Lima), July-August 1991, p. 33. By 1994 in recognition of these problems and of the failure of the economic boom to trickle down to the poor majority, the government began to spend some of its privatization windfall on social welfare programs.

3. Coca is a traditional crop in Peru, grown for centuries for local consumption, either as a tea or to be chewed. In both forms, it has a mildly stimulant effect and is estimated to be used habitually by about 15 percent of the population (Tarzona-Sevillano, 1990, p. 108). The government has traditionally allowed a certain amount of coca production and controlled its marketing (more for revenue than for any concern with its abuse) through a state corporation. Current legislation still allows private cultivation of limited amounts of coca for direct consumption. However, most production falls outside these limits and never enters the formal marketing system. See notes 22 and 23 below for statistics on the coca economy.

4. Discussions of styles of political integration in Peru (and other Latin American countries) have long focused on alternative informal institutions—patron/client relations and the like as opposed to parties and interest groups. See Bourricaud, 1969; McClintock, 1981, pp. 54-70. It was only with de Soto's (1986) work on the informal economy that the concept of informal institutions became a major analytic tool in discussions of Peru's economic, social and political crises. Although de Soto's work has been criticized for a lack of analytic rigor, especially in its definition of "informality," his notion as to the exclusionary nature of formal (i.e. legally recognized) institutions remains important.

5. Peru's birthrate has been steadily declining over the past three decades. It is still a relatively high 30 per thousand, down from 47 in 1960 (Webb and Baca, 1991, p. 28). The estimated life expectancy, which current sources list between sixty-one and sixty-five years, puts Peru in the low middle for the region, roughly in the same category as Guatemala, Honduras, and Brazil. Comparative figures from Inter-American Development Bank and Population Reference Bureau as cited in *La Nación* (Costa Rica), March 7, 1992, p. 30A, and *The New York Times*, March 8, 1992, p. E4, respectively. Other population statistics are from Webb and Baca, 1991.

6. Recent census figures do indicate a marked decline in monolingual speakers of Indian languages—from 35 percent of the population in 1940 to 9 percent in 1981, with a corresponding increase in monolingual Spanish speakers—47 percent in 1940 to 73 percent in 1981. Greg Urban, "The Semiotics of State-Indian Linguistic Relationships: Peru, Paraguay and Brazil", in Urban and Sherzer, 1991, p. 322. Unlike its neighbor, Ecuador, Peru has not experienced a recent national movement for indigenous rights. Although some commentators have identified such a movement with the late colonial rebellions and the contemporary Sendero Luminoso, neither example seems characterized by an attempt to establish a recognition of indigenous culture. While both use(d) an identification with certain indigenous symbols to justify their efforts, each had a more immediate political agenda of replacing the establishment in power. For a discussion of Sendero's agenda see footnote 28. For a discussion of Indian rights movements in the Andean region, see Urban and Sherzer, 1991, and Ayala, 1992.

7. This is an approximation for the last decade. See Webb and Baca, 1991, pp. 13 and 367. Given fluctuations in volume of production and international prices for all sectors of the economy, precise percentages vary substantially from year to year. In this and the following statistics on the economy only legal (i.e. noncoca) production is considered.

8. Figures on the informal sector are from de Soto, 1986, p. 13. His findings from research in the early 1980s indicate 52 percent in the informal sector. He estimates a rise to over 60 percent by the year 2000. Although de Soto argues that the informal sector represents one of the most vibrant parts of the economic scene, most of its members are small-scale vendors of products and services with little or no access to factors of production other than their own labor. Those who have scraped up the capital or training to do more may indeed be highly productive, but they represent a numerical minority.

9. Webb and Baca, 1991, pp. 303 and 367.

10. There is a long standing debate as to the size of Peru's population at the time of the Spaniards' arrival. Estimates have been as high as thirty-two million, but most recent figures downsize this to about nine million. Even so, Peru did not regain this population level until well into the current century. See Gootenberg, 1991, passim.

11. Recent findings and a discussion of post-colonial population trends in Peru are summarized in Gootenberg, 1991. As he notes, the increase in the "Indian" population may be both a biological and sociocultural phenomenon—i.e. an increasing proportion of the rural population may have found it more convenient to be considered Indians, or may have, given the difficult economic times, reverted to an Indian lifestyle. To this day, the term Indian as used in Peru is as much cultural as racial; a racial Indian who adapts more Europeanized habits becomes a *cholo* (mestizo) or even white (although probably not without a good deal of commentary as to his real origins).

12. Founded in 1924 by its leader for life, Víctor Raúl Haya de la Torre, APRA (American Popular Revolutionary Alliance) was originally intended to be a regional movement. Although it has influenced parties in other nations, (e.g. Venezuela's Acción Democrática) APRA itself took root only in Peru.

64

13. See articles in Bonilla, 1991, and discussion in Chapter 5.

14. By 1960, 50 percent of the urban middle class were said to be employed in the public sector (Nyrop, 1981, p. 90).

15. See, for example, Long and Roberts, 1978; McClintock, 1981; and Caballero, 1988.

16. It has been suggested that President Bustamante y Rivera was aware of and offered no opposition to the military's proposed action, once APRA abandoned its congressional alliance with him and otherwise obstructed his programs. In 1962, the losing party, Belaúnde's Acción Popular, was rumored to have acquiesced to a coup to prevent the APRA-UNO coalition from taking power. Such cases represent the traditional mode of military intervention in Peru (and in other countries of the region), whereby the civilian establishment invites in the military to prevent what it sees as a deterioration of the political situation. The 1968 coup broke with this model, although the 1975 internal coup (to form the second phase military government) is interpreted as a return to this style.

17. As recounted in García Rada, 1978, p. 215.

18. It has also been suggested that the timing of the military coup (like that of the Fujimori *autogolpe*) was precipitated by on-going investigations, this time of smuggling activities with findings likely to be embarrassing to the military high command.

19. This has been one of the most studied periods of Peruvian political history. See, for example, Chaplin, 1976; Cleaves and Scurrah, 1980; Lowenthal, 1975; McClintock and Lowenthal, 1983; Reid, 1985; and Thorp, 1978. Those authors writing in the early seventies are usually more sympathetic to the military than are later treatments.

20. "Exact" statistics on these changes vary considerably. These are the most common approximations as cited in Reid, 1985; Nyrop, 1981; and McClintock and Lowenthal, 1983.

21. For an earlier history of these bodies, see Hammergren, 1983, pp. 81-83; Caravedo, 1983, pp. 91-162. For their evolution under the military and after, see Hammergren, "Institutional Development of the CORDES," in Chetwynd et al., 1985.

22. Until the Fujimori period, the reprivatization did not progress far, although the fishing industry, mining, some banks, and the nationalized press were returned to their original or other private owners. It is claimed that the reluctance of individual military officials to cede their positions at the head of state enterprises was an obstacle in the early years. Two additional factors hindered a wider impact. One was the government's reluctance to privatize certain key industries (perhaps more a factor under García than Belaúnde). The other was the shortage of potential investors ready to take the risk given the economic and political situation.

23. The terms Indian, peasant, and *campesino* are used almost interchangeably since most of the poor rural population is culturally and racially Indian. Because the term Indian frequently has pejorative connotations, there is a tendency to substitute the less objectionable *campesino* (peasant, as in *comunidades campesinas*, in reality, Indian communities). The substitution also reflects the gradual loss of Indian culture; even *campesino* communities are rarely untouched by Western culture.

24. See for example, Webb, 1977, whose work provides an empirical basis for these arguments. His and later findings are summarized in Reid, 1985, pp. 42-64.

25. These are estimated to be about 60,000 families or 300,000 individuals. Of all the conflicting statistics on aspects of the drug trade, this is one facet on which most authorities agree. See Tarzona-Sevillano, 1990, p. 115. Although initially managed by non-Peruvians, nationals have gradually moved into the middle and upper management of the "export trade". They have been still more active in fomenting a domestic trade; here the picture is the usual one of a large number of petty vendors (those usually caught by the police) and a few large-scale traffickers, most of whom are never apprehended or convicted. Domestic drug use is still not widespread in Peru. The recognition of its existence has increased concern about the entire drug industry. See Prado, 1990.

26. The size of the drug economy and the amount of monies remaining in the country continue to be a subject of much controversy. While Tarzona-Sevillano, 1990, p. 113, estimates annual revenues to paste producers and local traffickers at $7.24 billion, or roughly one-fifth of the GNP, Webb and Baca, 1991, p. 425, set the figure at about $1 billion annually. For this and other controversies about the drug trade, see Palmer, 1992.

27. Although Peruvians were insisting on this point well into the 1980's, the Morales Bermúdez government was the first to turn U.S. pressures into a concerted, if not very effective, program to wipe out coca production in the highland jungle area of the Alta Huallaga. See Tarzona-Sevillano, 1990, p. 109.

28. The literature produced on Sendero by Peruvians and foreign authorities is almost endless. Whereas Sendero's criticisms of the injustices of contemporary Peruvian society once drew sympathy from foreign and Peruvian observers, more recent writings have found little to admire. For more information, but hardly a representative sample of that available, see Ames et al., 1988; Mauceri, 1989; Palmer, 1992; Pásara and Parodi, 1988; Peru, Senate, Comisión Especial, 1989; Reid, 1985; Tarzona-Sevillano, 1990; Woy-Hazelton and Hazelton, 1989. A review of the literature is found in Starn, 1992. One of Starn's most interesting contentions regards arguments offered by McClintock, 1984; Palmer, 1986; and some national observers, to the effect that Sendero was a peasant movement. Starn argues convincingly that the movement's base, both initially and into the 1990s, is essentially urban, and that it has always stressed class rather than race as the origin of social divisions. While admitting that peasant groups have supported the Senderistas, he does not see the movement as growing out of their particular concerns or any sort of Andean tradition. Tarzona-Sevillano's (1990) work is also interesting in its discussion of the connection between Sendero and drug traffickers. Her arguments have been cited to justify providing antiterrorist assistance as part of the antidrug war. See *The New York Times*, March 22, 1992, p. E2.

29. The preliminary count indicated that García had not won the requisite majority vote, thus requiring a run-off election. The United Left candidate Alfredo Barrantes withdrew his candidacy apparently believing he had little chance of winning. He had received 23 percent as opposed to García's 45 percent. After a month's study, the National Electoral Tribunal declared García the victor, with no need for a run-off.

30. For a sympathetic discussion of the heterodox strategy, see Pastor and Wise, 1992. Most views were not so sympathetic about the strategy's theoretical base or its implementation, depicting it as the Peruvian equivalent of Voodoo economics. Rumors about the Colombian strategy were circulating in Lima in 1988. Given the desperate straits of that period, it is likely that the idea came up, but there is no indication that it was ever taken seriously. Like many of the best products of Lima's notorious rumor mill, it never was repeated in any publicly available written form.

31. Fujimori was considered such a long shot that local media coverage of the campaign barely mentioned him until almost the eve of the election. A former rector of La Molina Agricultural University, he had no prior political experience. An overlooked key to his success was his use of a television program, *Concertando*, on which he regularly appeared for over a year and a half prior to the elections. By his own account, he used this program as the basis for his public appearances in small towns all over Peru where he was immediately recognized as *"el Señor Concertando"* *(La Nación* [Costa Rica], magazine section, April 26, 1992, p. 5). Post-election analysis of the vote also suggested a strong support from Peru's urban informal sector, from provincial nonelites, and, on the run-off, from Apristas and Leftists, the own candidates of which had been eliminated in the first round. As summed up by one source, it was the vote of the *cholos* and the Indians against White Peru *(Quehacer* [Lima], 64, May-June, 1990, pp. 30-50; and 65, July-August, 1990, pp. 4-10). For a blow-by-blow account of the campaign by the losing candidate, see Vargas Llosa, 1993.

32. Samuel Abad Yupanqui and Carolina Garces Peralta, "El gobierno de Fujimori: antes y despues del golpe," in Bernales, 1993, p. 98.

34. Wiener, 1996, p. 15.

35. The special (clandestinely published) April 10 issue of *Caretas*, a Lima news magazine, was already making these points. Subsequent editorials published outside Peru by national and foreign observers repeat these criticism. Still, many external and national observers have echoed the Peruvian public in claiming that there was no other way to tackle the problems of terrorism, drug trafficking, and corruption. Gorriti and Kerr, 1992, p. 20, have gone farther than many critics in claiming that the coup was being planned as early as mid-1990, immediately following the installation of the new government.

36. Wiener, 1996, p. 15.

37. Wiener, 1996, p. 17, notes that income from raw material exports was always subject to enormous fluctuations. He adds that only commerce, tightly linked to the surge in imports, has maintained a growth rate of 15 percent or better.

3

The Justice System: Institutional Overview

The following discussion focuses on the pre-1992 situation as a means of understanding the institutional context and objectives of Peru's reform efforts. Later chapters broaden this view with an examination of the operations of the criminal justice system and the societal and political factors shaping the reform movement. As regards the institutional overview, two initial clarifications should be made. First, even by mid-1991, some preliminary changes had been introduced in law, if not in fact, and others were pending approval. Second, despite these and subsequent de jure reforms, the following years saw more institutional continuity than might be expected, in part because of contradictions among the new provisions and in part because of a lack of interest in enforcing them. Just prior to the April 5 coup, Peru had approved three laws—a Criminal Code, Criminal Procedures Code, and Organic Law of the Judiciary—intended to alter substantially some of the relations discussed below. The Criminal Code and the Judicial Organic Law went into effect in April, 1991, and January, 1992, respectively. The procedural code was to become effective in July, 1992. This date was repeatedly deferred until late 1994, when a revised version was substituted for the approved law and discussions on its passage began. Before the necessary adjustments could be made to put the two approved laws effectively in force, or any preparation begun for the initial procedural code, there came the *autogolpe*, a series of decree laws producing immediate modifications, and finally the 1993 Constitution.

The new constitution leaves the structure of the judiciary open-ended, reserving almost all organizational details for secondary legislation. It makes certain other changes not necessarily compatible with those assumed or mandated by the preceding laws. These include the transfer of the appointment system and management of the judicial career (including that for prosecutors) to the National Council of Magistrates, the election of justices of the peace, the recognition of traditional law and authorities within native communities, the creation of the *Defensor del Pueblo* (Ombudsman) as a separate office, a modification of the appellate role of the Supreme Court, and the reservation of constitutional issues to the Constitutional Tribunal. Finally, in addition to the new draft Criminal Procedures Code, the post-1992 government also approved and put into effect a new Civil Procedures Code and an Arbitration Law, both of which implied further modification of the judiciary's new organic law. Many of the changes proposed by one or another of these documents appear very positive. There remain the questions of whether they will be implemented in fact, and of which of the conflicting variations will prevail. Since the resolution of these questions is likely to take several years, the following description of the preexisting institutional structure is in many of its aspects still relevant to de facto practices.

A Preliminary Note on Governmental Organization and the Role of Constitutional Change

Peru, like most of its neighbors, has had a series of constitutions over its independent history. These often introduced little real change in institutional arrangements and not even much in those formally mandated, but honored in the breach. As opposed to this function, Peru's constitutions, like those throughout the region, seem to serve three purposes: to signify a symbolic break with past administrations; to enshrine, perhaps equally symbolically, the values and strategic positions of new power holders; and to resolve, often unsuccessfully or irrelevantly, the institutional conflicts of the prior regime. Since executive-legislative relations are a frequent source of these conflicts, they usually figure prominently in each new constitution. The new formulations often control the symptoms and not the underlying problems, which eventually appear under a new guise.

In Peru as elsewhere, the real workings of institutions are determined at the interface of formal structures and political and historical forces. Peru's politically active population has traditionally been only a minority of its citizens. They and those striving for inclusion have shown a high level of sophistication in manipulating institutions to ends no constitution could foresee. This often leads to political impasses and a turn to unconstitutional regimes. It also means that mechanisms representing constitutional dead letters in other countries (e.g. congressional powers of interpellation) have been called into play in Peru. Whether this will remain the case under the 1993 Constitution is a critical question since it is one of those exceptional cases that offers the opportunity for a significant real break with the past.

As defined by the five constitutions in effect over the present century (1860, 1920, 1933, 1979, and 1993), Peru has a unitary government with three main branches: the executive, legislative and judicial powers. Subnational (departmental, municipal, and for a brief period prior to the *autogolpe*, regional) governments have traditionally been unimportant, responsible for only a minor portion of the public sector budget and often composed of officials appointed by the executive.[1] With the exception of periods (most notably from 1968 to 1980 and from April 5, 1992 to 1995) when the Congress was closed, this constitutionally defined structure has not varied. While Peru's government, has been characterized as presidential, the 1979 Constitution shifted the balance more toward the executive by limiting the legislature's ability to censure and bring down cabinets and so obstruct presidential programs. It also recognized and expanded the president's ability to issue legislation by decree when so directed by Congress. Both sets of provisions were retained in the 1993 Constitution. Although the new constitution does not noticeably broaden the executive's powers vis-a-vis the legislature, and eliminates some of its traditional controls over the judiciary, it introduces one transcendental change by allowing presidential reelection.

The growing recourse to decree legislation and the Congress's ex ante or ex post ability to limit its content have been a source of controversy over the past two decades. The development was necessitated by the Congress' inability to legislate rapidly in response to an increasingly difficult political and economic situation. However, the sheer quantity of laws enacted in this fashion, the executive's tendency to interpret the delegation of authority very broadly,[2] and a series of peripheral abuses had attracted concern even under the García administration.[3] In late 1991, following Fujimori's issuance of 126 legislative decrees in the areas of national defense and economic restructuring, the Congress took the unprecedented step of almost immediately nullifying ten of them and passed the Law of Parliamentary Control further circumscribing the executive's legislative powers as well as those regarding the declaration of states of emergency and siege.[4] The passage and initial application of this law by the opposition dominated Congress was a principal motivating factor behind the Fujimori *autogolpe*.

For most of its history, Peru has had a bicameral legislature. Its role vis-a-vis the executive has varied from rubber stamp to obstructionist, depending on the regime of the moment. Before its closure by Fujimori, it was composed of a 60-member Senate and a 180-member House of Deputies. Until 1968 both were elected by departmental districts, with the senators elected individually and the deputies on the basis of party lists. The 1979 Constitution introduced the election of senators on a regional basis, but the provision was never implemented. Among the most important changes in the 1993 Constitution is the creation of a unicameral Congress, limited to 120 members. This, in part, accounts for the greater brevity of the new constitution (206 as opposed to 274 articles), by eliminating the need to differentiate the powers of each house and by introducing means to resolve conflicts between them. As with the judiciary, the current constitution is also less explicit in describing the legislature's organization and internal operations.

While less relevant to the present discussion, it is worth mentioning that the 1993 Constitution reverses some of the statist ideology incorporated in its predecessor. The list of basic freedoms and political rights remains long, but the sections on social, economic, and cultural rights have been shortened, converting many guarantees into expressions of intent, and simply eliminating others. Had any of these guaranteed rights ever provided the basis for litigation, this would constitute a radical departure. Since they did not, the change is academic. The state's role in the economy has been cut back in line with Fujimori's well-advanced campaign to sell off almost all state enterprises. There is an explicit new emphasis on private enterprise and private initiative. All of this reflects an emerging consensus among the region's elites, but one which few other governments have been willing to declare so formally. Generally, the new document seems to offer certain advantages over the 1979 version, in the greater flexibility it for the most part allows, some very positive institutional changes (the emphasis on decentralization through existing structures, and the basis for a truly independent judiciary), the elimination of the least realistic aspects of the military ideology, and in its apparent reflection of a new consensus among a significant portion of Peru's political class. It remains to be seen whether the consensus can be pushed beyond a focus on the rules of the game to one on making institutions work. Over the short run, there is also the question of the extent to which the current government will be bound by its own rules. Anticipating the discussion in a later chapter, if the justice sector is any indication, the answer is "only insofar as is convenient."

Technically, until at least 1979, the Peruvian judiciary includes only two institutions: the ordinary court system and the virtually nonexistent "*Ministerio de Defensa*" (Public Defense). The Public Ministry (Attorney General's Office), once regulated by the Judiciary's Organic Law, and the National Council of Magistrates are now independent and have separate chapters in the 1979 and 1993 constitutions. A more complete definition of the justice system (as opposed to the judiciary) should include the Tribunal of Constitutional Guarantees (suspended by Fujimori, but reinstated in the 1993 Constitution and reestablished in 1996), the Ministry of Justice and the prison system it supervises, the Ministry of the Interior and the national police force under its control, the bar associations and law faculties, five systems of administrative courts, and the separate system of military courts. Two other court systems, the agrarian and the labor and industrial community courts, were separate under the 1968-80 military government, but have now been reintegrated into the ordinary court system. In terms of sectoral composition, to the extent there is a regional "norm," Peru falls within it, except perhaps for the separate courts created by the military government.

The executive and the legislature hold a number of powers that affect the justice system's operation. Until 1993, the most notable was their role in the appointments of judges and public prosecutors. Throughout Latin America, it is not unusual for one or both bodies to name members of the Supreme Court and the attorney general, or to intervene extensively in the selection of lower level judges and prosecutors. However, in most countries the executive does not, as it did in Peru, have a formal role in naming these lesser officials. All Peru's recent constitutions retain the executive and legislative roles in initiating and approving laws affecting sector operations, and the Congress' responsibility for approving institutional budgets[5] and initiating impeachment proceedings of Supreme Court justices, the attorney general, and the latter's three deputies. Despite these opportunities for executive and legislative intervention, until the 1970s, Peru's formal justice system, especially the judiciary, managed to maintain a considerable degree of institutional autonomy, albeit within certain closely defined limits. While this has been substantially eroded within the last two and a half decades, the survival of certain traditional perspectives and patterns of behavior has inhibited the sector's adaptation to a changing sociopolitical environment.

It should be emphasized that these institutions comprise only the formal justice system (i.e. that established by law). For much of Peru's independent history, this formal system has been less important to the majority of the population than have other parallel informal systems of justice. This is not an unusual situation in the region. It tends to be aggravated in countries like Peru with large unassimilated indigenous populations. These informal systems most obviously include the traditional practices of indigenous communities and less traditional variations adopted by community members as they come into contact with or migrate to urban areas. They also incorporate a variety of more restricted mechanisms created by the masses and elites alike to redress inadequacies of the formal structures. These range from paramilitary and vigilante groups to measures used by major economic interests to resolve conflicts outside the court system. To repeat an earlier observation,[6] justice in Peru was traditionally a middle class phenomenon; it never reached the masses and was easily circumvented by the elites.

For the most part confined to the more isolated areas of the country, these informal systems were conveniently ignored by official Peru until very recently. For a number of reasons, including their increasing contact with and impact on the formal system, the informal institutions have now become a matter of concern and study. They received brief mention in the 1979 and 1993 Constitutions. Members of the judicial establishment have often seen the informal structures as a threat to formal institutions and, thus, something to be eliminated. Other observers have argued that the formal system would in fact benefit from the incorporation of some aspects and traits of informal justice. The informal systems are further discussed in Chapter 5 in connection with the performance of the traditional justice system.

The Judiciary *(Poder Judicial)*[7]

The key institution within the formal system is the judiciary *(Poder Judicial)*, an autonomous branch of government that includes the ordinary court system *(fuero ordinario)* and its supporting administrative apparatus. Like the majority of Latin American nations, Peru has a unitary government and, thus, a single principal hierarchical chain of courts. The few exceptions to this rule were its separate system of military courts, the two court systems given independence by the military and since reincorporated, and the separate administrative courts (Customs, Fiscal,[8] Civil Service, Mining, and Government Contracts). With the 1979 Constitution, the decisions of all but the military courts and those resulting from arbitration[9] became subject to review by the ordinary court system. The judiciary (like these parallel courts) operates according to a civil law tradition with Peru's own particular modifications. These are most evident in the criminal process, especially after the 1982 creation of a separate Public Ministry with a major prosecutorial function. This change is part of a general trend in Peru and throughout Latin America away from an inquisitorial, written system, toward an accusatory, oral process. Although they are most visible and most advanced in the criminal branch and in the two court systems established by the military, comparable changes are contemplated for the entire procedural system.

Supreme Court

The judiciary is headed by the Supreme Court. Except as noted, the Court's organization, operations, and powers closely resemble those of its counterparts throughout the region. Peru's Court is slightly larger than average for Latin America, where current numbers vary from five justices (Uruguay) to thirty-one (Ecuador). From 1983 until 1992, it was composed of twenty-three justices or Vocales Supremos, twenty of whom sat in five-judge chambers (two for criminal and two for civil matters). The other three included the president and the *vocales* assigned to head the Office of Internal Control and to assist the president with administrative matters. The 1991 Judicial Organic Law added seven more *vocales* and a new chamber for constitutional and administrative matters. The selection of the new justices and the creation of the chamber were delayed by the *autogolpe*. In a decree law issued April 23, just before the reopening of the Court, Fujimori made his first, but not last, modification of the new organic law, reducing the Court to eighteen members and three chambers.

The permanent appointments of its justices[10] have guaranteed Peru's Court more continuity than is the case in many other countries. Its internal organization shows considerably less stability. The Court's president is elected internally, but his[11] term lasted an unusually short one year. This was increased to two years in 1992. It still contradicts a regional pattern of longer presidential terms, even for Courts that as a whole are changed with greater frequency. Assignments to the chambers or to one of the other positions were made each year by the Court's president. As at other levels, specialization of the *vocales* by substantive areas was only partially observed. A *vocal* who sat on a criminal panel one year might shift to a civil chamber in the next for reasons usually derived from the Court's internal politics. Outside pressures also played a role in the form of efforts to stack a chamber because of cases it was expected to hear. Among the changes introduced by the 1991 organic law is the requirement that judges declare a specialized area (civil, criminal, agrarian, labor or juvenile law) that they will maintain throughout their career and that will determine their assignments where relevant (i.e. when the assignment is to a specialized as opposed to a "mixed" tribunal or court). The 1993 Constitution is silent on the matter. The elimination of the two additional Supreme Court chambers envisioned in the organic law will make specialization difficult at that level. In any case, events since the *autogolpe* have precluded further attention to this detail.

The Court's president served as head of the entire judiciary, responsible for overseeing both its judicial and administrative operations. His decisions, however, were subject to approval by two-thirds of the whole Court or *sala plena*. Approval was not automatic. A Court president who was not careful in managing his position within the Court might be severely hampered as to the actions he could take. This became more difficult with the increase in the size of the Court and with the more overt intrusion of partisan politics. It was also complicated by the president's short term in office. Peru's chief justices have rarely if ever exercised the autocratic powers demonstrated by their counterparts in some other Latin American countries. The latter's power was generally enhanced by their longer terms; in these circumstances, being the candidate of the party in power was usually an asset as well.

All recent constitutions and organic laws make it clear that judges should be "apolitical.' The Spanish term *apolítico* is usually translated as "nonpartisan," but it tends to be interpreted (by judges in particular) in a much broader fashion.[12] While a significant number of *vocales* held to this view in at least the narrow sense, partisan politics have recently played an unprecedented role within the Court itself. Both the underlying principle and its increasing violation over the past decades are constants throughout the region. Especially during the 1985-90 García government, candidates to the Court presidency appeared to campaign as actively with the executive as they did with the other *vocales*. Greater executive involvement in this theoretically internal decision did not appear to enhance the power of the winner. However, García's ill-concealed attempt to stack the Court and the rest of the judiciary with Aprista judges did bring him some benefits. The chamber hearing a case brought against him for illegal enrichment dismissed it for lack of evidence. Anti-aprismo emerged as a dominant theme in Fujimori's own judicial clean-up and, in the first round of dismissals, appeared as important as alleged corruption.

Despite efforts by the 1978 Constituent Assembly to curb political control of the Court, such external influence was facilitated, even under normal circumstances, by the selection system for *vocales*. Under this system, the executive, either the president or by delegation, his minister of justice, chose new incumbents for vacant positions from lists prepared by the National Council of Magistrates. Appointments were ratified by the Senate. As described in more detail below, the selection of justices under the military government was similarly centralized, except that there was no Senate to ratify them. The system prior to 1968 allowed a more diffuse form of external influence in that the Senate made the final appointments from lists submitted by the executive. The process thus provided ample opportunity for interparty negotiation.

Like lower level judges, justices were usually selected from the "judicial career,"[13] that is, from judges or professional staff serving at the next lowest level in the system. Judges could also enter the hierarchy at any level, even that of the Supreme Court, by substituting teaching experience or private practice for years on the bench. Thus, a Supreme Court justice was to be at least fifty years old, and have served as a Vocal Superior for at least ten years, or have taught or practiced law for twenty years. Since judicial salaries were low and it was generally acknowledged that the best law students no longer entered the public sector, this practice had the advantage of attracting talented individuals at a later stage in their career, when the status of being a superior or Supreme Court judge could compensate for the limited material incentives. The practice was a source of conflict within the judiciary and had a further demoralizing effect on those entering at the bottom who saw their chances for advancement limited. The practice of lateral entry, combined with the absence of training programs for judges at any level, also reduced professionalism, making more credible the claims that many judges had an inadequate grasp of their responsibilities and, occasionally, of the law itself.

The Supreme Court is the court of last instance for all major civil and criminal cases, as well as for the administrative court systems; most appeals are heard by one of its specialized chambers, not by the Court en banc. In this sense, the reintegration of the nonadministrative labor and agrarian courts did not affect their operation. Even while separate, their cases were appealed directly from their second and last instance courts to the Supreme

Court. Contested decisions from administrative courts usually entered at the lowest instance of the ordinary court system. In theory, the 1979 Constitution provided that some administrative cases enter at the superior or Supreme Court level, but these were never specified in the required secondary legislation. The Supreme Court also has original jurisdiction in a limited number of other areas, most having to do with cases brought against high level officials, including its own members and those of the superior courts. These cases are tried by the Court's Criminal Chamber; if appealed, they are seen by the Court sitting en banc.

The appeals process itself and the Court's role in it are not unlike that found throughout Latin America. Traditionally, appeals were based on matters of fact or law (including both substance and procedures).[14] Where the Court found on matters of fact, its decision stood, except in overturning an acquittal in criminal cases. Here, as in matters of substantive or procedural law, in finding against a decision, it ordered a retrial at a lower instance. Changes introduced by the military and reinforced by the later civilian governments sought to reduce the burden on the Supreme Court by restricting its appellate jurisdiction to civil cases over a certain value or criminal cases involving major penalties. Their success was not notable and the Court continued to face a heavy caseload and backlog. The long-standing proposal that the Court's appellate function be limited to errors of law or its application (*casación*) was only partially incorporated in the new Criminal Procedures Code, organic law, and constitution. One notable problem here is the constitutional guarantee (maintained in the 1993 Constitution) that criminal cases be seen in two instances. This has normally been interpreted as meaning that cases tried in the first instance by superior courts should have a second trial at the Supreme Court level. In countries, including parts of Europe, where the Court's appeals functions has already been limited to *casación*, the effort to exclude factual review has proved difficult, if only because the distinction is sometimes hard to maintain. In Latin America, it is also hindered by a continuing distrust of trial judges' competence, the occasional introduction of new types of appeals,[15] and a tendency to include some exceptions within the laws regulating *casación*.[16]

Although appeals usually come at the end of a trial (and in criminal cases may be made by the prosecutor, defendant, or civil party), in Peru as elsewhere, civil cases in particular have traditionally involved the extensive use of interlocutory appeals. A variety of challenges to technical or procedural decisions, called *excepciones*, could be introduced at any point in a case and appealed separately up to the Supreme Court level. Recent Peruvian legislation attempts to restrict this practice by limiting the periods during which exceptions may be entered and requiring that they be handled simultaneously with, rather than prior to the resolution of the principal case. In the past, the use of exceptions could extend a litigation for years, if not paralyzing it completely. It has been observed that any civil case produced three separate trials, one for the matter of substance and two for the two major types of exceptions.[17]

Throughout Latin America, supreme courts are usually responsible for monitoring and evaluating the actions of all judicial and administrative personnel. In countries where judges have permanent tenure, this often produces some special mechanisms, for example the Costa Rican Court's "reelection" of lower level judges every four years.[18] In Peru, from 1920 to 1980, this took the form of the ratifications[19] required every five years for first and second-instance[20] judges. In effect the ratifications were at most a formality and according to observers, only took their legally mandated form once, in 1968.[21] The ratification process was eliminated under the 1979 Constitution. It was reinstated with the 1991 organic law and in the 1993 Constitution. The constitution extends the ratifications to Supreme Court justices, but removes them from the hands of the Court, giving the entire process to the National Magistrates' Council.

In 1977, the military government created the Office of Internal Control for the Judicial Power (OCIPJ) to attend to complaints and perform the monitoring process on a more systematic and permanent basis. Headed by a Supreme Court justice, the office was composed of six first and five second-instance judges and, thus, represented a review by peers. The OCIPJ was to receive and investigate all complaints about judicial and administrative employees. It was also to carry out its own monitoring and control functions, periodic audits, and any special investigations. While findings of criminal activities were to be submitted to the court system for trial, the OCIPJ could recommend disciplinary actions. These ranged from a written reprimand to destitution for noncompliance with procedural and ethical norms. Beginning with the 1933 Constitution, judges could be held criminally or civilly responsible for "judicial error," in effect, misapplication of the law. It was only with the 1991 Criminal Code that this was modified to stipulate intentional error. Judges could also be disciplined if they failed to meet the various deadlines for processing cases, or if too many of their findings were overturned by higher instances. Thus, although judges were legally "independent" in making their decisions (i.e. not subject to instructions from their superiors), and the OCIPJ was severely understaffed and inefficient, its presence and potential use for less official ends reinforced a conservative bias in judicial actions. Judges were well aware that, should the OCIPJ choose to make trouble, they were inevitably vulnerable on the point of delays and, still more seriously, could probably be challenged on various of their legal interpretations. This last issue was of particular concern to provincial judges who often lacked access to updated legal codes and who, if they received the official gazette at all, did so months after it announced new legislation.

For most of its existence, the OCIPJ was probably no better and no worse than the comparable offices in various of the region's countries, all of which are impeded by organizational weaknesses, political intervention, and a lack of clear standards for performance. Beginning about 1994, the OCIPJ became more active under the leadership of one of Peru's few reformist justices. Within two years, it had removed forty-four judges and judicial employees,[22] and was actively soliciting public cooperation. Rather ominously, its powers were cut back in 1996 and delegated to the presidents of the superior courts. The new policy may have more innocent explanations, but it is significant that the judiciary's first serious attempt to police itself was ended so abruptly.

In addition to its judicial functions, the Court, like the majority of its regional counterparts, has been responsible for the administrative management of the judicial system. This includes the formulation and presentation of the annual budget to Congress. Although the 1979 Constitution stipulated that the judiciary receive two percent of the central government budget, the amount delivered was rarely over one percent. The budgetary earmark follows a regional trend begun with the six percent of the national budget reserved for the Costa Rican judiciary in the late 1950s. While the trend continues elsewhere,[23] Peru's 1993 Constitution eliminates the earmark. However, it also removes the requirement that the Court's budget be included in the executive budget and, thus, presumably eliminates the additional regulations and cuts imposed by the executive budget office. One continuing problem has been the generally poor quality of administrative staff (who prepare the budget) and the court's general disinclination to invest any funds or effort in improving them.[24] The Court also had a reputation for inefficient use of what funds it received, creating a disincentive for giving them any more. The reputation was not entirely undeserved. In the mid-1980s, when judges who did not cash their paychecks on the morning they received them might find them unredeemable for lack of funds,[25] and when the Court could not afford to send copies of the national gazette to provincial judges, the *vocales supremos* were still reluctant to forego the formal trappings of their office (including private cars and drivers) and the part of the budget dedicated to maintaining them.

Superior Courts

Until 1994, Peru was divided into twenty judicial districts, one for almost every geographic department.[26] Each district has a superior court. As of 1991 they were composed of from three to sixty-six *vocales superiores* for a total of 246 in the entire nation. (Five of the sixty-six assigned to Lima served in the OCIPJ and, thus, did not hear cases).[27] There were an additional eight agrarian and twenty-two labor *vocales superiores*, who until early

1992 officially comprised their own separate second-instance courts. They have since been incorporated in the superior courts of their respective districts, forming additional tribunals. The superior courts all operate in the capitals of their districts. In the larger districts, the superior court is divided into three-judge tribunals specializing in either criminal or civil (including juvenile and administrative) cases. The new organic law not only adds the labor and agrarian tribunals, but also allows for specialized juvenile and administrative chambers. The latter have yet to be created and, even if surviving the expected further modifications of the law, are not likely to appear immediately. In the smallest districts there is only one unspecialized tribunal, a situation unlikely to change until more judges are added.

Although the number of court districts, superior tribunals, and first and second-instance judges has increased gradually over time, the distribution of the national population makes it difficult to rationalize their supply and their workloads. In the smallest districts, the courts may still have a light caseload. In the larger ones they may be completely overwhelmed. In 1991, Lima had 50 percent of the caseload,[28] but only a quarter of the *vocales superiores* and first-instances judges. Arguably the total number of judges could still be increased by a least one-third at both the first and second instances. Since 1996, the government has added about forty second-instance judges. However, many of them hold provisional appointments and occupy "transitory" positions, created as part of an emergency case backlog reduction program. In a pattern shared with most of its neighbors,[29] Peru's traditional solution was to add professional and nonprofessional support staff (clerks or secretaries, reporters, etc). As a result, these individuals increasingly controlled the flow of cases and assumed responsibility for many tasks that by law were reserved for the judiciary alone.[30]

Over the last quarter century, the increase in judgeships has not been the same at all levels. Between 1966 and 1989, the number of Supreme Court justices more than doubled (from eleven to twenty-three) and the number of professional justices of the peace more than tripled (from fifty-four to 171). At the first and second instance, growth was more moderate (only about one-third). While the increases at the bottom of the scale (i.e. professional justices of the peace who for the most part serve poor urban populations) respond to increased demand, the twofold increase in the Supreme Court has been criticized as unnecessary, uneconomical, and politically motivated. The same criticisms stand for Fujimori's temporary addition of seven more justices in early 1992.[31] The phenomenon is regionwide. Two recent examples are Nicaragua's expansion of its Supreme Court to shift control away from the Sandinista appointed justices, and Ecuador's increase to thirty-one justices, as a means of avoiding conflicts among its numerous political parties. In conjunction with its passage of a new Criminal Procedures Code, the Menem government also substantially increased the number of Argentina's federal appellate judges, a measure widely interpreted as a way of stacking the appellate courts.[32]

Until 1970, the superior tribunals were appellate courts for civil cases and trial courts for criminal ones. When the military granted sentencing powers to first-instance judges for a series of minor crimes[33] (eventually extended to about 80 percent of all criminal cases), the superior courts became the second and last instance for these matters. Cases could still be appealed for purported legal errors, *casación*, to the Supreme Court. Despite some initially radical proposals to further restrict appeals,[34] the new organic law, Criminal Procedures Code, and constitution do not appear to affect the existing system substantially.

Following the practice in the Supreme Court, each superior court as a whole elected its president annually. He was responsible for overseeing the judicial and administrative matters of all tribunals and lower level courts in the district. The district president was aided by an administrative secretary and by the president of any other superior tribunals in the district. Superior court judges were selected by the executive from lists provided by the National Council of Magistrates. Like the rest of the judiciary, they remained in their position until reaching the age for mandatory retirement unless they resigned, were dismissed for cause, or applied and were accepted for another judgeship. Thus, despite the periodic ratifications required under the 1920 and 1933 Constitutions, the various extraconstitutional or special ratifications practiced between 1968 and 1993, and the reimposition of periodic ones in the 1993 Constitution, Peruvian judges were considered to have permanent tenure. As noted, the ratifications conducted from 1933 to 1968 actually removed few judges.[35] Those performed afterwards had far more drastic results. Although the basic qualifications for *vocales supremos* were set in the 1979 Constitution, those for the *vocales superiores* were left to the Judiciary's Organic Law. The requirements under the 1963 and 1991 organic laws were that the candidate be at least thirty years of age, and have served for at least three years as a first-instance judge or for five years in private law practice. Until the 1970s most superior court judges were drawn from within the judiciary, either from among first-instance judges or other *vocales superiores* in less desirable districts. Subsequent governments tended to recruit more widely, although still choosing a majority from "the career."

First-Instance Judges

As of mid-1991 there were 468 first-instance civil and criminal court judges,[36] 120 of whom were assigned to Lima (six in the OCIPJ). There were also an additional 118 first-instance labor and agrarian judges who until 1992 formed part of their separate court systems. As part of its backlog

reduction program, the Fujimori government recently added about eighty
trial judges. As with the second-instance courts, the permanence of their
appointments or of the positions they occupy remains undefined. By law
there was a minimum of one first-instance judgeship in each of the country's 184 provincial capitals. In fact this position might not be filled or might
be held by a temporary or substitute incumbent. In the least populous provinces, the 121 *jueces mixtos* oversaw criminal, civil and juvenile cases. In
more heavily populated provinces, judges were assigned to one of the three
areas or combined civil and juvenile law. The integration of the agrarian
and labor courts did not immediately add more specialized judges. In areas
where agrarian or labor courts did not exist, *jueces mixtos* were to handle
these cases. Aside from the cases they try directly, first-instance judges also
see in second and final instance the minor civil and misdemeanor cases
handled by the justices of the peace in their jurisdiction. Under the 1940 and
1991 Criminal Procedures Codes, they also prepare major criminal cases for
trial in superior courts. Under the new code, preparation will not include
the investigative phase, which will be given to the Public Ministry.

First-instance judges served in one-judge courts *(juzgados)*, assisted by a
varying number of professional and nonprofessional staff.[37] In areas with
law schools, these were often unpaid law students doing their required
practical work. As discussed in Chapter 6, one of the more radical changes
currently being introduced is the restructuring and professionalization of
the entire support staff and, in areas with multiple *juzgados*, the introduction
of shared administrative personnel. Whether in a departmental or provincial capital, first-instance judges generally served under very difficult conditions. With the spread of terrorism in the rural areas, it became difficult
to fill these positions, which were often targeted for terrorist attacks. The
judges handling criminal cases were particularly vulnerable since they were
expected to make on-site inspections of crimes. The post-coup introduction
of "faceless" civilian judges for terrorist and drug cases and the government's channeling of most terrorist trials to special "faceless" military courts
did not immediately reduce the problem. Given their workload, first-instance judges were dependent on their auxiliary staff, especially their clerks
(secretarios), who were notorious for charging fees for doing their normal
work. Until 1988, the secretaries of civil first-instance judges were not employees of the court, and were in fact entitled to charge for their labors.
Their transition to court employees did not eliminate the practice because
no provision was made to pay their own, often large staffs, and because
they had a long tradition of surcharges despite the official fee schedule.[38]
Although secretaries and other personnel of first-instance criminal courts
were not legally entitled to fees, they often charged them anyway.

First-instance judges were selected by the executive from lists prepared
by the District Council of Magistrates. Requirements for inclusion on the

lists included being at least twenty-five years old and having been a professional justice of the peace, court reporter or secretary for at least two years, or having practiced law for three. In addition juvenile court judges (*jueces de menores*) were to be married, widowed, or have children. Juvenile court judges see both criminal and civil matters (the latter including adoption, appointments of guardians and the like).

Professional Justices of the Peace

Peru has two kinds of justices of the peace. As of 1991, there were 171 professional justices (*jueces de paz letrados*) who had law degrees and occupied the bottom rung (along with the court reporters and clerks) on the judicial career ladder, and 4,312 lay justices (*jueces de paz no letrados*). Unlike the lay justices, the professional JPs were salaried. By judicial districts, their numbers varied from one (Amazonas and Huancavelica) to fifty-two (Lima). While they were also concentrated in the provincial capitals, in larger cities (like Lima) they often had offices outside the major court buildings, frequently in the poorer parts of the city and in the vast urban slums. Their competence was and remains limited to misdemeanors and civil cases of minor value. They also handle child-support claims of minimum value. Given their location and the nature of their work, they serve predominantly the poor populations of the large urban centers or those located close to a provincial capital. Aside from the cases they are allowed to decide, they also prepare others for decision by a first-instance judge. Justices of the peace (of both types) may also act as notaries in areas where the latter are absent.

Professional justices of the peace, like lay justices and professional and some nonprofessional administrative staff, were appointed by the superior courts of their respective districts. To be appointed a professional justice of the peace, a candidate had to be twenty-five years old and have served two years as a lawyer or as a court reporter or clerk. Prior to the 1960s many judges entered the career as justices of the peace. The working conditions have become so unpleasant that only the dedicated or the desperate now chose this route. The 1993 Constitution provides for the election of justices of the peace, although it is not clear whether this will include the professional or only the lay JPs.

Lay Justices of the Peace[39]

Like their professional colleagues, the lay justices of the peace have their functions defined not only by the Judicial Organic Law, but also by the much revised, but still valid 1854 *reglamento* for justices of the peace. The lay justices were unsalaried and appointed for one-year terms, renewable for two years. The *reglamento* still stipulates a small fine for those who refuse to serve. The lay justices were to be twenty-five years old, reside in the area where they served, have completed their primary education, have property or stable employment and, in Quechua or Aymara-speaking areas, be fluent in one of those languages. Although appointed by the district superior court, they generally came recommended by local political authorities or other established community figures. An experiment in including the local peasant (Indian) communities in the selection was ended after two years, in 1977, following protests by the superior courts. As of late 1996, the constitutional stipulation that they all be elected had yet to go into effect.

In practice, as the selection procedures and criteria indicate, the lay justices tended to represent the upper, more established levels of their local communities. They were individuals who could be depended on to cooperate with the authorities and not to challenge them. This led to abuses and criticisms. The massive ten-year training program (1978-88) conducted by the Supreme Court's Center for Judicial Research and Training eliminated some of the worst problems by helping the JPs to understand and so better implement their role in the community and in the justice system. One interesting aspect of that role is the emphasis on conciliation (mentioned specifically in the 1854 *reglamento*, and repeated in the 1991 Judicial Organic Law and 1993 Constitution), as the first, and possibly final step in civil conflicts. The justices' role here is to help the parties reach agreement and resolve their differences and so avoid taking the conflict any further. Should conciliation not work, or in criminal matters where it is not allowed, the justice is permitted to deal directly only with very minor matters, defined by value, or limited damages. He must refer the rest to the local professional justice of the peace or a first-instance judge.

The center's course emphasized a basic grounding in the rules of the formal system and, especially, the duties and responsibilities, as well as the legal limitations of the justices' role. It also, rather more controversially, emphasized a consideration of local custom, especially in the conciliation stage. Since the lay justices generally had little formal education (some in fact were illiterate) the program worked toward filling a gap that had existed throughout the history of the office. The course also gave some important insights into how the lay justices actually operated. First, despite the official three-year limits on their appointments, it emerged that many served for much longer. Second, although unsalaried, and legally entitled to charge clients only for expenses, justices volunteered that they often charged additional minimal fees. Some were not aware that this was illegal; others saw this as only fair, given that they were expected to devote half their time to the office. While the training program only reached a portion of the justices (slightly over 5,000 in a ten-year period) and probably worked with the best of the total group, the participants demonstrated a strong interest in learning their jobs and in using this knowledge to help their communities. Finally, despite the controversy surrounding the course and its presumed encouragement of nonprofessional judges, a number of first and second-instance judges were strongly supportive, indicating an interest in replicating it independently in their own districts.

This concern with justices of the peace or other "local level" judges is a constant through most of Latin America. Peru's treatment of it has often taken a unique turn. Given the poverty of most court systems, the underlying problem is how to extend their reach to outlying areas. In some cases (Ecuador, Panama) the solution has been to rely on "administrative officials," usually the police or sometimes local mayors. Even where this is not an official remedy, it often becomes the de facto solution. Although such mechanisms are the source of considerable abuses, they may be no greater than those resulting from the actions of unsupervised, and often inadequately trained judicial appointees. A further problem, evident in Peru and elsewhere, is the tendency of such officials, whether judicial or administrative, to take their direction and orientation from local elites rather than from the upper reaches of their own organizations. In El Salvador, they became the local representatives of the national parties, making their judicial functions secondary to their political ones. In response to this situation, recent reforms often include a focus on these officials, most commonly insisting that they be lawyers and members of the judiciary. Nicaragua, for example, has made service as a justice of the peace a requirement for recent law graduates.[40] A second theme, visible in recent Peruvian legislation and culminating in a series of provisions in the 1993 Constitution, emphasizes the JPs' role as representatives of community values and, especially, their ability to resolve conflicts on the basis of the latter rather than through recourse to formal laws. While most proposals combine these two themes, Peru's current cut on the topic is unusual in its apparent preference for the latter one. Whether subsequent developments, and a judiciary that has traditionally worried about the deprofessionalization of the career, will continue in this vein remains to be seen.

Public Ministry (Attorney General's Office)

Until 1981, Peru's Public Ministry (*Ministerio Público*) was a function and not a separate organization. This is a common, if disappearing pattern within Latin America. Its members, the *fiscales*, were direct dependents of the court system, appointed by the same process as judges and assigned to the courts at all levels. In 1966, the Supreme Court had five *fiscales* assigned to it, and there were a total of fifty *fiscales superiores* assigned to the twenty superior courts. Their role was largely limited to writing nonbinding opinions on judicial decisions. After the brief elimination of the Public Ministry (1975-80) by the military government, the Court opposed its recreation, claiming that the *fiscales* contributed additional delays.[41] Although a few other countries had also eliminated their Public Ministries, the Court's overt opposition to its reappearance is unique to Peru. The sentiments behind it are hardly unusual. Even today there are many countries where the *fiscal* is conspicuous by his absence. Observers in Guatemala prior to its introduction of a new procedural code reported that when *fiscales* appeared in court, judges sometimes asked who they were and what they were doing there.[42]

Following the promulgation of the 1979 Constitution and of its own organic law (1981), Peru's Public Ministry reappeared as a separate institution. This also is a pattern in the region, although one that Peru initiated relatively early. The Public Ministry's *fiscales*, who in 1991 numbered about eight hundred, are organized by instances, districts and by specific courts, following the basic divisions of the court system. However, they are governed by their own hierarchical organization. *Fiscales* like judges are to operate independently, but only insofar as this involves external pressures. Unlike judges they are subject to the instructions of their superiors within the ministry as to whether and how they will prosecute a case. This constraint on their independence initially produced claims that the Public Ministry was more susceptible to executive interference and that its actions were guided by the interests of the party in power. There clearly was some truth in this during the ministry's earliest years. However, over its first decade it made progress toward developing an institutional identity and sense of direction, reducing if not eliminating its vulnerability to external control. The hierarchical organization of the ministry also made it a more dynamic institution as opposed to the Court, allowing it to implement internal changes and push aggressively for internal and external reforms.[43]

These developments were temporarily reversed by the decision, in late 1992, to conduct a reevaluation of all *fiscales*, dismissing those deemed unsatisfactory, and by the appointment of a *Fiscal de la Nación*, whose chief distinction was her unswerving loyalty to President Fujimori. The ratification, like that conducted on the judiciary, was widely criticized as a purge not only of the unfit, but also of the independently minded. Not all of the latter were eliminated. Three of the Ministry's *fiscales supremos* were among the most vigorous opponents of the government's 1996 judicial reform law. They were unsuccessful in their protests, but remained in office.

The Public Ministry is headed by the *Fiscal de la Nación* (attorney general), who until 1992 was chosen for a two-year term on a rotating basis from among four *fiscales supremos*. The choice was theoretically made by the group itself, but it is evident that the views of the executive had a major influence. The *fiscales supremos*, who now number six, were appointed by the executive from lists provided by the National Council of Magistrates. Under the 1993 Constitution, the council screens candidates and makes the final appointments. The Fiscal de la Nación will serve a three-year term, with a possible two-year extension, and will still be elected by and from among the *fiscales supremos*. The other *fiscales supremos* supervise the main areas in which the ministry works. These were initially criminal, civil, and administrative law. The two recent additions are responsible for constitutional cases and the leadership of the Fiscalía's newly created internal disciplinary office. *Fiscales supremos*, like *vocales supremos*, continue to enjoy permanent tenure, but this is now subject to ratification by the council at seven-year intervals. In the aftermath of the April 5 coup, the Fiscal de la Nación presented his immediate resignation. He probably anticipated his dismissal, based on his role as prosecutor in the attempted trial of Alán García. His rumored replacement was dismissed soon after, apparently in response to a widespread belief that he had ties with drug traffickers.[44]

On the next level are the twenty (now twenty-one) district *fiscalías superiores*, each headed by a dean (*decano*), the *fiscal superior* with the longest time in office. The dean of the *fiscales superiores* was also the head of the District Council of Magistrates, a body apparently eliminated or at least not mentioned by the 1993 Constitution. At the third level are the provincial *fiscales* or *agentes fiscales*. At each instance, the *fiscales* may be aided by *fiscales adjuntos* whose rank corresponds to that of the next lower instance. *Adjuntos* to *fiscales superiores* are, thus, at the rank of *fiscales provinciales* and so on. *Fiscales* like judges were appointed by the executive from lists drawn up by the national and district magistrates councils. The requirements for appointment were comparable to those for judges.

The burden of the work of the Public Ministry and thus of the majority of *fiscales* is that of representing the prosecution in criminal cases. For this reason, "*fiscal*" is most often translated as prosecutor and "Fiscal de la Nación" as attorney general. For those *fiscales* assigned to the criminal area, their responsibilities are described in the constitution, their own organic law and, by inference, in the Organic Law of the Judiciary. Since the version of the latter law in effect until 1992 dated from 1963, its specific sections on the Public Ministry were deleted as no longer valid. Its descriptions of the functions of the judiciary remained occasionally inconsistent with the role the Public Ministry claimed for itself. The principal point of conflict involved the respective responsibilities and duties of the judge, the *fiscal*, and the police in the investigation of a crime, both during and before the judicial investigation. Traditionally the first-instance judge (*juez de instrucción*) conducted the investigation (*instrucción*) and so presumably directed the police's part in it. (As noted in the section on criminal procedures, the judicial investigation is separate from the shorter, preliminary investigation conducted by the police.) However, various parts of the Public Ministry's Organic Law give the *fiscal provincial* authority to open a police investigation (Art. 94,2) and participate in the *instrucción* itself (Art. 94,4). Furthermore, the 1979 Constitution gave the Public Ministry as a whole responsibility for "overseeing and intervening in the investigation of crimes from the police stage" (Art. 250, 5). Although the 1991 Organic Law for the Judiciary and the 1993 Constitution reiterate this new role, some legal contradictions will remain until the new Criminal Procedures Code and a new Organic Law for the Public Ministry go into effect. Behavioral inconsistencies are likely to persist much longer.

While the specific role of the *fiscal* in the investigation may be uncertain, his presence is clearly required and it is he who decides whether an indictment will be made or not. Once a case is carried forward to trial in a superior court, the *fiscal superior* presents the arguments for the prosecution as does the *fiscal supremo* at the highest instance. In the new Criminal Procedures Code, the *fiscal* will be responsible for directing the investigation, presenting the indictment, and preparing and arguing the case. Like the *juez de instrucción* before him, he will be expected to investigate all relevant evidence, not just that needed for a conviction. The first-instance judge will only decide on guilt or innocence and pass sentence or, in the case of major crimes, coordinate the presentation of the case to the superior court. He will continue to have responsibility for authorizing preventive detention, searches and seizures, and other actions that have the potential of infringing on basic legal rights.

In carrying out their prosecutorial tasks, the *fiscales* faced obstacles similar to those facing judges—an uncooperative police force who might use the conflict between the other two institutions to avoid supervision by either, lack of resources, and an overwhelming caseload that might force them, like the judiciary, to rely on auxiliary personnel. The *fiscal*'s role in the investigation also included a responsibility for guaranteeing that legal rights were respected and other legal procedures (notably the time limits for each stage) complied with. While this had been a major part of their traditional functions, it offered obvious potential conflicts with their prosecutorial role. Under the new procedural code, the judge will assume these responsibilities, or until the Public Ministry's law is so revised, share them with the *fiscal*.

In fact the prosecutorial function is only one of a number of responsibilities assigned to the Public Ministry. A minority of *fiscales* are assigned to the civil and administrative areas, where their role has remained much as it was before 1980, the issuing of nonbinding opinions (*dictámenes*) on the courts' resolutions. The ministry was also responsible for "crime prevention," for guaranteeing the independence of the judiciary, and for ensuring a "correct administration of justice". Until the 1993 Constitution established this as a separate office, the Fiscal de la Nación was the national ombudsman (*Defensor del Pueblo*). Delays in the latter's creation occasioned the government's emission of still another decree of questionable constitutionality, extending the ministry's exercise of the function until 1996. Since the Public Ministry's Organic Law provided no further guidance as to how these additional responsibilities should be implemented, none of them was taken very far. The Public Ministry does *not* represent the state in litigation. In Peru, this responsibility belongs to a separate set of executive-appointed attorneys assigned to the Ministry of Justice.

Given the novelty of an autonomous Public Ministry throughout Latin America, there is no regional norm. Peru's ministry was created earlier and has advanced further in the new pattern. It continues to face many of the problems commonly encountered, ranging from inadequate resources to lack of clarity in its powers (compounded by incomplete or contradictory legislation) and, especially, in its relations with the courts and police. Its internal organization is more logical than some. It is still not evident that it is the most appropriate. For example, the ranking of *fiscales* by "instances," a practice common in the region, means that a single official will rarely handle a case from start to finish. Three partial exceptions to the general rule are Panama, the Public Ministry of which has for some years enjoyed what many consider excessive powers;[45] Costa Rica which, as with its adoption of a more accusatory system, began the process earlier and has taken a more gradual route (aided by the Public Ministry's participation in the judiciary's budgetary earmark); and Colombia, which following the passage of a new constitution and criminal codes in 1991, began a crash program, converting its *jueces de instrucción* into *fiscales*, adding more personnel, and financing the process with substantial national and foreign assistance funds. Fears have also been expressed that Colombia's Fiscalía General may hold excessive powers; whether this is true or not, the second Fiscal General enjoyed considerable popularity, topping the ranks of national figures in a recent survey.[46]

Legal Defense *(Ministerio de Defensa)*

This, like the old Public Ministry is a function rather than an organization. It is carried out inadequately by a few lawyers *(defensores de oficio)* named by the Ministry of Justice and paid by and assigned to each superior court where they are to provide free defense for those who cannot afford their own lawyers. Although a right to defense was guaranteed by the 1979 Constitution, it was often exercised only in the most perfunctory fashion. Aside from the quality of the public defenders, the most frequently cited problem[47] was that they were never involved until a case was actually brought to trial and, so, had no role whatsoever during the phase of investigation. The 1991 Organic Law for the Judiciary does establish a right to free defense for the poor from the start of the investigation. The system it describes is the current, woefully inadequate one. There is no suggestion, for example, of what appears to be a minimum condition for an effective public defense, a separate organization that selects, pays and supervises its defenders as opposed to the current system where one entity chooses them, another pays them, and no one provides any supervision. This general pattern, if not the specific organization, is evident throughout Latin America. The one outstanding exception is Costa Rica.[48] There are also indications that Panama's and Bolivia's services are improving considerably. Honduras and El Salvador have recently created separate offices, benefitting from foreign assistance programs. Their performance remains disappointing, constrained in large part by inadequate national funding. In El Salvador, for example, the 150 defenders manage only a fraction of the cases handled by Costa Rica's 160. Their inadequate salaries and working conditions combined with poor supervision and preparation encourage such widespread breaches of conduct as their acceptance of private cases or collection of fees for their official ones.[49]

In Peru and in many other countries, what the state cannot provide has been compensated in part by a network of legal clinics run by bar associations, law faculties, and human rights groups. These have the advantage of reaching defendants before they go to trial, which may be the first time the court appointed defender sees his client. However, they are often staffed by law students, who may not represent clients in court, or relatively inexperienced lawyers. The Peruvian Ministry of Justice also ran a group of popular legal clinics (*consultorios legales populares*) staffed with lawyers and law students. These clinics only gave advice and helped with paperwork, largely in civil matters. The program began in Lima, where most of the clinics are located and before 1992 had begun expanding into the major provincial cities.

Most would agree that the most effective defense services are provided through clinics run by human rights groups and other similarly oriented private organizations. These clinics tend to be highly politicized and usually define their role in terms of protecting the poor and other oppressed groups against the forces of a repressive establishment. This image is not likely to win them many friends in court. It has not prevented them from winning cases, helping the illegally detained get release, or educating community members in their basic legal rights. Many of these groups are also active at the international level, attempting to increase attention to human rights abuses in Peru. Although their legal clinics like those of the Justice Ministry were first formed in Lima, many of them now operate in other urban centers and in rural areas as well. Perhaps the most notorious of these groups was the Association of Democratic Lawyers (a branch of the Sendero Luminoso associated, *Socorro Popular*) who dedicated their efforts to defending accused terrorists and, especially, accused members of Sendero Luminoso. Some members of the group were themselves accused of and tried for terrorism. In recognition of the efficacy of the others, the government introduced special legislation in 1992, limiting the number of defendants a lawyer could represent in a single case.

Agrarian and Labor Courts

These agrarian and labor court systems, created under the military government, constitute one of Peru's unique contributions to the Latin American justice scene. Although the labor courts have not attracted much attention, the operations and ideology, if not the organizational independence of the agrarian courts has inspired imitation in several other countries. The 1979 Constitution provided for the reintegration of both court systems into the judiciary, a process only completed with the implementation of the 1991 Organic Law for the Judiciary. Reintegration will apparently not affect their operations, structure, or location since the new law establishes these as two areas of specialization for judges and courts. It has meant that in regions where no such specialized tribunals exist, agrarian and labor cases will have to be seen by other civil judges.

Although land judges, "*jueces de tierra,*" existed prior to 1968, the agrarian courts were virtual creations of the military. The labor court was the result of the merger of special courts created for the military's "industrial communities" (worker participation schemes) and the nonadministrative labor courts (for resolution of individual conflicts stemming from an employment relationship that had been terminated). There is also an administrative labor court system, overseeing civil service disputes, that remains outside the judiciary. Its decisions, like those of the other administrative courts may be taken into the ordinary court system once all administrative recourse is exhausted.

The agrarian and nonadministrative labor courts were established by the military to give special treatment to high priority policy areas. In addition to their favorable bias toward workers and peasants, the courts were organized with simplified procedures, oral trials and only two instances. Although both second-instance courts were originally located in Lima, first-instance judges were placed wherever most likely to be needed, in areas with industrial communities or in the countryside. The second-instance labor courts were eventually decentralized to five locations, including Lima. The second-instance agrarian court remained in the capital. Little has been written about the labor courts. The agrarian courts have been studied extensively.[50] Most observers conclude that they worked remarkably well in dealing rapidly and directly with a heavy caseload and avoiding the endless delays and formalism of the ordinary civil courts, where these matters would have otherwise been seen. This was the primary reason for the opposition to their reincorporation.[51]

Military Courts and the Military

Little has been written about the operations of the separate system of military courts in Peru, or elsewhere in Latin America for that matter. Considerable attention has been given to the issue of their jurisdiction vis-a-vis the ordinary court system. Under the 1968-80 military government the chief concern was the use of these courts to try civilians accused of political crimes. The military significantly extended the definition of these crimes to include sabotage of the agrarian reform, sabotage of communication services, and attacks on police officers. At one point they included verbal insults of a military official, whether in the government or not. With the re-introduction of capital punishment (eliminated except for treason by the 1979 Constitution, but reintroduced in the 1993 Constitution) and its use for political crimes, the issue of military jurisdiction over civilians literally became a matter of life and death. The potential for abuse was, however, more than the real abuses. With the 1980 return to civilian rule, the broad definition of political crimes and the use of military courts to judge them ended for the most part. The 1979 Constitution allowed civilians to be tried in military courts only for acts of treason during a state of external war.

After April, 1992, there was another partial reversal of the general trend when the Fujimori government ruled that terrorism constituted a variety of treason (D.L. 25659, August, 1992) and was thus subject to military justice. For this purpose it created a series of special military courts with "faceless" military judges and prosecutors. Initial preparation and investigation of the cases is, however, performed by ordinary *fiscales*. These special courts have become notorious for their unduly speedy trials that, critics claim, allow no time for a sufficient consideration of the evidence and often produce decisions contradictory to the initial findings and recommendations of the civilian prosecutors. Critics also note that, while the first-instance military trial judges and prosecutors are attorneys, the second-instance military tribunals reviewing the cases are composed of lay judges. The government also created "faceless" civilian courts to try these special crimes. They have been much less active and may remain so now that the use of military courts to try civilians accused of treason, genocide and terrorism has been made official with the new constitution. The reintroduction of the death penalty, first through special legislation and then in the new constitution, also makes the role of military justice still more ominous.

Military justice is not just an issue for military courts. If most civilians are not subject to formal military justice, the informal justice meted out by the military in areas under a state of emergency should not be overlooked. In these areas (not including Lima, where emergency decrees usually did not establish military control), the military was authorized to make initial detentions of suspected terrorists and to hold them for questioning before turning them over to the police. They also, as part of their "normal" operations, engaged in conflicts with "hostile forces" and carried out a variety of search and seizure activities directed at civilian populations whom they suspected of harboring terrorists. Especially during the dirty war[52] period of the mid-1980s, these "normal" operations often included abuses of human and legal rights, and out-and-out criminal activities—the pillage, rape, and murder of individuals or entire civilian villages. There are indications of improvements over the last years as the military command has attempted to exert more effective control over its own forces. However, while this eliminated the problem of freelance banditry, various human rights groups insist that human and legal rights abuses continued to be tolerated if not outright encouraged by the higher levels as a necessary response to a state of internal war. They also claim,[53] with some apparent justification, that the majority of Peru's *desaparecidos* (up to 300 annually) were the result of military operations, either summary executions in the field or detainees who perished in the military detention centers.

The frequently unpunished abuses of human rights perpetrated by military and police forces in the pursuit of terrorists, drug traffickers, and common criminals, aside from the immediate damages, has additional negative consequences. It undercuts efforts to build the credibility of formal institutions and further discourages the mass of the population from having any contact with them. The reputed involvement in drug trafficking of a number of military personnel including some at the highest levels (or at least their willingness to turn a blind eye, for a price, to such activities in regions under their control) has not helped to foster belief in the rule of law. It has also led to open conflict with the police, who are more generally responsible for the antidrug efforts.[54]

This raises a third related issue[55] as to the jurisdiction of military courts over military and police personnel who have committed crimes not necessarily related to their service functions. The question here is whether these individuals should be subject to military justice (where the action in question may not be treated as a crime, or handled as a much less serious one) or tried in the ordinary court system. During Peru's twelve years of near civil war, with the extensive civilian and military casualties; numerous massacres of civilian populations, some of them clearly attributable to the police or military; and many provinces and entire departments under military control, the issue became more than a theoretical one. The position within the military varied, just as it did among civilian groups. The argument was voiced by military leaders and some civilians that to hold the military and police accountable to civilian standards of justice in a war situation was to tie their hands unnecessarily. There were military leaders who stated that, if nine civilians had to die to catch one terrorist, especially if those nine were possible collaborators, the price was worth it.[56] Fortunately, this remained a minority view, but neither the law nor the Supreme Court, which must decide the issue of jurisdiction, provided clear guidelines. Law 24150 (art. 10), which was intended to set such guidance, only restated the obvious:

> Infractions typified in the Code of Military Justice which are committed in the line of duty are to be judged by the military courts, except those which are not connected to the exercise of duty.[57]

The 1993 Constitution is still more ambiguous omitting the exception regarding crimes not related to military functions (Art. 173).

An analysis[58] of Supreme Court decisions on this issue between 1980 and 1986 showed no consistent criteria. It did reveal a tendency to send cases involving the police to the ordinary courts and those involving the military to the military courts. As terrorist activities and police and military responses became more frequent in Lima, the issue received more attention. Opinions also became still more polarized. With the government's capture of the major terrorist leaders and decimation of their followers, the issue has become less urgent. One of the government's more controversial moves is an effort to resolve the question with an amnesty law, absolving military officials for common crimes committed in the line of duty during the period prior to 1995. At least one judge has refused to apply the law, although her decision was reversed on appeal. The amnesty is hardly a permanent solution, nor is it likely to be respected after a change of administration.

The National Council of Magistrates

First created in 1969 by the military government as the National Justice Council (*Concejo Nacional de Justicia*), this body was to select all judges except justices of the peace. Its creation (via D.L. 18061) was necessary to fill the role formerly held by the temporarily eliminated Ministry of Justice. The idea drew from European precedents. After Venezuela, Peru was the second Latin American country to adopt the council model.[59] The council was carried over into the 1979 Constitution as the National Council of Magistrates (*Concejo Nacional de la Magistratura*). The power of naming judges was returned to the Ministry of Justice, and the national and district councils were instead to provide lists of candidates for the Supreme and superior courts, and first instance judges respectively. The councils' powers in this regard were also extended to the Public Ministry; *fiscales* were to be selected following the same procedures used for judges.

In the 1991 Organic Law for the Judiciary, the Court seemed to be short circuiting the council, first by proposing that it manage the appointment system itself, and then, in the approved version, by returning final selection to the executive. The 1993 Constitution maintained the council and broadened its powers. It is now to be responsible for managing the entire judicial career, including the periodic judicial ratifications. It is to do this in coordination with the still embryonic judicial school (*Academia de la Magistratura*).[60] Presumably, since the council also maintains powers of appointment for the Fiscalía (with the exception of the Fiscal de la Nación, who is still chosen from and by the *fiscales supremos*), similar arrangements will be made with the Public Ministry's school.

Prior to 1993, the National Council was headed by the Fiscal de la Nación. Its other members were two representatives from the Court, one each from the Lima and the national bar associations and two from the nation's law schools. The council members were elected every three years by the organizations they represented. The district councils had a similar organization, headed by the senior *fiscal* in each district, and including the two most senior judges and two representatives from the local bar. The 1993 Constitution gives the Court, the Fiscalía, the bar associations, and the public and the private universities only one member each, and adds two representatives from other professional associations. Members are elected by their respective institutions or associations for five-year periods. If the council so decides, membership may be expanded to nine by the addition of representatives of labor and business associations. The new council was not seated until 1995 and did not begin its activities until early 1996. As discussed in more detail in later chapters, its future seems uncertain. By finally doing what it was supposed to do, it has entered into conflict with the government's latest judicial reform program.

The procedures used by the council to select their lists of candidates have varied over time. Under the military government and in the early 1980s, all that was stipulated was a "*concurso de méritos*," in effect a comparison of curricula, and a "personal evaluation." The results of the process suggest that it left substantial room for personal connections and recommendations, especially from the executive. In recent years, the procedure became somewhat more rigorous and, in theory, the national and district councils composed their lists on the basis of examinations and personal evaluations of candidates. Since the process, including the examinations, was conducted in private, there is little information on how criteria were weighed. Efforts to make the examinations public failed over protests by the judges. They contended this would be demeaning and even embarrassing to some of their members.[61] Despite these objections, the one set of lists (for the seven new Supreme Court vacancies) prepared under the 1991 Judicial Organic Law did result in a public ranking of the candidates' scores, based on their curricula and performance on (private) oral examinations.[62] President Fujimori rejected all of the lists claiming that they were politically influenced.

To date, the participation of the council in any of its various forms has not noticeably improved the quality of the judges and *fiscales* selected, or reduced the impact of political pressures and personal connections. A part of the problem may be that many council members, as products of the system they were to improve, never understood this as their role. Those who did attempt a new approach may have found political pressures overwhelming. The council temporarily disappeared following the *autogolpe*, and its functions as regards appointment and evaluation of the judiciary were passed first to a *Tribunal de Honor* and then to the newly created Council of Government for the Judiciary. Both organizations attracted the participation of a few reform-minded judges (including members of the "New Law" movement[63]) who seemed to take a more active interest in these tasks. Their performance suggests the potential role for either kind of council, given the "right" membership. The Council of Government also benefitted from the administration's temporary loss of interest in the judiciary following its first purge of suspect judges and *fiscales* and its creation of special courts for terrorist trials.

Peru's experience with its councils is unfortunately unusual only in the variety of forms they have taken. As common elsewhere, the councils are most often proposed in good faith by national jurists with some familiarity with the European models. Perhaps with greater familiarity they might have foreseen more problems.[64] Once introduced, the resulting bodies have been plagued either by inertia or immediate politicization and, sometimes, a combination of the two. The two worst case scenarios may be Venezuela, the council of which originated as a way for the recently ousted Christian Democrats (COPEI) to retain control of the judiciary,[65] and Colombia. In the latter country, a council composed of eminent jurists and ex-justices was unfortunately given responsibility not only for the selection of judges, but also for control of judicial administration.[66] Critics blame many of the problems in implanting Colombia's 1991 judicial reforms on the council's obstructionism. Other councils have been less spectacular failures, but have so far done little to resolve the problems they were supposed to address. They have been particularly disappointing as regards reduction of political intervention in appointments and, if less frequently, of the Supreme Court's excessive powers over the rest of the judiciary. Where they enjoy real power, they become immediate targets of politicization in their own right. Where they do not, they may become rubber stamps for the preexisting informal mechanisms. Two potential solutions, which still have flaws, are to use the councils, as in pre-1993 Peru, to screen candidates for final selection by some other body, or to make councils internal bodies, composed of representative members of the various judicial instances and administrative staff. The latter seems more appropriate if the council is to supervise judicial administration, but offers problems as the main means of appointments.[67]

Tribunal of Constitutional Guarantees

The hierarchy of laws in Peru and the various constitutions indicate that a judge who finds a law in conflict with the constitution should not apply the law. However, a specific function of judicial review or some other form for challenging the constitutionality of legislation did not exist prior to the 1979 Constitution. The Court's proposal to the Constituent Assembly argued both for the creation of the function and its embodiment in the Court itself. Only the first part of the proposal was accepted. In lieu of the Court, the function of judicial review was given to a new organization, the Tribunal of Constitutional Guarantees (TGC). The tribunal had nine members, three designated by the Court, three by the Congress, and three by the executive. They were appointed for six-year, renewable terms, with the replacement of one-third of the members every two years. Requirements for members of the tribunal were the same as those for *vocales supremos* with the added stipulation that they have demonstrated support for democratic practices and the defense of human rights. The TGC's two main functions were to review and rule on the constitutionality of any national, regional or municipal law or regulation submitted to them for this purpose, and to act as a court of *casación* for requests of habeas corpus and *amparo*[68] that had been denied by the last judicial instance.

In reviewing the constitutionality of legislation, the tribunal acted only on requests submitted by the president, the Supreme Court, the Fiscal de la Nación, sixty deputies, twenty senators or a petition signed by 50,000 citizens whose signatures were verified by the National Electoral Tribunal. The TGC's decisions on constitutionality were not retroactive. Where the legislation in question came from the Congress, the latter had forty-five days to pass a law nullifying it. If they did not do so, the law was nullified directly by the TGC. In the case of legislation from other sources, the TGC published its decision in the official gazette. The decision took effect the day following its publication.

The tribunal also heard procedural appeals of habeas corpus (illegal detention) and *amparo* (infringement of all other constitutionally guaranteed rights) after they had passed through the normal court system. When the tribunal upheld the lower courts' denial of a request, it might be submitted to the Inter-American Commission of Human Rights, the United Nations Committee on Human Rights, or other entities that the Peruvian government recognized as competent for this function. While the tribunal's creation represented an important innovation, its composition and the procedures governing its actions, guaranteed it a potential for far less activism than comparable bodies created elsewhere in Latin America, a region not noted for this kind of activism in any case. This apparently was the intention of the 1978 Constituent Assembly, which rejected a number of more radical variations. It did not, however, protect the tribunal from the effects of Fujimori's *autogolpe*. This was one of the justice sector institutions immediately closed. It did not reappear until mid-1996 and, even then, last minute changes in its organic law substantially reduced the likelihood that it would strike down legislation.

The first draft of the 1993 Constitution eliminated the tribunal, passing its functions to a Constitutional Chamber of the Supreme Court. The final version reinstated it as the Constitutional Tribunal (*Tribunal Constitucional*) with much the same powers as before. Two changes were the elimination of the forty-five-day waiting period for the declaration of the unconstitutionality of a law emitted by the Congress and a specification that the tribunal would also decide on conflicts of competence among institutions arising in the constitutional definition of their powers. It also sees in final instance two new mechanisms for protecting constitutionally guaranteed rights, the writs of habeas data (requests for information managed by a public entity) and of "compliance" (*acción de cumplimiento*). The latter protests an infringement by omission or failure to act. Further, less positive changes were made to its enabling law in 1996, following the congressional opposition's successful blockage of several government candidates to the Tribunal. These are discussed below and in Chapter 6. The new tribunal has seven members, all elected by two-thirds vote of the Congress and serving five-year terms with no immediate reelection. To establish further its separation from the judiciary, *fiscales* and judges who have not been out of office for at least one year are ineligible to serve.

Since judges retain first instance jurisdiction for cases involving the alleged violation of individual rights and are still instructed to not apply an unconstitutional law, Peru maintains a partially decentralized system for the protection of constitutional guarantees. This appeared to be an advantage as observers saw little hope that the tribunal's relative lack of efficacy in the past would change over the short run. It also seemed unlikely that the retention of a separate constitutional court rather than the delegation of its functions to the Supreme Court would make much difference. Indeed the general pattern in Latin America continues to suggest that of itself the choice among these three major alternatives (decentralization, centralization in the Supreme Court, creation of a separate constitutional court or chamber) makes little difference. It cannot override more fundamental factors like the inclination of judges, whether because of political pressure or institutional norms, to avoid their role in defending constitutional principles or the unwillingness of institutional and political elites to tolerate let alone encourage more activism. It can be argued, however, contrary to the reigning theoretical preference for decentralized systems, that an activist Supreme Court, chamber, or constitutional court is a more potent source of change. Only after one of the latter takes the lead, and proves it possible, can the majority of judges be expected to follow suit. Peru's Constitutional Tribunal has proved more willing to take this role than its Supreme Court. Some of its first decisions unexpectedly struck down the administration's pet laws, including one permitting Fujimori's second reelection. This is particularly surprising given the tribunal's composition and because, thanks to the last minute modifications, six of the seven magistrates are now required to declare a law unconstitutional. However, the short term victory for constitutionalism does not bode well for the court's future; in fact, the Congress removed three of the justices in 1997.

The Ministry of Justice

In Latin America, the Ministry of Justice is almost as varied in form and function as the Public Ministry. In a few countries it does not exist, and in many others, its only sectoral function is running the prison system. In Argentina, until recently, it exercised far greater powers over the federal[69] judiciary than even in Peru—responsible not only for appointments, but also for the judiciary's budget and other administrative activities. The Colombian ministry managed the judiciary's budget and administrative offices until 1989; however, it never appointed judges. In Peru, the ministry has had three direct sectoral functions: its role in appointing judges, *fiscales*, and public defenders; its role in overseeing the state of national legislation; and its responsibility for the prison system. The ministry was eliminated under the military government—reportedly as a means of evening out the distribution of ministerial positions among the various armed forces. During those twelve years, prisons were managed by the Ministry of the Interior, appointments were made by the National Council of Justice, with a good deal of input from the president and his advisors, and legislation was left to proliferate on its own. The Peruvian rumor mill attributes a similar plan to the Fujimori administration, as part of its program to reduce the size of the public sector.

From 1980 until the 1993 Constitution transferred the entire function to the National Council of Magistrates, the executive made appointments of *fiscales* and judges based on the lists provided by the council. The ministry's role in appointments consisted of standing in for the president in the case of those appointments (usually the majority) where he did not wish to intervene directly. This put the minister of justice in a very critical position vis-a-vis the composition of the judiciary and the Public Ministry. After 1980 several ministers took full advantage of these powers, despite the theoretical restraints posed by their limitation to the council's suggestions.[70] This was especially true in the early 1980s when the executive also had partial control of the National Council of Magistrates through its direct appointment of three of its members (the two Supreme Court representatives and the Fiscal de la Nación) and when the civilian government was replacing a good portion of the military-appointed judiciary. Until the April, 1992, coup, the council had become more independent. Still, if the executive no longer controlled the lists of candidates, individuals on those lists found it advisable to make a courtesy call on the minister before he made his selection. A closer look at the eventual appointees also suggests at least occasional executive intervention in the formation of the lists. Many would never have made the first cut without such assistance. As the section on public defense should make clear, the ministry's role in appointing public defenders is hardly worth mentioning, although it probably reaped some benefits in patronage for otherwise unsuccessful attorneys.

The ministry's role in overseeing the state of legislation is poorly defined and even more poorly executed. In theory its Division of Legal Affairs reviews all laws prepared by the executive, with particular attention to possible contradictions with existing legislation and to constitutionality. It is to maintain an official archive of all laws and resolutions of a general character, cross-referencing them as they are issued. Specifically, in the justice sector, it is also to centralize and coordinate commissions charged with revising the major codes and organic laws. Unfortunately, shortages of staff and other resources severely constrain its ability to perform any of these functions, not to mention its more ambitious pretensions to being the ultimate authority on existing legislation. As a consequence, and because there is no other public or private entity that fills this role, in Peru as in most of Latin America, it is often very difficult to determine what is the law.[71]

The ministry's major responsibility, in terms of effort invested if not formal priority, is the supervision of the prison system. Especially since 1980, the frequent turnover in ministers of justice can be directly attributed to problems faced in this area. A series of riots and the military-led massacre of 266 suspected or convicted terrorists in Lima's three major prisons forced the 1986 resignation of Alán García's first minister of justice and close personal advisor, Luis González Posada. Their inability to resolve the continuing prison crisis was also a critical factor in the resignations of two of the ministers who succeeded him under García. Although Peru's prison situation is hardly unique, it may be one of the worst in Latin America. Prisons are understaffed, overcrowded and filled with inmates who have yet to be tried or sentenced. Estimates over the past ten years routinely report that these untried and unsentenced prisoners represent over 70 percent of the prison population.[72] The new Criminal Code (in effect as of April, 1991) seeks to reduce this problem by discouraging the use of pretrial detention. So far its impact has been minimal.[73]

In Lima, the major prisons or large portions of them have been controlled by the inmates; the function of the guards is to keep them inside.[74] Mistreatment and torture of inmates by guards or other prisoners is not uncommon. Prison budgets are so meager that inmates usually depend on family members to bring them food and other basic supplies (although in that regard, they were no worse off than patients in all public and some private hospitals). Guard duties are shared by police (who guard the perimeters) and Ministry of Justice staff who supervise internal operations of the prisons.[75] Neither group receives special training for this function, and poor working conditions and low salaries produce frequent strikes. While there have been experiments with halfway houses and provisional liberty, these have generally proved unenforceable and subject to abuse and corruption. Given this general situation and a woefully inadequate budget, the minister of justice and the ministry officials charged with prison policy often find the most they can do is arbitrate conflicts among the various warring factions. Corruption is rife throughout the entire system, and even the most idealistic ministers have found the situation near hopeless.

Ironically, Peru's Criminal Codes (1924 and 1991) and the 1979 and 1993 Constitutions espouse the view that prisons should be places of rehabilitation and training for inmates, preparing them for their eventual reintegration into society. Under the military government, the minister of the interior began a program of prison reform based on this same philosophy. In substance this only got as far as the construction or partial construction of a series of modern prisons. All of these by now are as shabby and overcrowded as the prisons they were to replace. For a variety of reasons, most discussion of these issues in Peru has focused on the larger prisons located in and around Lima, which house about 50 percent of the total prison population, and which arguably demonstrate the most dramatically awful conditions. The remaining prison facilities scattered throughout the country demonstrate a far greater variety in terms of size, structural characteristics, and even basic professionalization of staff, although they generally share the common problems of overcrowding in inadequate facilities. One conclusion resulting from a series of studies[76] done in the 1980s is that Peru may have too many jails and prisons, and that many of the smaller more rustic provincial facilities might be better eliminated. While this would certainly not resolve the problem of overcrowding, the proponents of the argument conclude that it would at least allow prison authorities to concentrate their efforts on facilities with some possibility of improvement.

The Ministry of Interior and the Police

Although given control of the prison system under the military government, the Ministry of Interior's current role in the justice system comes through its control of the National Police Force. Until the end of 1989, when they were unified by the García administration, the country had three separate police forces. Of the three, the largest was the Guardia Civil (now General Police), numbering about 25,000 in 1980. There was also a smaller (about 5,000) Peruvian Investigative Police (now Technical Police), which was responsible for conducting criminal investigations and a Guardia Repúblicana (now Security Police) of about the same size. The Guardia Repúblicana's functions were mainly custodial, protecting buildings, forming a border patrol and guarding the prisons. By the early 1990s, the new national force numbered about 86,000, maintaining roughly the same numerical and functional divisions among the three groups.[77] However, its unification had so far involved only changes of names and a new uniform. Most of the problems characterizing the three forces remained and appeared to have been exacerbated under the new system.

One contributing factor was the presence of special divisions (most of them left intact by the unification of forces) with prominent and controversial roles in the antiterrorist efforts. The PIP's antiterrorist force, DIRCOTE (now DINCOTE, a division of the Technical Police), had been a target of criticism for its selection and treatment of terrorist suspects. Although current antiterrorist legislation allows the police to hold a suspect incommunicado for fifteen days (as opposed to twenty-four hours for suspects for conventional crimes), the DIRCOTE was less than fully observant of the additional requirement that they notify a judge and *fiscal* of the detention. Reports of the torture and other mistreatment of such detainees were not uncommon, if difficult to substantiate. The Guardia Repúblicana had its own special organization of commando style antiterrorist police, the State Security Force, more commonly known as the *Sinchi* Battalion. Although based in Lima they could be mobilized nationally and had also come under severe criticism for their operations in terrorist zones. For example, in a case sent by the Supreme Court to the ordinary courts in 1984, forty Sinchis were accused of massacring a group of peasants in Soccos, a community in Ayacucho. In 1986, the Superior Court of Ayacucho found ten of them guilty of *homicidio calificado* (first-degree murder).[78]

Whether with three forces or one, the failings of the police system, if more violent and dramatic in form, were similar in substance and origin to those of the rest of the justice system. Police salaries were low and budgets for basic supplies (from transportation and arms to paper and typewriters) almost nonexistent. Even in Lima it was not uncommon for police officers to offer to file a report on a complaint if the interested party gave them money to buy paper, or to have to ask the complainant to give them a ride to the site of the crime. While such requests for "collaboration" might be limited only to dire necessities, the practice of stopping or detaining individuals to solicit bribes had become almost an institution. This was aided by the semi-legal figure of the "intervention,"[79] a practice whereby individuals might be stopped and questioned or held for up to several days (usually over a week-end or holiday when the official in charge of bookings was not on duty) without ever being formally detained. Reliable figures are nonexistent. During the 1980s the ratio of interventions to actual detentions was apparently about four to one. However, there are famous examples, usually linked to terrorist actions in Lima, where up to 45,000 individuals were "intervened" in a single day, resulting in only a few hundred actual detentions. These mass interventions usually involved another near institutionalized practice, the mass round-up (*remada* or *batida*) or cordoning of urban neighborhoods with house-to-house searches for suspects or suspicious materials. The abuses associated with these actions are easily imagined.

Although extremely low salaries and difficult work conditions have been blamed for a major part of police misconduct, there are other contributing factors. Promotion systems were rumored to be ruled by favoritism, corruption, and political interference. While all three forces had training centers that were to be unified under the single national force, these were heavily influenced by the military government, leading to a further militarization of the police. Human and legal rights would not appear to have a role in the curriculum, producing not only the frequent charges of police brutality, but also in the case of the ex-PIP (now Technical Police), claims that their investigations often produced evidence that had to be thrown out of court. As with the other sector institutions, the situation and the performance of the police worsened notably in the last twenty-five years, a result of increasing crime, terrorism and drug trafficking, the decrease in public funds available to combat them, and the generalized breakdown of social cohesion and trust. If the judges and *fiscales* distrust the police, the disrespect is mutual. It's worth noting that until very recently the written report on the police investigation, the *atestado*, was not admissible as evidence. It now may be accepted, but only if signed by the *fiscal*, as evidence of his participation in the gathering of evidence and any interrogations.[80]

Police strikes for better wages and working conditions became more frequent and violent from the mid-1980s on, as did outbreaks of conflict among members of the different forces. Relations between the police and military, especially over their respective roles in combating terrorism and drug traffic have also been strained and have led to mutual charges of corruption. Finally, the unification itself and the resulting deterioration of lines of control may have further exacerbated police misconduct through the early 1990s. This was more than simple corruption, involving cases where police bands terrorized the communities where they operated, indulging in robbery, kidnaping and out-and-out murder.[81] In response, isolated communities have attacked police installations to force out individuals or groups whom they accused of being worse than the common criminals they were supposed to control. Another response was an increasing reliance on paramilitary or parallel police forces. For the wealthy this involved contracting of private police or, it was rumored, sponsorship of paramilitary vigilantes; for the poor it might be support for or participation in the officially recognized *rondas campesinas* (groups of peasants organized and sometimes armed by the military to patrol rural areas)[82] or less formal self-protection groups, merging into vigilantism.

There are some indications that the post-1992 government's law-and-order emphasis (and thus greater attention to the police) combined with its efforts to counter accusations of human rights abuses has curbed some of the more egregious examples of police lawlessness. The current administration has its own unique stand on human rights, but it is not one that tolerates a police force run amok. In any case, press reports of out-and-out police banditry have declined, and there have been moves to improve salaries and equipment, encourage higher levels of professionalism, and strengthen internal control. The reduction of the terrorist threat has also improved general service. Police now patrol the streets rather than staying locked away in their stations and venturing out only in groups. In late 1996, a substantial revision of the Organic Law for the National Police was under discussion in the Congress, although agreement on its content seemed a long way off. A more dependable police force, and one more susceptible to centralized control will be an important element in reducing the administration's dependence on the military and so countering any aspirations it may have to a more decisive political role.

Bar Associations and Law Schools

Throughout the 1980s, Peru had two major bar associations, the Lima Bar Association (*Colegio de Abogados de Lima*, CAL) and the National Federation of Bar Associations. The latter has since disappeared, missed only by the Aprista lawyers who had come to control it. The Lima Bar Association was the more prestigious and influential. While practicing lawyers must belong to it or one of the several other local bar associations, admission is based on payment of a fee. No examination is required. The bar associations have been known to disbar lawyers, but this is fairly infrequent—despite a common complaint that unethical lawyers are a major factor in encouraging judicial corruption.[83] The bar associations and, especially, the CAL are most important as intellectual fora and as lobbies for changes in key legislation, especially, but not exclusively that affecting the justice system. They and their members were important contributors to discussions on the new Organic Law for the Judiciary and on various proposals for revising major legal codes. In fact earlier delays in the implementation of the new law were largely due to objections to its content raised by the CAL.[84]

Because CAL did not rely directly on the state for its existence, it often acted as a more independent source of criticism and ideas than the Court itself. While generally seen as a politically conservative organization, it has provided a forum for a variety of ideological views, including those of the remaining members of the reform-oriented New Law group from the military period. At least until recently, the CAL's president, elected for a one-year renewable term, was arguably the single most distinguished and prestigious member of the national juridical community, displacing in this respect even the president of the Court and the Fiscal de la Nación. The latter were more frequently seen as having attained their position through political pull (or even occasionally corruption) whereas these factors were usually not viewed as influencing the Colegio's election of its leader. The Federation of Bar Associations was a more highly politicized institution and, as a result, lacked the prestige of the Lima Bar. In this the federation more closely resembled the majority of bar associations throughout Latin America, with CAL being a more interesting exception to the general rule.

CAL has not escaped the Fujimori period completely unscathed. The controversies surrounding the government's policies in the sector eventually affected even its operations. As discussed in more detail in a later chapter, its financial security had depended on a lucrative contract with the Court for notice serving. The contract was terminated in 1996, leaving the association on the verge of bankruptcy. The fate of the contract was linked to a more fundamental division within the association between the elite lawyers who had dominated it and the majority membership who in 1995 captured its presidency. The outcome of this conflict is likely to affect not only the future of CAL, but also the direction and success of judicial reform in Peru.

As noted above, the major bar associations and the law schools have representatives on the National Council of Magistrates and, while they existed, on the district councils. They also often run free legal service clinics. The law schools of course are the primary training centers for the major sector professionals. As such they have come under increasing criticism for a curriculum and teaching methods that encourage a formalistic, theoretical approach to the law. As is the unfortunate rule throughout the region, in recent years Peru has also seen a proliferation of private law schools. These are often simply diploma mills, contributing to the general decline of the profession's image and its poor performance. Some few universities have tried to introduce a more varied, nontraditional curriculum and approach. Their students, drawn from the more privileged social groups, usually go on to lucrative private law practices and not to the public sector. A minority have been influential in forming free legal clinics and advocacy groups to defend the interests of marginalized peoples.[85] Because these schools also harbor the remaining New Law or reformist faculty, they continue to produce studies critical of the established justice system. This line of thinking is usually not well received at the higher levels of the court system. It has found a small following among more junior members of the judiciary.

Summary

The foregoing has described many of the weaknesses and shortcomings of individual sector institutions. The following two chapters examine their interactions, first in the context of criminal justice and then as the focus of several decades of attempts at reform. For the moment, several general comments are in order. First, as should be evident from the lengthy discussion above, while the judiciary occupies stage center, it is only one of a series of separate, but interdependent institutions comprising the sector, each with its own set of individually determined rules, behaviors, and operating procedures. As regards their internal performance and interactions, institutional autonomy is a legal fact and still more of an operational reality. Even where legislation stipulates cooperative or hierarchical relationships among the various institutions this has rarely been achieved. This lack of coordination is a major factor contributing to poor performance in the sector as a whole and of the individual institutions within it. It is also a vice few Latin American countries have escaped. Perhaps only Costa Rica, by including the courts, defense, prosecution, and the investigative police under the Supreme Court's control, has avoided the problem. This solution, however, has other drawbacks and hardly seems advisable for Peru or the rest of the region.

Second, aside from insufficient coordination, most evident in the criminal justice area but also visible elsewhere, there are other common problems. These include inadequate funding for both operational and investment budgets that translates into the inadequate quantity and quality of human and material resources; political interference, especially in the selection of personnel but also in all other activities; antiquated operational and administrative systems and procedures; and institutional missions increasingly out of touch with the larger social, political and economic environment. These complaints are echoed throughout the region, although Peru, despite its history of reform efforts, seems to suffer most of them in extreme forms. For all of Fujimori's criticisms of sector performance, his efforts to provide remedies have been slow to arrive and his earliest actions only aggravated the situation. The few exceptions might include those entities directly involved in the antiterrorist efforts (the special courts and DINCOTE). However, such selective special attention is an often counterproductive method of achieving wider reform. It is doubtful, in any case, that this objective motivated these actions.

Third, the combined effect of all the above elements have meant that the quality and quantity of services provided, both among the various institutions and to the wider public, is increasingly deficient. This tendency, here as elsewhere, has been compounded by societal changes—including but not limited to the political activation of large segments of the urban and rural poor—which have expanded and qualitatively changed the demands on the sector. Although the attendant problems of terrorism, drug trafficking, and economic decline focused most attention on the failings of the criminal justice system in particular, these same failings to a greater or lesser extent pervade all aspects of the sector's operations.

Finally, as serious as they are, the sector's failings cannot be separated from those of the wider political system that both mirror and reinforce them. For example, corruption has become endemic to all justice sector institutions and can be explained by sector specific (although often externally initiated) characteristics. However, it is also a societywide phenomenon in which the sector's participation may be seen as just one localized example. Consequently, although sector reform may be implemented as a single program, it is difficult to envision much in the way of permanent improvements absent corresponding changes in the broader political environment.

Notes

1. Municipalities have been the most stable in their organization and powers. Until rather recently, they alone had their own locally derived governments. Even these were often centrally appointed. Between 1923 and 1980, elections for local (provincial and district) councils were held twice, in 1963 and 1966. From 1980 to 1989, they occurred at regular three-year intervals, and resumed again in 1993. A series of localized disasters and generally worsening conditions in the provinces led to experiments with departmental boards in the late 1960s. Under the military and second Belaúnde governments these evolved into the departmental development corporations (one for each of the twenty-four departments) that were to serve as prototypes for a lesser number of regional governments. After lengthy debates and several false starts, twelve regions were introduced in 1990, each headed by an elected assembly, council, and president. They disappeared with the *autogolpe*. The 1993 Constitution leaves open the possibility of their recreation, but the current administration seems content to work with elected municipal governments. See Hammergren, 1983, pp. 81-83; Caravedo, 1983, pp. 91-162; Hammergren, "Institutional Development of the CORDES," in Chetwynd et al., 1985; Bernales, 1996, pp. 679-702.

2. Executive decrees were of two types. Legislative decrees required delegation of authority by Congress. The delegation included a deadline and general thematic limits. As part of his responsibility for overseeing public finances, the executive could also issue extraordinary decrees when national interest so required. As observers note of the 667 decrees issued between 1980 and 1985, the term "extraordinary" was hardly appropriate (Rubio and Bernales, 1988, p. 410).

3. One of the earliest controversies involved President García's attempted nationalization of a series of private banks and financial institutions. Here for a change, the judiciary weighed in by granting temporary restraining orders (*amparos*)

to several banks. García was forced to retreat and rely on Congress's passage of a law, enacted in much diluted form after lengthy delays. See Ashehov, 1988; Maxfield, 1992.

4. The law required that legislative and extraordinary decrees be reviewed by the congressional Constitutional Commission and stipulated that the duration of emergency states be specified along with the rights affected. The 1993 Constitution preserves the original wording, thus eliminating these statutory constraints.

5. However, a recent decree requested by the sector reform commission seems to reduce Congress's powers in this regard.

6. Pásara, 1988, pp. 42-43.

7. With the exception of a few articles written in the 1960s and early 1970s (e.g. Cooper, 1968, 1971; Murray, 1987), studies of the operation of Peru's "judicial power" are virtually unavailable in English. Published sources in Spanish for the most part are either formalistic treatments, essentially commentaries on legislation, or the series of very critical studies coming out of the New Law movement of the 1970s. The latter deal less with the overall institution and its internal politics than with "judicial sociology" (i.e. the background and opinions of the rank and file judges, and the interface between judicial culture and the public at large). There are a few exceptions, among them Ramírez's (1985) very polemical book on the politicization of the Court under the military and after, Rubio and Bernales' (1988) work on the constitution, and sections of Valdivia, 1986, but none of these gives a basic overview. They instead cover themes that presuppose a knowledge of the fundamental operation of the system and the issues it raises. Another important source are the "memoirs" of ex-magistrates, sometimes published as such (e.g. García Rada, 1978), but often appearing as part of their learnèd commentaries on the justice system (e.g. Olivera, 1986). While such works are too anecdotal to constitute systematic evidence, they offer important insights, found nowhere else, into the internal workings of the justice sector. The information included here is, thus, based on three principal sources: the constitution, organic laws and other legislation that set out basic structure and functions; writings of Peruvians either directly or indirectly discussing the system's real workings; and my own observation and interviews.

8. The tax courts, along with the executive department responsible for collecting taxes, received early and substantial attention from the Fujimori government. Both are said to be very efficient, although little is known about the courts' operations.

9. While Peru has always recognized some arbitration, it was only in late 1992 with Decree Law 25935 that it approved a General Law of Arbitration. Three years after its passage, reports were that it had little effect.

10. Peru is one of only six countries with permanent appointments for its Court. The others are Argentina, Brazil, Chile, Colombia, and Mexico (until 1995). Permanent or "lifetime" (*vitalicio*) tenure is, however, accompanied by a mandatory retirement age; changing the age of retirement is one means of forcing renewal of the Court. Permanent tenure, sometime subject to periodic ratification, is slightly more common for the region's lower level judges.

11. There is little point in gender neutrality. No woman has served on the Supreme Court and very few have even reached the rank of superior court judges.

12. See discussions in Chapter 5 on judges' dismissal of their responsibility for the sociopolitical consequences of their decisions.

13. To this day, there is still no official judicial career in Peru—that is, a formal career path in which individuals' entry, transfer, promotion, and dismissal operate according to predictable, transparent rules and where these rules establish prorammed patterns of movement through the career ladder. When Peruvians speak of the judicial career (*carrera judicial*), they are usually referring to the seated judiciary as opposed to outside recruits—as in the distinction that someone is chosen "from the career." Sometimes tenure has been confused with the career, but this is really a minimal condition. A judge with tenure may spend his entire time on the bench in one isolated judgeship, lateral or horizontal movement depending not on any formal criteria, but rather on whom he or she knows.

14. In detail, the situation is considerably more complicated. See Chapter 4 for a discussion.

15. One of these is the Chilean *queja*, in effect a complaint about an irregular judicial decision. As discussed by Cappalli, 1990, and in articles in Valenzuela et al., 1991, this has evolved into a fast-track appeal, replacing the normal *apelación*.

16. This is apparently a regional tradition, but it also follows Spanish jurisprudence. See Sojo Picado, n.d.; Albán Gómez et al., 1994.

17. The statement was made in the introduction (*Exposición de motivos*) to the 1912 Civil Procedures Code. Cited in Monroy Gálvez, 1967, p. 170.

18. As discussed in Chapter 7, the process was recently eliminated in Costa Rica.

19. Introduced by the dictator Leguía (1919-1930) as a means to control the Court, this was first used effectively against one of his own candidates in what is widely regarded as the last time the Court openly and overtly opposed a president.

20. Although Peruvians still distinguish types of judges by "instances," the term has lost its initial neat correspondence to trial and appellate levels. Currently "first-instance judges" may serve as trial or investigating judges in criminal matters. For major criminal cases, "second-instance" courts are trial courts. Similar changes have been made on the civil side.

21. Universidad Católica, 1991, p. 126.

22. Interviews, Lima, 1996.

23. More recent additions include El Salvador's judiciary with six percent of the national budget, and Ecuador and Honduras with two percent. In most cases, the amount actually dispersed is less than the earmark.

24. Interviews, Lima 1988. For an analysis of the administrative structure and needs around 1991, see Universidad Católica, 1991, pp. 86-127.

25. For a while the situation was so difficult that it was impossible to hold meetings with the judges on payday since they all wanted to get to the bank early. In addition to their cars and drivers, the *vocales supremos* also received a generous *bolsa de representación* (entertainment allowance) and expected to be accompanied on trips by an extensive entourage. Power apparently went to their heads easily. In the late 1980s, one president ordered that his (daily) entrance into the Judicial Palace be announced by a military band playing the national anthem. Interviews, Lima, 1988.

26. In that year, a second superior court was added for Lima's northern section; further additions are likely.

27. Based on statistics in Universidad Católica, 1991, p. 80.

28. Interviews, Lima, 1988.

29. Merryman and Clark, 1973, p. 392. The conclusion is based on statistics for five countries, Chile, Colombia, Costa Rica, Peru, and Spain, over the period from 1945 to 1970.

30. Interviews, Lima, 1988. This is a common complaint throughout Latin America and one of the primary justifications for moving to an oral system.

31. After the coup, Fujimori ordered the restructuring of the Court to include only eighteen justices.

32. See Verbitsky, 1993, and articles in Stotzky, 1993.

33. The military also introduced single-judge sentencing tribunals in an effort to clean up the backlog of criminal cases. This mechanism was preserved by the subsequent civilian governments, although it has also been criticized as violating due process.

34. One proposal was to limit the Supreme Court to *casación* and direct other appeals to the superior courts. Another was the creation of regional supreme courts. Interviews, Lima, 1988.

35. In effect, the only ratification performed strictly according to law was that done in 1968. Otherwise, ratifications remained a tool for dismissal of individual judges, but were never conducted systematically. Universidad Católica, 1991, p. 70.

36. In 1987 (following the 1985 passage of the *Ley de Ejecución Penal* or sentencing law), a second category of first-instance judges, *juez de ejecución*, was added. The judges were assigned to the various prisons where they were responsible for overseeing the execution of sentences (i.e. prison terms) and the implementation of provisional liberty, halfway houses, etc. Their performance was generally not considered satisfactory, in part because of the disorganization and other failures of the entire prison system and in part because of their own susceptibility to bribery and other forms of pressure. Under the 1991 Judicial Organic Law, these judges were to become ordinary criminal judges of the first instance. For a short discussion of the problems associated with the *jueces de ejecución*, see Universidad Católica, 1991, p. 28.

37. Not all of these worked in the *juzgado*; in areas like Lima with numerous *juzgados*, some were assigned to a separate reception desk or *mesa de partes* where they processed documents and filed cases as they arrived. The secretaries of civil first-instance judges often maintained their own offices with separate staff, one of the unforeseen obstacles to their complete incorporation into the judiciary.

38. Interviews, Lima 1988. The situation in Lima was so notorious that, in the mid-1980s, the superior court ordered an investigation of all secretaries in first-instance courts. They found at least one-third of the total liable for dismissal on the evidence and testimony collected; the rest were not above suspicion, but their guilt could not be established so concretely. Unfortunately, the report was never made official—and the secretaries were all left in place. Apparently, political pressure from above and from the employees' unions posed too great an obstacle to make the findings public or to act on them.

39. Because of the externally financed training program discussed in this section, these officials have also been the subject of numerous studies. See for example,

Brandt, 1987, 1990; Chunga Lamonja, 1986; Mejía et al., 1987. Comments in this section are also based on my own observation of one of the training programs and discussions with participants.

40. However, a new organic law, under consideration in the Nicaraguan Assembly in early 1997, may terminate this practice, by requiring that local judges be certified lawyers. It is not clear whether the drafters of the law, who drew on the Dutch model, had fully considered the consequences.

41. Rubio and Bernales, 1988, p. 432. No reason is cited for the military's elimination of the ministry, but one suspects that like the Ministry of Justice (also eliminated), it struck them as superfluous.

42. R. Smith et al., 1990.

43. This is the author's view. The judiciary was more critical of the ministry's performance, as were many local observers. While the ministry was never accused of the rampant corruption associated with the judiciary, in individual cases prosecutors were allegedly subject to political or other pressures. For example, in the dismissal of the case against ex-President García, the Fiscal de la Nación was criticized for not having acted aggressively enough. *Caretas* cited rumors that this had been a trade-off for a position on the APRA slate for senators in the next general elections. Whether more honest or not, *fiscales* have been less critical to the outcome of cases than have judges and other judicial employees. Thus, it may make less sense to bribe or pressure them. See *Caretas* (Lima), March 23, 1992, pp. 25-26.

44. *Caretas* (Lima), May 4, 1992, pp. 46-48.

45. This conclusion stems from its ability to order detentions, searches and seizures, and other measures usually requiring prior judicial approval.

46. The favorable responses were 67 percent of those surveyed. In terms of recognition (82 percent), the Fiscal, Alfonso Valdivieso, was third. The same survey indicated a 63 percent confidence rate for the Fiscalía, as opposed to 47 percent for the judiciary and 35 percent for the national police (*Semana* [Bogota], January 1, 1996, pp. 44 and 46).

47. Interviews, Lima, 1987-1988. See, also, Ferrandino, 1993, for a more complete description.

48. Costa Rica's public defense program has existed and functioned remarkably well for years, so much so that individuals capable of paying for their own defense often prefer a public defender. Panama's program made rapid strides between 1991 when Salas and Rico, 1993, described it as woefully inadequate and 1993 (see Wilson, 1993), increasing its staff from twenty to 120.

49. National Center for State Courts, 1993, passim.

50. See for example Cleaves and Scurrah, 1980; Pásara, 1978; Pásara, "Perú: Administración de justicia?" in de Belaúnde López de Romaña, 1984, pp. 257-258; Zeledón et al., 1989. Seligmann, 1995, pp. 62-69, also provides relevant observations.

51. Interviews, Lima, 1988. While critics have accused the agrarian courts of adopting the more static mentality of the rest of the judiciary, these interviews also indicated a sense of common purpose and esprit de corps not visible elsewhere. For example, using their normal budget and their own funds, the agrarian judges had maintained a system of training programs and seminars throughout the districts where they operate. Meanwhile, the Supreme Court, even when offered external

funding, was hard pressed to create its own training program, spending several years debating such details as who would run it, where it would be located, and whether long-term training was preferable to short courses.

52. For a vivid account of one soldier's participation in the dirty war, see *Quehacer* (Lima), June-August, 1991, pp. 54-62. The same issue has two other articles on the *guerra sucia*, one referring to events of the late 1980s.

53. Interviews, Lima, 1991. The military insists that most of the *desaparecidos* have chosen to go underground, are artifacts of the notoriously poor recordkeeping systems of various government agencies and the absence of an adequate documentation system for a large portion of the national population, or may have left the country. For a rebuttal, see Amnesty International, 1991, 1992; Youngers, 1992.

54. This is not to suggest that the police are not involved on the criminal side of the drug traffic. The charges arise from police and military involvement in the Upper Huallaga area, the center of coca cultivation. Because the military held an antiterrorist function, they consciously chose to ignore coca cultivation so as not to antagonize potential allies among the peasant small holders. Whether aside from the strategic differences, military officials are more direct collaborators with the drug traffickers remains to be proven, but it is an accusation frequently made by the police. For the views of Alberto Arceniega, one of the military generals criticized for being overly tolerant of drug trafficking, see *Quehacer* (Lima), December-January, 1990, pp. 38-43. Significantly, increased involvement of the military in antidrug activities was terminated by the Fujimori administration in early 1996, specifically to discourage this source of corruption.

55. This issue has received considerable attention. See for example, Rubio and Bernales, 1988, pp. 440-444; Ames et al., 1988, passim.

56. This remark is attributed to Luis Cisneros, a retired general and former minister of defense. More recently (July, 1991), a minor scandal erupted when a Peruvian television station tried to run copies of a military training film on how to kill subversives. The military acknowledged the film, but as the product of an individual, not the institution *(Miami Herald*, International Edition, July 21, 1991, p. 15A).

57. The 1991 Judicial Organic Law (Article 14) attempts more precision on this issue, stipulating that military courts will only try officials for infringement of their military responsibilities and functions. An official, even on duty, who commits a civilly defined crime is subject to prosecution by civilian courts.

58. Rubio and Bernales, 1988, pp. 440-444; *Quehacer* (Lima), No. 35, February-March, 1987.

59. See Rico, 1993, for a discussion of experiences in Europe and elsewhere in Latin America.

60. The judicial school had been under discussion for years. Prior to the writing of the new organic law, it had begun to function at a very rudimentary level. While both the organic law and the constitution establish it as a legal fact, it was not until 1996 that the government gave it funding and encouragement to begin a "normal" program. However, its first task was an evaluation of the seated bench that many believed to lie outside its legal mandate.

61. Interviews, Lima, 1988.

62. Since data on the scores of Fujimori's new appointments to the Court (from examinations taken previously—his appointments were made outside the regular procedures) have been published, the scoring system evidently predated the new law, but had not been made available to the public. *Caretas*, which published the scores, gleefully noted that most had been so low as to prevent the candidates from appearing on the lists presented to the executive for final selection (*Caretas* [Lima], April 6, 1992, pp. 16-17, 82-84; April 27, 1992, p. 22).

63. See Chapter 5 for a discussion of this group during the military government.

64. See Rico, 1993, for a discussion of the evolution of various European councils and the problems of politicization affecting them.

65. See Pérez Perdomo, 1988, for a discussion of its history.

66. See Chapter 7 for details.

67. Costa Rica introduced two such internal councils in 1993. See Chapter 7.

68. Prior to 1979, habeas corpus was used to protest infringement of all legal rights. It was only with the 1979 Constitution, that it was limited to illegal detentions, with *amparo* introduced to cover all other individual rights.

69. Readers are reminded that Argentina is one of the few countries with both federal and provincial or departmental courts and that the ministry's direct powers extend only to the former.

70. Ramírez, 1985, pp. 85-97 is especially critical of appointments under the second Belaúnde government.

71. Throughout the region, the situation is further complicated by the practice of issuing legislation with the closing disposition that it "revokes all previous legislation in conflict with its contents." Since no government entity is capable of checking through all previous laws to determine which are thus repealed, there are an undetermined number of laws on the books that are in effect invalid.

72. See Carranza et al., 1983, p. 22; Cooper, 1971; Webb and Baca, 1991, p. 352; and Perú, Senate, 1989, pp. 324-325.

73. Although no statistics have been made available, it is claimed that at least in Lima, these provisions have had some effect. One suspects that in the provinces their effects have been nil.

74. Following a series of prison riots and massacres the Fujimori government temporarily replaced the guards with soldiers and worked to restore order in the affected prisons. Once the emergency (and international attention) had subsided, the situation returned to normal. With the construction of special prison facilities for captured terrorist leaders, the incentive for maintaining order, if not improving conditions, in the normal prisons also disappeared—a phenomenon not unlike the impact of the special terrorist courts on government interest in improving the normal administration of justice.

75. The 1985 *Ley de Ejecución Penal* (Sentencing Law) created a new body, the National Prison Institute (INPE) to run the prisons and provide staff for internal operations. By the early 1990s it was already regarded as so corrupt and inept that the military and/or police were frequently brought in to assume these functions in the major prisons around Lima. The March, 1992 comment by a deputy that INPE was the most corrupt governmental institution in the country would probably be challenged by few who knew it well (*Caretas* [Lima], March 30, 1992, p. 82). In 1996,

the government had extended its sectoral reform program to INPE and was working on a new law to regulate its operations. Given the administration's tendency to contract out services to private sector entities, it would not be surprising to see the adoption of this mechanism.

76. See for example, Peru, Ministry of Justice, 1981.

77. There is also a small body of Judicial Police who are part of the Technical Police, but restrict their activities to delivering summons and bench warrants. In this they respond directly to judicial orders (and in Lima, have their office in the Palace of Justice) unlike the rest of the Technical Police who for the most part conduct their investigations and other activities independently.

78. Rubio and Bernales, 1988, pp. 443-444.

79. These and other aspects of the intervention/detention system are discussed in Eguigueren, 1991. While the intervention is a legally defined measure, it has been extensively abused by the police—since it is not supposed to involve any restrictions of personal liberty. Interventions often differ from detention (arrest) only in being shorter term (a maximum of a few days) and never involving the booking of the person held. One informant reported that police sometimes "intervened" housekeepers and maids on their way home from work, holding them so that they could clean up the station house and then releasing them. Although complaints about the semilegal or illegal activities of police go back at least thirty years, the situation reached crisis proportions in the early 1990s. As reported in a *Miami Herald* (International Edition, Oct. 31, 1991, p. 1A) article entitled "Peruvians terrified of their police," one part of the problem was the difficulty of recruiting new police to replace the hundreds killed annually in terrorist attacks. As a consequence, recruits were increasingly drawn from among poorly educated youths, given a three-month (as opposed to the former two-year) training program and put out on the streets.

80. Interviews with judges and *fiscales* indicated their incredulity as to the possibility of accepting an arresting officer's testimony as evidence since "everyone knows" they will lie.

81. While possibly just unfortunate coincidence, one day's reading of the Lima papers (October 8, 1991) produced three stories on crimes allegedly committed by police: the kidnaping and murder of a rancher in Trujillo, the unexplained escape of twenty-six accused officers from a prison (guarded by fellow police), and the shooting-murder of a twelve-year-old child when police stopped her parents' car and tried to rob them.

82. The *rondas campesinas* have an interesting and controversial history. Reputedly based on indigenous tradition, their creation has been encouraged by government authorities throughout the rural areas. The controversy arises both in the official encouragement of what has sometimes become little short of a lynch mob and the dangers posed to the *campesinos* participating as targets for terrorist attacks. The two lines of criticism are not entirely compatible; those favoring the second argument often contend that the situation would be improved if the government would arm the *rondas* adequately. Obviously, those fearing rampant vigilantism are not in agreement. An article form the *New York Times* (Oct. 6, 1991, p. 3A) outlines both views, stressing that Sendero had targeted an estimated "80 percent" of its military actions at the *rondas* as opposed to the conventional security forces. At the

same time, it notes that the *rondas*, whether armed or not, had engaged in attacks on other peasant communities, claiming that the latter, if they had not formed their own rondas, must clearly be Sendero sympathizers. For a more sympathetic portrayal of the rondas, see *Quehacer* (Lima), 69, January-February, 1991, pp. 76-92.

83. Like many countries in the region, Peru's only substantive requirement for entrance to the bar is a law degree from a recognized law school. Valdivia Pezo, 1986, p. 118. Corruption within the legal profession has been less documented than that in the judiciary. It is apparently widespread and clearly either a cause or effect (and probably both) of judicial corruption. Even "honest" lawyers admit to knowing which judges can be bribed, and presumably less honest ones act on this information (Pásara, 1982, pp. 155-157).

84. Interviews, Lima, 1989.

85. An anonymously authored report, prepared for USAID/Peru is the source of this comment. The report, while generally positive about their activities does offer a series of more critical comments on their overall impact and possibility for expanding it.

4

Criminal Justice Process

Of all aspects of its operations, it is the justice system's handling of criminal matters that has attracted the most criticisms and provided the most impetus for reform in Peru and throughout Latin America. This is also the area involving the widest variety of sector actors and, thus, offering the best demonstration of how the institutional strengths and weaknesses play out in practice. It is in criminal justice, as well, that one can best appreciate the often enormous gap between formal and real procedures or their intended and real effects. The present chapter explores these themes. The following chapters elaborate on them, examining the wider sociopolitical foundations and impact of sector performance, the efforts that have been made to reshape them, and the consequences of these reform programs.

Peruvian criminal procedures, both as written and applied, are still more "typical" of the region than its institutional structure.[1] This is a logical consequence of the widespread practice of copying codes from other, presumably more advanced countries. Even when countries varied their choice of models, the alternatives selected had usually been developed in the same fashion. That is to say, they themselves were already imitations. Earlier in the century the preferred models were European codes; more recently, those of other Latin American countries or the Latin American "model codes"[2] have been used, as well. The lack of variation is also a consequence of the limited interest in the codes. Whereas other political actors might see some benefit in tinkering with institutional relations, code writing was left to a small group of jurists. Finally, since most countries faced the same obstacles in applying their progressive codes, even the subsequent deviations from the new legal norm are similar. As has been observed, Peru began its process of code modification somewhat earlier than many other countries, especially as regards the movement toward oral, accusatory procedures. However, the initial gap is closing and the situation described here, and that currently in effect in Peru, is arguably more similar to the regional "norm" than it might have been ten years ago.

The major legal documents shaping Peruvian criminal procedures are the Constitution, the Organic Law for the Judiciary (1963 and 1991) and for the Public Ministry (1981), the Criminal Code (1924 and 1991), and the Criminal

Procedures Code (1940, 1991, and the 1994 draft code). Following the civil law tradition, the Criminal Code defines ("typifies") specific crimes and establishes punishments for each. It also defines conditions under which criminal responsibility may be waived or sentences reduced, and controls such actions as the use of pretrial detention. The Criminal Procedures Code, as its name suggests, sets out the general principles guiding criminal procedures (e.g. due process rights) and describes in detail the means by which criminal cases will be handled. It also incorporates the rules of evidence and the appeals process. The Judiciary's Organic Law sets the general structure of the court system; the roles, responsibilities and privileges of its major actors; and otherwise defines basic operating procedures. The Public Ministry's Organic Law and those for other institutions where relevant have a similar content.

The earlier versions of both codes and the Judicial Organic Law have been subject to modification almost since their passage. It was only in 1991 that completely new versions were finally approved. A comparable version for the Public Ministry is still pending. Only the Judicial Organic Law and Criminal Code went into effect on schedule. The implementation of the procedural code was repeatedly delayed until late 1994, when a slightly modified version was substituted and discussions of its approval commenced. Thus criminal procedures remain regulated by the 1940 code, its later modifications, and a variety of special legislation defining the treatment of crimes like terrorism. This situation has impeded full implementation of the other two laws. If implemented as written, the three will substantially change the criminal justice process, furthering its longer term evolution away from a written, inquisitorial process to an oral, accusatory one. They will also work significant changes in the definitions and punishments for specific criminal activities. The latter changes include the incorporation of nonconventional crimes (e.g. terrorism, drug trafficking and white collar crimes), still treated under special legislation, and the decriminalization of certain activities, largely those that the authors believed more appropriately regarded as offenses to conventional morality. The effective, as opposed to formal, implementation of the three laws is likely to take years. If attempted, it will require additional modification of their content. In part this is due to contradictory provisions already introduced in complementary legislation or the 1993 Constitution. However, as experience elsewhere has already demonstrated, such new codes usually maintain more continuity with past practices than their authors realized or intended.[3] Unless subject to further modification or clarification, they often reinforce practices their proponents had hoped to eliminate.

Another reason for viewing the proposed changes cautiously is Peru's history of introducing legislation the implementation of which has been partial at best. The 1924 Criminal Code was considered a model document at the time of its writing, although this view was for the most part limited to national and foreign academics. The Peruvian judiciary was less complimentary, terming it extreme and dangerous.[4] In the regional tradition, it drew heavily on foreign sources, most notably the draft Swiss Criminal Code of 1915 and 1918; the Italian, Spanish and Swedish codes of the era were also influential.[5] Some sections, such as the one on the rehabilitative and readaptive role of the prisons, seem progressive by today's standards. It is not surprising that they were never successfully implemented. Others, like the special treatment[6] to be given "less civilized" indigenous peoples and "savage tribes," while expressing the more advanced views of their era, were perhaps just as well ignored. More recent criticisms of the code and those accounting for its ultimate replacement were its design for crimes of an era long past and its basis in a theory of criminality hardly in touch with contemporary reality. This, combined with the traditional belief that the judges should stick to the letter of the law and thus not make interpretive adjustments for changing circumstances, further limited the code's adequacy for present conditions. In recent times, piecemeal modifications have included legislation addressed to terrorism, drug-related crimes, white collar crime, and a variety of other crimes against the state, most of which were not treated in the original code. The modifications have often been infelicitous and not infrequently inconsistent with the basic document itself.[7]

General Outlines and Principles

Even before 1991, modifications of the codes and complementary legislation had introduced substantial changes in the basic procedures. Most notable were the enhanced role of the Public Ministry, the further development of the oral trial (first introduced in the 1920 procedural code, but in a very rudimentary form), and the passage of the responsibility for the bulk of minor crimes to lower instance judges, working with a new summary procedure. In these areas in particular, Peruvian criminal procedures, at least in the abstract, embodied some of the most progressive trends in the region. However, the 1940 procedural code, as written and as practiced, was also based on certain assumptions that arguably no longer hold. These range from a judge's average caseload and the types of crimes most normally dealt with to the availability and reliability of certain kinds of evidence. The tendency to hold to a strict interpretation of the contents of both codes and the Judicial Organic Law also obstructed efforts to modernize and rationalize even purely administrative practices. Examples include the long delays in accepting the substitution of typewritten for handwritten documents and the resistance to replacing the massive books of registry with some more efficient means of recording the initial filing of cases.[8]

The gap between law and reality is also evident in the 1979 Constitution's numerous guarantees on the rights of the accused in criminal proceedings, virtually all of which are retained in the 1993 Constitution. These rights are incorporated in contemporary constitutions throughout the region and, unfortunately, are often subject to the same incomplete realization in fact. In addition to the basic rights to be considered innocent until proven guilty, not to be held without cause, and not to be tried or sentenced for crimes not legally defined at the time of their commission, all detainees must be brought before a judge within twenty-four hours of their arrest. The only exceptions involve terrorism, espionage, or drug trafficking. In these cases, the suspect may be held by the police for up to fifteen days. Prior to the end of this period both the judge and *fiscal* who will handle the case must be notified. This exception is a recent addition to the code and an obvious response to Peru's special problems in these areas.

Detainees must be informed immediately in writing of the reasons for their arrest, they have a right to defense, and they cannot be held incommunicado except in certain cases specified by law. Even in these cases, their presence must be made known to the judge and prosecutor. Forced confessions are not allowed, nor are individuals obliged to testify against themselves, their spouse, or close relatives. No one may be tried by special courts or commissions. In both the 1979 and 1993 Constitutions, the sections addressed to the judiciary guarantee public trials (except where public morality, national security, or the interests of minors dictate otherwise), the right to an interpreter, indemnization for judicial errors or arbitrary detention, and a plural instance (that the case will be heard by at least two judicial instances). They also prohibit being tried twice for the same crime.

Unfortunately many of these guarantees have been violated, in some instances, routinely. This is especially true of the time limits for notifying a judge of the detention of a suspect, the requirements for the presence of a *fiscal* during police interrogation, the prohibitions on forced confessions, the right to defense, and, especially, free defense for the indigent. Furthermore, certain of Peru's "atypical" legislation, including that establishing special courts for terrorist cases, and the introduction of the summary process (investigation, trial and sentencing by the same first-instance judge) appears inconsistent with the basic constitutional guarantees. Finally, under "exceptional situations"—states of siege or emergency—certain of these rights and especially those regarding restrictions on personal liberty may be waived. As much of the country was permanently or periodically under one or both of these exceptional states for a good part of the last decade, these guarantees were frequently not in effect.

Under the 1940 procedural code, ordinary criminal proceedings (reserved since the 1970's for major[9] crimes, about 20 percent of the cases tried) had three theoretically distinct stages: the investigation (*instrucción*) conducted by the first-instance judge (*juez de instrucción*), the trial and sentencing (conducted by a three-member panel of the superior court or correctional tribunal), and the second instance or appeal to the Supreme Court. The constitutional guarantee of plural instances meant that the Supreme Court considered matters of fact and law, and might reverse the findings of the superior tribunal on either basis. The Supreme Court's findings on matters of fact usually stood as final decisions (*cosa juzgada*). If they found legal errors or overruled a not-guilty verdict for whatever reason, the case was remanded to another superior court for retrial.

Although this discussion focuses on the ordinary procedure, it should be noted that there were also special procedures for libel, slander and crimes against sexual honor. One of their most important features is the requirement that the criminal action be initiated by a private party rather than the public prosecutor. This is common throughout Latin America, as is the belief that many of these issues, which might be handled as civil cases under the common law tradition, are more adequately dealt with by criminal courts.[10]

More importantly, in terms of quantity of cases, there was the summary procedure introduced in the 1970s and most recently used for about 80 percent of criminal cases. Various observers have argued that this innovation violated the guarantee of a public trial, because the whole procedure except the sentencing was conducted in private by the investigating judge. This measure was an innovation for contemporary Peru. In some sense, it moved back in the direction of an older Peruvian and Latin American tradition (still in effect in many countries, including El Salvador and until recently in Guatemala) of having the same first-instance judge investigate and sentence. Under the summary procedures, the defense and prosecutor could participate in the investigation. However, they frequently did not view it in detail until the judge's findings were turned over to them for their comments, prior to sentencing. The 1991 procedural code maintains the distinction between major and minor crimes, with the former tried by a superior court and the latter by a first-instance judge. However, a member of the Public Ministry (a *fiscal*) will now conduct the investigation and present the case for the prosecution to either the trial judge (former *juez de instrucción*) or the superior court. The change will eliminate the conflict of interest inherent in the existing system and ensure a separate public trial for all criminal cases.

A still thornier problem is posed by the "special" courts introduced prior to and during the Fujimori administration to try drug and terrorist cases. Those created within the common court system are less problematic; with a few exceptions (notably the "faceless judges" introduced in 1992),[11] they remained subject to the normal procedural rules. The military courts, however, have their own procedures that are widely regarded as violating the most minimal due process standards. In some sense they also circumvent them. One of the principal complaints is overly speedy justice and insufficient time allowed the defense for consultations with their clients or adequate preparation. Additional problems include the use of military officials without legal training as judges at the appeals level, the use of anonymous witnesses, and the "legal" but still questionable ability to hold defendants incommunicado for up to fifteen days prior to their presentation to a judge. While the presence of these courts and of legislation allowing their continued use remain among the most controversial aspects of Peruvian criminal justice, they are not treated in detail here. They are best seen as an alternative to, rather than a focus of the broader reform movement.

The Investigation and Preparation for Trial

Under the 1940 procedural code, the investigative stage for ordinary cases began with the detection or complaint of a crime. Once brought to the attention of the *juez de instrucción* (in effect, a first-instance judge serving in that capacity), the latter had ten days to conduct a preliminary investigation and decide whether to open a case. The appropriate judge was the one assigned to the district where the crime occurred. If there were two or more *jueces de instrucción*, they generally alternated tours of duty, each one receiving and handling all the cases that entered during his tour. If a suspect had been arrested, he was to be brought before the judge within twenty-four hours so that the latter could take his statement and decide whether this and the other elements of the case merited his being held in provisional detention (for up to ten days) or released. The same held true if a suspect was arrested at any point in the initial investigation. In fact, the requirement for notification of the judge within twenty-four hours (fifteen days for terrorism, drug cases or treason) was commonly violated. Among other considerations, this gave the police time to collect evidence and extract their own confession from the suspect.[12]

Up to this point, the process did not vary significantly from that in place until recently throughout most of Latin America. One major change introduced with the 1982 creation of a separate Public Ministry was that it was often the *fiscal provincial* (the level corresponding to the first-instance judge) who received first notification of the crime[13] (usually from the police or the victim) and who then notified the judge and requested him to take action. According to the Public Ministry's Organic Law (Art. 94.2) the *fiscal* once notified could either contact the judge immediately or open police investigation prior to doing so. He could also decide to set aside the case, if he felt there were insufficient grounds and evidence for proceeding further. This was most often done if no suspect could be identified, ending the long-standing practice of opening judicial investigations against "suspects unknown."[14] In countries that have not introduced similar measures, such cases (called *sobreaveriguar* in Guatemala and El Salvador) often make up the bulk of the judges' case files.

By law, a member of the Public Ministry (the *fiscal provincial* or his representative) was to be involved in the police investigation from its initiation and to be notified within twenty-four hours of an arrest.[15] At this time he or his representative was to meet with the detainee to guarantee that the latter's legal rights were respected. The *fiscal* was to be present when the detainee was questioned by the police and his signature was to appear on any statement taken. These norms were also commonly violated. It appears that *fiscales* were often involved earlier in the police investigations than were judges, and that this had improved the collection and presentation of evidence in the *atestado policial* (charge sheet) There are several reasons for this. First, with the *fiscal's* signature, the *atestado* became legal evidence and not just a point of reference for the judges. Second, in Lima and some other cities, the pool of legal assistants (*abogados auxiliares*) attached to the *fiscal's* office, visited the police stations daily, thus encouraging cooperation. Both measures are unusual in Latin America and are demonstration and cause of the Peruvian *fiscales'* more active role over the last decade.

Although there is no legal reason for this limitation, the active police investigation usually ended with the opening of the judicial investigation, or even with the notification of the judge via the presentation of the *atestado policial*.[16] This document, bearing the signatures of the *fiscal* and the police investigator, might run to 100 pages and included transcripts of any testimony and documentation of all other evidence collected. It was the principal basis on which the judge formed his decision as to whether to open an investigation (*instrucción*). To do this, the judge had to determine that a crime had been committed, that there was a suspect, and that a penal action was in order (i.e. that there were no mitigating circumstances or other reasons for not holding the suspect criminally responsible for his actions). A negative answer to any of these questions meant that the case could be dismissed (*archivado*) with or without prejudice. Although the judge made the decision, the *fiscal* or the aggrieved party (who would become the civil party if the case went forward) could appeal it to the appropriate superior court. The police had no direct means of appeal if the judge decided not to open the case. This was a major incentive for ignoring the legal deadlines and preparing their evidence as completely as possible before it reached the judge's hands.

Upon the opening of the *instrucción*, the defendant was to be notified in writing of the charges against him and was usually ordered to appear before the judge to deliver his statement (*instructiva*) if he had not already done so. At this point a defense attorney was to be identified, whether paid by the defendant or appointed by the court. As noted, public defenders were usually not assigned at this stage, often on the formal if fictitious pretext that the defendant had waived this right.[17] The defense was entitled to participate in all aspects of the judicial investigation, even those where the defendant did not appear. Defense attorneys provided by the state rarely did so. At this point, if he had not already done so, the judge could order provisional detention for up to ten days. Any time in police detention did not count, since this was theoretically only twenty-four hours. In theory as well, provisional and definitive detention (ordered after the first ten days) were only used if the defendant was a recidivist, or if his minimum sentence would be over four years. Even in the latter case, he was to be detained only if there was already considerable evidence against him and if on release he was likely to flee or tamper with the evidence. In fact, detention was used almost automatically. In Peru, as in most of Latin America, this practice accounts for the extremely high percentage of pretrial detainees among the prison population. It has also been claimed that Peruvian lawyers favored it as a way of extracting fees, legally or illegally, from the defendant.[18] While this phenomenon has not been documented elsewhere, it is probably not unique to Peru. Detained suspects were usually held incommunicado for up to the full ten days allowed by law or until the *instructiva* was completed. During this period they could only meet with their defense in the presence of a third party.

Aside from the suspect's statement, the judicial investigation was largely composed of the judge's (or more frequently, if illegally, his staff) taking testimony from witnesses or others who could shed light on the case. These witnesses might be those suggested by the *fiscal*, by the accused, or those identified as important by the judge himself. The judge also collected testimony from expert witnesses, usually employed by the state, and whatever physical evidence might be relevant. Throughout Latin America, criminal trials tend to place enormous emphasis on witnesses' testimony as opposed to other kinds of evidence. This poses particular problems both because of the common legal restriction on who may testify (e.g. the exclusion of relatives, minors, and people of "bad character") and unsophisticated interviewing techniques used by judicial personnel. The emphasis on testimony also includes the use of mechanisms like confrontation (of a witness and the defendant, the defendant and the victim, or of two defendants) and the reconstruction of the crime with the participation of all the affected parties.

Peruvian critics contend[19] that the judicial investigation generally duplicated that already done by the police, and that this was often repeated a third time at the trial phase. It is debatable whether this duplication or triplication of efforts led to any more certainty as to the truth of the matter; it undeniably lengthened the process. The *instrucción* was limited to four months, with a possibility of a two-month extension ordered by the judge, and up to two months more at the request of the *fiscal provincial* and the superior court and Fiscal Superior. It was usually drawn out much longer, if for no other reason than because of the judge's heavy caseload. The most common case assignment system tended to aggravate the problem, giving one judge all cases beginning within a single period, and leaving the next set for another judge. Figures on the real length of ordinary *instrucciones* indicate they averaged two to four years. Comparable figures from the summary process for minor crimes show that the legal limits of sixty days, with an extension of up to ninety days, normally had a real duration of eight months to two years.[20] The figures are comparable to those from other Latin American countries, despite a substantial variation in the length of time legally allowed.[21]

The 1991 procedural code converts the *juez de instrucción* into a *juez penal*, who will monitor the *fiscal's* investigation and then either decide and sentence or present the case to the superior trial court. The transformation should eliminate a major source of delays, confusion, and abuses. It should, thus, shorten the time required for the investigation and for the first-instance trial as a whole. It may also eliminate some of the opportunities for cases to be "misplaced" or pretrial detainees forgotten,[22] and may make better use of the police investigation while guaranteeing a closer supervision of the latter by the *fiscal*. It will not by itself eliminate other problems like that of guaranteeing an adequate and timely defense (i.e. one initiated when an investigation begins and not when it is finally taken to trial). Nor will it eliminate the custom of extending police detention until a confession is obtained, reduce the recourse to pretrial detention, or improve the quality of the investigation itself. Some of these traditional abusive practices are also addressed by the new codes, but the intended remedies seem less practical or less likely to be implemented.

The *instrucción* was largely devoted to the judge's investigation of the case, leading up to a recommendation as to whether or not it should go forward to trial. There were other details to be covered. Many of these involved the arrangements with any civil party[23] to the case (the victim, or others directly or indirectly affected). Although these individuals could also initiate their own civil suit, awards for damages were a normal part of any criminal sentence. Aside from identifying and conferring with the civil party, the judge also made an estimate of the damages to be awarded and guaranteed, if necessary by embargoing the defendant's assets, that they would be paid. The civil party was entitled to participate in parts of the investigation and could appeal the judge's decision not to open the *instrucción* or not to take the case to trial. Criminal trials generally took considerably less time than civil ones, which could be interminable. One unfortunate consequence of the opportunity for the civil party's participation and the award of damages was a tendency to request criminal action, when civil action might be as appropriate.[24] Since the civil party retains the same rights under the 1991 code and the new Civil Procedures Code is reported to have changed little in that area, this incentive also remains in place. This problem is also not unique to Peru. It may in fact be aggravated by a tendency for reformed codes to include a substantial strengthening of "victims' rights."[25]

On completing the *instrucción*, the judge reached a decision as to whether or not the case should be tried. The case file (the *expediente*), including written transcripts of testimony and all other relevant documents, was made available to the *fiscal* and then to the defense. Each had three days to add observations or objections. Following the creation of the Public Ministry, it was the *fiscal* who decided whether to send the case forward to the superior court, to send it back for further investigation, or to dismiss it, with or without prejudice. If there was a disagreement between him and the judge on this decision, it had to be settled separately by the superior court that would hear the case, in consultation with the *fiscal superior*. If both the judge and *fiscal* agreed to dismiss, they could do so and release the suspect without prior consultation with the court. This decision could still be contested and appealed by the victim or civil party. It has been claimed that this unconsulted decision to dismiss was not infrequently the result of outside pressures or bribes, especially in cases of drug trafficking.[26]

If the case went forward, it was first filed with the corresponding superior court and then sent to the *fiscal superior* who had from eight (if there was a suspect in detention) to twenty days to enter an indictment, to order that it be dismissed with or without prejudice, or to request another extension for further investigation. If the *fiscal superior* moved to indict, the oral process began regardless of the court's opinion on the matter. The court then had three days to issue a resolution scheduling the trial or, in the case of an *acusación formal*, note that it would begin once additional police investigation was completed. The resolution also identified the accused, the crime, the defense, and the civil parties and listed the witnesses and experts who must appear. If there were other suspects who would not be tried for lack of sufficient cause, the court could simultaneously order the permanent retirement of their records.

As one observer notes, it was during this "intermediate stage"[27] that case files tended to "disappear," never to be seen again. This was more likely if disagreements among the various representatives and levels of the judiciary and Public Ministry required further consultation. It was also common for agreements on some compromise solution, like temporary dismissal or the extension of the investigation. The loss could be intentional or accidental. Unfortunately in the latter case, if the suspect was already under detention, he could remain there for years, especially if he had no friends or lawyers to push aggressively for his release. One of the factors allowing both intentional and accidental abuses of the system was the continuing lack of clarity on the respective roles of the court and the Public Ministry, and the various ad hoc solutions that had been adopted as conflicts emerged. Such solutions might conform to the letter of the law and allow each institution to maintain the powers and rights it thought it ought to have. They often did not make sense from the standpoint of moving cases through the system in a rational and fair fashion.

The Trial

Once a trial started, it theoretically moved forward rapidly. By law, it was to continue, with interruptions of only up to eight days, until completed. This did not prevent some trials from going on for years,[28] largely because of the difficulty of assembling all the required participants, including all members of the three-judge panel. Not infrequently, the defendant or defense created intentional delays by refusing to appear in court, or creating disturbances once there. Failure to appear was not always intentional. Recent investigations have uncovered a veritable mafia of guards and police whom defendants had to pay for the privilege of being transported to the courtroom.[29] Unprepared judges were another source of delays; if they had not read the *expediente*, they might resort to the so called *"audiencia de minuta"* (*pro forma* hearing) in which they asked a few questions and then called a recess, rescheduling the trial for another day.

Unlike the judicial investigation, the trial had a definite order as established in the procedural code. It began with the *fiscal's* statement of the charges, his questioning of the accused, and the latter's recounting of his own version of the events. The accused had the right to maintain silence, but this did not halt his consequently one-sided interrogation by both the *fiscal* and the president of the tribunal. In theory his silence would not be held against him. However, the presiding judge was to encourage him to respond, and his refusal to answer any question or to offer his explanation of events was recorded in the written record of the proceedings. Following the civil law tradition, evidence belonged to the court, not to the parties, and thus was presented as a single effort to arrive at the truth of the matter.[30] The trial was also public unless special circumstances moved the court to decide otherwise. Since this was an oral trial, evidence collected in the police and judicial investigations was presented once again, orally. In major trials, witnesses were called to testify. In many other countries it is more common for the parties to read the depositions appearing in the *expediente*. Following an uninterrupted recounting of their testimony, witnesses and the accused might be questioned by the defense, the prosecutor, the civil party, and the members of the three-judge panel. As all parties had access to the case file, questions often focused on discrepancies between the written depositions and oral testimony. The civil party might be required to give testimony or choose to do so voluntarily. This stage, the presentation of the proof (*probatorio*), also included any expert testimony or physical evidence. The trial concluded with oral expositions delivered by the *fiscal superior*, the civil party, the defense and any third party with responsibilities for damages. The last to speak was the accused.

The *fiscal superior* in his presentation was limited by the terms of his initial accusation. He could neither vary the crime nor the sentence requested without asking for either a new trial (based on a new accusation) or a new *instrucción* (should additional crimes be involved). The *fiscal*, the defense, and the civil party also presented their conclusions in written form. The decision of the trial court was by majority vote. It was to be reached the same day as the accused was heard. The judgment or verdict addressed questions of fact (essentially guilt or innocence) and was a written response to the various questions posed in the case. Within twenty-four hours of its reading, the sentence (determining the penalty) was issued, also in written form and by majority vote of the three-judge panel. In both cases, the judges were required to explain how they reached their decision, summarizing both the facts and the law on which it was based. These documents became part of the *expediente* and thus a key element in the appeals process.

Appeals

As in common in Latin America, even in reformed systems, the defense, prosecution, and the civil party all had a right to appeal the decision (verdict or sentence), asking that it be overturned for reasons of fact or legal errors. Both types of appeal were incorporated in the single *recurso de nulidad* that was filed with the superior court hearing the case at the reading of the sentence (orally) or in written form within twenty-four hours. The civil party could also appeal the damages awarded. The superior court could refuse to process the appeal, a decision subject to its own appeal. Under the 1991 code, there are three appeals of lower instance decisions: *casación* (specific questions of law, seen only by the Supreme Court), *apelación* and *revisión*. *Apelación* (formerly used for appeals heard by superior courts) is the appeal to the next higher instance (e.g. *juez penal* in the case of decisions by a *juez de paz*, Supreme Court in the case of superior court decisions). It includes both verdict and sentence, as well as decisions on pretrial or interlocutory motions. As in the past, its most frequent use will be to provide the constitutionally guaranteed second instance trial for all criminal cases. It consequently covers both factual and legal matters, except for those specifically reserved for *casación*. *Revisión* is only heard by the Supreme Court, and is subject to no deadline. It can be requested years after a trial and even after the death of the defendant. It is available only to the convicted party or his relatives or the *fiscal supremo*, and is used only when new evidence, changes in the law, or new developments (including indications that the judge may have been pressured or bribed) suggest that the verdict or sentence was in error. The Court can reverse a guilty verdict or modify a sentence, but in overturning a verdict of not guilty it must order a retrial. *Revisión* existed under the 1940 code but was limited to appeals of a finding of guilty.

Under the 1940 code, and presumably in the future, the appeal once passed to the Supreme Court (or the relevant lower instance) may require the opinion of the *fiscal supremo* (or the comparable lower level *fiscal*), depending on the nature of the case. It is then scheduled for hearing. The hearing is based for the most part on the written records, the *expediente*, although the defense, fiscal and civil party may also offer oral arguments. The Court's vote must be unanimous to overrule decisions involving the death penalty or maximum prison sentences. Otherwise, a vote of four of the five-judge panel is sufficient. Where this does not occur, additional magistrates will be brought in until the necessary agreement by four is reached.

The constitutionally guaranteed second instance (unaffected by the new code) and the tendency to resort to appeals as delaying tactics, have ensured an enormous caseload for the Supreme Court. Although the hearings themselves are usually not lengthy and the Court must come to a decision within eight days, the backlog is such that the average case takes over two years to be resolved.[31] Since the same 20 percent of major cases will still have the Court as their almost automatic second instance, the new code will not affect this part of the caseload. However, in limiting the terms and origin (for the most part from the superior courts only) of *casacion*, additional appeals from still lower levels may be substantially reduced.

Proposed Changes: The 1991 and Draft 1994 Procedural Codes

As mentioned above, the major change to be introduced by the 1991 procedural code and the 1994 revised version is the elimination of the judicial investigation and the transfer of the investigative function to the *fiscal*. The latter will open the investigation on his own initiative, but must inform the first-instance judge (now *juez penal*) that he has done so. While the *fiscal* will direct the investigation and the police role in it, and decide what actions should be taken, he must consult with and receive the authorization of the judge for actions possibly infringing individuals' legal rights—for example, the detention of a suspect, embargoes of goods or evidence, the search or surveillance of private property. He must also inform the judge if he decides to suspend the investigation, needs an extension of the time limits, or, on its conclusion, whether he will enter an indictment. The time limits themselves will be shortened to four months for the investigation with a possible fifteen day extension. This change, with the acceptance of a corroborated confession[32] as sufficient reason for cutting short the investigation and taking the case to trial, should move cases ahead more rapidly.

The 1991/1994 code will also simplify matters by vesting the Public Ministry with the sole responsibility for the *acción penal* (indictment) and, thus, for moving a case forward. As a result, it will eliminate the convoluted procedures through which the *fiscal* and judge decided whether or not to indict. Under the new rules, if the *fiscal* enters a formal accusation, the case will proceed to trial, regardless of the judge's opinion. Should the judge disagree with a *fiscal's* decision to dismiss the case, he may refer the matter to the *fiscal superior* for the latter's binding opinion. The issue of who decides whether a case goes to trial has given rise to a variety of arrangements throughout Latin America and the discussion as to the best solution continues. In some cases (El Salvador, Costa Rica) the judge retains more say in the matter. In El Salvador, the victim may also override a *fiscal's* decision not to order a trial. In others (Honduras, Colombia), the decision is solely that of the *fiscal*. The underlying dilemma is how to reconcile a number of different values and concerns motivating the codes' authors—the recognition of the rights of both the accused and the victim, an emphasis on greater efficiency and on more transparency, and, last but not least, a continuing lack of faith in the judgment or honesty of any of the actors and, thus, a tendency to cover as many bets as possible.

Both versions of the new code also provide that all trials will include an oral hearing, either by the *juez penal* or the superior court. A more radical earlier proposal to make the latter into appellate courts and have all cases tried in the first instance by the *jueces penales* was discarded. This has been another problematic area for all reformed codes, stemming again from lingering doubts about the abilities or honesty of the new legal actors. In Peru, major crimes (essentially the same 20 percent) will still be heard by the superior courts, preserving the problem of assembling all the necessary participants in the departmental capitals where they sit. The new codes do include provisions aimed at eliminating some prior obstacles and abuses, making appearances of some participants mandatory, allowing for substitution of some court officials, and making more difficult intentional interruptions of the process caused by the absence or disruptive behavior of the defendant or defense.[33] The format of the trial itself is not changed substantially. As is common in Latin American, the new code retains the practice of a single presentation of evidence, the order of which is decided by the presiding judge(s) in consultation with the parties. To guarantee an adversarial treatment, the parties may question witnesses before and during the probatory stage, and present their own arguments as to how the evidence should be interpreted (the *"oralización de la prueba"*). As under the present system, all parties offer concluding arguments and the accused is the last to speak. In line with the notion that the *fiscal* should pursue the "truth" in his investigation and courtroom appearance, he will be allowed to request an increase *or decrease* in the penalty or the civil damages and may recommend acquittal if the proceedings have convinced him it is most appropriate. The practices are new, but the general principle is a holdover from the inquisitorial system and, in theory, currently guides the actions and decisions of the investigating judge.

The code's authors have portrayed their creation as the most advanced in the region.[34] In reality, both versions share many flaws with the "competition," and add a few questionable innovations of their own. It is likely that many of the efforts to legislate out problems will produce their own unforeseen complications. In addition, certain details like the format for the trial itself will require rethinking. Most of the new "accusatory" codes retain hearings that look fairly inquisitorial, although Peru's *oralización de la prueba* is a uniquely cumbersome wrinkle. Moreover, although the *expediente* is not discussed in detail, it is apparent that all parties, including the judges, will have access to it before and during the trial. The obvious question is how much it will influence the judges' appreciation of what occurs in the hearing, thereby undermining the explicit emphasis on orality and immediacy.[35] Still, the authors' faith in the superiority of the oral, accusatory system may be no more warranted than their belief that they have introduced one.

Most of the code's more evident failings lie less in its overall structure than in an overspecification of details, many of which will prove impractical or contradictory. These are probably best identified and corrected by those who must apply the code, through prior consultation, simulated exercises, and real experience. However, for this to happen, these individuals must be engaged in the process, as active participants in rather than mere targets of change. The major obstacles to effective implementation of any new procedural code are those of preparing and reorienting personnel for their new functions and ensuring they have the human and material resources to carry them out. Although the Public Ministry supported the change, when the first code was approved in 1991, they indicated that their staff and resources were inadequate for their new role and that police cooperation was far from guaranteed. Outside observers have concurred with the view, noting that the *fiscales* as late as mid-1993 still seemed unclear as to what directing the police investigation really entailed and how that differed from what they or the judge had been doing all along.[36] The judiciary has been relatively silent on the matter, possibly because the implied changes seem to touch them less directly. The workload of the judges will not be increased and, actually, should be reduced by the new code(s). Nonetheless, if the system is to work, judges will have to learn a new set of functions and rules, in addition to adopting the new philosophy behind them.

One additional concern, although one that has produced few comments, is the lack of attention in the procedural code, the organic law, or for that matter, the constitution, to the minimal organizational and material requirements to ensure an effective defense. All three documents guarantee the right to defense and to free defense for the indigent, but there is no indication as to how this would be achieved. It appears that no one has given much thought to why the present system works so poorly, or to the critical role of defense in a system that purports to be more adversarial. For a country that has normally been in the forefront of code revision, the oversight is hard to explain.

The continued decisions to postpone the implementation of the procedural code even in its latest version apparently respond less to these foreseeable difficulties than to the current administration's simple lack of interest. So far, its post-1994 reform program has produced no alternative proposal for procedural change, instead focusing on the special courts and a few measures to shore up the existing ordinary system. Following its initial post-coup purges, the government has increased the number of *fiscales* and authorized still more appointments. It had otherwise left the Public Ministry largely untouched through late 1996. Defense has not been an issue and the few improvements here have depended on donor-financed NGOs. The program directed at the courts has been highly selective in its targets. As regards criminal justice, its principal emphasis has been reducing the current case backlog and establishing a new system of drug courts. This has required the creation of additional judgeships, but the majority of the appointees are provisional and their positions (except in the drug courts) temporary. For the moment, Peru's official reformers seem disinclined to be limited by any general legislative guidelines and, especially, not a five-hundred article code, the underlying philosophy and considerable detail of which would only impede their *ad hoc* inventions. Over the longer run, some of the code's proposed innovations—most notably the elimination of the investigating judge, the primacy of the oral hearing, and the expansion of the *fiscal's* role—are bound to be adopted, but more in the interests of efficiency than any concern with due process rights. If the administration's reformers can find someone to scale down and simplify the latest draft, it may eventually be enacted. However, in another reversal of regional trends, it will be the culmination rather than the blueprint of their program, guided not only by a different set of values, but also by a distinctive approach to identifying and resolving the problems posed by the sector. So long as the current administration or its ideological successors remain in power, conventional procedural reform will remain a dead letter.

Notes

1. One apparent, but relatively insignificant exception is the terminology used in its codes. What Peruvian jurists call the (*declaración*) *instructiva* is termed the *inda-*

gatoria elsewhere. Peru's *etapa de instrucción* is called the *sumario* in other codes; this produces some confusion in that Peruvians speak of a *jucio sumario* instead of a *jucio abreviado*. Other countries have similar quirks; Bolivia, for historical reasons, uses the term *juez de partido* for what everyone else calls the *juez de jucio* or *juez de primera instancia*. What to outsiders is a simple question of semantics is taken very seriously by many local jurists. Complaints that a code drafted by outside experts does not correspond to "national realities" often means that it uses different names for what are essentially the same concepts.

2. See Llobert, 1993, for a discussion of the Latin American model codes.

3. One example is Colombia's retention of the *indagatoria* (statement by the suspect) as an obligatory stage in the investigation, subject to many of the requirements in effect under the inquisitorial system. Where the *indagatoria* is not realized in the form dictated by law, the investigation is temporally paralyzed. In a similar fashion, many other stages and events from the inquisitorial system are often transferred to the new codes where their presence is irrelevant or counterproductive.

4. Hurtado, 1980, pp. 115-116.

5. As Peruvian experts now admit, while there is nothing intrinsically wrong with using foreign models, the adapters seem disinclined to consider what kind of infrastructure or environment is necessary to make certain mechanisms or entire codes work in their countries of origin. Unfortunately, the characteristics required of an expert code writer are more a voluminous knowledge of other codes and relevant doctrine than a familiarity with their real life application. See Prado, 1991, and Hurtado, 1979, for a discussion of the "importation of foreign law."

6. Articles 44 and 45. The provisions allowed the sentence to be served on a prison farm and reduced to two-thirds of that served by a "civilized man." See Hurtado, 1979, pp 67-84. The problem of what to do with cultural minorities or majorities, who may not share the common legal tradition, continues to plague Peruvians and other Latin Americans. The solution offered in the new Criminal Code is to admit that a crime has been committed, but waive the sentence if it can be established that, for cultural reasons, the perpetrator did not understand that this was a criminal act. In the civil law tradition such distinctions are allowed, since the criminality of an act (*tipicidad*) is determined separately from responsibility (*culpa*) or criminal intent (*dolo*).

7. This has been the case with legislation to deal with terrorism. Various laws attempting to define terrorism as a crime had to be modified because they were unworkable or because of questionable constitutionality. For a discussion, see Peru, Senate, Comisión Especial, 1989, pp. 315-320. Another example is a law on early release, passed in 1980, which, it was subsequently realized, allowed individuals sentenced for the maximum prison term to be freed after serving only one-third of their twenty years. After 1987, accused or convicted terrorists were excepted from the program, although only those charged after the change were affected.

8. Language introduced in the 1991 organic law attempts to resolve this problem by eliminating many specific references to "books" to be kept.

9. The criteria for separating major from minor crimes do not lend themselves to facile summary. Minimum length of sentence is one criteria. Under the 1991 procedures code, three and five years are two common cut-off points. The degree of

violence is another; superior courts handle homicides and robberies committed with extreme violence or cruelty. Less violent homicides and robberies, manslaughter, and theft go to first-instance judges. There are additional criteria, the origins of which lie in cultural historical sensitivities. Patricide is a major crime, as is genocide, including "means destined to inhibit births" or the "forceful transfer of children from one group to another."

10. Many of the arguments given revolve around the notion that suing for damages is pointless if the offending party has no resources. There also may be some resistance to the idea of putting a monetary value on such things as honor and public image. Curiously, many of those advocating the decriminalization of status offenses or payment of damages for crimes against property resist the extension of these measures to offenses to honor.

11. Peru had experimented with special courts before 1992, but simply in the form of courts that handled only drug or terrorist cases. The judges were not "faceless" and unfortunately, were not given much in the way of extra protection. Proponents of the prior system argued that, with better safeguards for the judges, it would have worked, without violating due process rights.

12. Interviews, Lima, 1988. This is in fact a common complaint throughout Latin America.

13. This is not required by law. The Public Ministry's Organic Law introduces the possibility of notification through the *fiscal* and, at least in Lima, this appears to be more common practice than notifying the judge (Olivera, 1986, pp. 28-30).

14. Earlier modifications of the 1940 code had finally eliminated the practice of trying and sentencing suspects *in absentia*. At present, suspects can be tried *in absentia* and may be absolved, but not found guilty. The most famous recent case was the *in absentia* trial of Sendero leader, Abimael Guzmán, just prior to the *autogolpe*. The Supreme Court's upholding of a lower court acquittal was much criticized since it meant he could not be tried again for the same actions.

15. Police could arrest anyone caught *en flagrante*, although just what that meant was subject to broad interpretation.

16. Interviews, Lima, 1988. One effect of the new procedural code may be that the police, under direction of the *fiscal*, will continue the investigation beyond this point.

17. See Ferrandino Tacsan, 1993, for a discussion.

18. Cooper ,1971, p. 618.

19. Interviews, Lima, 1988.

20. Statistics from Universidad Católica, 1991, pp. 31-33.

21. Nicaragua and Guatemala, under the codes in effect in the early 1990s, gave eight days and fifteen days respectively. The region's longest period is six months (Argentina). However, the usual real length is estimated at about two years (Salas and Rico, 1993, p. 66).

22. For a discussion of these problems, see Olivera, 1986, pp. 254, 275-303. One other innovation in the new code, which should save time if adopted, is the acceptance of an uncoerced confession, with corroborating evidence, as sufficient reason for terminating the *instrucción* and proceeding to trial. This is a hard won point. Many Peruvian jurists, like those throughout Latin America, continue to

insist on the full-blown, full-term *instrucción* as part of the accused's rights of due process. Unfortunately, this increases court congestion, thus virtually guaranteeing that all investigations will run over time. Given the frequent use of pretrial detention, it also guarantees that many of the accused, whether ultimately found guilty or not, will have more than served the maximum sentence before the trial begins.

23. Under Peruvian law, all criminal cases have a civil party. In effect, there are often two or more civil parties, the *parte civil* (victim or anyone else directly affected, for example, the family of a homicide victim) and the *tercer parte civil* (those with indirect responsibility who may also be liable for damages). An example is the legal owner of a gun or car used in the commission of a crime. Both civil parties are full participants in the case. If a civil suit is also brought, the civil damages may not duplicate the criminal ones.

24. Interviews, Lima, 1989.

25. Here again, two legal traditions have been mixed with possibly undesirable consequences (i.e. the civil code tradition of the civil party and the victim's rights movement, especially as developed in the United States). A number of European countries have also expanded victims' rights, but they are usually more selective than the Latin Americans in how they combine this with the traditional participation of the civil party.

26. Olivera, 1986, p. 254.

27. Olivera, 1986, p. 303.

28. One recent study indicates an average length of between nine months and four and a half years for trials conducted by a sample of superior courts (Universidad Católica, 1991, p. 31). Surprisingly, this seems less of a problem in other countries with semi-accusatory ("modern mixed") systems. In El Salvador, for example, jury trials usually last a day or two and bench trials, once they occur, are also dispatched fairly rapidly. In Salvador, however, while the trial ends quickly, the judge may delay months in issuing his written sentence, thus leaving the prisoner in limbo. Costa Rican trials, with the exception of the most notorious ones, also tend to end more quickly.

29. Interviews, Lima, 1996. In response to the situation, the government has built courtrooms in some of the major prisons. This also reduces the risk of escapes.

30. See Damaska, 1997, for a discussion of the use and role of evidence in inquisitorial and accusatory proceedings.

31. Universidad Católica, 1991, p. 9.

32. See note 22 for and a discussion of this change.

33. This was a particular problem in trials of suspected terrorists (at least until the advent of the special courts). Defendants would refuse to appear (aided by the near absence of means for transporting them), or they or their lawyers would cause disruptions in court. The 1940 code offers no provisions for dealing with this.

34. Interviews, July, 1995.

35. Damaska, 1997, pp. 70-73, notes that this continues to be a problem in the efforts of European countries to move to more oral procedures, although he also sees it as offering some advantages.

36. This is one of the unforeseen problems of the rush to introduce accusatory systems throughout Latin America. In mid-1994, as El Salvador began to look seri-

ously at its proposed new procedural code, one observer noted that many prosecutors seemed to feel they would be issued badges and guns, and accompany the police on all their investigative work. In other countries it has been contended that the new *fiscales* are just investigative judges with a different title, and that the intended improvement in the quality of investigation has thus not been realized.

5

System Performance and Impact: The Crisis, Its Origin, and the Efforts to Induce Change

Peruvian's concern with the performance of their justice system long predates the past decade. As early as the 1920s the gap between expected and real performance had attracted attention from a small group of concerned critics. Nevertheless, it was only during the 1960s that the system's growing dysfunctionality became more widely apparent. In terms echoing or anticipating those heard throughout most of Latin America, the system as a whole and its various parts—courts, prosecutors, police, prisons—were increasingly characterized as corrupt, incompetent, inefficient, or simply irrelevant. The Peruvian reaction was earlier than most and has precipitated three decades of efforts to reverse these trends. Where the resulting reforms did not actually accelerate institutional disintegration, they still proved inadequate for the burgeoning demands on the sector. The efforts to revitalize the formal justice system have not ended. They have been increasingly obstructed by the sector's internal weaknesses and by an unusually difficult collection of wider social, economic and political crises. They may also be hampered by an incomplete appreciation, even among the most progressive would-be reformers, of the extent of the underlying problems and of the depth of the transformation required to resolve them.

Both the focus of complaints and the proposed remedies have changed over time, in line with shifting societal expectations and demands. The unfortunate common factors have been the exceptional resiliency of the sector's institutions in the face of externally imposed reform and their inability to promote reform from within. In part, the institutions have been protected by the moving target of criticism and the continuing lack of popular or elite consensus on the nature of the problem and the measures required for improvement. These tendencies have been exacerbated by the accelerated rate of sociopolitical transformation over the past decades and the explosive increase in the number and variety of groups affected by the sector's operations. This dynamic environment would appear to increase the chances of effective reform. It has more often produced reform measures motivated by political expediency and by concerns having little direct relation to long-term improvements in system performance. The tension between external "reformers," who seem most concerned with exerting control over some aspect of judicial operations, and the judicial community's resulting emphasis on institutional independence has created a schizophrenic reform process, discouraging a more broadly focused discussion of the nature of the sector's problems and possible solutions. The process has damaged the institutions. It has also encouraged a defensive attachment to the surviving elements of their traditional culture, further inhibiting an effective response to the widespread dissatisfaction with their performance. Thus, although Peru's traditional justice system was a prominent fatality of the 1968 military coup, its effects live on as a source of current institutional problems and obstacles to their resolution.

The Traditional System

Before examining the workings of the system, it should be noted that, during its heyday[1] (roughly the late nineteenth to the mid-twentieth century), its composition and organization was much simpler than that described in Chapter 3, dominated by if not coterminous with the judiciary. That domination has been eroded by the emergence of new institutions (e.g. an independent Public Ministry, national police forces), by the internal development of others, and by the increasingly complex pattern of relationships within the sector and with its wider organizational environment. Even before the military's death blow to judicial leadership, more evolutionary change had already begun to undermine the judiciary's role as the sector's institutional center and, thus, the key to its stability.

Peru's traditional justice system has been characterized in a variety of ways, but almost all observers conclude that its role was secondary to that of other political institutions. The system's staunchest defenders might phrase this differently, but their own emphasis on the independence and apolitical nature of the judicial role is not inconsistent with this description. In response to criticisms of the courts' actions, defenders usually argued that the judiciary could not go beyond the law, but should simply apply it, and that the law's content and impact was the responsibility of other (political) actors. While the judiciary participated in the formulation of some legislation, there were always those laws that most directly affected it, including major substantive and procedural codes, as well as organic laws and other legislation regulating the sector. Despite the legislation's broader impact, its drafters saw their function as technical, rather than political.

The system's traditional secondary role should not be confused with subordination or external control. Until well into the present century, the justice system, or at least the judiciary, enjoyed a good measure of institutional autonomy, made possible by conscious and unconscious limits on its sphere of action, on the issues it treated, and on how it chose to handle them. This is not an unusual situation. Observers in other countries have reported similar phenomena, often couched as a kind of nostalgia for the "good old days" when judges were less identified with partisan politics and were more professional. In some cases (Colombia, Costa Rica), this was the result of explicit political pacts. Fruhling[2] argues that a tacit agreement among Chile's political elites in the 1920s left the courts to handle their internal affairs so long as they stayed out of political matters. In Peru, and arguably elsewhere, three factors interacted to produce similar, if less consciously imposed limits: recruitment and promotion mechanisms that reinforced shared values and perspectives, internally and with national and local elites; the traditional limitations on the role of the state and, thus, the decisions and issues it affected; and the effective exclusion of the majority of the population from access to the system. What may be different about Peru, and account for the extent of its subsequent institutional collapse, were the factors' exaggerated development and the sharp break with tradition wrought by the post-1968 military government.

The contention that selection and recruitment practices enhanced institutional autonomy would surprise traditional observers, who usually argue that they encouraged control and manipulation by political elites.[3] This they see as the inevitable consequence of the selection of the judiciary by other branches of government. From 1860 to 1969,[4] Supreme Court justices were selected by the Congress from lists of ten candidates (seven to eight career judges and the rest practicing lawyers) prepared by the executive. Second and first-instance judges were selected by the executive (usually the minister of justice) from lists presented by the Supreme Court. The lists for first-instance judges were most frequently prepared by the respective superior court. From 1969 to 1979 and from 1982 to 1992, the executive filled vacant positions from lists prepared by a Magistrates or Judicial Council. In the latter period, congressional ratification was required for nominees to the Supreme Court. (The 1993 Constitution leaves the entire appointment process in the hands of the council, but does extend ratifications to the justices.)

Under all these variations, would-be candidates to the Supreme and superior courts usually lobbied the president, the minister of justice, or the Congress to guarantee their selection, or even their placement on a list.[5] Despite the frequent criticisms of this practice, prior to 1969 it does not seem to have guaranteed control of subsequent judicial decisions, except for a minority of high political significance,[6] or damaged the judiciary's prestige. In fact until that date, it helped maintain the profession's status by ensuring their connection with national elites and their common pro-establishment outlook. A comparable practice held for candidates to lower level positions.

Pásara[7] notes that an aspiring justice of the peace or first-instance judge was advised to invite the members of the relevant superior court to dinners or lunches. Contacts with local elites were also critical; courts often relied on the recommendations of community officials or other notables in selecting lay justices of the peace.

Three other factors set significant limits to external intervention in the selection process. First, despite the absence of an official judicial career, the formal requirements and informal biases of the system favored a high rate of internal recruitment. Even political elites attempting to place their own candidates generally selected them from existing members of the judiciary. Second, for most of the present century, efforts at political intervention only occurred when natural vacancies arose. The most determined dictator never had the opportunity to fill more than a small portion of the total positions. It was not until 1969 that a government dared to use the ratification process to create its own vacancies or simply fired judges en masse, a history of self-restraint uncommon in the region. Finally, although during some periods, most notably the Leguía (1919-30) and Odría (1948-55) dictatorships, the process and the selection of Supreme Court justices, in particular, was tightly managed by the executive, it usually had no single point of control. It was instead subject to a diffuse set of influences. Since the Supreme Court conducted the periodic ratifications of sitting judges, formed the lists for superior court vacancies, and reviewed those for first-instance judges, they maintained control over key aspects of the selection process and, through it, over the composition of the judiciary as a whole.

The control was admittedly weakest for the lowest level positions and, especially, those in far-flung rural areas. The Supreme Court was unlikely to know the candidates and, thus, had to depend on recommendations from the superior courts, who were in turn susceptible to those of local elites. This was the weak point in the system in as much as these unknown candidates were a part of the pool from which the higher level judiciary would eventually be recruited. It was also an evident source of abuses when local judges proved too cooperative with the local power structure. The Court had no means of preventing these situations and seemed inclined to address them after the fact, only when an individual's behavior became so outrageous that local notables themselves complained. For those who fit too well with the local culture, the more common response was to leave them there. The policy prevented their having a wider influence, but tolerated whatever abuses the community was willing to accept or encourage.

The Court's role might have been challenged more directly and more often had it not been for important formal and informal limits on the nature of issues handled by the judiciary. The jurisdiction of the formal justice system was in effect that of the formal state. In functional terms this meant that the issues it saw were as limited as the policy-making role of the latter, and that elites often found more effective, informal alternatives for resolving their conflicts.[8] As compared to many other Latin American countries, Peru was unusually late in expanding the state's role and, thereby, altering the composition and power base of its political and economic elites. Of the three case studies discussed in Chapter 7, it more closely resembles El Salvador in this regard than it does Colombia or Costa Rica. It was only in the 1970s that effective control of a greater range of judicial decisions became important in Peruvian politics, with predictable consequences for institutional autonomy. Until that time, the fact that most judicial personnel either came from or at least identified with the traditional elite groups further reduced potential conflicts.

When such conflicts did arise, the judiciary's usual response was to impose further limits on its own involvement, avoiding substantive issues in favor of a focus on technical and procedural details, often referred to as "legal formalism." The most famous of these cases involve writs of habeas corpus related to the imprisonment or persecution of political enemies of the administration. Here, the Court generally supported the government (by ruling against the request) for reasons having to do with procedural irregularities in the presentation of the case.[9] In so doing, justices and judges often resorted to some amazingly twisted legal reasoning. They justified this, and the accompanying lack of attention to the substance of the case, as in accord with their apolitical role. In one famous case from 1955 (during the Odría administration), the judge writing the dissenting opinion (ruling against the government) consciously avoided questioning the constitutionality of the Emergency Law involved, preferring to couch his dissent in terms of formal procedures.[10] The justices' lengthy deliberations on this case, their extensive consultations with political actors, including the president, and the advice they received, most of it urging caution to avoid political reprisals, are significant. They suggest not so much a controlled Court as one aware that its liberty of action depended on not transgressing certain political limits. However, the perceived limits were probably fewer and less important than the judiciary's unconscious biases— for example, a tendency to treat and sentence individuals differently according to their social class.[11]

Conflict was also limited by the effective exclusion of up to 80 percent of the population from contact with the formal system. Once more, this is not an unusual pattern, but one most frequently carried to extremes in countries with large, unassimilated Indian populations. Until well into the present century, the formal justice system, like most formal institutions, was coterminus with modern, urban, non-Indian Peru. Demographic trends brought some change, but urbanization and greater physical proximity to formal structures could not eliminate the cultural and economic barriers. The first attention to this phenomenon, especially as it occurred in traditional rural areas, stressed not the lack of access, but rather the use of the formal system as a tool of the rural elites and large landowners (*gamonales*) to reinforce their repression of the Indian or *campesino* (peasant) community. This characterization originates with the *indigenista* social critics of the 1920s and the literary genre of social criticism they inspired. Peruvian literature is replete with examples of the local judge or justice of the peace who belonged to the *gamonal* and administered justice according to his whim. If "in Peru, Indians never win lawsuits," it is because, in the words of a fictional hacendado, "the judge is on my side because he owes his job to me."[12] While this picture apparently contradicts the arguments on institutional autonomy, it overemphasizes the extent of contact between the formal system and the rural masses. It also underestimates the ways in which the system's own biases and values made such manipulation superfluous. This is not to deny the doubtlessly numerous cases of collusion between judicial officials and *gamonales*, who were often relatives or business partners as well. However, the formal system's more basic flaws were its complete disregard of the different needs and condition of the popular majority and its inability or unwillingness to monitor the actions of its more far-flung representatives.

For most of this century contacts between the formal system and the rural masses were in fact the exception. For most of the population and for most conflicts, effective "jurisdiction" fell to an alternative informal system, either that of the *gamonal* administered on his own estate or the traditional community. On his land, the *gamonal* was the law and, at least until the 1960s, effectively controlled his workers' access to outside structures.[13] Since these structures included education, it is doubtful that most hacienda residents had much if any knowledge of the formal justice institutions. As late as the 1960s about 20 percent of the rural workforce lived permanently on one of the large estates and another 20 percent worked there as temporary laborers.[14] For this 40 percent of the rural population, the formal justice system had little relevance and perhaps no existence. Another 40 percent still lived in indigenous communities, where traditional authorities most often administered their own system of justice without the intervention of either the *gamonal* or the state. With the opening up of the rural areas from the 1920s on and the increasing conflicts over scarce land, both the communities and the other 20 percent of small and medium landholders were increasingly drawn, willingly or unwillingly, into contact with the formal system. This has only been at the cost of overcoming nearly insurmountable problems of distance, language, and a basic unfamiliarity with and distrust of formal institutions and procedures.

Given these obstacles, the increasing incidence of *campesinos'* recourse to the formal system in conflicts over land represents a substantial step forward, and one for which the formal authorities can take little credit.[15] This is an important exception to the general statement on the judiciary's limited jurisdiction. Land cases were important, although their depiction as an area where the courts served only as a tool for exploiting the peasants is a gross oversimplification. This image was advanced by the ideologues of the 1970s agrarian reform. It is summed up in the statement by one of the agrarian reform leaders that no Indian had won a case in the Supreme Court in the first one hundred and fifty years of the Republic.[16] The statement may be true, but the fact is that at lower levels, they did win some cases, in as much as many of the disputes were between *campesino* communities. In a study of land disputes in the department of Junin between 1874 and 1943, Contreras[17] finds the communities involved in litigations against individuals, their own members, state officials (governors and subprefects), other communities, mines, *gamonales*, and hacienda officials. Less than half of the disputes identified by Contreras were against large land owners and, in some cases, one community might ally with an hacienda to pursue its battle against its own members or a second community. The conflicts took place in a context where land continually changed hands in all directions, and where the break up of a small number of communities into a large number of smaller ones was a major source of friction among them, as was the increasing shortage of arable land.

Dissatisfaction with the outcome of these encounters would produce a proliferation of land invasions in the 1950s and 1960s. The *campesinos'* frustrations were as much a result of the slowness and unintelligibility of the formal procedures as of any belief that they were doomed to lose. Even after the introduction of the pro-*campesino* agrarian courts in the 1970s, observers[18] reported that the community leaders and members were often uninformed and confused as to the status of their lawsuits, perplexed by the delays, and convinced that any delay meant that their rights would not be recognized. Judges in these courts were in fact instructed to counsel peasants on their rights and proper legal procedures and, if necessary, to go beyond the letter of the law. Without this special attention, the peasants' cases would founder on purely formalistic grounds. The rare efforts to access the formal system for non-land related conflicts met with similar problems. The *campesinos* were frequently confused as to the roles and responsibilities of the local political and judicial authorities and the police. These authorities themselves were often no better informed, or, in the worst of cases, willing to take advantage of the *campesinos'* ignorance.[19]

Decades of rural to urban migration have decreased the relative proportion, if not the absolute numbers, of rural residents on haciendas and in traditional communities. The land reform conducted under the military government in the 1970s effectively destroyed the hold of the landholding elite and distributed much of their land to the hacienda workers. However, the other obstacles of distance, cultural and linguistic differences, and a generalized distrust of formal institutions still inhibit access by rural residents and rural immigrants to the urban centers. To this should be added another obstacle, cost. If justice is "free" in Peru, it is not without a price tag. This may take several forms, ranging from the time and expense involved in reaching the appropriate official (a problem even for urban residents), lawyer's fees, and the legal and illegal fees charged by various judicial personal for processing documents. The "free" justice system combined with the low salaries of its employees has demonstrably increased the incidence of these illegal fees. Free justice also meant a system without resources even for such basics as paper and pencils. Employees often either had to pay for their own supplies and transportation or charge clients at least a minimal fee to cover these costs. Certain functionaries (notably the secretaries to first-instance judges in the civil area) were allowed to charge for their services since, until 1989, they were not direct employees of the courts. Particularly at this level, on both the criminal and civil side, the collection of additional completely illegal fees was not at all uncommon. There is little systematic evidence on these abuses, especially from the earlier period. Still, it appears that the levels of corruption reported in the 1980s are a more recent phenomenon, a product of the formal system's expanded contact with formerly excluded groups and of measures taken to accommodate the new demand for services, especially the greater reliance on auxiliary court personnel to handle routine procedures.

In summary, until the late 1960s, Peru's formal justice system, like the rest of its formal political institutions, was directly relevant to only a small, if expanding portion of the national population. Recruitment procedures that guaranteed an identification with, if not membership in the traditional elite, an established if informal career system, and a series of externally and internally imposed constraints, allowed the judiciary, its core institution, to maintain a considerable level of autonomy and to preserve its basic patterns of organization and procedures with only minor adjustments. This is not an unusual situation for Latin American judiciaries. Peru's case is remarkable only in the relative absence of challenges to this arrangement and in its judiciary's consequent ability to maintain its institutional self-image and culture impervious to the surrounding signs of impending change. However, the very tactics that allowed its survival and bounded independence, and the institutional identity they protected, would in the end prove unsuited to the radically changed political and organizational environment of the late 1960s and beyond. The result has been a rapid decline in the performance and institutional integrity of the sector, further aggravated by the series of externally and internally generated reforms that followed.

The Military Reforms

Prior to the 1968 military coup, formal efforts to redress the sector's problems had been largely limited to the seemingly endless reworking of Peru's

basic legal codes. Such measures might have addressed the emerging dissatisfaction with the inefficiency of the system or its inability to prevent the
endemic increase in crime and social disorder. However, these did not
figure as major considerations. Instead, the continued revisions represented
a desire to bring the codes into line with more "modern" versions, essentially those of European or occasionally other Latin American countries.
Presumably, modernization would improve performance, but the connection was an abstract one. The code writers' orientation was more
ideological or doctrinal than empirical. Similarly, other concerns—the complaint as to the elite bias of the formal system and the judiciary's own desire
to protect or expand its autonomy—saw no substantive translation into concrete programs. It thus remained for the military, shortly after their take-
over, to connect these various themes for the first time, combining a
scathing criticism of sector performance with the promise of an integral
reform. Their attack had a lasting impact on public perceptions of Peruvian
justice. Unfortunately, the comprehensive reform never materialized.

When the military came to power in 1968, the judicial system was one of
the few institutions they did not immediately target for change. Two considerations figured here: the lack of importance initially attached to the
judiciary, and a desire to avoid further damaging the new government's
image within the international community. Within months of the October
3 coup, the government was forced to change its mind on the first point and
reevaluate the risks assigned to the second. By early 1969, the Supreme
Court had made it clear that neither it nor the lower level judiciary would
operate with unquestioning support for the new government's policies and
that, at the very least, they would use the time honored tactic of passive
resistance to slow the process of change.[20] When discussions with the chief
justice proved fruitless, the military issued a decree law (D.L. 18060) of
December 23, 1969, announcing the reorganization of the judiciary. This
included the replacement of the entire Supreme Court (D.L. 18061), the
creation of the Concejo Nacional de Justicia to select all magistrates except
justices of the peace, and the creation of a separate agrarian court system.

The government justified its actions with a series of speeches and declara-
tions stressing the corruption and inefficiency of the traditional system and
its lack of political independence. They also emphasized the system's ties
with the traditional establishment, especially in the rural areas, and its use
to maintain the elite's position. Aside from the formation of the agrarian
courts and the later courts for the industrial community, the military added
nothing new to resolve these problems. They instead relied on the replacement of existing personnel with those assumed to be more ideologically in
tune with the government's aims. They did make a series of minor changes
in existing civil and criminal procedures, aimed at simplifying and ac-
celerating them. Over the long run these did little to decrease court con-

gestion. They also had the probably unintended effect of undercutting guarantees of due process, especially in the creation of single-judge sentencing tribunals and the granting of sentencing authority to first-instance judges for a number of minor crimes. The introduction of harsher penalties for a number of crimes, the stiffer legislation regarding freedom of the press, the broader definition of political crimes and their transfer to military tribunals also suggest that due process and protection of traditional legal rights were not high priorities for the government. Finally, despite its public objective of creating a new form of justice, the government continued to cut the portion of the national budget assigned to the sector, which for most of the period remained less than 0.5 percent.[21]

Although the judiciary received the brunt of its attention, the military made a few other changes, temporarily eliminating the Ministry of Justice and the Public Ministry, and giving a decidedly military orientation to police training programs. Only the police training had any lasting impact on the sector, and none of the decisions was a conscious part of their larger plans for sector reform.[22] The one potentially positive change in sector policy was a short-lived effort to improve prison conditions. Its only lasting effect was the construction of a new prison in the Lima area.

In its efforts to change the composition of the judiciary, the military abruptly broke with two traditional practices: that of waiting for natural vacancies to occur and of recruiting almost exclusively from the judicial career. The agrarian and industrial community courts were staffed almost entirely by noncareer judges and, not surprisingly, deviated dramatically from traditional patterns of judicial behavior and decisions. If the military had less success with the mainstream courts, it was not for lack of trying. Aside from the replacement of the entire Supreme Court in 1969 (four members were actually reinstated, but only after their formal removal), the destitution of an entire five-member chamber in 1973, the replacement of various other justices through periodic ratifications (now extended to the Supreme Court as well), and the filling of normal vacancies, the new government also replaced 504 of the 643 lower level judges by 1975.[23] Over one hundred more vacancies were created with the lowering of the retirement age in 1975. Still more appeared in 1977 when a series of new courts and judgeships were opened, most of them in Lima. For countries more accustomed to overt political intervention in appointments, the impact might have been less dramatic. For Peru, the break with tradition was decisive, and it did not end here.

Working through the Concejo Nacional de Justicia (the membership of which it controlled), the government increasingly made appointments outside the career judiciary, bringing in lawyers from independent practice and from elsewhere in the public sector. The sheer quantity of the appointments and the military's limited ability to discriminate among the candidates, or to define what it was seeking, in the end defeated efforts to create a new, or even a captive, judiciary. Perhaps with more time, they would have suc-ceeded, but the immediate result was an increasing factionalism within the judicial branch. Most favorably interpreted, this took the form of an ideological split between the supporters of the traditional neutral judicial role and the proponents of the activist "New Law" (*derecho nuevo*).[24] Less favorably viewed, it was between the holdovers from the old regime and the military's sycophants.

Despite the increased pressures, capitulation to the military line was not universal. For the most part the reaction of the judiciary was a further re-treat into formalism or an abject submission to what it assumed to be the wishes of the government. In contrast with past dictatorships, the dra-matically expanded role of the state increased the incidence of the tradi-tional politically sensitive cases (e.g. habeas corpus) and the variety of actions they affected; it also added whole new areas of legislation that the judiciary would be expected to apply. Simple passive compliance was no longer the best survival strategy. At least until the mid-1970s, there was evident pressure to demonstrate active support, in word if not in deed. Some of the professions of revolutionary zeal drew on ideological convic-tions; most appear less nobly motivated, further damaging the judiciary's self image and external prestige.

The experience with the two new courts, especially the agrarian tribunals, was more positive. The agrarian judiciary also toed the military line, but apparently more out of conviction than convenience. The new courts worked with streamlined procedures and were under instructions to move rapidly, take an activist stance, and be sympathetic to the peasants and workers. They advanced with unprecedented speed in resolving new cases and eliminating the tens of thousands that had accumulated from as far back as 1920.[25] The courts had a simplified structure of only two instances. The sixty-six land judges worked alone under extremely difficult condi-tions. Unlike their civil court counterparts, they were required to make on-site inspections of disputed lands rather than simply dealing with cases in their offices. Especially in the early years, while the mystique (and a higher pay scale) lasted, the courts were an example of what the "New Law" strived to produce. Unfortunately, a comparable model was never developed for the ordinary justice system.

Perhaps that model would have been found, had certain developments of the mid-1970s been allowed to continue. In 1975, with a near balance between its traditional and New Law members, the Supreme Court re-quested the creation of a Judicial Reform Commission (formed with D.L. 21307, November 11, 1975). The commission was to "work with social reali-ty and motivate itself with the principles of the Revolution, and on this basis reformulate the problem of the administration of justice in Peru." To tilt the balance further the government in December of that year lowered the age for compulsory retirement of the judiciary to sixty-two years (D.L. 21354). The move temporarily gave the leadership of the judicial reform and the Supreme Court to noncareer proponents of the New Law. Victory was short-lived, as the Revolutionary Government had already entered its second phase. New appointments to the Court shifted the balance against the New Law group by early 1976.

Still, the reform commission continued its work. By the end of 1975 it presented the prime minister with proposed legislation modifying the criminal and civil procedural codes, adapting the judicial organization to the regionalization of the country, introducing professional and staff training programs, and improving the organization of systems of statistics. The commission also contracted a series of studies on existing conditions and sponsored training seminars for judges using many of the new materials. With the change of regimes, most of the recommendations and studies were shelved. The commission was dissolved in 1978. Its remaining functions were transferred to the newly created Center for Judicial Training and Investigation. Although the center retained some of the commission's sense of mission, underfinanced, understaffed, and under close scrutiny by an unsympathetic Court, its activities and impact were severely limited.

Notwithstanding the curtailment of its broader efforts, the commission introduced a few innovations. One was the creation of an Office of Internal Control (*Oficina de Control Interno del Poder Judicial*, OCIPJ), which transferred back to the Court the disciplinary and control function temporarily assigned to the Concejo Nacional de Justicia.[26] A second important change was the greater attention to the role of the lay justices of the peace. Beyond a short-lived (1975-1977) experiment with including the *comunidades campesinas* in the selection of these officials, the most important result was a ten-year program to train the lay justices. With the change of Court personnel in 1980 and the departure or elimination of the New Law contingent, this program fell into disfavor. Because of its external financing, it was allowed to continue. The more traditional members of the Court, the overwhelming majority after 1980, claimed the program encouraged the proliferation of nonprofessional judges and threatened the integrity of the court system.

The other surviving remnant of the commission's efforts were the studies[27] it sponsored, many of which were published privately. They provide an unprecedentedly systematic analysis of the inner workings of the justice system. Their audience and impact were limited by their very critical and ideological biases. Within the information they provided were findings on the changing outlook and composition of the judiciary, based on a survey of eighty-one first and second-instance judges done in 1977-78.[28]

Two sets of findings are especially relevant. The first relates to the impact of the military period on the judiciary's outlook and self-image. The group surveyed recognized and accepted the criticisms directed at the traditional justice system, especially those on its inequitable treatment of different social classes. However, they had no suggested remedies and were generally defensive as to their own responsibilities, citing legal limitations on their actions and the traditional apolitical role of the judge. The second set of findings describes what the researchers called the "devaluation of the judiciary." Contrary to the profession's traditional image, most of those sampled came not from well-connected families, but from "the lower and middle ranks of the petite bourgeoisie, with a distressed family economic situation, and with grand expectations about secure employment in the judicial career."[29] The researchers contended that part of these trends were visible at least as early as the 1920s, the last period in which the Court made serious efforts to challenge the political elites. However, while it may be true that, "with few exceptions, judges and justices...[of the period were] named from among those professionals who have not been successful in private practices,"[30] this is still a far cry from the "devalued" composition depicted by the researchers in the late 1970s.

As a whole, the military's policies escalated and aggravated trends that had begun decades earlier, leaving in their wake a justice system bereft of leadership, discredited in the eyes of the wider public and of its own members, and divided as never before by political and personal conflicts. At the same time, despite berating the system for slowness, corruption, and an elitist bias, the military did absolutely nothing to resolve these long-standing problems, which only continued to worsen. The few bright notes were the advances made in extending and tailoring the system to the needs of rural populations via the agrarian courts and the justices of the peace. The fate of these changes, like that of the entire structure, now depended on the decisions of the new civilian leaders.

Redemocratization: The Politicization of Reform

The opportunity for substantive change, or for reversing some of the military's damage, was lost on their successors. The new civilian government instead fell prey to more immediate interests, most of them having little to do with sector performance. Civilian leadership, both within and outside of the justice sector, was more bent on eliminating any trace of the military's policies, and those who had collaborated with them, than they were on global reforms.[31] The Court drafted a proposal for a section on the judiciary to be included in the new constitution. It also ignored the broader issues. It instead sought to increase judicial economic and political independence through a self-managed selection and promotion system, the elimination of the periodic ratifications, permanent tenure with compulsory retirement at age seventy, and a guaranteed two percent of the national budget. The proposal also introduced formal powers of judicial review to be vested in the Court sitting as a whole.

The Court's proposal was partially incorporated in the new constitution with some important modifications. The two percent of the budget was included, but this was calculated against operating expenses and not the budget as a whole. The selection and promotion system was not left to the Court. Instead, the newly created Concejo Nacional de la Magistratura and its district subcouncils were to prepare lists from which the executive would make its selection. Finally, although introducing formal powers of constitutional review, the constitution vested them in a separate body, the soon to be created Tribunal de Garantías Constitucionales. Significantly, these modifications cannot be attributed to specific objections to increased judicial autonomy. Instead they were a result of struggles between the Aprista and social democratic factions of the Constituent Assembly. The parties' fundamental concern was the distribution of powers between the executive and the legislature, which would be indirectly affected by those functions vested in the Court.[32]

The 1979 Constitution made only two significant changes in the organization of the judiciary, stipulating the eventual incorporation into the judicial branch of the separate labor and agrarian court systems and the creation of a separate Public Ministry responsible for the prosecutorial function, as well as for the defense of legal rights. The constitution included a more lengthy and varied description of constitutional and human rights than did any of its predecessors. It also established four major means for protecting these rights: challenges to the constitutionality of laws, legislative decrees, regional norms and municipal ordinances (seen by the Tribunal de Garantías Constitucionales); requests for habeas corpus (against illegal detention) and *amparo* (covering all other rights), both of which could be entered with any judge regardless of normal case assignment procedures; and popular action (*acción popular*),[33] questioning the constitutionality of resolutions, decrees and administrative norms, seen by the judiciary.

A final issue addressed by the constitution was the question of what to do with the existing judicial personnel, most of whom had been appointed by the military, and with those who had been dismissed under the military government. Thus, one of the closing dispositions allowed the reintegration of all magistrates so dismissed, so long as they were not beyond the retirement age. Another instructed the Senate to proceed with an extraordinary ratification of the entire Supreme Court. Following this, the newly constituted Court was to ratify all remaining judges, except for justices of the peace.

The two ratifications, conducted in 1980 and 1982, were highly controversial proceedings, leaving little doubt that many decisions were motivated by political and personal antagonisms. Although the Constituent

Assembly had been split between Aprista, social democratic and leftist factions, the new government and legislature were dominated by Popular Action (AP), the party of Fernando Belaúnde (who had been deposed by the military in 1968) in coalition with the Social Christians (PPC). Since both parties had cooperated with the more conservative Morales Bermúdez government in affecting the transition to democratic rule, they ratified all but one justice chosen by the latter. They also ratified two justices who had been chosen, but then dismissed under Velasco's first phase. However, they refused to ratify almost all the appointees from outside the judicial career, losing their opportunity only in the case of four "New Law" justices who resigned before they could be fired. The final count was eight ratified, eleven not ratified, and four prior resignations. As one observer noted, "the New Law had been swept out of the judiciary."[34]

The ratifications of the lower level judges were still more controversial.[35] To accomplish its work, the Court divided itself into six commissions to study the 600 individual files. Unlike the ratifications under the military the judges were entitled to know the charges against them and could speak in their own defense, but the process was fraught with problems. Not surprisingly almost all the labor and agrarian court judges were not ratified. Of the eighteen second-instance judges not ratified in Lima (of a total of thirty) three cases in particular were roundly condemned in the press, by members of the Court itself, and by such political figures as the ex-president of the Constituent Assembly. The selection of replacements for the 232 judges not ratified nationwide received even further criticism, in part because of the unusually high proportion of outsiders (i.e. practicing lawyers as opposed to judicial careerist) named. The unusually direct and partisan involvement of the minister of justice in the selection of first-instance judges and of the president in that of superior court judges was also criticized. Thus, despite complaints that the new constitution was too strict in its limitations on the political activity of the judiciary, partisan identification emerged in the 1980s as a primary factor in naming and promoting judges. To an extent never seen before, judges were identified as sympathizers with one or another party. Even strictly internal decisions, for example, the annual election of the Supreme Court president, took on partisan dimensions and incurred increased outside intervention. Partisan concern with controlling the composition of the Court reached such heights that it was widely believed to be the main reason behind the 1983 decision to add five more justices, raising the total Supreme Court membership to an unwieldy and arguably unnecessary twenty-three.

It is frequently argued that the politicization of the court was motivated by the interest of individuals and factions in ensuring favorable outcomes for their cases. However, there were other factors at play. These included the desire of the political ins to punish those who had collaborated with and still maintained any loyalty to the first phase policies. Ideological differences drove a part of this, but one should not underestimate the strength of personal animosity, which in some cases still raged ten years later. Another factor was the changing nature of party organization and competition, and the new value of judgeships as rewards for party loyalists and as positions from which to further enhance the party's, as opposed to an individual's, power. Partisan identification or personal connections had always influenced appointments. They now were often the only criteria. This development, already criticized during the post-1980 Belaúnde government, would become still more evident under García. The Apristas, in power for the first time in their party's history, made an unprecedented grab for government positions, including those in the judiciary. In this Peru demonstrates, if somewhat tardily, a trend visible in a number of Latin American countries, an unprecedented entrance of partisan politics into the heart of the judicial appointment system as a direct result of the emergence of and conflict among mass-based parties.[36] Whatever the mix of motives, the partisan colonization of the judiciary only served to increase the divisions and overall demoralization within the institution, and further discredit it in the eyes of the public. It also aggravated and distracted attention from the more basic weaknesses identified by the military, but now taking on still more disturbing proportions.

The Justice Sector on the Eve of the *Autogolpe*: Dimensions of a Crisis

It was only well into the Belaúnde government that the broader question of sector performance received much attention. By then the series of problems criticized by the military had worsened, complicated still further by the demoralization of the judiciary and the generally deteriorating economic and political situation. The immediate solutions were largely legal ones—a renewed effort to rewrite the basic codes and the Judiciary's Organic Law and, in the interim, a series of laws of more limited application. Aside from legislation implementing institutions and procedures created by the constitution (Organic Law of the Public Ministry, Law of the Tribunal of Constitutional Guarantees, Law for Amparo and Habeas Corpus), all of which were promulgated in the early 1980s, these interim measures included modifications of the details of certain civil and criminal procedures that appeared too urgent to await the fully revised codes.[37]

In the criminal area, this sense of urgency also produced a series of laws defining or redefining specific crimes, or the means through which they would be handled. Not surprisingly, most of these were the so-called modern or unconventional crimes—economic crimes, terrorism, and drug trafficking. The area that saw the greatest surge in legislation, especially after

1985, was that regarding states of emergency and special procedures for handling suspected terrorists. Of the thirty-two laws (including decree laws) passed on this theme between 1932 and 1989, twenty originated under the García government.[38] Here, as in the case of the other interim legislation, a sense of urgency did not necessarily produce satisfactory decisions. The piecemeal approach often led to contradictory or unforeseen results requiring further legislative modification.[39] Significantly and despite the humanistic bent of the proposed new criminal codes, most of this interim legislation had a repressive, law-and-order orientation. In this it was arguably more in tune with the tenor of public opinion.[40]

Little of this interim legislation focused on wider concerns with overall sector performance or on the fundamental weaknesses identified by the military. Also completely forgotten were the military's criticisms of the sector's structural biases and its links to the traditional establishment. None of these themes were addressed by the would-be reformers, the wider public, or even by groups applying similar analyses to other traditional institutions. Their eclipse is puzzling; whatever the reason, when attention again focused on the larger issues, it was based on more conventional notions of the sector's role and its failure to perform it adequately. The weaknesses here can be summarized as the dysfunctionality of the formal justice system in serving its traditional clientele and mandate and, as well, the mass of new participants introduced over the course of the military regime.[41] This radically expanded nontraditional clientele was itself a source of the problem in that their entrance on the scene overwhelmingly increased the number and variety of demands to be attended. Access remained limited and, thus, another source of complaints for a majority of the rural and urban poor. Still, enough of them were brought into the system, voluntarily or by force, to overtax its physical, financial, human, and organizational resources. The few efforts to meet their special needs were of some help. However, the additional justices of the peace and support personnel, the popular legal clinics, and, under the military, the agrarian and labor court system were hardly adequate given the dimensions of the increased demand. Meanwhile, its traditional clients—the middle and, to some extent, upper classes—were chafing at the routine slowness, inefficiency, and formalism[42] of a system apparently not designed for a more complex and rapidly moving modern society. Whatever satisfaction they may once have derived from the cumbersome rituals of formal institutions was also diminished by the burgeoning presence and participation of the popular classes. It was soon a common complaint that the formerly majestic Palace of Justice in Lima had become a *tugurio* (slum) where sidewalk vendors and curbside lawyers openly plied their trades.

The sector's dysfunctionality was more than a question of excess demand. Short of resources, riddled with corruption, constrained by archaic procedures designed for an epoch long past, beset by conflicts between and within its major institutions, disdained by public opinion and by the more talented professionals who formerly might have joined its ranks, the justice system was widely acknowledged to represent the worst of the public institutions in a country where the entire public sector was in crisis. As measured against any of the usual criteria, the justice institutions were not delivering justice. This was evident in the criminal and civil case backlog,[43] the time needed to process cases (on an average well over the legal limits for criminal cases and seemingly endless for civil ones), the percentage of cases carried to completion (as opposed to those suspended, dismissed for technical reasons, or simply lost in the system),[44] respect of fundamental human and legal rights, as well as the basic provisions of the major procedural codes, pretrial detainees as a proportion of all prisoners, the situation in the prisons themselves, the incidence of police and military brutality, and the general public opinion of the system. The absence of adequate statistics on any part of the system's operations was just another of its failings. This made it impossible to track or document changes, but did not diminish the general sense that the situation was worsening from day to day. Finally, just as excess demand was only part of the problem, the remaining contributing factors were so intertwined as to make it extremely difficult to separate causes from consequences, or to determine where one might begin to seek a solution.

Whether as cause or effect, one major aspect of the crisis was (and continues to be) the quality of sector personnel, both in terms of initial aptitudes and skills (who is recruited) and on-the-job performance (the system's impact on shaping behavior). This is a constant across all the sectoral institutions and at all levels of each of them. Low salaries, diminished prestige, and inadequate provision of basic supplies and equipment had taken their toll, but at least in their contemporary dimensions were relatively recent developments and could not adequately explain trends that were already visible three decades earlier.[45] Some of these trends may not have been perceived as, or even constituted, problems when they first appeared. Carried over into the contemporary setting, the underlying attitudes, behaviors, and organizational cultures produced a widening gap between societal expectations and institutional outputs.

A substantial injection of resources might narrow that gap in some cases. This is most effective where the problem is not institutional culture itself, but rather the institution's inability to enforce it. Thus, better salaries, adequate equipment, and longer training programs might go a long way toward reversing the criminalization of the police. It is unlikely to affect their militarization or their unwillingness to cooperate with the *fiscales* and judges. Elsewhere, additional resources might only allow institutions to promote goals and values at odds with the wider sociopolitical environment. For example, within the court system, the traditional role model is the eminent jurist, versed in legal doctrine and philosophy, and able to quote line and verse not only of Peruvian legislation, but of that of a variety of other countries. Conceivably, could the Court afford to attract or train a judiciary composed of such scholars, the public might be still more disenchanted with their performance. There was also no guarantee that improvement of human resources would be a first priority use of a budgetary windfall, or that institutional leadership would have the insight and capabilities to design effective programs to this end. Indeed, the scant attention to training and incentive systems in most recent reform proposals suggests a very limited understanding of their role in changing behavior.

Thus, while the problem has been defined as one of human resources, it goes far beyond the question of attracting and retaining "good people" to one of the specific roles and behaviors that the institutions encourage and reward, and how effective they are in doing this. As suggested above and further elaborated below, the larger issue is that the behavior and roles, the traditional institutional culture, are no longer adequate to contemporary expectations and demands, and that a major process of institutional reorientation is in order. Many of the most recent reform proposals attempt to address this need, although not as profoundly as might be desired. Furthermore, their effectiveness will continue to be obstructed by the second part of the problem, the whole set of unofficial actions unintentionally encouraged or allowed by the institutional setting. While the universe of actions is clearly larger,[46] the major issue here is corruption.

If not evident before the Fujimori coup, popular support for the *autogolpe* made it clear that the vast majority of Peruvians agreed with the president's contention that the entire justice system was riddled with corruption. Popular perceptions may not match reality, but a variety of events over the last few years certainly lent support to their beliefs. The police and the National Prison Institute (INPE) represented the worst-case scenario, combining pervasive corruption with outright criminality and an apparently near total loss of institutional control over the actions of their members. These were never very effective organizations, even under the best of circumstances, and were further hampered by woefully inadequate resources and external and internal political pressures and intervention. However, in the late 1980s and early 1990s, the almost daily revelations of scandals involving all aspects of their operations suggested that extralegal behavior had become the norm and that even the most routine activities required a bribe or a kickback to move them forward. Still worse, although fortunately not as widespread, were the instances of overt police criminality, the involvement of bands of officials in kidnappings, robberies, and murders. While the military had been less frequently accused of the petty, endemic corruption associated with INPE and the police, it had long been rumored that some of its members were unnecessarily, but profitably, cooperative with drug traffickers in the coca growing regions.

If not in these dimensions, a certain amount of irregular behavior by the forces of law and order is less damaging to the sector's performance and popular image than is that same behavior when exercised by the judiciary itself. The issue of judicial corruption is a delicate one. While everyone "knows" that judges are corrupt and can cite figures on the extralegal take-home pay of civil and criminal authorities, the basis for such calculations remains a mystery.[47] The theme of judicial independence (for the judiciary as a whole and for individual judges), the Court's insistence that it police itself, and its evident inability or unwillingness to do so further complicated matters. However many judges accepted bribes or let other pressures influence their decisions, those actually identified and disciplined by the Office of Internal Control were too few to be more than a token sampling. The Court's failure to purge its ranks of the corrupt, like the failure of individual judges to convict the "obviously guilty" or make other decisions more in line with popular perceptions of justice, had legitimate as well as suspect explanations—a respect for due process, the inadequacy of evidence, and the constraints imposed by the law itself.[48] This is often forgotten by the public and by members of other branches of government in their outrage over the outcome of specific cases. Still, the judiciary has been its own worst advocate in responding to these reactions, when it has even bothered to do so.[49] Their apparent belief that no explanation was needed was one more indication of the gap between their perception of their role and that held by the public.

If the level of corruption was less than total, it was still more than the Court was willing to acknowledge. At least until Fujimori's purge of their ranks, comments from individual judges and from members of the public based on their own direct experience provided ample if unsystematic evidence of a widespread and probably growing problem.[50] Although the widely cited low conviction rate (less than ten percent of detentions for terrorist cases)[51] might have been more indicative of police incompetence than of legitimate or illegitimate judicial error, a number of highly publicized criminal cases reinforced popular opinion. Among them were the Supreme Court's decision to dismiss the case brought against ex-President García for illicit enrichment,[52] several trials of alleged major drug traffickers and terrorists,[53] and, just prior to the *autogolpe*, the Supreme Court's finding of not guilty in the in absentia trial of Sendero leader Abimael Guzmán.[54] To these should be added the February, 1992, disclosure that, over the prior four years, up to 200 suspected and convicted terrorists had been released annually from a maximum security prison near Lima, most under fairly suspicious circumstances.[55] The releases attracting most public outrage, those of a minority of convicted Sendero leaders, had apparently been in conformity with a little known early release law. However, almost all releases had been authorized by a single *juez de ejecución*, who had not officially notified the prison authorities or the respective trial courts. Both omissions indicated that the process was at least highly irregular. Public reaction can be summed up in the newspaper headlines, "Whose Side are the Judges on?"[56] Judicial corruption was certainly not new or unique to Peru, but it had assumed truly disturbing proportions over the past decade, as, it should be noted, had corruption in all aspects of public life.

To the extent the judiciary can be separated from this broader phenomenon, a part of the blame lies with the political purges and interventions of the military and following civilian governments. The García administration was especially noteworthy in this regard, not only for its effort to stack the Court with party loyalists, but for its attempts to use public officials, including the judiciary, to promote decisions and actions favorable to its friends. The collapsing economy and the increased incidence of terrorism and drug trafficking also contributed their part. All three phenomena substantially expanded the demands on the sector's institutions by multiplying the incidence of crime and civil disorder. Economic decline and the galloping inflation undercut the value of the public budget, reducing already inadequate salaries to ridiculously low levels and virtually eliminating even the most basic supplies. This diminished the ability of the organizations to operate effectively, further undermined morale, and increased vulnerability to corruption.

The growth in terrorism and drug trafficking[57] also had a variety of direct and indirect impacts. These were further complicated by the often controversial measures taken to combat them. Such measures placed additional burdens on the judges and *fiscales*, posed threats to their personal security and, because of their frequently questionable constitutionality, may have further heightened cynicism and disillusionment.[58] Both terrorists and drug traffickers made judges and other sector officials targets of bribery and of violent attacks; if too honest to succumb to the former, the judiciary may have found the latter sufficiently intimidating to influence their actions and decisions. However, the most serious damage to internal morale and to its external image, may well have been the system's demonstrated inability to deal effectively with these new threats to public order. Mismanaged police investigations, ineffectual prosecutorial action, and judges whose decisions seemed to dwell on irrelevant formalities and so miss the point of the case created an overall impression of ineptitude even when they tried to work to the letter of the law. Added to this was a leadership, especially that of the court system, that appeared to ignore both the external problem and the difficulties faced by their institutions' members. In short, corruption, rather than the root of the problem, was an effect and symptom, albeit so severe as to merit special attention and solutions.

Reform Revisited: New Prospects for Change

As grim as the situation appeared, the possibility of reform had not been discarded. By the early 1990s there were some interesting new developments and programs, if no noticeable improvements. Most of these efforts were temporarily paralyzed by the *autogolpe* and, even by 1996, had not recovered momentum. Still, the programs merit examination both for what they attempted and for their influence on subsequent events.

From the mid-1980s onward reform efforts had been notable on two levels. The first aimed at improving institutional, if not always sectoral, performance; the second was more concerned with transforming the sector as a whole, although often with less concern for intra-institutional change. The emphasis in both was functional, not political. No one was talking about changing the sector's political role or powers, but only about making it do better what everyone agreed it was intended to do. Ideally, the institutional and sectoral programs would complement each other. Their different origins and response to different pressures were not obviously producing that effect. Events of the late 1980s and early 1990s made it evident, for example, that the situation of the police, perhaps the most thoroughly discredited of the key institutions, would no longer be tolerated by the wider public, and that something would have to be done.[59] Nevertheless, the complaints and, thus, the focus of change addressed the criminal activities of police officers, common but increasingly violent crime, and corruption. They seemed less likely to emphasize ways of enhancing the police's role in the overall administration of justice. The same type of pressures and, especially, the campaigns of national and international human rights groups had already produced a visible effort by the military to curtail the more excessive human rights abuses of their members. Once again, this was a partial reform. While it reduced specific kinds of abuse, it did not involve a more global view of justice sector problems and the military's role in them. Thus, the military established its own registry of suspected terrorist detainees to counter complaints about its production of *desaparecidos*. It showed marked reluctance to share this information with other sectoral institutions.[60] Human rights groups were also active in criticizing the conditions in the country's prisons, if with little noticeable effect. Here, even more than in the case of the security forces, it was obvious that effective reform would require a systemic approach. This would work first at keeping people out of prison, by reducing recourse to pretrial detention and encouraging alternative sentencing, and thereby reduce the purely institutional problem to more manageable dimensions.

In contrast, the Public Ministry's efforts to improve its own performance did begin with a broader vision of change. It promoted an accusatory system, with a more aggressive role for the ministry, but also with implications for the roles of at least the courts and the police. Although subject to the same severe budgetary limitations as the other institutions, the ministry found ways to improve training and material support for its employees. This allowed them to implement the new role and to introduce procedures to coordinate their activities with the police investigations. Two factors undoubtedly aided the ministry in these efforts. The first was its recent creation. This left the organization relatively resource poor, but it also provided a chance to start afresh in shaping values and behavior. The other was the ministry's hierarchical chain of command and its small and relatively permanent leadership body, the four Fiscales Supremos. The latter, once appointed, held office until retirement, rotating the position of Fiscal de la Nación among themselves. These two factors were in marked contrast to the situation of the Court with its long entrenched practices, diffuse power structure, and more rapidly changing and far larger group of leaders. Although traditionally seen as the key institution in the sector, the Court was far less active in promoting its own internal changes. There were members of the judiciary who showed concern for the courts' poor performance and image, but they tended to be at the middle levels of the hierarchy. The uppermost leadership, the Supreme Court, usually down-played the extent of the problem, or, some would charge, were very much a part of it.

These efforts at institutional reform received impetus from international critics and were frequently supported by international assistance programs. If still on a small scale compared to the dimensions of the problem, these programs provided two key elements, the absence of which had hindered purely national efforts. The first and most obvious were financial resources. Resources alone are not the solution, but it is difficult to envision any remedy that does not involve a substantial increase in funding. Donors could not compensate for inadequate operating budgets. They could fund such exceptional expenses as training, technical assistance, and one-time equipment purchases. The second and often overlooked element, was the introduction of new ideas and approaches. Although often not well received and, occasionally, as misguided as the traditional solutions, these attempts at innovation broadened the spectrum of reform possibilities beyond the traditional repertoire.[61]

Among early examples was the program in the 1980s to train lay justices of the peace, funded by the German Naumann Foundation. As mentioned, this external support undoubtedly saved the program from the Court's opposition to its objectives. Prior to this, in the late 1960s and early 1970s, the Ford Foundation financed efforts to improve legal education in selected universities.[62] This was part of the so-called "Law and Development" movement,[63] which had U.S. government support in other countries. While often dismissed as a failure, the movement produced a group of reform-minded lawyers in Peru, many of whom have reemerged periodically to support change programs. The lower salaries and stifling atmosphere in the public sector kept most of them in private practice. However, to this day members of this group are among the country's most prominent reformers.

Beginning in 1986, the U.S. Agency for International Development (USAID) worked with the Court, the Public Ministry and the Ministry of Justice in developing a series of activities to strengthen these institutions.[64] The vehicle was a two million dollar, grant funded, Administration of Justice Project. Most of these activities were on a fairly small scale and have been justifiably criticized for having little immediate and still less long-term impact. They ranged from support for the Ministry of Justice's legal clinics to development of a training program for the Public Ministry and the purchase of small amounts of equipment for all three institutions. The project also financed a series of studies, including one intended as the basis for an improved court administration program, and made an undoubtedly ill-advised effort to create a computer data base of all existing legislation. Had the latter continued it would easily have absorbed the entire grant. The project had its greatest impact in giving reform-minded members of the institutions an opportunity to experiment with new ideas and approaches. Of the three institutions, only the Public Ministry took full advantage of the support. In the Court and the Ministry of Justice, constant changes of leadership and a frequent suspicion that the assistance hid some other agenda proved major obstacles to closer cooperation. The situation was further complicated by the constant threat that the project, and other U.S. assistance, would be terminated owing to Peru's nonpayment of arrearages on earlier loans. However, like the Law and Development program, the USAID project expanded the interest in and perspectives on reform. Many of the ideas it introduced and the individuals with whom it worked have most recently reemerged in the Fujimori administration's post-1994 reform.

Other governments, notably the Italian and the Spanish, as well as the United Nations, were also exploring the possibility of assistance to the judiciary. The United States was also active in supplying technical and financial assistance in counternarcotics activities, especially to the police and military.[65] These latter efforts have been criticized for the lack of coordination among the various U.S. government agencies involved. Another obstacle was the continuing Peruvian insistence that terrorism, not drug trafficking, be the priority area for assistance. Until just before the Fujimori coup, the United States appeared reluctant to entertain this argument, in part because of its own priorities and in part because of the political risks of involvement in Peru's civil war.

One major obstacle confronting all of these assistance efforts was the inability of sector institutions, and most notably the Court, to develop programs suitable for external financing, or to use funds once they were provided.[66] Administrative weaknesses were partly to blame. The phenomenon was also indicative of leadership's failure to grasp the dimensions of the situation or to expend much effort in considering how it might be resolved. Lack of coordination among actual and potential donors, and even among agencies of the same government, also impeded progress, further aggravating the sector's inability to develop its own coherent program.[67] While external assistance programs produced no dramatic successes, interest remained high. It is possible that the deepening crisis itself, combined with lessons learned even from unsuccessful experiences would have inspired a second more fruitful round of assistance. The April 1992 coup put all such assistance on hold while external donors and the Peruvian government decided whether they could work together and on what terms.[68]

These efforts at reforming specific aspects of institutional performance were accompanied by another, more broadly focused attempt to effect systemwide change through the introduction of new procedural and substantive codes. The first of these was the new Civil Code, promulgated in 1984, although immediately the subject of criticism. The second were the two new criminal codes (procedural and substantive) and the new Organic Law for the Judiciary, all approved in 1991 and scheduled for staggered implementation. Discussions of the need for a modification of the Civil Code were accompanied by efforts to rewrite the Civil Procedures Code. This undertaking was supported or allowed to continue by the post-coup administration so that a completed code went into effect in late 1993. Its impact was reported as minimal several years later, a consequence of the lack of resources for implementation and a general ignorance of its very existence.[69] The production of new legislation often drew on foreign examples and experts, but it was not a focus of external assistance. Prior to and after the coup, donors were showing interest in assisting in programs for its implementation.

Peru, like the rest of Latin America, has placed excessive faith in the effectiveness of purely legal reform. However, the new criminal codes in particular could be a useful base for more fundamental change. (Observers are more skeptical about the Civil Procedures Code, which seems to have been elaborated in undue haste and without any thought to its implementation.) The major role assigned to the Public Ministry in the Criminal Procedures Code is a case in point to the extent it strengthens the hand of the sector institution with the broadest perspective on the problem. A stronger Public Ministry with a more clearly defined role may be able to redirect the investigatory functions of the police, while also taking a stronger stand against human rights abuses. By reducing the responsibilities of the judiciary, the code eliminates a number of bottlenecks and may allow judges to focus their efforts more effectively on a more limited range of activities.

The two criminal codes also introduce innovations aimed at eliminating other problems. Most notable are the restrictions on the use of preventive detention and the increased emphasis on alternative sentencing. Both measures should substantially reduce the prison population, as well as the additional abuses associated with the almost automatic utilization of pretrial detention. The new procedural code arguably errs in the direction of excessive and perhaps unimplementable detail. This and the retention of some seemingly unnecessary procedural steps are the lingering effects of the formalistic, inquisitorial mind set.[70] On the positive side, the code includes numerous measures designed to protect suspects from abusive interrogation practices, to guarantee them an adequate and timely defense, and to otherwise safeguard their human and legal rights.

Both the procedural and substantive criminal codes were intended to correct the injustices of the existing system as they affect the rights of accused. They show far less interest in or attention to two other major targets of criticism—the inefficient and archaic operations and the alleged inability of the system to bring the guilty to justice. In this they follow regional trends, but are less attuned to concerns voiced by the Peruvian public and elites. It has been argued that the transition to a more purely accusatory system will automatically increase efficiency and effectiveness by simplifying and streamlining the investigative stage. However, it is also conceivable that the codes' overall effect in these areas will be negative because of the difficulties of documenting or even complying with their detailed provisions on human and legal rights protection.[71] The consequent opportunity for the dismissal of cases on what the public, the prosecutors, and the police perceive as pure technicalities could produce its own reaction, eventually undermining the attainment of the human rights goals. Such considerations have already surfaced in other countries and have been blamed for the delayed passage of El Salvador's new criminal codes.

The codes also give only the most formalistic attention to the issue of corruption. In fairness, this is more appropriately addressed by the third element of the package, the new Organic Law for the Judiciary. Predictably, the law's treatment of the theme is equally elusive. On reading it, one would never guess that corruption is as widespread a problem as commonly held. The law is equally disappointing in its treatment of the Court's administrative functions, although it at least recognizes the complex set of administrative offices created over the last three decades[72] and charges them with the further modernization of administrative processes. However, the new Judicial Council of Government, originally introduced to take on the full Court's oversight of administration, was reduced to an advisory role, suggesting a continuing reluctance to delegate administrative decisions even within the Court. Whatever the merits of the proposed changes on the judicial side, they will not be adequately implemented without a substantial strengthening of the basic administrative processes. Aside from the delegation of responsibilities, this means a willingness to invest scarce resources in these areas, a theme conspicuous by its absence in the law as well as in the Court's other actions. As discussed in the following chapter, the post-1994 reform, whatever its other shortcomings, has for once adequately treated this issue.

The new organic law experienced an interesting evolution which provides additional insight into the obstacles confronting would-be reformers. Almost from the passage of the prior law, in 1963, discussions of the need for its modification and eventual replacement had begun. These became more critical with the passage of the 1979 Constitution, the new role accorded to the Public Ministry, and revisions of the basic legal codes. The Court itself was extremely interested in developing a new law, if only as a means of regaining the privileges and prestige it saw itself losing. Finally, if only incompletely absorbing the concept, the judiciary was increasingly aware of the need for modernizing the court system, to bring it into line with changes in other public and private sector institutions.

Work on the organic law began in early 1985 and was carried out by a commission composed of judges, practicing lawyers, and law professors. The text accompanying the initial (1986) version offers an excellent analysis of the fundamental failings of judicial performance, their causes, and the provisions included to address them. Even this version was already two projects. One established a framework of organizational principles, procedures and structures that, if implemented gradually (as the project seemed to dictate), might have produced real improvement in the judiciary's performance. The other comprised a welter of details, some apparently addressing oversights in the procedural codes, and others relating to the rights and privileges of the judiciary.[73]

The revisions made in the following five years further weakened the reformist thrust. The final version softened or removed the most radical innovations and those with the greatest potential for redirecting the institution. Among these reversals were the elimination of the election of lay justices of the peace (reinstated, however, in the 1993 Constitution); the substitution of an advisory role for what was first the delegation of the full Court's policy and administrative decision-making authority to a Council of Government; the reduction of the Court president's term from three to two years; and the removal of a policy facilitating the transfer of judges from less desirable to more sought-after locations.[74] In their initial form, these four provisions alone would have created more dynamic leadership within the Court, while also effecting significant changes in the situation, orientations, and expectations of lower level lay and professional judiciary.

Meanwhile, the revisions complicated the already ambitious and costly restructuring[75] outlined in the first versions. This is especially obvious in the establishment of specialized chambers, tribunals and courts at all instances; the addition of seven more justices to make a total of thirty in the Supreme Court (reduced to eighteen following the *autogolpe*); and the provisions for the creation of additional judgeships. While the resulting structure has a certain elegant logic, the financial and human resources it would require are incalculable, or simply uncalculated. The wealth of extraneous details, either further defining tasks and responsibilities or protecting the traditions, rights and privileges of the judiciary, also proliferated. Despite the section on the right to defense, the guarantees of due process, free justice and equal treatment, the various deadlines imposed to assure the forward movement of cases, and the admonitions to modernize, the final document no longer seems driven by these concerns. Although the basic elements of a true reform remained buried within the law, the scope of the changes it mandates is so far beyond what is possible, as to require a very selective implementation. The weakened leadership structure and the general evolution of the law's content suggest that, left to the judiciary, the final selection would be more motivated by special interests and such lowest common denominator issues as judicial salaries than by any overarching vision of a new, radically different role for the institution as a whole.

Viewing the three pieces of legislation together, it is evident that, even had they gone into effect as written, their implementation would have been fraught with problems, both for the difficulty of what they proposed to do and for the factors they completely overlooked. While at the time representing Peru's most ambitious effort to restructure its justice system, the legislation suffered from a familiar set of weaknesses. First, even under the best of circumstances, which were hardly those prevailing in Peru, the proposed changes and the implied results were far more than could be achieved over the short or medium run. Aside from the complexity of the immediate changes, there were the additional problems of cementing the new pattern of relationships among the various sector institutions and the considerable quantity of human, financial and material resources that would be required. A series of interviews[76] conducted in mid-1991 revealed concern among judges and *fiscales* as to their own ability to implement the basic procedural changes under current conditions. The judges also expressed particular doubts about the willingness of their counterpart institutions, especially the police and Public Ministry, to play the new roles indicated for them.

Second, none of the proposed reforms included a hint of a transition plan, prioritizing changes and setting guidelines for the host of specific decisions that would have to be made at all levels. It was apparent that even the most accelerated implementation schedule would require several years and that some provisions would be needed for treatment of cases already begun under the old system;[77] no such scheme had been elaborated. The restructuring of the court system, especially as it relates to decisions most appropriately made within the judicial districts, would also require general guidelines to avoid twenty different, potentially incompatible variations. Here again, it was not obvious who would make the decisions, let alone what criteria they would apply. In this, the Peruvian proposal resembled others in the region in far more than ideological content. Improvisation has long been a vice of Latin American reform planners, and not just those in the justice sector. However, the latters' tendency to ignore the whole question of implementation, or to trust that things would simply work out takes this characteristic to an entirely different plane. It suggests that their interest begins and ends with the plan or law and with the moral or symbolic victory its approval represents.[78]

Third, in addition to the virtual absence of financial, institutional, and related analyses to test feasibility and identify possible implementation bottlenecks, the laws were conspicuously weak in their treatment of complementary actions essential to effective implementation. They are virtually silent on critical elements like training, technical assistance, and supervision and control systems. Given the extent of the changes proposed in organization and procedures and in the substance and ideological thrust of the law, the absence of any provisions for the orientation and reorientation of all personnel was at the least, disturbing. The same set of mid-1991 interviews indicated that a large portion of judges had not yet seen the new procedural code or organic law, and that many were completely uninformed as to their content.

Fourth, the inattention to administrative systems, either in the organic law or complementary legislation, suggested that administrative weaknesses would continue to obstruct change. A judiciary, with a planning office that did not plan and a budget office that could not draw up its 1992 annual budget, seemed uniquely unprepared to undertake any of the proposed reorganizations.

Fifth, related to the fourth issue, but deserving special mention was the laws' limited attention to administrative and support staff *within the courts.* They do get more attention then those in the systemwide administration, but this is the traditional description of job qualifications and responsibilities. The description is sufficiently close to what already existed to indicate minimal thought to the laws' own implications that their jobs would henceforth be radically different. It also ignores the frequent contention that their lack of training, inefficient use and performance, and outright corruption were major sources of problems.

Sixth, although representing improvements over past legislation in this respect, all three documents still demonstrated a centralized, inwardly focused, occasionally elitist perspective. As such, they appeared insufficiently sensitive to the situation either of lower level officials, especially those in the provinces, or of the urban and rural poor. This characterization is in line with all prior attempts to modernize or reform Peru's justice system. It is particularly inconvenient in an effort that emphasizes bringing justice closer to the people and to the lower level courts. The legislation, especially the procedural and substantive codes, did acknowledge the special needs of marginalized populations. Examples include the requirements for interpreters and public defenders, and a special section reducing or eliminating sentences for individuals whose culture or customs prevented recognition of the criminal nature of an activity (*error de comprensión culturalmente condicionada*, Art. 20). However, Peru's own experience with agrarian courts and that in other countries[79] suggest that this did not go far enough in recognizing the inability of such culturally marginalized groups to deal with the formal system without special help. Furthermore, there was the problem of the extent to which officials throughout the sector would internalize and, thus, act on the philosophical and ideological bases for the new provisions. The various other changes in the substantive code, including those in the nature and presumed purpose of sentencing and in the definitions of various types of criminal activities, posed similar difficulties. Some of them imply a fairly sophisticated understanding of economic, financial, and environmental issues. It is worth stressing that the point here is not that Peru's judiciary should become political or social activists or revolutionaries (which certainly is not the goal of any of the regional reforms), but rather that in a society like Peru, if justice is to be a truly *public* service, then more effort must go into getting it to the public and the public to it.

Finally, and perhaps most critical in the existing political circumstances, the legislation gave little if any attention to the issues apparently of most public concern—the increasing incidence of crime and especially terrorism, the belief that criminals, even if apprehended frequently went unpunished, and the perceptions of widespread corruption within sector institutions. The immediate problem was more one of packaging than content. It may have been less necessary to introduce specific measures to address these issues than to acknowledge their existence and link proposed reforms to their resolution. By virtually ignoring them, the laws' authors opened the way for others to introduce more direct measures that, at the very least, were likely to undercut their fundamental objectives. Those others were not slow in accepting the invitation.

Conclusions

Although the pre-1992 legal reform-package remains on the books, the *autogolpe* and subsequent events have made it largely irrelevant. The Criminal Code and the organic law have been selectively implemented and substantially modified in line with political priorities having little to do with their original intent. Neither the 1991 Criminal Procedures Code nor the 1994 revised version has ever gone into effect. What finally occurred was almost a mirror image of the proposed reform, filling in the areas it ignored, and ignoring much of what it proposed to change. However, both before and after the coup, there was a brief opportunity to move the reforms ahead. As a prelude to the next chapter, it is worth exploring why nothing more happened.

Most obviously, this was the least propitious moment for the type of reform proposed. In light of Peru's prospects in the early 1990s, efforts to modernize and humanize its justice system seemed of secondary importance, if not entirely quixotic. While the justice sector's problems were tightly linked to the larger crisis, both as a consequence and contributing factor, it was hard to envision much success in their resolution until economic conditions improved, terrorism was brought under control, and the wider crisis of political and social disintegration was halted if not reversed. The immediate efforts to resolve these larger problems involved the justice sector, but the direct effect was limited to institutions like the military and the police for reasons having to do with their overall efficacy and not as part of a concern for their role in administering justice.

However, aside from the higher priority accorded these other issues, several additional factors stood in the way of the initial reform proposal. One was the government and the general public's loss of faith in the sector's ability to reform itself. Whether because of presumed incompetence, irrelevance, or their vested interest in leaving things as they were, the leaders of the various institutions and, especially, those of the Court were decreasingly seen as having sufficient political will or vision to take the institutions in new directions. If President Fujimori's actions before and immediately after April 5 were the strongest indication of this loss of confidence, the trend was already evident in the words and actions of previous administrations. Thus, while Fujimori's temporary inattention to most of the sector and a number of constitutional provisions appeared to give the judiciary the lead in remaking itself, there was no indication of broader support for any decisions they might take.

Another related obstacle was the long-standing inability of the sector's core institutions to come up with much in the way of reform aside from the old standards: new codes, higher salaries, a bigger share of the budget, and control of their own appointment and selection system. Most of these are necessary accompaniments to any large-scale reform. None of them addressed the series of more fundamental problems increasingly attributed to the sector. Given the government's preference for compliant judges and *fiscales*, those who make no problems, the post-1992 leadership was still less likely to develop innovative programs.

Finally, behind both of these complaints was the failure of these same institutional leaders to demonstrate an understanding or even a recognition of these problems. This is not a new criticism. Both New Law researchers and the conservative Lima Bar Association had commented on the leadership's apparent inability to understand either the complaints directed against them or the public expectations giving rise to these criticisms. The two groups characterized these expectations quite differently. However, underlying their comments was the common notion that the institutions would be evaluated by the products and services they delivered. This, unfortunately, has not been where the sector's own reform efforts have focused. Instead, a near obsession with regaining lost respect produced reform proposals where prestige, rather than performance, appeared as the primary goal. This reverses the normal sequence where prestige is a result of performance. It also vastly underestimates the level of popular discontent with sector performance, the sense that the entire system does not work.

Speaking as individuals, in their frankest moments, many judges, *fiscales*, lawyers, and other sector professionals seemed quite aware of the public disenchantment with the justice system and with the reasons behind it. Their inability to convert this awareness into a collective, credible program of action was equally a product of intra and interinstitutional politics, the lack of support from political elites within and outside the sector, and an institutional and professional culture that deemphasized, when it did not ignore, a service provision and problem solving orientation. A change in any one of these areas might have been sufficient to break the impasse and start the sector in the direction of more fundamental changes. However, the Court and the rest of the judiciary, as the center of both the political and sociocultural obstacles, continued as followers rather than leaders in the change that eventually occurred. Thus, the apparent decision to leave things in their hands was tantamount to an agreement to live a little longer with the status quo.

Notes

1. Prior to this period, while Peru was still consolidating its political structure, the judiciary had a more independent role and was an active, if not very powerful player in the various interinstitutional conflicts. The Supreme Court was established in 1823, following the conversion of the *Alta Cámera de Justicia* (High Court of Justice), successor of the *Real Audiencia*, into the Superior Court of Lima. There followed the creation of a series of departmental superior courts and provincial judgeships. The method for naming Supreme Court justices varied. The 1828 decentralist constitution provided for the appointment of one for each major department. Although in 1855 justices were first given permanent tenure, the various military *caudillos* often insisted that seated and new justices declare their loyalty to the executive, and the 1867 dictatorship removed several justices who refused to do so.

Months later Congress reinstated them. It was not until 1860 that a system of appointments, similar to that exercised until 1969, was constitutionally established. Although the political battle took its most dramatic form in the issue of appointments, the judiciary exercised its independence in two other areas: first, in its active and passive resistance to executive pressures on its decisions, and second, in a much more active role in drafting major legislation shaping its own powers, organization, and functions. In three periods, 1904, 1922, and 1940, when such major legislation was drafted, members of the Court were prominent on the commissions charged with the task. The Mining Code of 1900 was the product of two magistrates, and the 1940 Criminal Procedures Code is attributed largely to one justice, Carlos Zavala Loayza. This contrasts with the more recent situation where the major intellectual powers behind the new codes are either ex-justices, or still more frequently, prominent jurists who have never served on the Court. See Valdivia Pezo, 1986, pp. 231-234.

2. Fruhling, 1993, discusses this as "internal autonomy," arguing that a perpetuation of this tacit agreement protected the institution, but reenforced its conservative outlook during the Pinochet government.

3. See, for example, Rubio and Bernales, 1988, pp. 425-429; Pásara, 1982, pp. 103-117.

4. The earlier selection system was more varied as might be expected given the unstable political conditions. Military and civilian dictators often attempted to appoint their own Courts, regardless of constitutional provisions, but at least in theory, appointments were permanent until retirement.

5. García Rada, 1978, pp. 205-206, speaks of candidates to the Supreme Court standing outside the Congress with ballots with their names on them to be passed out to the members. Since each vacancy had a separate list of candidates, the list on which one appeared was, and continues to be important. Assuming multiple vacancies, it thus paid off to be on the list with the weakest candidates. Consequently, it was necessary to campaign with the judges or court responsible for making up the list.

6. These most frequently dealt with the detention of political enemies of the government in power.

7. Pásara, 1982, p. 156.

8. Pásara in de Belaúnde López de Romaña, 1984, p. 206.

9. For a systematic study of the differential treatment of political and nonpolitical habeas corpus, see García Belaúnde, 1979, and Rubio and Bernales, 1988, pp. 209-223. One of the more notorious cases was a refusal to grant a hearing because the wife of the detainee had not submitted "adequate" documentation to prove her relationship. Constable and Valenzuela, 1991, describe similar incidents from the Pinochet period in Chile.

10. García Rada, 1978, pp. 171-191.

11. See Pásara's essay "La ideología de un juez," in Pásara, 1988, pp. 169-184, for an analysis and examples.

12. The first quotation is from Manuel Scorza, *Historia de Garabobo, el invisible*, and the second is from Ciro Alegría, *El mundo es ancho y ajeno*, as cited in Pásara, 1988, pp. 24, 27. Translations are mine.

13. For an elaboration of these points, see McClintock, 1981, especially pp. 64-83.

14. Figures from McClintock, 1981, pp. 64-68.

15. Given their conclusion that peasants do not expect to be treated well by the courts, authors who have studied this issue have developed some interesting hypotheses as to why they would voluntarily access the formal system. See for example Pásara, 1982, pp. 26-37; Pásara, 1988, pp. 73-112; Brandt, 1990, pp. 126-130. The explanations range from an inability to resolve problems within their own communities to a growing sense of their own competence. For a discussion based on existing literature, see Drzewieniecki, 1995.

16. Guillermo Figallo, as quoted in Cleaves and Scurrah, 1980, p. 156. Revilla and Price 1991, p. 63, attribute a similar comment to Roberto Garmendía, chief justice in 1963.

17. Carlos Contreras, "Conflictos intercomunales en la Sierra Central en los siglos XIX y XX," in Bonilla, 1991, p. 203.

18. See Brandt, 1990, pp. 153-163; Pásara, 1988, pp. 73-112.

19. Brandt, 1990, pp. 124-126.

20. The military's hand was strengthened by two scandals involving the judiciary: a case brought against a former administrative director for misuse of funds and the arrest in New York of a former justice, traveling on a diplomatic passport with $75,000 worth of contraband in his luggage. It is doubtful that these incidents played a major role in defining the military's position, but they probably firmed their resolve (see Ramírez, 1985, p. iv).

21. Pásara, 1982, p. 148, indicates that the percentage went from 0.39 in 1975 to 0.21 in 1979, and only rose to 0.45 in 1981, the first budget completely prepared under a civilian government. Figures from Universidad Católica, 1991, p. 101, coincide although indicating that from 1970-1974, the military gave a slightly higher 0.59 percent to the judiciary, over the 0.52 average for the five previous years.

22. These complementary actions were never mentioned in any of the military's explanations of its plan for the sector. They most probably responded to considerations having little to do with sector performance. For example, it is believed that the Ministry of Justice was eliminated to even out the division of portfolios among the branches of the armed forces. Since the Public Ministry had only minor and largely formal responsibilities, it was probably seen as superfluous.

23. For a detailed discussion of these changes, see Ramírez, 1985, pp. 3-10, 31-34; Pásara in de Belaúnde López de Romaña, 1984, pp. 249-268.

24. While the New Law group worked with the military, it should be clarified that they did not draw their views from the latter. Rather, they represented long time (if formerly more silent) critics of the traditional system, who saw this as an opportunity to implement their views. They added substance and concrete direction to what had first been the government's unguided criticisms of a set of institutions they did not understand, but knew they did not like. The New Law movement was also fed by Law and Development programs simultaneously implemented in Peru, for the most part by the Ford Foundation. See Gardner, 1980, for a discussion of Law and Development's history in Peru and elsewhere.

25. Cleaves and Scurrah, 1980, p. 158. Pásara, 1978, p. 59, estimates the backlog in the thousands only.

26. The Concejo retained responsibility for ratifications, and the courts for the periodic evaluations of lower instance judges under their jurisdiction. The OCIPJ was responsible for responding to complaints from the broader public, and for undertaking investigations and disciplinary action at the request of the Concejo and courts as well as on its own initiative.

27. The works published by DESCO and CEDYS are most important. See all sources by Pásara (the most prolific and arguably the most insightful of the authors), which also include a more complete bibliography.

28. As reported by Ciudad and Zarzar in de Belaúnde López de Romaña, 1984, pp. 294-409. A further finding, which can only have alienated the judicial readers, was that the eighty-one judges and *fiscales* did relatively poorly on tests of their legal knowledge and analytic skills, scoring lower than students at any one of the better private universities.

29. Pásara, 1982, p. 191. Translation mine.

30. José A. Encinas, 1920, as cited in Pásara, 1982, p. 138. My translation.

31. Ramírez, 1985, pp. 36-37.

32. Ramírez, 1985, p. 37.

33. *Acción popular* relates to the constitutionality of decrees, resolutions, municipal ordinances, etc. (everything below the level of a law promulgated by the Congress). It has been infrequently used and, consequently, remains controversial. Some argue that it must only be associated with a pending case, while others believe it can be applied abstractly. *Acción popular* is different from *amparo* in that it challenges the legislation itself, and not its specific application. See Rubio and Bernales, 1988, pp. 223-225, and Sousa Calle and Daños Ordoñez in Eguiguren, 1987, pp. 322-330.

34. Ramírez, 1985, p. 46.

35. Ramírez, 1985, pp. 58-64.

36. Peru is hardly the worst case scenario. In Honduras, under the Callejas administration, a national presidential hopeful was made president of the Court so that he could sit out his wait in an advantageous position. He was later dismissed when found to be using Court funds for his presidential campaign. In the mid-1980s, partisan fighting found two Honduran Supreme Courts seated simultaneously, one backed by the executive, the other by the opposition dominated Congress. In Ecuador between 1984 and 1990, interparty strife twice led to the naming of three separate Courts within less than three years. In 1994, El Salvador remained without a Court for one month while members of the newly elected Assembly battled over control of the Court presidency. Ironically, in this last case, the country was initiating a system to depoliticize appointments. Partisan and ideological considerations affect all appointment systems. The problem in countries that have emerged suddenly and explosively into mass-based electoral competition is the tendency for the Court to become wholly and without exception a tool of the party factions. In such circumstances it is difficult for the institution or its members to retain any sort of integrity.

37. For a list and brief treatment of this legislation, and a comparative listing of that from the military period, see Prado, 1990.

38. Prado, 1990, pp. 79-81.

39. The attempt to write legislation "typifying" (describing) acts of terrorism is a prominent example. Especially during the García period a heated debate was waged as to whether such crimes were covered by the existing Criminal Code and, if not, how they ought to be described. See Ambos, 1989, pp. 60-69, for a brief discussion. Much of the debate is summarized in Ames et al., 1988. Peru, Senate, Comisión Especial, 1989, pp. 309-329, is also relevant.

40. Analysis from Prado, 1990, pp. 92-93.

41. Increasing access to the justice system was not a prominent goal of the military, except as regards the agrarian and labor courts, but their efforts at politicizing the masses increased awareness of and demands on sector institutions. Other developments of this and later periods, especially the increased rural to urban migrations and the enlargement and bureaucratization of the state, also expanded contacts and demand.

42. These groups, and the masses as well, were also affected by the increased incidence of crime and the visible inability of the sector institutions to deal with it.

43. Figures on the backlog vary and are not available in any meaningful form. A survey of judges as to the number of cases they were processing indicated a range between 100 and 2,000, with an average of 500. The judges tended to agree that 250 was a more manageable number (Universidad Católica, 1991, pp. 83). It has been argued by observers, in Peru and elsewhere, that the real problem is not the quantity of cases, but rather overly complicated procedures and inefficient handling and organization. Much of the backlog consists of cases that have not moved for years.

44. For a discussion and some illustrative statistics, see Universidad Católica, 1991, pp. 30-36.

45. For a series of essays dealing with these trends, see Pásara, 1988. Complaints about police and judicial corruption and their inability to deal with increased levels of conventional crime are evident as early as the 1960s.

46. Aside from corruption, the sector institutions have long been characterized by their own informal system of behavior, much of it introduced as short cuts, to deal with excessive workloads, or to find a way around legislation impossible to implement. Examples include the use of support staff to carry out tasks for which a judge or *fiscal* is legally required, the charging of illegal fees to cover costs for which no budget resources have been allocated, or certain biases in judicial decisions, when a law is perceived as too harsh. It has been claimed that judges attempted to avoid applying the death penalty (when in force), even if this involved some questionable interpretations of laws, most often as regards the crime committed. Excessive formalism, often interpreted as a means of distorting decisions, is sometimes just a way of reducing workload. A Costa Rican judge reported that one colleague routinely read *expedientes* to find technical reasons for returning them, thus keeping his own desk clean.

47. Figures are often cited with amazing detail. In addition to Fujimori's accusations in his April 5 speech (see Chapter 1, note 1), there are such examples as a Fiscal Superior who cited a figure of $6,000 to $7,000 as the additional monthly take-home pay for civil judges. He claimed that a criminal judge could make much more. Furthermore, people in the know claimed to be able to identify the corrupt judges,

fiscales, and lawyers. This last point is important as to the extent corruption exists, private lawyers are an important contributing factor. They know whom to bribe and what is the going rate. Interviews, Lima, 1988.

48. The extent to which bad laws contribute to the problem is debated. So far as judges are willing to defend the decisions of their peers, they note that substantive law and, especially, that on evidence and decisional criteria often ties their hands. Another argument blames judicial inability to interpret the law adequately, for example, an unwillingness to use indirect or circumstantial evidence in their decisions. Interviews, Lima, 1988-1989.

49. Two factors contribute, the judiciary's sense of its own special expertise and the theme of judicial independence. In regard to the latter, because both the judiciary as a whole and individual judges are accorded independence in their decisions, there is a reluctance for the others to comment, seeing this as a violation of their independent sphere of action.

50. Interviews, Lima, 1988.

51. Figures for other crimes showed a higher conviction rate, but given the concern with terrorism, the fact that as few as 6.0 percent of the detainees were finally convicted was often used as a sign of judicial incompetence or corruption. See Eguiguren, 1991, p. 152, for figures on terrorism.

52. Just prior to April 5, 1992, the Fujimori government had apparently decided to appeal this ruling, charging that the Supreme Court Criminal Chamber had failed to open an investigation before making its decision. Complaints were also directed at the Fiscal de la Nación, responsible for prosecution, who, it was charged, had done an inadequate job. See *Caretas* (Lima), March 23, 1992, pp 25-26.

53. While most of the criticism has been directed at terrorist trials, the trial of Peru's "godfather," Reynaldo Rodríguez López, in 1987 was also criticized. It was widely rumored that the Supreme Court chamber hearing the appeal had been bought off or threatened into submission. For a discussion of other controversial terrorist cases, see *Caretas* (Lima), March 30, 1992, pp. 34-47.

54. Guzmán was charged with assault, robbery, and threats to public security. The Supreme Court chamber hearing the appeal had the additional options of sending the case back for further investigation or ordering dismissal without prejudice. By upholding the initial acquittal, they guaranteed that Guzmán could never again be tried for the same criminal actions (*Caretas* [Lima], March 23, 1992, p. 22; March 30, 1992, pp. 34-47).

55. *La República* (Lima), February 4, 1992.

56. The headline was from *Expreso* (Lima); cited in an interview.

57. In contrast to much conventional wisdom, the economic decline and terrorist movement may have had a greater impact than drug trafficking, the first because of its effect on working conditions, the second because of the measures taken officially and unofficially to combat it. It was terrorism that placed up to 50 percent of the national territory under military control, invaded the most important population centers, increased the incidence and violence of police and military brutality, placed the civilian population in jeopardy, and occasioned the most controversial laws and practices. It also attracted far more government and popular interest than the drug issue, which continued to be perceived as a secondary problem.

58. The Court commonly provided neither special protection nor even transportation for judges, who if they did not have their own cars, got around in buses or taxis. Only the *juez de turno* (the one on duty to receive complaints filed) had a guard assigned to his or her house. Judges hearing cases had no assigned protection for themselves or their families. Judges have also been critical of the antiterrorist laws they were expected to apply, noting that they violated aspects of due process or other individual rights. Interviews, Lima, 1991.

59. It is worth repeating that the 1989 unification of the three national police forces, which was supposed to solve many problems, made them worse over the short run. One reason was the further complication of the lines of control within the presumably unified bodies.

60. Prior to this, the International Red Cross and the Public Ministry had been granted access to military detention facilities through a decree issued by the executive. The military eventually agreed to share the list when the detainees registry was made a condition for further U.S. military and economic assistance.

61. While much the same might be said of the traditional reliance on "imported law," the difference here is the introduction of reform areas and techniques often overlooked by national reformers. These include attention to purely administrative structures and processes, internal control systems, management information systems, training of judges, *fiscales* and police in investigative techniques, and training in the handling and evaluation of nonconventional evidence.

62. See Pásara, 1988, pp. 215-41, for a discussion of the first years of this program in Lima's prestigious Universidad Católica.

63. One example was Costa Rica. Here, despite positive impacts on the quality of legal education, and the introduction of participatory teaching methods, it ran afoul of university politics and charges of imperialist intervention. As in Peru, its overall dismissal as a failure seems exaggerated and shortsighted. Interviews, Costa Rica, 1991.

64. The first program began in 1986 and officially ended in 1991. For a fairly critical view, see Mudge, 1993. Youngers, 1992, offers a less detailed, but equally critical summary.

65. See J. Smith, 1992, passim.

66. As the country moved into hyperinflation, this failure to spend became particularly critical, as funds once disbursed were converted into local currency and immediately began losing value. It is further indicative of the Court's lack of touch with reality that, on one occasion, the *Vocal* in charge proudly reported that he had not spent a cent of the disbursed monies, but had left them all in the bank!

67. One of the unanticipated obstacles was the total unfamiliarity of most institutional leaders with foreign aid programs. They often could not understand why they were being offered funds and sometimes suspected this was meant to buy them off. Peru's Court, the most difficult institution in this respect, has come around to the extent of recognizing coordination with donors as one of its responsibilities, as stated in the 1991 organic law.

68. As of early 1997, the U.S. government was still considering assistance, but planned to focus on human rights groups and public defense. The World Bank had finally signed a project agreement, under study since 1992. Because the Bank main-

tains that its programs are apolitical, it faced fewer constraints in working with the Peruvian public sector. However, human rights clearly raised concerns, as did doubts about the Fujimori government's own commitment to reform. After a short period of activity, the Bank's project was again halted in mid-1997.

69. The Civil Procedures Code was modeled on the Uruguayan code, adopted in the early 1990s. Uruguay accompanied this event with substantial investments in construction, the hiring of new judges, and training. The code's preparation was also well publicized and supported by private sector groups. It appears that in Peru there was no conscious intent to keep the new code a secret. Instead, it attracted little attention given such simultaneous occurrences as the debate over the new constitution.

70. As discussed elsewhere, one example, common to most "reformed" codes is the retention of the *instructiva* or *indagatoria*, the suspect's formal statement made during the prosecutor's investigation. In Peru this remains as a mandatory step and the procedures for its realization and content are set out in painstaking detail. This made sense under an inquisitory, written system when it was a key piece of evidence; its retention defies the logic of accusatory, oral procedures.

71. The code, for example, supplies a kind of script for initiating the taking of a suspect's statement and specifies such details as the provision of a rest period for an overtired interrogee. While one appreciates the sentiments behind these additions, they also leave considerable leeway for error in not following the instructions to the letter. In countries where such reforms have been adopted, problems, and a backlash, have occurred when judges begin to throw out entire cases because of the violation of one step in the stipulated procedure. For example, the failure to provide a defender "immediately" on the arrest of a subject has been used by Salvadoran judges as a reason for releasing suspects and invalidating all evidence, even that collected at the time of arrest. Critics have gone so far as to suggest that "someone" may be paying off public defenders not to show up. The problem is more likely the result of a very ineffective Public Defense Office. The complicity of some judges cannot be discounted, however. In the most notorious cases, they have allowed the investigation to proceed for some time so as to be able to nullify a good deal more evidence. Interviews, El Salvador, 1994.

72. For a more complete description of what is included, see Universidad Católica, 1991, pp. 86-127. The authors conclude that the missing details on administrative organization might be better left to internal regulations. The same might be said of many details on purely judicial organization and powers that *were* included. The comparison makes it clear that the Court still sees its administrative support structure as a necessary evil, not a vital service.

73. Among these are provisions setting salaries for judges, the establishment of special housing credit plans for the judiciary, guarantees of police protection, reimbursement of medical expenses for judges and their families, and establishment of special prison facilities for judges found guilty of a crime. All but the section on salaries were removed from the final version, but they have been replaced by a series of other rights.

74. This may appear trivial, but it addresses a perennial complaint of provincial judges who often find themselves tenured for life in some backwater. Since upward

mobility is usually contingent on getting the attention of judges in a district capital or Lima, movement to a more visible posting, even at the same level, is critical for career advancement.

75. In one respect, the later version of the law is an improvement since it reduces the number of specialized areas and courts from the initial eight to only five, and makes mixed (general jurisdiction) courts a normal rather than a special case.

76. Universidad Católica, 1991, pp. 16-17.

77. Uruguay introduced its Civil Procedures Code over a three-year period, assigning certain judges to the new system, while keeping others managing the cases introduced under the previous one.

78. I would not want to take this observation too far, but comments from reformers in Peru and other countries do lend support to the idea that improving reality may not be their first priority, and that there is something in the way law is taught and perceived that encourages this view. Thus, when the authors of the first version of the organic law were queried as to its budgetary requirements, they had no idea and were struck by the oddity of the question. Similarly, when El Salvador promulgated its new Family and Juvenile codes, comments were often made, and apparently intended as positive, that in twenty years the two laws might see real implementation.

79. See for example, material on Mexico's experience with special defenders for indigenous groups, Magdalena Gómez, "La defensoría jurídica de presos indígenas," in Stavenhagen and Iturralde, 1990, pp. 371-388.

6

The Fujimori Reforms

The separate treatment of Peru's post-*golpe* period may appear to signal a complete break with the past. To the contrary, it is interpreted here as demonstrating considerable continuity. It obviously builds on almost thirty years of frustrated reform efforts and on their cumulative identification and analysis of the sector's failings. In terms of content, almost nothing initiated by the Fujimori administration had not been attempted, or at least proposed before. Moreover, there are strong parallels between the evolution of the Fujimori program and those of prior administrations. They are particularly evident as regards the initiatives of the two phases of the military government. In short, the sense of deja vu remains.

Nonetheless the post-1995 strategy does represent a significant departure from the conventional reform model as applied in Peru and elsewhere. It is characterized by important tactical differences that guarantee a greater impact than any of Peru's prior programs. It will produce change; improvement is another story. The two most apparent deviations are in the reform leadership and the government's support of their efforts. For once, the legal community has been excluded from a determining role. Its members may collaborate if they wish, but the direction and the details of change are being set by planners, administrators, and organizational designers whose notion of how it should be effected and the terms of success have defined an unaccustomed pace and mix of actions. Still, even with their emphasis on producing results, the new reformers would have accomplished little had it not been for a second element—the administration's broad delegation of authority to them along with unprecedented financial resources. The new reformers have been issued a blank check, literally and figuratively.

This second element raises a question as to a third factor, the nature of the government's interest in justice reform. This question, which is explored but not answered below, will define the real extent of deviation from the past, as well as the likely outcome, sustainability, and wider political significance of the current program. Taken at face value, the Fujimori reforms already pose some thorny political issues. Their implied political neutralization of the judiciary in the macro as well as microsense leaves a gap in the separation and *balance* of powers as defined in the new constitution. It weakens governmental accountability and strengthens the authoritarian thrust of the new institutional arrangements, threatening their sustainability over the longer run. It also may endanger the purely functional performance of the sector institutions and the legitimacy they are accorded. However, the larger issue is whether a face value interpretation is sufficient, or whether the government retains additional objectives that are inconsistent with their explicit goals.

If the reforms adhere to their explicit agenda, they will represent a partial break with the past. They will be a novel, if highly questionable effort to define and implant a new functional and political role for the sector. If they do not, they will become Peru's most recent and most costly attempt to subvert that functional role to short term political ends.

The Early Years: 1992 to 1995

From 1992 to 1995, it appeared that the Fujimori government would leave the justice sector, and the courts in particular, to their own devices. If the administration had its own ideas about judicial and justice sector reform, it was not ready to discard measures already underway. For a time, it gave them room, if not financial support, to continue their development. The result was a curious mixture, the orientation of which was still evolving two and a half years after the coup. President Fujimori did not revoke any of the new fundamental legislation and, in fact, substantially accelerated the preparation and promulgation of a new Civil Procedures Code. According to some reports, the law produced a few early changes in the operations of the Lima courts. Once the initial enthusiasm dissipated, past practices were resumed. The only enduring change was the addition of several new first-instance courts and the attempt to move those situated in Lima out of their already cramped quarters to the building formerly occupied by the Ministry of Education.

The entrance into effect of the Criminal Procedures Code (approved in 1991) was repeatedly postponed. A new draft was eventually substituted. After an announcement in late 1995 of its imminent passage, it also disappeared from sight. While allowing the new Judicial Organic Law and Criminal Code to remain in effect, the administration did not push for the full implementation of either, and almost immediately began to issue decree laws amending their content. A decree issued on April 23, 1992, reduced the Court from thirty to eighteen members and its chambers from five to three. A series of decrees dealing with terrorist cases gave the latter a treatment hardly compatible with the *garantista* (due process) thrust of the two laws in effect or the still suspended procedural code. It modified the new judicial structure to allow the creation of special courts with "faceless" judges and private or semipublic hearings (D.L. 25475, May 6, 1992). Confronted with the judiciary's apparent inability to organize these special courts,[1] terrorism was defined in a subsequent decree (D.L. 25659, August 8, 1992) as a type of treason, hence liable to military justice. Cases were redirected to newly created military courts with their own faceless judges and prosecutors.

Finally, beginning immediately after the coup, the government ordered a series of purges of judicial personnel, including court administrative staff and members of the Public Ministry. After the formation of an evaluative commission, the efforts of which led to "the largest mass firing of judges and support personnel in Peru's history"[2] and a comparable "special ratification" in the Public Ministry, existing judicial staff was left pretty much alone.[3] Those who survived the purge or were appointed to replace the dismissed staff remained in provisional status, meaning that virtually all judges and prosecutors did not enjoy even minimal job security. While this may have discouraged corruption, it provided judicial staff with little incentive for taking a more activist approach to their jobs. Neither public opinion[4] nor government pronouncements suggested any greater satisfaction with sector performance, but there were too many other issues crowding the agenda for anyone to pay attention to its improvement.

Although these emergency measures enjoyed considerable domestic support, they were the target of immediate criticism by international observers, bringing the indefinite suspension of external assistance to the sector. Equally critical to the future of continued reform efforts, they alienated a good portion of the reform-minded legal community within the country. This caused further resignations from the bench and made it seem unlikely that those who had backed the pre-1992 reform movement would offer any cooperation with officially sponsored programs. Many of the "progressive," as well as independently minded judges and *fiscales* were already victims of the special ratifications. This general reaction only further complicated the task of finding replacements. High levels of unemployment initially provided a large pool of lawyers willing to volunteer for the jobs. However, they were not guaranteed to be the most capable. Moreover, by mid-1992 there were reports that some of the replacements were already disenchanted with their working conditions, as well as with their still temporary appointments.[5] On the positive side, the executive crackdown had temporarily created a more honest Supreme Court and perhaps reduced corruption at other levels. This was not because the government's hand-picked personnel was intrinsically any more honest, but because, under existing conditions of uncertainty, the risks of petty corruption were far greater. However, a series of decisions by the Court and Public Ministry, including their willingness to undertake the special ratifications, made it evident that susceptibility to political intervention was at an all-time high.[6]

The government never officially revoked the reform programs embodied in the new codes and organic law. Their initial actions merely ignored them when they did not actually override them. The first months' decisions were instead guided by the government and public's shared concern with terrorism and corruption and, thus, by a preference for expedient measures that had little to do with the procedures, structures, and philosophies embodied in the new laws. Since these measures created a special set of courts to handle the antiterrorist program, the continued suspension of the new Criminal Procedures Code probably had nothing more behind it than a lack of interest in its content combined with a reluctance to initiate a complicated and expensive implementation program. In these early measures, there were clear parallels with the reform programs of the 1968-1975 military government. These can be summarized as a broadly focused attack on the sector that, nonetheless, reduced its concrete impact to two principal policies: a special set of courts to meet the government's immediate political objectives, this time the elimination of terrorists rather than of the landed oligarchy, and the removal of a good portion of the seated bench and prosecutors. As before, the purge seemed equally inspired by an anticorruption campaign, a preemptive attack on potential resistance and opposition, and a drive to cement popular support among the majority of Peruvians who believed that the judiciary deserved this anyway.

A second set of parallels to the military period began to emerge with the convening of the Constituent Assembly and the serious discussion of the future of the sector. Here, despite their apparent lack of approval for the first months' "reforms," the government was gradually able to draw in some of the more distinguished members of the legal community, either as participants in the assembly's special commission on the judiciary or as members of the newly formed Judicial Council of Government.[7] Like their military predecessors, the Fujimori administration apparently had no special agenda for further judicial reform. These individuals were thus attracted by the possibility of finally effecting the changes they have been advocating for years if not decades.[8] Not surprisingly, some of them had participated in the New Law programs of the late 1970s and were instrumental in the preparation of the new criminal codes and Judicial Organic Law. Although necessarily bound by an implicit understanding that it would not criticize current government policies, the group appeared to share in the philosophy behind the new criminal codes and, to the extent it had one, behind the new organic law. The latter, as the least internally consistent of the laws, was likely to undergo the most revision, especially as regards the organization of the court system, procedures for selection of judges, and perhaps the powers accorded to the council itself.

The group's further elaboration of their vision for justice reform shaped the relevant sections in the 1993 Constitution. These were as important for what they did not say as what they said. The constitutional provisions on the judiciary, the Public Ministry, the National Judicial Council, and due process guarantees set important parameters on the functions and powers of each. For once they are relatively silent on much organizational detail, leaving this to be determined in secondary laws and internal regulations. Thus, both the territorial and functional-hierarchical framework for the judiciary and Public Ministry are left open-ended, as are the qualifications for any but the topmost officials of each. The constitution stipulates that justices of the peace will be elected and leaves open the possibility that this be extended to first-instance judges. While the term and manner of appointment of the Fiscal de la Nación are set, those for the president of the Court are undefined.

In line with the emphasis on separation of powers, but still surprising given the political environment, the constitution significantly reduces the formal ability of the other branches of government to interfere with judicial and prosecutorial independence. By enhancing the role of the National Magistrates Council, it likewise attempts to protect lower level officials from the upper reaches of their own institutions. As noted earlier, it makes such critical determinations as the removal of any role in selecting members of the judiciary and Public Ministry from the executive and its transfer to the National Magistrates Council, and the reestablishment of a separate Constitutional Tribunal with original jurisdiction on challenges to the constitutionality of legislation and final jurisdiction on other actions protecting constitutional rights. It also neatly resolves the issue of judicial tenure by making judicial appointments and those of *fiscales* permanent, but subjecting both groups to ratification by the National Council every seven years. The council's members are appointed or elected by the organizations they represent. Neither the executive nor the legislature has a direct role in selecting any of them. The legislature can remove members for cause with a two-thirds vote. Since the council and the Constitutional Tribunal are renewed every five years, apparently to coincide with or follow legislative and presidential elections, they are likely to be influenced by the same political trends shaping the latters' outcomes. This is of most concern in the case of the Constitutional Tribunal's direct election by Congress.

With this last possible exception, the constitutional framework appears to facilitate rather than inhibit reform and to leave it in the hands of the affected institutions. The government's lack of involvement in the elaboration of these sections further suggested that, so long as no threats were posed to its antiterrorist policies (almost completed in any case) or its economic liberalization programs, it was disinclined to place any ideological constraints on the reformers' future work. Whether it would make available the resources to allow implementation was another question. This was a critical point. What emerged from the reformers' discussions, combining the pre-1992 concern with due process and procedural "modernization" with a greater emphasis on human resource and management development, was no less ambitious or costly than the pre-1992 proposals. In this sense, the government's lack of opposition to the constitutional changes struck an ominous, as well as a positive note, an indication of the lesser priority it assigned to the sector, translating into a freedom to plan reforms, but little interest in paying for them. This, combined with the fact that many of the constitutional provisions, including those on judicial independence, had not gone into effect a full year after their promulgation,[9] was already eroding the enthusiasm of the new reformers and their supporters. Some remained on the bench where a few, by 1994, had risen to relatively important positions. Others who had been incorporated from private activities returned to the latter.

The Origins of the Fujimori Reforms

As has been noted of other aspects of the Fujimori administration's policies, apparent inactivity can signal lack of interest or a major change in the making. In retrospect, some observers claim to have identified an ominous escalation in the president's criticisms of the sector as early as late 1994, with increasing references to the courts' corruption and inefficiency. Whether their perceptions were accurate or not, by mid-1995 something was visibly afoot. Working with considerable secrecy, the United Nations Development Program (UNDP) brought several foreign consultants to Lima to confer with government officials on a possible reform program and began to negotiate a small grant with the Japanese government to finance its initial development.[10] In October of 1995, the president of the Supreme Court took an unprecedented, and allegedly unconstitutional step,[11] by presenting a reform proposal to the government and requesting the intervention of a reform commission representing all three branches of government. The rest of the Court awoke from its somnolence for long enough to protest the move. The proposal was adopted in a modified form (D.L. 26546), resulting in the creation of an internal reform group, an Executive Commission composed of three justices. Once created the commission took another unexpected step by choosing as its executive secretary a retired admiral, José Dellepiane Massa. Dellepiane was a stranger to the sector, but he had important contacts within government circles. An engineer by training, his prior government experience had been in the Ministry of Energy and Mines where he had conducted a series of reorganizations and administrative reforms, working closely with several key government figures.[12] As indicated by the title of the decree law creating it (the Law of Administrative Reform), the commission's mandate was to be limited to administrative reorganizations and improvements. It was to be active for the space of a year. Thus while the move, and the role of Dellepiane brought some objections, no one was yet terribly alarmed about the innovations.

As of this writing, twenty months after the creation of the commission, it is still unclear whether the government had in mind as ambitious a program as was to result, or why in fact it decided to act when it did. It is likely that what was envisioned in late 1995 fell far short of what eventually developed. Apparently, what was to become the country's most ambitious judicial reform effort to date began with a far less global agenda. Even so, the reason for the move continues to be debated. Judicial reform, as one of the pretexts for the *autogolpe*, was an unfinished item on the Fujimori agenda. This alone may have been sufficient excuse for the initial intervention. Those favoring this interpretation have suggested that the Court's inability to work its own reform, acting on the tools provided by the initial intervention and the 1993 Constitution, eventually motivated the government to take control. The captive Court, with its largely undistinguished membership, had spent two years debating how it would proceed. Despite some advances, the government it was said, was fed up with their incompetence and inertia. No one in any case believes that the Court president made his request on his own initiative, or that the appointment of Dellepiane as the commission's executive secretary was a fortuitous accident.

More Machiavellian interpretations, which credit the government with a more ambitious agenda from the start, offer several alternative explanations.[13] Some observers emphasize the presence of a number of foreign donors, and especially the IDB, World Bank and USAID. All three had shown interest in financing a judicial reform program, but only one with full government support. In this view, the government was anxious to access these funds and, thus, instituted the reform as a sign of good faith. Those favoring this explanation suggest that the government's announced intent to provide over $100 million of its own funds was not to be taken seriously. They predict that if the ploy does not attract external financing, the reform will never see these monies.

Another set of explanations stresses the need to improve judicial performance and, especially, to reduce corruption and malfeasance as conditions for attracting private foreign investment. This interpretation is not incompatible with the first one. Both the World Bank and the IDB seemed principally interested in commercial law. Hence, the initial program would serve two purposes. It would create the conditions for encouraging private foreign and domestic investment and attract external loans and donations to finance the reform itself. Ironically, as of late 1996, the only international agency actively cooperating with the reform was the UNDP, which presumably was most concerned about the implications for judicial independence and human rights. The World Bank had initiated negotiations for a large loan and begun some preliminary work. It was still withholding further advances pending resolution of its own concerns about the significance of the new developments.[14] USAID continued to withhold support except for its remaining commitment to the National Detainees Registry, a project it had begun in the early 1990s. The IDB's reading of the new situation was unknown and in some sense irrelevant. Its relative lack of involvement was primarily due to its having prioritized projects in other countries.

Finally, in contrast with these first interpretations, there are those who credit judicial progress in beginning a reform as the motivating factor. Evidence here includes the actions of a few judges who had taken decisions against the government on a number of minor cases[15] and the incipient advances in such areas as judicial ratifications, discipline, and training. This progress had been slight, but there were signs that it might escalate. Those favoring this explanation argue that the government was afraid the judiciary might overcome the initial setbacks, start taking its self-improvement seriously, and thereby establish a basis for further independent action. The reform-minded members of the Court and the rest of the judiciary remained a minority. Still, there were signs of change, including the reactivation of the Office of Internal Control under the leadership of one of the few remaining reformist justices,[16] the formation of the Judicial Academy, and the actions of the *Tribunal de Honor*[17] in reviewing the cases of judges dismissed in April of 1992 and beginning to ratify provisional appointments. The government may have decided to seize the initiative before it faced a less than fully subservient court system. Proponents of this interpretation suggest that the administration foresaw future problems with its economic and investment programs if the courts were called upon to rule on any of them. A more activist court might also begin to take seriously its role in questioning the activities of certain highly place officials. Thus, the argument concludes, the government moved to reassert control before this could occur.

The Early Stages

It is probable that the explanation will never be determined to everyone's satisfaction. The immediate consequences are less debatable. The creation of the Executive Commission in November of 1995 effectively took control of the judiciary's further development out of its own hands and placed it in those of a body that quickly became dominated by its executive secretary, Admiral Dellepiane. Dellepiane had the power and the backing of the government to proceed. It was apparent, as he himself continued to claim, that he began without much idea of where he was heading. In the first months he took a number of actions that elicited the reluctant approval of some of his critics. Most of these were innovations that had been suggested before, but had been left unimplemented, most often because of opposition from the judiciary itself. Among them was an attack on the justices' traditional practice of hiring their relatives to fill sensitive positions. This practice had come under frequent criticism, but had been defended by prior Courts as the only way of ensuring confidentially in their work. This time the attack was successful. It temporarily placed Dellepiane at odds with his official sponsor, the Court president, who had hired his own daughter as his personal secretary. Dellepiane, nonetheless, exercised a free hand in making his own appointments. Within the first months of his tenure he had placed a group of fifteen new employees, five to oversee general administration and ten to work on a reform program. The UNDP-administered Japanese grant allowed him to avoid the public sector salary ceilings and the variety of regulations that most often frustrated attempts to attract qualified contract and permanent employees.

For the first six months of his tenure, until April of 1996, Dellepiane remained a figure of much speculative interest, but gave few indications of the direction he would take.[18] His working group grew to almost forty. In addition to his control of the normal judicial budget (established with Law 26546), the government increased the allocation by 50 percent, to be used in reform activities. The Executive Commission began to issue a series of administrative resolutions intended to produce changes in the details of operations of the courts and their administrative organs. Some of these escalated or facilitated changes already under way. They included the relocation of the civil and criminal trial courts in Lima, changes in the operations of the Office of Internal Control, and the creation of more judgeships in Lima and in the provinces. Others responded to what may have been real necessities, but were the targets of considerable scorn and sarcasm. The local press had a field day with the reformers' contracting of a modeling school to teach proper etiquette to judicial employees, the elimination of the informal vendors from inside the Palace of Justice, and the installation of a corps of "hostess-guides" to provide information to those seeking services. Dellepiane and his group probably merited this reaction. They announced these cosmetic improvements with the same seriousness and occasionally more fanfare than moves like the buy-out program for voluntary retirement of administrative staff or the introduction of a permanent duty judge.

Initially, the measures introduced were less striking for their content than for their variety and the speed with which they were taken. The full Court traditionally had labored months or years over a single proposal. Dellepiane quite literally was limited only by the time required to draft a resolution. In April and May of 1996, the series of almost random directives began to take a more definite shape. Dellepiane produced his first operational plan, moving into a new phase of action. It was now clear that his goals went far beyond administrative reform.

In the meantime and after considerable delay, the government had introduced the additional entities mandated by the 1993 Constitution. The new National Magistrates Council was installed in March, 1995, although it remained relatively inactive for almost a year. This was followed, after lengthy negotiations, by the appointment of a Human Rights Ombudsman in April, 1996 and, finally, in June, the naming of a Constitutional Tribunal. In as much as the last two sets of appointments required a two-thirds vote of Congress, the government was prevented from naming its first choice candidates. However, in the case of the tribunal, the administration took a second tack by having its organic law modified in the midst of the negotiations. Thereafter it would take the vote of six of the seven members to establish the unconstitutionality of a law; such decisions could only be made in the first six months of a law's entrance into effect. It was explained that this would augment juridical security. It was also clearly a way of protecting the government's own programs.

In February of 1996, the National Magistrates Council, recognizing that inaction now had real costs, began a program of vetting all provisional appointments. By late October, it had ratified all Supreme and superior court judges and prosecutors. By the end of October, as it prepared to begin the process with the mass of first-instance judges and *fiscales*, it entered into conflict with Dellepiane and his group. The reformers suggested that such actions be postponed for a year, pending further decisions on the judicial career and requirements for appointment to it. Even given the signs that Dellepiane's reform program had superseded his initial mandate, the debate had still more ominous portents for the judiciary's future, reactivating concerns over the real purposes of the reform. This gave weight to rumors, circulating a year earlier, that the government already had 150 magistrates slated for dismissal.[19]

Consolidation

In May of 1996, the reform took another turn with the suggestion that a new Sectoral Coordinating Commission be created with a mandate extending beyond the judiciary to the entire justice sector. Once again, objections of unconstitutionality brought a modification of the initial proposal. A late night session of the assembly and the reworking of a counter-proposal submitted by an opposition congressman resulted in Law 26623 (June 18, 1996), which was to be the basis for further reform. The five-article law mandated the creation of the Sectoral Coordinating Commission. Its members would include the maximum authorities or their representatives from the Supreme Court, Constitutional Tribunal, Public Ministry, National Magistrates Council, prison authority, police, and private bar. The commission was charged with overseeing and coordinating reforms initiated within these entities and, in itself, seemed unobjectionable. However, the law included two pages of transitory dispositions that radically changed its immediate significance.

The full commission was only to be created in 1998, or later.[20] In the meantime, a smaller commission consisting of representatives of the first three entities and an executive secretary, with voice and vote in most decisions, would oversee the reform. The commission was chaired by Dellepiane as the representative of the Court and head of its newly created Executive Council.[21] Its executive secretary was Miriam Schenone, a former vice minister of justice, and one of Dellepiane's followers. The law creating the commission also removed control of further reforms and their constitutionally mandated "legislative initiative" from the Supreme Court and six Fiscales Supremos, locating it in the executive councils of the Court and Public Ministry and in the commission itself. It placed both the National Magistrates Council and the Judicial Academy under "reorganization," entrusting this to the Coordinating Commission. The promulgation of the law brought immediate objections from several Court justices and their counterparts in the Public Ministry, and attempts by each group to provide substitute legislation. Lacking support from the chief justice and Fiscal de la Nación, neither effort prospered. When the dissenting justices introduced their proposal in a scheduled en banc session, the chief justice abstained from voting, three justices voted against it, and several Court members simply failed to appear.

The creation of the commission was quickly followed by the presentation of a three-year reform program for the judiciary with total funding of roughly $100 million.[22] The government put up the first $40 million for the effort. It was argued that donor funding might fill out the entire amount, but that it would only be accepted on the government's terms. Should the donors not choose to cooperate with the plan, the government vowed to fund it itself. With the commission, the plan, and the first year's funding in place, the following months saw a flurry of activity. Including activities beginning in January of that year, expenditures on the reform already totaled $20 to 25 million by November, 1996.[23] Accounting for the expenditures was hardly transparent. Dellepiane reported that a large portion was going into the voluntary retirement program for administrative staff. Participants and observers spoke of 250 or more reform activities divided into twenty or more projects. The plan worked on three main areas: improvement of the administrative management and offices of the court system; improved court administration; and establishment of a judicial career and new recruitment and personnel policies. Progress in these areas advanced in this order. By October of 1996, Dellepiane claimed to have almost finished his work on the administrative systems, where the initial reform was to have begun and ended. While the declaration of victory was premature, a number of transcendental changes had been effected. Staff had been reduced, a new move to contract out basic services had begun, ending the Lima Bar Association's long-time monopoly on notice serving, the Office of Internal Control was further reorganized and some of its powers delegated to superior court presidents, and Dellepiane had requested complete budgetary autonomy for the judiciary. What exactly the latter meant was uncertain. It would at least eliminate the legislature's traditional paring and reshaping of the budgetary request and the Finance Ministry's control over the disbursement and use of approved funds.

Work on court administration was well underway with the design of computerized management and case tracking systems, the introduction of a centralized notification system, and initial moves to replace the bulk of courtroom support staff with newly trained law graduates.[24] Many of the 250 or so activities were in this area, constituting a series of innovations in courtroom functions. Case files (*expedientes*) were redesigned, a manual registry was introduced for courts that could not yet be automated, judicial assistants and law clerks were introduced, and pools of administrative staff were provided for courts operating in the same locales. Most of these activities were introduced on an experimental basis in a few courts, and slated for wider replication if they proved successful. The primary pilot programs were begun in the central offices of the new antinarcotics courts that had been installed in a building formerly occupied by the first-instance civil courts. Within a month of their opening, by October of 1996, the Lima second-instance drug court (the head of the system) and its two trial courts were fully functional under the new system. The reformers proposed to extend the system to the other four second-instance drug courts and sixteen trial courts by the end of the year.

One of the reform group's basic assumptions was that corruption had been encouraged through excessive contact between judges or administrative staff and lawyers and their clients. Thus, they began to introduce measures to reduce this contact, in the process moving outside their administrative mandate into areas affecting the functional operations of the courts and the traditional practices of the bar. In the drug courts, contact with the public was limited to the reception offices (*mesas de partes*) and a room where lawyers could read case files under supervision by a clerk and police guards. Furthermore, the judicial Executive Council issued a resolution (095-CME-PJ, May 14, 1996) forbidding ex parte conversations between lawyers and judges involved in the same case. This resolution was applicable to all legal cases, not just those involving drug trafficking. It was extremely controversial. Even lawyers who were generally assumed to have no interest in buying justice believed that such conversations were necessary to "help judges understand the laws" they were applying.[25] Another measure taken to reduce such contacts was the rotation of administrative personnel among courts. A series of resolutions moved administrative staff not only among courts in the same area, but also from province to province. While the measure was advertised as a way of breaking up possible circles of influence or rings of corruption, it may also have been a means of persuading staff to resign. The reformers were guarded in their prognostications, but it was evident that they hoped to remove a large portion, perhaps up to 80 percent, of the courtroom staff.[26] Existing staff would be replaced with the newly graduated lawyers who were being trained in short courses on court administration in universities throughout the country. Changes such as these, which were announced from one day to the other, brought considerable criticism because of the lack of consultation with the judiciary, the bar, and other affected parties.

The final part of the judicial reform, the status of the judicial career and of the existing judges remained unresolved. This was the area that aroused most concern. Given the replacement of auxiliary staff, it was only logical to ask whether a similar plan was being contemplated for the judges, and if so, whether the criteria would be technical or political. As noted, the Magistrates Council's plan to move ahead with the vetting and permanent appointment of the mass of provisional judges had been discouraged by Dellepiane's group. No one doubted that they were buying time while they decided what direction to take. Utilizing his new powers under Law 26623, Dellepiane did direct the Judicial Academy to begin an evaluation of existing judges, testing them not only for probity (the normal grounds for suspension) but for their knowledge of the law. Objections were made that this violated the academy's mandate, to train and form judges. Despite his own reservations about the move,[27] the school's director proceeded to develop examinations, promising to begin their administration before the end of the year.[28]

Dellepiane did not have the authority to terminate judges definitively. He did claim the ability to suspend them, using a controversial interpretation of the powers granted him under Law 26623. He further contended that suspension could be based on insufficient knowledge of the law, as well as on the usual criterion of misrepresentation of credentials. Many saw the move as a transparent ploy to attack the politically unacceptable, as well as the insufficiently prepared. Other observers suggested that the fears were misplaced, and that the emerging goal was one of improving the overall quality of the bench by eliminating the hopelessly incompetent. The predominance of the latter, it was widely acknowledged, had been the unfortunate consequence of three decades of highly politicized appointments. In this interpretation, the government's goal for the judiciary was similar to its objectives in other parts of the public bureaucracy. There, most notably in the tax offices and tax courts,[29] it had sought to place highly qualified, apolitical appointees who would do an excellent technical job and restrain any impulses to political activism.

To this end Dellepiane was already talking about increasing judicial salaries to their dollar level in *soles*, that is, a factor of 2.4 to 2.6 times their current value.[30] It was also evident that more judges would be needed and that the overall salary bill could be expected to increase. However, the accompanying plan was to reduce administrative staff, increase the salaries of those who remained, and effect a fee system for all but the poorest users. The revenues thus generated were intended to make up the difference. The reform group argued that after the initial investment in new equipment and the buy-outs of administrative personnel, the normal operating expenditures for the reformed court system would be lower than current levels.[31]

In the meantime, two other reform areas, the Public Ministry and further law revision, remained on the back burner. Dellepiane's powers did not extend to the former and he argued that, until the Public Ministry was reformed, efforts to enact new criminal legislation made little sense. The Public Ministry had formed its own Executive Council and issued a reform plan. In the absence of a group of technicians like those in the Court, the proposed program appeared to be little more than the usual endless reorganizations, equipment purchases, and increased automation of basic procedures. Dellepiane had in fact provided the Public Ministry with a group of his own advisors. They were fired by the Fiscal de la Nación after two months, when the head of the group made several impolitic and highly public statements about conditions within the organization. Not one to give up easily, Dellepiane subsequently provided a second group, the fate and success in its task of which is still to be determined. Meanwhile, reforms of both the National Prison Institute (INPE) and the police were under discussion. It had already been suggested that the prisons might be removed from the Ministry of Justice and turned over to the courts. Discussions of an improved public defense system were conspicuously absent. The most effective legal assistance services remained those offered through NOGs, often with the support of foreign donors.

The Political Response

As the reform ended its first year, the controversy surrounding it continued, but effective opposition remained at a minimum. After the Court's abortive effort to substitute an alternative reform plan, and a similar attempt by a few of the Fiscales Supremos, neither institution offered significant resistance. The majority of their members had never been known for their political activism and their provisional status probably silenced any judges and *fiscales* harboring doubts about the undertakings. The most likely source of external opposition, the Lima Bar Association, was temporarily neutralized by divisions among its own members and by its loss of the lucrative contract for process serving for the courts. Since the contract had been the association's main source of income, its loss threatened near bankruptcy.[32] The termination of the contract was precipitated by a falling out between Dellepiane and the association's president, Vladimir Paz de la Barra, who until then had been one of Dellepiane's informal advisors. In any case, Paz was an unlikely rallying point. His humble origins, questionable political credentials (including his earlier friendship with Dellepiane), and overall lack of political finesse had alienated the elitist lawyers who traditionally dominated the association and whose support for the reform was distinctly qualified. The bulk of the membership shared Paz's less distinguished background and conceivably had still more to lose from the proposed changes. They were apparently reluctant to register opposition, especially if this meant uniting with and thus following the leadership of their elitist colleagues. For the bar as for the bench, such class divisions worked to the reformers' advantage. The prior reform movements, largely in the form of law revision, had been backed by a small but prestigious group of judges and lawyers. Their attitudes toward their increasingly "massified" (*masificados*) colleagues had at best been perceived as paternalistic and at worst as antagonistic. Thus, although the reformers were targeting many of the vices already identified by the elite bar and frequently attributed to the "bad habits" of the masses, the latter undoubtedly took pleasure in the elites' fall from grace.

The reformers were also able to undermine the more principled opposition within and outside the public sector because, apart from their questionable political motivation, many of the specific reform measures were those that had been favored for some time. For every debatable action (e.g. the prohibition of *ex parte* conversations), there were perhaps nine others, the content and explicit purpose of which were unimpeachable. Those remaining unconvinced frequently found themselves saying that they agreed with the objectives, but merely questioned the style or form of the reform. The opposition's greatest weakness may have been their failure to provide a viable alternative plan. As time went on, an increasing number of critics signed on as advisors to the reform movement. Whether motivated by conviction, or the rumored lucrative fees paid for their services,[33] their decision sacrificed their moral edge and removed their credibility as opponents. Some, like the director of the Judicial Academy, argued that they had joined forces with the reform on their own terms.[34] The subtly of the argument was lost on most observers, who simply interpreted their actions as selling out. As more of the former critics joined the reform group, the incentive to stay outside continued to diminish. By late 1996, the question became less one of why the protesters had joined, than of what the few holdouts sought to accomplish by their principled opposition.

By then, it appeared that nothing could stop Dellepiane and his band of reformers. The remaining doubts were not whether they could work the changes they intended, but whether the government would continue to give them a political and financial blank check. What had been accomplished was impressive. Replicating the various experimental programs on a nation-wide basis would take every bit of the government's promised $100 million and perhaps considerably more. A distinguished Chilean expert[35] had developed figures to demonstrate that the reformed sector would cost less than its unreformed predecessor. His arguments were not entirely convincing and, in any case, the savings would be over the long, not the short run. The imponderable factor was thus not the aims of Dellepiane's group, which arguably were fairly transparent. The critical issue was what his bosses really hoped to accomplish by letting him proceed with his plans and what value they placed on his success.

The Wager

In an interview appearing in a local journal,[36] the head of the Judicial Academy, a prominent jurist known for his independent views, answered the inevitable question as to why he chose to cooperate with the reform group by referring to his situation as a wager. He explained that he had retracted the resignation he tendered with the appearance of Law 26623 in the belief that he could retain his independence in his current position, contribute to those aspects of the reform he supported, and perhaps help to save elements that might be endangered by reformers with less than a complete appreciation of the judiciary's ideal functional and political roles. In some sense, this figure of the wager characterizes the reform program as a whole. Certainly in its methods, and possibly in its goals, Peru's current reform represents a unique approach among the various regional efforts to improve their judiciaries. The Peruvian reformers are thus betting on the efficacy of a completely untested strategy and on their own ability to hold together the elements needed to carry it out. There are several elements of chance involved in the current program and consequently a good measure of unpredictability as to what will result.

This interpretation differs from that of many external and some internal critics, who see the reform as little more than a political ploy to appease external political forces (and major donors) while creating a completely politically subservient judiciary. These critics view the current set of administrative and technical reforms as a prelude to the real agenda, the removal of any remaining elements of judicial independence, if necessary, by the replacement of the majority of the seated bench. This may be part of the program, but it seems doubtful that the government would dedicate so many resources and so much effort to achieve an objective that was already within its reach. Even assuming an additional goal of getting external donors to pay for the bulk of the reform, the initial investment, in both financial and human resources, hardly appears justified by the likely returns. The logical conclusion is to accept at least a portion of the program at face value, as an effort to create a modern, efficient, technically oriented justice system and, thus, as a part of the larger strategy for modernizing Peru's entire public sector.

For the reform leaders, who for the most part are not jurists, the judiciary is essentially a public service provider, not a political power. Its mission is to provide that service as efficiently and effectively as possible, and with the highest degree of technical expertise. There is no question that, for at least the last three decades, Peru's courts and other sector institutions have performed disastrously in this sense and that many of the reformers' proposals offer solutions, for the most part highly reasonable ones, for specific aspects of this abysmal record. The issue is whether a performance-oriented judicial reform can be accomplished as a kind of turn key operation, choosing and imposing the best technical solutions to increase efficiency and improve services, vetting incumbents to ensure that those who remain in or enter the system are capable of working in the new environment, and finally, entrusting them with the reformed institution in the expectation that modern technology and rationalized procedures will drive future behavior.

This strategy has enjoyed some measure of success with other institutions, both in Peru and elsewhere. Dellepiane and others had applied it in their administrative reorganizations in various public sector entities. Peru's tax office, SUNAT, is a prime example and one which is generally regarded as highly successful. The approach also resembles programs implemented by international donors in remaking police forces in Panama, Haiti, and El Salvador. However, the courts by themselves and the justice sector as a whole represent considerably more complex institutions. It is questionable whether what a judge needs to know and do can be as easily reduced to a set of procedures and basic formulas as can the skills of a tax inspector or police investigator. Furthermore, unlike these other institutions, the judiciary does not have a functional hierarchy. Judges work in greater isolation without direct supervision. Their decisions may be reviewed and reversed by higher instances, but it is the law, not the latter's anticipated reactions or direct orders, that is supposed to guide them.[37] Hence, assuming a better system is designed, its sustainability will depend on higher levels of internalization by the mass of individual judges than is the case for the police or tax officials. In short, a turn key operation is likely to be more difficult here, even if the reformers decide to enhance their chances by replacing virtually the entire professional as well as auxiliary staff.

In working toward their goal form, thus, is important, not only for ideological, but also for practical reasons. The limited judicial participation in the reforms, while facilitating the rapid imposition of change, may well work against its sustainability. Over the medium run, the reformers face a choice of either extending their presence to force compliance or accepting a substantial erosion of their improved system in practice. Their overwhelming confidence in their ability to design logically compelling systems of action is evident in the absence of efforts to draw change out of the institution, through consultations and discussion, and in the format and content of training programs. Those mounted by the reformers (especially the courses for auxiliary staff) tend to be of very short duration and dedicated largely to imparting new knowledge and skills. The underlying assumption is apparently that behavioral change has an essentially cognitive base and that a rational appreciation of improved methods will automatically promote their adoption. This is a completely technologically driven vision of organizational change. As such, it ignores the importance and difficulties of altering mentalities and predispositions shaped by a larger culture within which the institutions will still have to operate. Consequently, the pilot projects are not an adequate test. They will help the reformers identify technical errors, but will provide far less indication of how the new methods work under less controlled conditions. Still, this is a wager, and they may succeed. There are, however, a number of reasons to doubt their success will be as great as they anticipate.

If the greatest wager entails the feasibility of a technologically driven strategy, there are a number of other factors adding their own element of uncertainty. One of these is the availability of adequate resources and continued governmental support. Regardless of the claims that, over the long run, Peru's justice system will be more cost effective, if not less costly, over the short run, the reform will be very expensive. The $100 million budget, whether provided wholly by the government or partially financed by donors, is only an estimate. It is almost certainly an unrealistically low one. For the time being the reformers have a blank check and are limited only by the speed with which they can invest resources. In the next year or two, the government, faced with numerous high priority programs, may decide to be less openhanded. Whatever the technical feasibility of the effort, it will not work without funding. Despite the prevailing optimism, there is no guarantee that it will be available. Thus, the second part of the wager is the continued availability of resources to carry it out the reform.

Funding restrictions will not negate all reform, but they will certainly limit the reformer's reach. The most likely outcome is a reform that concentrates on the high visibility components of the system and leaves the rest relatively untouched. Perhaps the pilot courts will be extended to the rest of the drug jurisdiction and the ordinary courts in Lima and a few other major provincial cities,[38] but never reach the rest of the country. This will produce a situation where excellent services are provided to those who can reach them, while others are left with a more traditional system. This does not necessarily imply a cynical approach to reform, a sort of Potemkin Village of modern courts. It is one inevitable conclusion of a strategy that emphasizes going first class until the funds run out.

The situation of the Human Rights Ombudsman is suggestive of what such a future could hold. Currently seated in a refurbished colonial house in the center of Lima, the ombudsman's office is a showcase of modern technology put to the service of its clients and employees. With carpeted offices, computers and communication equipment, and private cubicles for attending the public, it puts to shame the Ministry of Foreign Affairs located across the street. The office is not lavish, but it is hardly what one expects to find in Peru's public sector. Nonetheless, the proposed budget and future staffing of the organization indicate that it will be able to duplicate these settings in only a few provincial cities, that its scope will necessarily be less than its open-ended constitutional mandate, and that its services will have to be rationed. As even its leaders admit,[39] there is no way it can attend to the potential universe of human rights, legal, and administrative abuses. Thus, it will have to be very selective as to what it undertakes. Peru will have a "model" Human Rights Ombudsman in both senses of the word. Where it operates, it will do so in an exemplary fashion, but its further political reach and clout will be limited by the inevitable resource constraints. The office has already undertaken some very important activities, including the formation of a commission to review the cases of prisoners held for terrorist activities. It will doubtless be the recipient of considerable foreign assistance. Despite its obviously highly dedicated staff, one wonders whether the government's primary objective in creating the office might not be improving its external image and coopting some potential critics rather than any real concern with human rights.

Assuming the reform strategy can work and is given the funds to do so, there is another unpredictable factor that may also alter its outcome, or bring it to an untimely end. This is the political element about which so many of the critics continue to express concern. To date, there are few indications that the government and reformers have a hidden agenda of replacing the entire judiciary with political loyalists. Nevertheless, there remains a certain ambiguity on the government's side as regards a desire for real judicial neutrality. If, as several informants suggested, the government's goal is a Chilean style judiciary, one with a high degree of technical efficiency and a political perspective that transcends neutrality to sheer avoidance, it still appears to draw the line when technical efficiency puts its own programs and people in danger. The performance of the Public Ministry and its head during the "Vaticino" trial of 1996 is a case in point.[40] When the defendant threatened to implicate Fujimori's chief advisor, Vladimiro Montesinos, in corruption and drug trafficking, the trial took on a decidedly political cast, with official participants risking flagrant violations of ethical standards and legal norms to pursue the administration's interests. The defendant's last court appearances brought rumors that he had been roughed up or drugged to discourage further outbursts, documents requested by the lawyer for a second defendant were "lost," and the Fiscal de la Nación publicly stated that Montesinos was above question. The fact that the Public Ministry itself has been allowed to pursue its reform absent its own Dellepiane also raises questions. With a Fiscal who has been so unswerving in her backing for the government, the obvious conclusion is that political loyalty is still the paramount objective and the preeminent criterion for determining whether or not an organization will be intervened.

If the government perceives many more instances where neutral technical criteria lead to inconvenient decisions, it may find itself in conflict with its own reformers, or with that portion of them who believe their mandate is to advance modernization and efficacy. Should this happen, the reformer's plans could be sabotaged by their own backers. Insufficient internalization of the reform values is one thing. Judges, prosecutors and staff who see their chief responsibility as acting in accord with the government's instructions on each case, are still less likely to accept their new roles and duties in the spirit in which they were designed. The reform group and those judges and lawyers affiliated with it already include a measure of opportunists and individuals more notable for their political and personal connections than their technical competence. This is inevitable and not unduly damaging in its current proportions. The real threat is that for whatever reason these conditions come to prevail in the design and implementation of the judicial career. Alternatively, the government may decide to postpone any such career, preferring to keep tenure contingent on political compliance. With either of these outcomes, technical and administrative improvements will have still less effect on the quality of services provided, or on the judiciary's contribution to a wider respect for the rule of law.

The Judiciary as a Political Power

As most observers agree, the new reform strategy by focusing on the judiciary's public service role, has chosen to ignore its political functions. Here both judicial independence and the judiciary's role as a counterbalance to the other branches of government have been conveniently forgotten. Whether oversight, preference, or a little of both, this "macro-depoliticization" of the judiciary runs counter to regional and world trends. That does not make it wrong. It does raise concerns about the consequences for the attainment of the immediate official goals of more effective, efficient performance; its rumored aims of impressing foreign donors and investors; and its impact on overall political development.

Assuming the reform does continue and that the temptation of "micro-politicization" is avoided (i.e. the incumbents are not replaced with a host of sycophantic opportunists), the reformers are forgetting that the public's evaluation of a service depends not only on what is offered, but on how it is received and perceived. Here, they might reevaluate their apparent preference for the Chilean model, widely recognized as a judiciary that has based its survival on a mastery of technical detail and an avoidance of political issues. Chile's judiciary is regarded as remarkably honest. It is also criticized for an isolation and elitism that make many of its decisions at best irrelevant and at worst contrary to broader societal values.[41] As regards its isolation if not elitism, similar criticisms have been directed at the more bureaucratized European judiciaries, like that of France.[42] Interactive videos, corps of hostess-guides, or opening the Palace of Justice for Sunday tours will not bridge this gap, especially if the public has doubts about the real interests being served. The question is whether the public, Peruvian or otherwise, want their judges and other legal officials to be as cold and impersonal as the tax inspector, another of the apparent models. It is also whether these same officials can provide adequate service for a public from which they are increasingly and intentionally isolated.

Other Latin American reforms have worked to increase contact with the public, on the assumption that this humanizes and improves the administration of justice. The Peruvian reformers are moving in the opposite direction. It is an interesting strategy, but one which may be missing an important dimension of reform. Ending corruption, emphasizing equal access to and treatment before the law, and increasing predictability are all important goals. Yet, reform is also supposed to produce intelligible, satisfactory decisions that strike people as just and, hence will be an acceptable means of resolving their conflicts. Mass-produced decisions, offered by almost faceless bureaucrats according to immutable rules, may not provide that satisfaction and, thus, will afford a less than optimal improvement in the underlying public service. One may keep judges honest by isolating them from the public; that still may not produce very good judges.

This development may be more favorably received by foreign donors and investors. The former, lacking in-depth contact with the system, tend to evaluate progress on the basis of what is made visible. The latter are often said to value speedy, predictable decisions over slow, erratic ones. Presumably, they can lose more awaiting a favorable decision than they lose with an unfavorable one that is made rapidly. Foreseeable losses can be factored into higher prices and passed on to the consumer. However, for those whose contact with the courts is less routine and for whom a single decision is thus more critical, the quality of that decision should count far more. Results count, but the way they are presented and explained have a good deal to do with determining quality.

This consideration raises a second and more clearly political aspect of the judiciary's role, its function as an integrative force. The judiciary does not just resolve conflicts; it does this as an ultimate authority, determining which of a series of contradictory and potentially legitimate interests and values should prevail. When this authority is recognized, it should also prevent conflicts from escalating or being diverted into less widely recognized forms of resolution. Its authority and, thus, this function are undermined when they are perceived as based in a biased or less than holistic treatment of the interests at stake. As suggested above, predictable and even adverse biases may be acceptable when the parties' real interest is getting beyond an immediate conflict to the business at hand. Win or lose, their underlying concern is in removing an obstacle to further action. However, for most users, the conflict is the real issue and an inadequate treatment of the interests involved, whether because of perceived bias, incomplete attention, or decision-making rules that are not understood, will not bring its satisfactory resolution.

Throughout Latin America this has been a perennial complaint vis-a-vis the judiciary's normal performance. It is a primary reason for viewing the institution as an "the weak pillar of democracy" and a contributor to political disorder. The current reformers may not be much worried about democracy; stability is a different question. Their reform does not necessarily run against the judiciary's integrative, stabilizing role. In its current form, it certainly does not enhance it. A speedy, technically impersonal judiciary may indeed facilitate the resolution of the multitude of questions confronting Peru's investors and business class in their dealings with each other or with the government. Even for them, the decision may represent no more ultimate authority than the flip of a coin or a roll of dice; it is just convenient. But a coin toss is a poor base on which to create national values or make decisions on the interests they will represent. Here the reform may be missing a chance to use the judiciary more creatively, as a means for forging a national consensus and incorporating a disparate population in it. To do that, it will have to allow the judiciary more rather than less contact with the population, and a more dynamic rather than a constrained stance toward the interpretation and application of the law.

A coin toss at least is neutral. The new judiciary, it is feared, may not be. This introduces the most obvious question about the judiciary's political role relative to its status as a co-equal branch of government. It would appear that the reformers are avoiding this issue, possibly because they recognize the administration's ambivalence or just plain opposition to it. They also may believe the institution cannot assume this role until it is reformed internally and, thus, that it is best ignored for the moment. Whatever the reason, Peruvians are well aware that the judiciary, reformed or not, is not an independent power and that it applies the rules differently for the administration's favorite sons and daughters. This is one of the weakest points of the reform, whether from the standpoint of altering the attitudes of the judges themselves, convincing the public of their honesty and fairness, or using the judiciary as a source of legitimacy for the regime. It is not worth discussing the judiciary as a check on governmental abuses and illegalities. It clearly is not and is not intended to be one. The corollary questions arising from this undisputed fact are legion. Who besides the government will be interested in this kind of reform and how will it affect the more limited goal of increasing technical efficiency? What kind of legitimacy will be accorded the decisions of an institution that is perceived as an extension of the executive branch? How will judges within this system view their own roles? And finally, what kind of political system will result when, even in the narrowest technical sense, the judiciary may not override executive actions and decisions?

There are as yet no answers to any of these questions. The current reform's explicit and implicit objectives contain some obvious contradictions. Over the longer run, these will have to be resolved. In the worst case scenario, Peru will get a politically subservient body with a veneer of technical skills. In the best case, its judiciary will adopt a professional self-image that will subordinate decisions to technical rather than wholly political criteria. The issue is not political activism but an independent decision-making base. In the civil code tradition, the judiciary has never aspired to political activism and has often been accused of going easy on the government[43] in cases involving its interests. What is being asked of the Peruvian judiciary may go far beyond that and, hence, be considerably more damaging to internal morale and external image. As for providing an active check on the executive, there is no reason to expect the judiciary to accomplish what no other Peruvian institution has been able to do. If the reform's emphasis remains more on technical neutrality and less on political subservience, that is a possible later development that may again put it in line with trends elsewhere in the region.

If the reform opts for political subordination, the past may still be the best indication of what will follow. The parallels with the military efforts of twenty years before are uncomfortably strong. The sequence has been accelerated and the content and leadership has changed, but the basic pattern holds—first a purge of the existing personnel, then a series of partial reforms of expediency featuring new laws and new courts, and finally the beginning of a global overhaul to change the institutions once and for all. The different leadership, an administrator already practiced in reengineering the public sector instead of distinguished jurists, has speeded up implementation as has the government's commitment of funding. Tactically, the current reform is an improvement over the military's program. Strategically, especially as regards its more limited vision of its objectives, it may be much weaker. Both reforms hinged on the persistence in power of a small reform group and, thus in the end, on the survival of the government that had authorized their actions. The military reforms were commencing as that government was preparing its departure. The current

reforms do not face a similar deadline. Still, if Fujimori or a chosen successor extends the current administration for another term, there is no
guarantee that their blank check to the reformers will remain in force.
Should the government withdraw its support, there will not be much
protest. The true believers are few and like their predecessors in the 1970s
would find their exit greeted with overwhelming relief.

Notes

1. Although the government issued the law soon after the *autogolpe*, as of mid-
1992 people were still wondering whether the special courts would become a reality (*Caretas* [Lima], June 22, 1922, p. 28-35). The courts, in both a civilian and military
version, did go into effect, but only the latter were used for the "important" terrorists, including Abimael Guzmán. The courts' operations, in both forms, confirmed many initial doubts as to their independence and respect for due process.
Observers also questioned the adequacy of protection for the faceless civilian
judges, prosecutors, and witnesses. With the trials of the major terrorists for the
most part completed, these questions remain largely academic, but they could have
a lasting negative impact on public notions about legal rights.

2. Bernales, 1996, p. 545.

3. With the issuance of Decree Law 25446 of April 23, 1992, the final count was
the destitution of 41 superior court judges, 6 Fiscales Supremos, 53 first- instance
judges, 24 provincial *fiscales*, and 10 juvenile court judges, all from the Lima and
Callao districts. The entire Supreme Court had already been dismissed with an
earlier decree (Bernales, 1996, p. 545).

4. A survey conducted by Apoyo in December of 1993 indicated that only 5
percent of the population rated the judiciary as trustworthy and 14 percent as
"somewhat trustworthy." In discussing the institution's major problems, 51 percent
mentioned corruption, 12 percent political interference, and 9 percent an inadequate
budget (*Debate* [Lima], December 1993-January 1994, pp. 43-47).

5. Despite some initial success in securing replacements for the judges fired, the
government by mid-1992 had run into problems as the newcomers began to leave,
disappointed by the low salaries and lack of adequate office space, staff, and equipment. By late May, forty-four of the sixty superior court positions in Lima were
filled by temporary appointees; keeping them temporary also seemed to be the
government's preference over the short run. The figures were still worse for the
lower levels (*Caretas* [Lima], May 25, 1992, pp 40-41). With higher salaries and a
decision (still largely unimplemented) to make permanent appointments, by 1994
the apparent shortage of candidates seemed to have been resolved.

6. The new magistrates were an unimposing group, chosen for their willingness
to comply with orders from above. While the initial purge removed several of
dubious character, it and subsequent resignations, saw the loss of several justices
who might have provided leadership for real reform. Unlike the purges conducted
by the military and post-1980 governments, the immediate political situation discouraged the cooperation of seriously minded jurists, although over the next year
their reluctance to participate began to disappear.

7. Created by the new organic law, the council temporarily became the planning body for further reform and held responsibility for selecting or purging judicial personnel. It coordinated closely, to the extent of sharing members, with the Constituent Assembly's special committee on the judiciary.

8. Interviews with participants, 1993.

9. Much of this independence depended on the creation or reformation of key institutions (most notably the National Magistrates Council) and their ability to exercise such powers as the ratification of judges and *fiscales*.

10. The first information comes from one of the invited consultants, who among others, met with President Fujimori's brother, Santiago. The negotiation of the grant, to be administered by the UNDP, obviously began far earlier than the date it went into effect, in late 1995.

11. Decisions of this nature correspond, constitutionally, to the full Court and not to its president alone. Also, the request for intervention by a body including the two other branches of government violates the judiciary's constitutional independence.

12. These included Jaime Yoshiyama, Daniel Hokama and Amado Yataco.

13. The source is a series of interviews conducted in Lima in October, 1996. Virtually everyone interviewed, except active participants in the reform, discarded the idea that the government's frustration with judicial inaction had any part in shaping the decision.

14. By the end of 1996, it had signed the agreement for a larger project and begun implementation. In mid-1997, the project was again halted. At that time two explanations were circulating. The first credited the bank's continuing concern with judicial independence. The other claimed the government was fed up with bank conditionality. To the extent the conditions may have stressed independence, the explanations are not incompatible.

15. One of the most famous of these was the Judge Saquicuaray who refused to apply the Amnesty Law, excusing members of the armed forces and police from responsibility for alleged human rights abuses connected with their antiterrorist activities prior to 1995. The judge remains on the bench, but as a "reward" for her actions has been assigned to one of the new "sentencing courts" created to process the cases of the large number of tried but unsentenced detainees. In November of 1996 a second judge who defied the government by accepting a habeas corpus against the military courts was also rewarded by a similar transfer. The case in question was that of General Rodolfo Robles who was being held in connection with his statements on military death squads (*Caretas* [Lima], December 5, 1996).

16. The justice in question was Carlos Ernesto Giusti Acuña, the sole civilian fatality of the government's attack on the terrorist held Japanese Embassy in April, 1997. Giusti had also opposed the executive's intervention in judicial reform and the use of military courts to try military officials charged with human rights abuses.

17. The tribunal was a temporary creation of the Constituent Assembly. Among its recommendations were the ratification of five of the seated justices and the dismissal of the rest. The tribunal's report was eventually tabled without subsequent action (Bernales, 1996, pp 545-546).

18. An editorial in *Ideele* (Lima), the journal of a local human rights organization, thus notes that while his initial actions had reduced some criticisms, there was a

lingering "uncertainty as to where his power would go and how independent he would be of the executive" (*Ideele* [Lima], July, 1996, p. 4).

19. Cited in *Caretas* (Lima), November 16, 1995.

20. A postponement of its creation could be effected by the interim commission.

21. The council originated with the new organic law; however, its formation was subsequently modified to allow its being chaired by its executive secretary. It replaced the Executive Commission mandated under the initial reform law and was to have a counterpart organization in the Public Ministry.

22. Information on financing comes from interviews with reform participants and the *Plan Integral de Reforma*, updated to October, 1996.

23. One further criticism is that no one except the government seems to know how much money is being spent or on what. Reports indicate that much of the initial amount has gone to consulting firms for studies and designs for new systems. Another substantial amount has gone to the purchase of computers and other equipment. While no one has yet suggested misuse of funds, critics have hinted that the reformers may be less interested in economizing than in "buying" support.

24. This information comes from interviews and the summary of progress contained in the *Plan Integral de Reforma.*

25. Although not making this argument, Javier de Belaúnde, a highly respected lawyer and a participant in prior reform efforts, also debated the wisdom of this move. He argued that it would unduly isolate judges and might encourage corruption (as cited in *Ideele* [Lima], July, 1996, p. 7).

26. In interviews, members of the reform group were guarded about this, but did mention the figure of 80 percent. As one of them said, "we know who the corrupt ones are."

27. The director, Francisco Eguiguren, expresses some of these reservations in an interview in *Ideele* (Lima), October, 1996, pp. 25-29. For a still more critical view see the interview with Javier de Belaúnde, cited in note 25 above.

28. In an unanticipated show of independence, the Constitutional Tribunal declared the move unconstitutional and temporarily brought it to a halt in early 1997.

29. This interpretation was offered by interviewees both within and outside the reform group. As one of the latter noted, what the government wants is a Chilean style judiciary; when asked whether this meant apolitical or politically manageable, he just smiled.

30. Interview with José Dellepiane, October 17, 1996.

31. Interview with member of the reform group, October 16, 1996.

32. Interviews, Lima, October, 1996.

33. Here again the reformer's secrecy as to how they were spending funds left this only as a rumor, but one which was cited by most external informants.

34. Cited in *Ideele* (Lima), October, 1996, pp 22-29.

35. Iván Vera, a consultant hired by the World Bank, as cited in *Expreso* (Lima), July 24, 1996, p. 4A.

36. *Ideele* (Lima), October, 1996, pp. 22-29.

37. Of course, many judges take such reactions into consideration, even in civil law countries. The point is that they are usually not required to do so and should not be motivated by fears of reprisals. See Damaska, 1997, p. 9.

38. They in fact have another pilot project in Chimbote, a city to the north of Lima.

39. Interviews, Lima, October, 1996.

40. Information on this is taken from issues of *Caretas* (Lima), August and September, 1996.

41. See Fruhling, 1993. Others (e.g. Galleguillos, 1997) have been far more critical, characterizing Chile's courts as an antidemocratic force.

42. See Jacob et al., 1996, pp. 221-239.

43. See Jacob et al., 1996, for a discussion of French judges' treatment of cases involving government interests. In Europe, judicial activism in the defense of constitutional rights may be increasing, encouraged by public pressure and the influence of the European Court of Human Rights.

PART THREE

Justice Reform as a Regional Phenomenon

7

Other Latin American Experience

The running comparison of Peru's experience with that of other Latin American countries has identified similarities in the shortcomings of their justice systems and the programs most frequently adopted to remedy them. It also has highlighted some common obstacles to implementing reforms, a topic that will be more thoroughly addressed in the last chapters. Before reforms reach the stage of implementation there are also significant differences in their political treatment These differences help to explain why such movements are more viable in some societies whereas in others, such as Peru, they hit impasse after impasse. Their viability is less relevant if one concludes that conventional reforms are misdirected, but here too, their political origins are crucial. Although Latin American justice or judicial reform movements may look the same, and purport to resolve some of the same problems, the more specific conditions giving rise to them, the alliances behind them and, thus, some of their objectives demonstrate critical variations. As we have seen in Peru, the combination has not been particularly propitious and has led, as discussed in the preceding chapters, to an apparent abandonment of the conventional model. In a number of countries the conventional efforts have been more successful. The present chapter examines the reasons for that success in further detail. The concluding chapters return to the fundamental question of the broader consequences of reform, for the justice sector itself and for the surrounding political system.

The following discussion focuses on the experience of three countries—El Salvador, Costa Rica and Colombia. They are chosen because, in sustaining reform programs, they, unlike Peru, are relative success stories. They owe their individual success to a different mix of three factors: the pre-existing strength (or weakness) of sector institutions and, especially, the judiciary; the attitudes of political elites toward the sector and toward reform; and the availability of external resources and political support. In each of these cases, the individual and combined values of these factors were different, leading to three distinct scenarios for reform, each with its own implications for impact. There is also a fourth potential condition and scenario, resting on the sustained involvement of nonpolitical elites or the broader public.

Throughout Latin American, and perhaps universally, this seems to be a largely hypothetical possibility. Nonetheless, the reasons for and implications of its absence merit further consideration.

Unlike Peru, where until very recently the other factors (a relatively weakened sector, elite attitudes that were at most opportunistic if not simply uninterested, and a relative absence of external support) worked against reform, each of the three countries enjoyed sufficiently positive values in one or more of these areas to initiate and maintain momentum. All three reforms face their own obstacles, many of which are increasing. There is, thus, no guarantee that the early momentum will be sufficient to lead them to their logical ends. It is here that wider elite or public involvement might play a role. That theme is left for the concluding chapters.

In presenting these three cases, I am making no attempt to cover the historical and institutional setting in detail. In part this is unnecessary because the brief interpretations offered here are fairly conventional ones and because the factors selected for closer examination, the details that count, are relatively few. Also, at the most general level, their wider institutional structures and those specific to the sector are not that variable. Where that rule does not hold, the exceptions are noted. Readers interested in additional background on any of the cases are referred to the list of sources noted at the beginning of each section.

El Salvador: Externally Induced Change

Background[1]

It should come as no surprise that of the three countries, El Salvador had the least developed justice sector and the political elite whose attitudes were least conducive to resolving its classic set of sectoral problems. On both counts it was arguably worse off than Peru, although not unusual for the region. It may thus be of more practical interest than the other two cases. For these reasons, a slightly longer background discussion is offered.

El Salvador is a small country with a relatively uncomplicated economy. Although the distribution of resources among its fairly dense population (5.6 million in 1995) is highly unequal, this is not aggravated by intense racial and cultural divisions or by extreme geographic isolation. Development of its economy came fairly recently. After a reliance on the production and export of *añil* (indigo, a natural dye) dating from its pre-independence days, it was only in the last decades of the nineteenth century that the coffee boom began. This brought the emergence of a new economic elite, many of whom were European immigrants or members of the urban middle class.[2] The government of Rafael Zaldívar (1876-85) attempted to stimulate an agro-export economy, focusing on coffee. This led to the distribution of *ejido* lands, formerly held in common and administered by the municipalities.

This development further cemented the hegemony of the new economic class of coffee growers. It also established a pattern of highly unequal[3] land ownership that has been the basis for many of the nation's subsequent political problems. As the economy diversified, the coffee growers successfully expanded their interests into other areas. They and their descendants continued to dominate economic life, as the famous "fourteen families" of El Salvador.[4]

Politically, El Salvador's trajectory has not been dissimilar from that of many of its Central American neighbors and, in the early years, from much of South America as well. Its membership in the Central American Federation lasted from 1824 until the latter's dissolution in 1839. This was followed by a chaotic period of governments headed by military leaders, but hardly representing the military as an institution (which in large sense it was not[5]). In a pattern common to the region, the last decades of the nineteenth century and the first three of the twentieth constituted what is usually called the consolidation of the Liberal State. This was characterized by competition among a small elite, in El Salvador's case, often a few families; one of them, the Meléndez Quiñónez dynasty, remained in control from 1913 to 1927. In the latter year, Pío Romero, a candidate imposed by the elite, assumed the presidency. Much to their surprise, he began a democratic opening, allowing the participation of a wide variety of social groups. This period saw the emergence of El Salvador's Communist Party under the leadership of Farabundo Martí.

This brief democratic experiment soon fell victim to the worldwide Depression. The agricultural economy was hard hit. Lacking the revenues it generated, the government was unable to make its payrolls, including that of the military. A chain of further economic collapses and internal unrest followed. The Araujo government, the product of the country's first open elections, was felled by a military coup in 1931, nine months after it took office. External pressures and the U.S. threat to cut off assistance and diplomatic relations led to the "reinstatement of democracy" via the assumption of the presidency by the elected (and temporarily jailed) vice president, General Maximiliano Hernández Martínez. In January of 1931, within less than two months of assuming office, Hernández Martínez was faced with an armed peasant rebellion. He responded with repressive measures that left 20,000 peasants dead and their leader, Farabundo Martí, a martyr to the popular cause.

Hernández Martínez brooked no further political opposition, closing out all political parties except his own Pro Patria. Through the latter he was able to control elections and the National Assembly. By twice modifying the constitution to allow his own reelection, he remained in office until 1944. A national strike and U.S. pressures forced his resignation. Hernández did impose economic order and enjoyed some initial popularity for such measures as a debt moratorium, which extended to the country's masses, and a program of employment-generating public works. His exit and replacement by his vice president were followed by fifty years of governments dominated and usually headed by military leaders, some of them "elected" and some the results of military coups. Civilians sometimes participated in these governments, but the military's usual heavy handedness with popular agitation increasingly drove many into more radical opposition.

Political repression was not always accompanied by unenlightened social policies. The head of the 1948 "revolutionary" junta and later elected president, Colonel Oscar Osorio, maintained an interest in social development as embodied in the 1950 Constitution, the introduction of labor laws, the creation of a social security system, and the nation's participation in a variety of international organizations. The civil and military junta in power from 1979 to 1982 promulgated important agrarian, banking, and trade reform legislation that was enacted by the subsequent elected civilian regime. The junta ceded power to a civilian head in 1980 and called national elections for 1982. Although a civilian candidate won, the civilian opposition had already opted for armed struggle, thus beginning twelve years of civil war. After the deaths of some 75,000 countrymen and the flight of another million into exile, many of them poor and displaced rural workers, the signing of the Peace Accords ended the war in 1992. The members of the FMLN (Farabundo Martí National Liberation Front) guerrilla forces were reintegrated into a democratic process, participating as a united front in the national presidential elections of 1994. Each of the front's factions, however, fielded its own slates of candidates for the simultaneous congressional elections.

Their long exclusion from electoral politics left the ex-guerrillas at a decided disadvantage, especially since the majority conservative parties (PDC, ARENA, and PCN) had learned to live together in the interim. The three formalized this cooperation in the 1982 Pacto de Apaneca, which produced a common provisional president in that year and a new constitution in 1983. The national elections were won in 1984 by the PDC and in 1989 and 1994 by ARENA. The leftist electoral alliance, like that of the three conservative parties, eventually broke down, further enhancing the advantage of the now majority ARENA. The Peace Accords did incorporate a number of the Left's requests for reform, some of which were in turn included as amendments to the 1983 Constitution. A few of them, like the requirement of a two-thirds vote of the Assembly for such decisions as the selection of the Supreme Court, the newly created Judicial Council, the attorney general, the human rights ombudsman, and the Procurador General (the head of an office providing legal and social services to the poor) did allow more influence to opposition parties. Other legislation, like the winner-take-all elections of municipal councils, only served to cement ARENA's power.

The negotiation and signing of the Peace Accords and their subsequent implementation involved substantial participation by the United Nations and a variety of foreign governments (most notably, and traditionally, the United States). A land redistribution program for former military and guerrilla combatants and the formation of a new civilian police are two key areas where foreign pressures and financing have been decisive. Another key area is judicial reform, as discussed below. U.S. economic assistance[6] during and after the civil war allowed the government to initiate or extend social welfare programs, expand public employment, and begin to modernize and rationalize its own structure. In conjunction with the massive remittances from the one million exiles, it also permitted a high rate of economic growth, moderate inflation, and the stability of the local currency.[7]

Unfortunately, the economic benefits, if more widespread, are still unequally distributed. Unemployment and underemployment remain high. CEPAL[8] figures indicate 74 percent of the population lived in poverty and 56 percent in extreme poverty in 1990, an increase from 68 and 51 percent, respectively, in 1980. According to government estimates,[9] between 1988 and 1993 there was a slight decline in the proportion of the urban population living in poverty, from 55.2 to 50.4 percent, but those living in "extreme poverty" actually increased, from 23.3 to 29.6 percent. The already dense population makes land redistribution at best a partial remedy. Alternative sources of income for a people whose resources and skill levels suffered the additional setback of twelve years of civil war are not easily found. Although international pressures and assistance brought a record turn out in the 1994 national elections, public opinion polls indicate that the initial euphoria and optimism accompanying the end of the war is declining. This is also true of trust in democratic institutions, which was never very high. Organized and common crime are now widespread problems, fed by the literal armies of now unemployed ex-combatants, and even by the former death squads.[10]

The Institutional Framework and the Place of the Justice Sector

On the basis of its legislative and formal history, El Salvador looks far better off and more stable than it is. Its 1886 Constitution was replaced only in 1950. With some modifications, the 1950 Constitution remained in effect until 1983. The current constitution in large part resembles its predecessor. It has been criticized by the political Left, but it is characterized by a respectable number of legal guarantees, a dedication of the state to the furtherance of social welfare, and an apparently reasonable division of institutional powers. In addition to the changes noted above, amendments dating from

1991 and afterwards introduced such positive features as a Human Rights Ombudsman, an Electoral Tribunal with multiparty representation, the civilian police, staggered terms for the Supreme Court (ending the prior practice whereby each entering administration selected a new Court), the elimination of military jurisdiction over civilians, and the public prosecutors' supervision of the police investigation of crimes.[11] However, as the prior historical account suggests, the constitutional and other legal structure has for most of El Salvador's independent existence provided only a very rough guide to real institutional and political behavior. Where provisions were not voided by states of emergency, they were simply ignored. When neither voided nor ignored, they were manipulated to ends hardly apparent in their content. Elections were held, but their results were controlled, either through outright fraud or limitations on who could participate. When that did not work, a coup disposed of the objected victor. The National Assembly, which remained open for most of the period, was rarely more than a rubber stamp and source of patronage for whomever was in power. Political parties were formed for the purpose of advancing one candidacy and then disbanded. Those representing more radical views were eliminated or driven underground. While the military played politics, sometimes with civilian participation, the other real power holders, the economic elite, stayed behind the scenes to manage their own interests in relative peace.

If part of this situation has changed post-1991, many of the general outlines remain. In politics as in the economy, there has been some opening, but the newcomers are hardly the majority of the population, nor are they more than junior partners. The military has apparently withdrawn from an active role in politics. Its budget remains high, and many believe it to exercise significant power behind the scenes. Many of the most applauded additions to the new constitution have been only partially implemented, and some have been virtually ignored.[12] Aside from the universal truth that real power is harder to withdraw than its formal representation, there is a more contextual challenge. This is the lack of practical preparation and cultural base provided by the country's long history of irregular governments and more recent civil war. The newly empowered legislature is still grappling with its constitutional role. Only since 1994 has it begun to function as something more than a mouthpiece for the executive. Even when its official functions, internal rules, and composition encourage more activism, its members, many of them further disadvantaged by scanty educational preparation, have risen to the challenge with difficulty. It is not infrequent for them to admit that they approved legislation that they neither understood, nor even read.[13]

Moreover, old practices die hard, and both the 1984-89 Duarte government and that of his successor, Alfredo Cristiani, were plagued with rumors, many substantiated, of corruption. If noting else, this proved that newcomers to power learn some skills more quickly than others. Under the Calderón administration (1994-99), some of these cases have been investigated and suspects identified and arrested. It is also commonly argued that the few individuals singled out for this treatment are either scapegoats or victims of intraparty rivalries. One of the military governments' more questionable but least deniable accomplishments, the creation of a middle class dependent on public employment for its livelihood, has fed these tendencies and, with them, the continuing inclination to use public positions for political patronage and patronage positions to press partisan advantages. As noted, the expansion of public employment was continued by the post-1982 governments. However, many of the newcomers were uniquely unprepared to carry out their functions. All of this has complicated the further development of such basic institutions as political parties, the Electoral Tribunal, municipal governments, a modern public administration, and last, but hardly least, the courts and other elements of the justice sector.

As regards the justice sector, the situation offered a paradoxical advantage in the relatively narrow view of its functions held by political and other elites. Political elites have reluctantly given up control over judicial appointments. Once this was underway, they remained fairly unimaginative as to the additional opportunities for manipulation. In El Salvador, broader political and, especially, economic power never had much to do with the judiciary. Hence a variety of substantial and fairly radical changes have been proposed and adopted with remarkably little opposition. What opposition has occurred came largely from within the sector itself and from those individuals most directly affected by the proposals.[14] In many cases, the acquiescence of the broader political elite seems a consequence of simple inattention. Since formal institutional arrangements never meant much in the past, no one was accustomed to examining them very closely. If they did, they likely assumed that the proposed changes were not to be taken seriously. They sometimes were unpleasantly surprised. This was apparently the case of male legislators who found they had approved a law giving them financial responsibility for their children born out of wedlock and that a variety of interests intended to see it enforced.[15] However, in most instances, their tranquility remains unperturbed by the pattern of slow adoption and even slower implementation of the proposals. Thus, discounting the resistance from within the sector itself, the political leadership's general lack of concern allowed a small minority of would-be reformers to operate relatively unopposed.

Left to themselves, however, it is unlikely that this group would have made much progress. Most came from within the legal community and shared the sector's general weaknesses. The prior history of El Salvador's justice sector is less well documented than that of other political institutions. What is known replicates familiar regional patterns. The country never had many distinguished jurists and still fewer who found incentives to seek public employment.[16] As elsewhere, informal observers frequently comment on a golden period twenty or thirty years ago when judges were more professional and enjoyed greater prestige. This seems unlikely except on one count. A rather unfortunate reform from 1968, "democratizing" education, and a follow-on reform of several years later introducing automatic promotions (*promoción automática*) unquestionably lowered the quality of high school and university education.[17] The proliferation of private law schools, supported by their own legislation, continued the damage, guaranteeing that lawyers graduated after that date were much poorer prepared than their predecessors. Thus, although the institutions may have been no stronger in the past, their members, both professional and staff, were undoubtedly better educated and possibly more professional in their outlooks. They were undeniably better suited to a situation where they were not expected to do much except analyze the application of the law to the concrete cases before them. The judiciary is not the only subject of nostalgia. In the current climate of increasing crime, it is not unusual to hear a certain preference for the old police forces, who, despite their lack of concern for human rights and domination by the military, are portrayed as more "effective" than their civilian replacements.

This special handicap simply exacerbated a situation that was never conducive to high levels of professionalism or to attracting highly qualified professionals. Prior to the 1983 Constitution's introduction of permanent tenure for first and second-instance judges, both of these groups were appointed for very short periods (usually three years). As one observer notes,[18] while judges might be reappointed, they found their relations with and ability to please the Court the most important conditions for acquiring and keeping their positions. There were no formal criteria aside from the usual requirements of age and education. The Court had no system for keeping track of judicial performance, except for whatever complaints might be directed its way, usually by well-connected individuals soliciting their intervention. It is possible, as another observer claims,[19] that partisan as opposed to personal ties became more important after the midcentury. In any case, the extreme insecurity of tenure for these judges made "professional" behavior the least of their concerns. The selection of justices of the peace was still more overtly political. Appointed by the Court for three years and not required to have a law degree, they have in recent times been the product and vehicles of political patronage. When the Court naming them represented several political parties, the appointments were divided up proportionately.[20] The practice extended at least through 1993. In short, the general quality and public image of most of the Salvadoran judiciary made its members a still less likely and less credible source of reform proposals than their pre-1980 Peruvian counterparts. Even after the removal of some of the structural impediments, their lingering impact would continue to hinder reform efforts.

The Justice Sector on the Eve of Reform

By the 1980s, when its current reform can be considered to begin, El Salvador had in place, if only on paper, the basic institutions required to implement it. These included an ordinary court system, divided into three instances and the additional body of justices of the peace; a Public Ministry composed of a prosecutors office (Fiscalía General) and an office of social and legal welfare for the poor (Procuraduría General) that after 1986 incorporated legal defense; a prison system supervised by the Ministry of Justice, which also ran the national registries and was the official executive liaison with the courts; and the police in their investigative capacity. The two principal forces, the Policía Nacional and Guardía Nacional, were under the supervision of the Ministry of Defense (military). A smaller fiscal police (Policía de Hacienda) reported to the Ministry of Finance. The 1983 Constitution introduced a National Judicial Council to run the Judicial School and preselect candidates to the judiciary for subsequent appointment by the Assembly (Supreme Court) and the Court (lower level judges[21]). The council, however, was not installed until 1989. It also remained under the effective control of the Supreme Court[22] until further changes were made in the legislation setting its composition. The basic procedural and substantive codes, while targeted for revision, were not unusually backward for the region. Oral and occasionally jury trials[23] were officially in effect, the prosecutor was to assist the *juez de instrucción* in his investigations and argue the criminal case in court, and the right to defense was supposedly guaranteed through a system of bench-appointed lawyers (*defensores de oficio*) and after the mid-1980s, by the new Public Defense Office.

Reality, not unexpectedly, was different. Most sector professionals, including even judges in the mid-1980s,[24] worked only part time. Their salaries rarely justified a full-time job. This is still true of the Procuraduría General's staff, the worst paid in the sector. Judges at all levels succumbed to the usual range of traditional vices, from delegating responsibilities to their staff, to receiving and requesting bribes, when their staff did not usurp the prerogative. They also added some of their own. These included the practice on the part of first-instance judges and justices of the peace of retaining valuable physical evidence—largely vehicles and weapons—for their own use or that of their friends.[25] Just as in Peru, the provisions on pretrial detention were given the most extreme interpretation, with the predictable effect on the composition of the prison population. Unsentenced prisoners represented up to 90 percent of the total. On the other hand, if the suspect had a lawyer who knew whom to pay (a *sacador*[26]), he might avoid pretrial detention and could expect his case to be forgotten. Oral bench trials were simply nonexistent. Jury trials usually involved the prosecution and defense reading the *expediente*[27] (if they were lucky, only parts of it) to the jury that then made its decision, by majority vote, almost immediately. Unlike the rest of the procedures, jury trials, except those involving paid counsel, were conducted with lightning speed. The usual goal was to select a jury, hold the hearing, and have a verdict within twenty-four hours, a practice generally conceded not to produce optimal results.

While case loads were not unduly onerous[28] for judges, defenders or prosecutors, lengthy delays were frequent, especially during the *instrucción*. A 1993 study[29] indicates that 50 percent of criminal cases and 68 percent of civil were over two years old. Figures for those over four years old were 36 and 50 percent respectively. Salvadoran prosecutors were less numerous and less active than the Peruvian *fiscales* despite the earlier creation of a separate Public Ministry.[30] Court appointed defenders were and remain notorious for requiring payment for their "free" services, a practice less widespread but not unknown in the new Public Defenders Office. Until a 1992 modification to the Criminal Procedures Code made nonprovision of defense a reason for dropping charges, they were rarely called by the police or judge, and frequently never saw their client until the trial. Appeals of judgments were rare, except in cases handled by private, paid counsel and, thus, neither the appellate nor the Supreme Court received many filings. This did not prevent long delays in dealing with those that were submitted.[31] A habeas corpus might take a year to process! Finally, since the confession was still regarded as the "queen of evidence," the traditional police forces had no compunctions about beating it out of suspects. For this reason they also avoided the code's instructions to present the suspect to the judge within seventy-two hours. It bears noting that such practices seem to have been largely eliminated with the creation of the civilian police and the presence of national and international groups devoted to monitoring abuses.

The Salvadoran legislation had its own unusual quirks, which to the wary might have signaled problems. Its Criminal Code included a number of "presumptions of guilt," situations from which guilt could be inferred absent direct evidence. Thus, possession of stolen property was proof of theft. It also allowed detention on the basis of suspicious character or dubious actions, the "dangerous state" or *estado peligroso*. Preventive detention was virtually mandatory for suspects facing potential sentences of only three years. As discussed, the absence of judicial tenure prior to 1983 and the irregular situation of the justices of the peace were also good indications of what lay behind the institutional facade. Finally, the Court and its president exercised an usual amount of power, even for the region. The post-1983 reforms actually aggravated this situation. Following the 1991 amendments, the Court manages the six percent of the national budget now reserved for the judiciary, a regional record.[32] It continues to select all lower level judges and also admits and disbars lawyers. Its Constitutional Chamber, created in 1983, exercises powers of judicial review and is headed by the president of the Court, who is himself designated by the Assembly. Although until 1994, the Assembly elected the entire Court by majority vote with each change of national administration, the Court once seated could operate relatively independently or, more often, arbitrarily. The Court's power did not translate into effective control and supervision of the lower levels of the judicial hierarchy. It could intervene when problems were called to its attention, but lacked the ability and apparently the interest to monitor what its judges were doing on a day-to-day basis.[33]

The Reform Program

If, for the most part, not in the public sector, there were Salvadorans with an interest in changing this situation. Their presence and contact with European and Latin American reform movements account for the fact that, however poorly implemented, the country's legislation had more or less kept up with regional trends. Even before 1983, it thus reflected some of the latter's emphasis on procedural modernization, due process guarantees, and enhanced judicial independence and professionalization. Members of this group, largely lawyers in private practice and law professors, were instrumental in the drafting of the 1983 Constitution and, especially, of the parts altering the sector's structure. They contributed many of the more specific ideas on sector reform included in the Peace Accords and subsequent constitutional amendments. In this they drew on their own and others work in CORELESAL (Revisory Commission for Salvadoran Legislation). This governmental creation, financed with foreign assistance funds, conducted studies of the sector and began to prepare draft legislation in the mid-1980s. The CORELESAL staff was aided by a number of foreign advisors who supplied more specific ideas on reform measures. Their work included empirical analyses of the state of sector operations. These were never as critical, or as ideologically oriented, as the studies growing out of Peru's New Law movement. They also were less widely circulated, remaining for the most part as unpublished internal reports.

The draft legislation and other proposals were the work of a small group of concerned jurists, only a few of whom were actively engaged in politics. They might have met the fate of Peru's reform programs had it not been for another element. This was the continued presence of foreign pressure and support—first the U.S. government with its Administration of Justice projects[34] beginning in 1984, then the United Nations during the Peace Accords negotiations, and eventually its Mission in Salvador (ONUSAL) after 1991.

How these external actors came to focus on justice sector reform as a key element of their programs in El Salvador is a subject worthy of far more than the few comments offered here.[35] The important point is that they did and that their initial emphasis was on eliminating human rights abuses and impunity, especially as it related to abuses of power by the military and paramilitary groups. None of these external institutions had any experience in promoting this kind of reform. They were, thus, amenable to adopting the proposals of the local reform advocates. However, their involvement, increasing reliance on foreign experts, and focus on government institutions represented a pyrrhic victory for the local reformers. This group was gradually sidelined from the more detailed development of programs, where the expertise was provided by outsiders and the negotiation of terms occupied the foreign donors and government actors. This development did not dilute the reform goals, which retained much of their initial focus on human rights, due process and depoliticization. It did, however, eliminate the only individuals with sufficient knowledge of the target institutions to detect emerging problems as reform proposals, including many of their own, clashed with local reality. Those who did not withdraw entirely retained less than effective participation. They became junior partners in the reform design teams, or external critics, concerned less with the mundane details of implementation than with the programs' doctrinal purity.[36]

Both the U.N., and through it a number of other governments, and the U.S. provided financial support for the reform package and monitored its progress. The U.S. made the meeting of certain reform benchmarks a condition of broader assistance funding. The U.N. did not impose conditionality, but through its periodic progress reports to the broader international community, may have exercised still more leverage. Pressure also came from a number of domestic and international human rights organizations, which like the U.N. were an important source of information for potential donors. Conceivably, El Salvador's sector reform may be the most closely monitored in the world, but it owes its advances to this continuing external attention combined with the external resources, both financial and technical, to carry it forward. In effect, the Salvadoran government's principal responsibility was to pass legislation, and occasionally to create new institutions. Even in the latter case, their further development was most often in the hands of external assistance programs. Only in the area of human rights violations by police or military was the government held to more concrete benchmarks. In other areas, substantive progress was more difficult to measure, improved justice being a fairly debatable and highly subjective quality.

The reform program had two major components: the creation of a new civilian police force and the restructuring and reorientation of the rest of the sector. The creation of the police force was an expensive, but arguably more straightforward exercise. It essentially threw out what went before and started anew. Most of its design and implementation was also left to foreign donors, and, in particular, the U.S. government and the United Nations. A complicated formula allowed the inclusion of ex-combatants and some members of the prior forces, but only after they had passed through a training program in the newly created and donor-financed police academy. After an initial period of optimism, doubts have begun to emerge on such critical themes as the ability and willingness of the Salvadoran government to assume full financial support, the ability of the force to retain its civilian orientation, especially in a period of rapidly rising crime, and its overall efficacy.[37] Still, the undeniable accomplishment is that the old police forces were eliminated and a new single civilian force substituted in relatively record time.

It is in the second component that the challenges have been most difficult and the progress most problematic. Nonetheless, a series of fairly dramatic changes were introduced in relatively little time. The Judicial Council, first formed in 1989, was reorganized in 1993 to reflect the independence stipulated by the Peace Accords and the 1991 constitutional amendments. While it has benefitted from little financial or technical assistance, except for U.S. support of its judicial school, and had problems attracting qualified members, it has slowly begun to assume its new responsibilities: the selection of candidates to the judiciary, and the evaluation of the seated bench. The Human Rights Ombudsman, also the recipient of limited amounts of foreign funding, has begun to assume the monitoring process formerly exercised by ONUSAL. The government amended the constitution to include new procedures for the selection of the Supreme Court and the rest of the judiciary. By 1994 it had put them all into effect. The Court entering in 1994 is the last selected in its entirety, and the first elected by the two-thirds vote of a multipartisan Assembly. This did not produce the sought after nonpartisan Court. It did allow the inclusion of justices identified with the opposition. The government has approved and passed into effect two new substantive and procedural codes, one governing family and the other juvenile cases. The final drafts of a new criminal, criminal procedures, and sentencing code remained stuck in the Assembly until early 1997. They were finally approved with minor modifications and scheduled to go into effect in a year's time.

Passage of these three codes had been defined by many as the core of the reform package. Fortunately, there was already considerable room for improvement under existing legislation, including that approved since 1991. The judiciary, with the benefit of its six percent budgetary earmark, began its own internal modernization program, automating its offices, redesigning its internal systems of governance, and supporting the creation of new family and juvenile courts. In part in response to external criticisms and possibly to wrest some power from the Judicial Council, the Court elected in 1994 initiated an evaluation of seated judges with the end of rooting out the incompetent and corrupt.[38] The government increased, if not adequately, the budgets of the public prosecutors and public defenders. Further preparation of these officials for their enhanced functions lay largely in the hands of foreign assistance programs and particularly the USAID judicial reform projects. Their respective institutions were cooperating with the drafting of new organizational (organic) laws to ease the process. Still, both entities remain very weak, inadequate to the performance of their current responsibilities let alone those proposed under new legislation. This is partly a function of inadequate staffing and operational budgets, but it is also a result of inappropriate organizations and operating procedures. There is also some question as to the government's real interest in strengthening either of them, and especially in giving a more independent role to the Fiscalía.[39]

The government and the sector have shown an interest in continuing the reform programs, especially with external financing. They began negotiating with the Inter-American Development Bank (IDB), World Bank, United Nations Development Program (UNDP), and a series of foreign governments to create new grant and loan-funded projects. In the second half of 1996, a twenty-three million dollar loan program with the IDB was initiated. Much of this will be used for new infrastructure and equipment, but a part will continue the organizational reforms begun by the USAID projects. Meanwhile foreign assistance agencies also offered financing to the numerous human rights and other nongovernmental organizations (NGOs) that had expressed an interest in the program and a concern that it was not going far enough or in the right directions.

In this flurry of activity, the government and the sector have thus not been entirely passive participants. However, those of their members who have come to support these measures often seem longer on opportunism than conviction. The new Family Code and Juvenile Offenders Law became President Cristiani's (and ARENA's) "gift to the nation's children" on the eve of the 1994 presidential elections. Support for the due process criminal legislation has been a way for a few Arenista justices to cross party lines and garner the political Left's support with an eye to the upcoming election of a new court president. The Left, meanwhile, found itself in a quandary vis-a-vis the conservative parties' support of legislation it might have preferred to introduce. This inter and intraparty jockeying for position accounts for some of the delays in the passage of the criminal justice package, with the Left trying to salvage something out of what appears to be an ARENA victory.[40] More recently, problems also emerged with the realization that the Christian Democrats had taken over the Judicial Council and filled its staff with party loyalists. No one is sure what this means, but ARENA, which had ignored the council in favor of a more traditional focus on the Court, obviously did not like the implications. Finally there is the Court's budgetary earmark, obviously in excess of its needs, but something it is unlikely to sacrifice, even faced with the relative poverty and resulting weak performance of the Fiscalía and Procuraduría.[41] The past Court president had offered to make a one-time gift of part of this largesse to both institutions until the government found a way to increase their budget. The current Court has identified other uses for the excess and is equally determined not to relinquish it. The earmark, combined with its new autonomy and the powers it retains over the rest of the bench and bar, make it potentially one of the most powerful Courts in the region. It, thus, is no surprise that its prior president was contemplating an advance to national office, although in the end he was unable to guarantee even his own reelection.

In short, whatever its effect on the quality of justice, the reform has altered the face of institutional politics both within and outside the sector. This apparently was not anticipated by any of the participants, explaining why some of them have been so slow to react. Because the process has generated more winners than losers and remains subject to external monitoring and pressure, efforts to undo the changes are unlikely. However, further progress will increasingly depend on national political elites, some of them holding sectoral office, as opposed to external supporters. Whether the apparent enthusiasm for new political and financial resources can be translated into one for making the new system work is still another question. Its answer remains far from certain. If that is to happen, it may well hinge on increased involvement by the two missing elements, a wider variety of members of the affected institutions and of the public, including nonpolitical elites and the authors of the initial reform proposals.

Costa Rica: Reform from Within

The Costa Rican experience can be seen as the judiciary's ideal reform, one it produces with the compliance of but little intervention by political elites, and with external support that follows the judiciary's lead rather than imposing its own conditions. It is also, from the reformer's standpoint, a model in that change has been incremental, studied, and effectively implanted. Whether or not one agrees with the ends sought, it is also apparent that the method is unlikely to be duplicated by many other countries. It has required, on the one hand, a judiciary that is sufficiently enlightened and independent to attempt such a move and, on the other, levels of political consensus and stability that few of the region's countries can match. The only nations that might duplicate these conditions are present-day Uruguay and Chile, and during some periods of its modern history, Colombia. Consensus and stability are relative, of course. Currently, Costa Rica shows signs of losing some of these qualities, threatening to fall into the same kind of institutional decay that has plagued much of the region for decades. While they lasted, and particularly from the 1950s on, they allowed the judiciary to take charge of its internal development, and whether intentionally or not, to alter its political role.

Background[42]

Costa Rica's self-image as the "Switzerland of Latin America" is generally regarded as an exaggeration. The country is unusual in its low levels of internal unrest, high levels of political participation, and an apparent cultural preference for settling conflicts by compromise. Costa Rica experienced a typically turbulent early independence period. It had ten constitutions prior to 1871,[43] passed in and out of the Central American Federation, and experienced a moderate share of irregular governments. It subsequently settled into a pattern of constitutional regimes, and after 1902, suffered only two lapses, the brief Tinoco government (1917-1919) and the events surrounding the 1948 civil war. In avoiding the more serious conflicts characterizing its neighbors, Costa Rica drew on some unlikely advantages. It was underpopulated, isolated, and its inhabitants were so dispersed that an early constitution experimented with rotating the seat of government among the four major population centers.[44] It also entered early into the coffee trade, and owing to the availability of land and shortage of labor and capital, into a pattern of small and medium sized agrarian holdings. There was a coffee elite who controlled larger holdings, processing, and export, but the benefits of the coffee economy continued to be more widely distributed than in the rest of Central America.[45] Costa Rica's economic leaders never enjoyed the immense fortunes and influence of their neighboring counterparts. These developmental patterns have been credited with unifying the nation's socioeconomic foundations, discouraging polarizing class conflicts, and allowing the gradual incorporation of a greater variety of political participants.[46]

During its early independent history, Costa Rica avoided the intense conflict between conservative and liberal factions of the elite characteristic of the region. Its relative underdevelopment during the colonial period left little attachment to traditional institutions and facilitated the transition to a more liberal economic and political system. Communal land holdings and ecclesiastical privileges were eliminated early. By the end of the century, even militarism was in disfavor, as the upper and middle classes came to perceive its conflict with their interests.[47] The 1871 Constitution, embodying principles of individualism, laissez-faire economics, and a strong but non-interventionist civil state, remained in effect for over three-quarters of a century. This did not prevent the reemergence of unconstitutional, authoritarian regimes, one of which produced the constitution, but they tended to be brief and did not reverse such positive trends as the expansion of the national education system.

The liberal state was not spared its bouts of violence and repression. It was also not immune to internal criticism for its failure to take a more activist role in addressing the needs of the poor and protecting national sovereignty. The effects of the Depression exacerbated the problems and invigorated the critics. This gave rise, on the one hand, to the creation of the Communist Party in 1931 and its expanding influence on the emerging labor movement and, on the other, to calls for more interventionist economic policies to stimulate growth and employment and to control foreign investment. Backed by an unlikely alliance of members of the traditional elite, Communists, and the Church, the Calderón government (1940-44) began to act on some of these criticisms, introducing a broad range of social reforms. In 1942, it seized the sugar and coffee holdings of families of Italian and German descent, a move widely interpreted as an attack on private property. Upper class opponents of these programs were joined by middle class groups calling for electoral reform, control of fiscal corruption, and an end to general mismanagement. Although the opposition could not prevent the victory of the calderonista candidate in the 1944 elections, his inability to deal with any of these problems, or with the economic aftermath of the Depression increased their discontent. The calderonista controlled Legislative Assembly's invalidation of the 1948 presidential elections was the final straw, producing the outbreak of civil war twelve days later. The brief (two-month) war ended with a pact between the two contending factions. It gave control of the government for eighteen months to a junta presided by the opposition leader, José Figueres. Afterwards, it was turned over to Ricardo Ulate, the winner of the nullified elections.

During the eighteen months, Figures and his junta ruled by decree and introduced several important changes, nationalizing the banks, eliminating the army, and drafting a new constitution. The Assembly refused to approve the draft and, after Figures' departure from government, substituted its own version. Modeled on the Constitution of 1871, it included at least a part of the philosophy promoted by Figueres' National Liberation Party. Although the judiciary was neither a party to nor a particular target of the larger conflict, the constitution represents a major shift in its internal workings and larger political role, and the beginning of its assumption of responsibility for its own self-reform.

The Constitution of 1949

The prelude to the constitution was not a positive one for the judiciary. Arguing that its restructuring was essential, the junta issued Decree Law No. 8 of 1948, dismissing all judges and judicial employees for presumed acts of commission or omission in support of the prior regime. They were replaced temporarily with the Tribunals of Immediate Sanctions (*Tribunales de Sanciones Inmediatos*) and of Administrative Probity (*Probidad Administrativa*) introduced to root out and take actions against other collaborators. Still, the judiciary's eclipse was short-lived. Once the new constitution went into effect, the temporary tribunals disappeared and normal institutions were reinstated.

It is generally accepted that the judiciary was the branch of government most strengthened by the 1949 Constitution. Apparently, this was less out of a concern for its independence than an effort by each of the conflicting factions to keep it out of the hands of the other. A first important change was the extension of tenure for justices from four to eight years and their automatic renewal in their positions absent a two-thirds negative vote of the Assembly. This was intended to place the Court outside direct partisan control. Other changes included the transfer of management of the courts' administrative systems to offices of the Supreme Court, the definitive decision that only the Court (and not the legislature) would rule on the constitutionality of laws,[48] and the establishment of the contentious-administrative jurisdiction within the ordinary court system to decide on the legality of administrative acts. The Court was also given responsibility for selecting the members of the Electoral Tribunal. Finally, the judiciary was guaranteed that it would be consulted on any proposed legislation affecting it. If it registered an objection, this could only by overridden by a two-thirds vote of the Assembly. The final step in the process did not occur until 1957 when the constitution was amended to give the judiciary six percent of the national budget. Following its passage, the Court immediately began a construction program to rebuild its facilities and raised the salaries of all employees. Interestingly, its program did not include a dramatic increase in the number of its dependencies, and over the next two decades, the proportion of tribunals to population actually declined.[49]

For over a decade the Court's attention seemed directed to recuperating from the events of the late 1940s and using its new resources to resolve problems caused by its prior relative poverty. During this period, several new legal codes were introduced. They had little affect on judicial operations, and were limited for the most part to aspects of the civil code, including the Public Health Code (1949), the Electoral Code (1951), the Mining Code (1953), and the Commercial Code (1964). However, from the late 1960s and extending into the 1970s, the judiciary began to initiate more substantial changes. Starting in 1967 and ending with the establishment of an office under the Court's control, a system of public defense was created. This made good on the constitutional guarantee (repeated in the Judiciary's Organic Law and the 1971 Criminal Code) to a free defense for the accused in criminal cases. In 1973, the public prosecutors, formerly part of the

Ministry of Justice's Procuraduría, were transferred to a new body, the Public Ministry, also incorporated into the judiciary. A protest from the Procuraduría let it retain responsibility for prosecution of crimes against the state. In fact it has tended to delegate most of these to the judiciary's *fiscales*. In December of the same year, a judicial investigative police, the Organismo de Investigación Judicial (OIJ) was created, separating the administrative from the investigative forces. This encountered some opposition from the executive and the Court, which found the initial draft law unconstitutional. It subsequently approved a revised version.[50] The judiciary's internal development was accompanied by the drafting of new procedural and substantive legislation, most notably the Criminal Code (1971), the Criminal Procedures Code (1973), and the Family Code (1978). Here the Court joined with concerned members of the legal community, and drew on foreign experts to guarantee that the products reflected the most progressive trends in the region.[51]

Consolidation of the Post-1949 Programs

By the time this stage ended, the Costa Rican justice system had taken on a radically new shape, with much of it under the direct control of the judiciary. The latter included the ordinary court system, divided into a seventeen-member Supreme Court, seventeen Superior Courts (with both appellate functions and original jurisdiction in major criminal trials), eighty-four first-instance courts (*juzgados*), and over one hundred *alcaldías* (the equivalent of the justices of the peace).[52] It also encompassed the Public Ministry, Public Defenders Office, and Judicial Police, organizations that throughout the rest of the region are usually autonomous or under the control of other governmental bodies. The inclusion of the public prosecutors and defenders within the judiciary was also important in allowing movement of professionals among the three institutions. The arrangement has been criticized for creating occasional conflicts of interest. However, by permitting an informal joint judicial career, it arguably attracted more qualified candidates and gave them a better understanding of their individual and mutual roles in the criminal justice process. It also discouraged the common practice of paying defenders or prosecutors far less than judges. Salaries for all remained high compared to the regional average. Discounting the nonsalary benefits (representation allowances, cars and drivers, etc) accruing to the justices, the differences among the various levels was also less marked than elsewhere.

While receiving less notice, the judicial administrative offices were also expanded and reorganized. Additions include the 1981 creation of a separate Direction of Administration to centralize and rationalize the administrative systems, the creation of a Judicial Inspection Office in 1982, and of the Judicial School in the same year. Costa Rica was one of the first countries in the region to develop a school and, to this day, has one of the best entry-level and in-service training programs. These three institutions remained under the direct control of the Court, and in effect of its president. Policy decisions affecting their operations usually required the vote of the Court en banc.

This pattern of development put the country at the forefront of Latin American judicial reforms, especially in the criminal justice areas, but also in others. Because of the maintenance of the judges' investigatory role, Costa Rica still had a mixed accusatory and inquisitorial system, but it was one of the first countries to make this transition, and arguably the first to implement it so completely. Even under the mixed system, Costa Rica's *fiscales* have taken an increasingly active role in the investigation and prosecution of crimes. Its public defenders are so known for their efficacy that individuals able to afford their own counsel sometimes prefer them.[53] Until 1994, defense services were provided free regardless of the clients' economic situation.[54] Costa Rica's family code and its agrarian courts have become models for other countries. The principles informing both might strike the U.S. observer as unduly paternalistic or simply uneconomic,[55] but they are viewed by many Latin American jurists as very progressive and highly compatible with local culture. More importantly, they tend to shape real practices and decisions, contrary to the usual rule in the region.

Needless to say, the judiciary's financial autonomy and generous budget are the envy of other courts, which have used its example to argue for their own earmarks. It should be noted that Costa Rica had some other advantages not common in the region. First, was the high quality of legal education in the country; this had been aided by its inclusion in the U.S. sponsored Law and Development program during the 1970s. Student protests and accusations of CIA involvement eventually forced its termination, but it left the National University with very strong graduate and postgraduate programs. A second influence was the presence of the Inter-American Court of Human Rights in San Jose. Its members focused attention on human rights and due process issues among the local legal community. The 1974 establishment of the United Nations Latin American Institute for Crime Prevention and Treatment of the Delinquent (ILANUD) in San Jose was also important. The institute remained underfinanced until the U.S. government decided, in 1984, to use it as a channel for its Regional Administration of Justice Project.[56] However, even in the first years, its presence brought visits by a series of foreign jurists who strengthened interest in human rights, due process, and code modernization.

If the target of fewer complaints than judiciaries elsewhere, Costa Rica's justice system was not immune from them. Corruption, incompetence, and malfeasance in office were apparently at a minimum. However, the country's increasing use as a transhipment point for drug trafficking produced some scandals that touched even the Supreme Court.[57] More common were complaints about slow, costly, and overly formal justice. Although the 1949 Constitution made clear the Court's powers of judicial review, there was concern that it did not use these adequately and that, in their application, justices often succumbed to political pressures.[58] There were also complaints both from within and outside the system about the judiciary's increasing bureaucratization and its oligarchic outlook.[59] Observers claimed that the Supreme Court's management of the entire judicial system, especially the appointment process, had created an almost closed caste that was less and less attentive to outside opinions and values, whether of the elite or the popular masses. Even the judicial budget came under criticism for what some considered the inordinate amount spent on special allowances and privileges for the justices.[60]

Concerns were also directed at the criminal justice system, in particular, its slowness and the low, but still significant percentage unsentenced detainees represented in the total prison population. During the 1980s, rising rates of common crime also brought some criticisms of the prison system itself, as overly lenient. This responded to developments in the 1970s, whereby the Ministry of Justice had adopted its own reform, introducing prison farms and other low security facilities, and generally trying to humanize its operations. Criticisms of the police forces were usually limited to the administrative police. The confusing number of separate forces (at one point as many as seventeen!) remained a source of political patronage and, thus, subject to a turnover in personnel with every change of government. One predictable consequence was the sudden upsurge in police activity just before national elections, as members struggled to amass as many bribes as possible before they lost their jobs. Unlike the OIJ, which was the occasional target of complaints about human rights abuses, the administrative bodies merely remained an atypical and remarkable island of petty corruption, nonprofessionalism, and general inefficiency.

There were also criticisms from within the system. The lack of a tenured judicial career, and the Court's consequent ability to place and remove judges and other professionals almost at will, was a key issue. While abuse was not frequent, lower level judges, prosecutors, and defenders were well aware that crossing a member of the Court could result in a nonappealable dismissal when they came up for the reelection[61] that was required every four years. The selection of the Court itself was also criticized; the two dominant parties (National Liberation and Social Christian Unity) had reached an informal agreement to alternate appointments. This did not often produce poor candidates, but there were occasional exceptions. Moreover, it was alleged that the political loyalties of the justices entered into their appointment and reelection decisions vis-a-vis the rest of the judiciary, and to their occasional pressures on the rulings of lower level judges. The critics admitted that the pressures were not frequent and that judges were able to carry out most of their work without higher level interference. Specific problems most often occurred when a judge who had repeatedly ignored higher level "suggestions" sought advancement in the system, or in the very occasional case of outright defiance.[62] Internal critics also complained about over centralization, favoritism, and, on a more intellectual level, the failure to adopt still more progressive legal codes.

The Second Stage of Judicial Reform

Whether the changes from the 1980s on constitute a new stage or simply a continuation of the first is debatable; whether they should be termed reform or just directed development, is as well. In any case, following the first period of growth and consolidation, Costa Rica's judiciary began a new round of changes. Here, three objectives figured prominently: continued modernization of the basic legal codes; restructuring of judicial governance and internal organization and, most recently, its enhancement with modern communications and computer technology; and further development of the constitutional jurisdiction or judicial review. In the first area, the transformations continued to be driven by regional trends and, thus, featured the adoption of legislation patterned on that developed elsewhere. In the latter two, they have been marked by more innovation. Even where the inspiration for change had external origins, the reforms have involved a greater adaptation to local conditions. The entire reform process has continued to be driven by the judiciary itself in collaboration with members of the local legal community. It has drawn on some external assistance, both technical and financial. Especially in recent years it has also tried to attract broader public support, undoubtedly spurred by the criticisms of its bureaucratization and oligarchic isolation. Although many of these changes were too specific to the sector to draw the interest of political elites, those involving the constitutional jurisdiction had important political implications. That the judiciary was able to advance them without broader opposition was in part a result of the elite's distraction by such pressing themes as the economic crisis of the early 1980s and the political upheavals of its subregional neighbors.[63]

The passage from the first to second stage of reform began with the promulgation of a new Civil Procedures Code in 1990. Imitating the model Latin American code and, thus, attempting to introduce more oral procedures, it was not a great success. Its impact is generally regarded as minimal.[64] Apparently learning from this failure, the next effort, a revision of the Criminal and Criminal Procedures codes was organized differently. The reformers were clear from the start that they wanted to introduce more accusatory processes, with a more active role for prosecution and defense; insert more contemporary approaches to criminality and especially modern crimes; and include such innovations as alternative sentencing and alternative dispute resolution. However, the experience with the Civil Procedures Code and observation of events in neighboring countries[65] created an awareness that the obstacles lay not in the grand themes, but rather in the details of design and implementation. Thus, drafting of the new codes was envisioned as a more participatory, iterative process. An initial draft would be passed to a series of internal commissions that themselves would undertake broader consultations inside and outside the institution. The process has been lengthy and, in the end, the consultations had to be truncated in the face of impending national elections. However, by early 1996, a new Criminal Procedures Code, revised sections of the Criminal Code, and accompanying secondary legislation were finally approved. Very wisely, the procedural code was allowed an eighteen-month transition period, during which some further consultation, extensive training, and the preparation of the basic institutions would be effected. There are still minority opinions that find the mandated changes either too radical or not radical enough. A debate over the new role for the Public Ministry was one of the factors leading to the resignation of its long time head.[66]

In addressing questions of its internal organization and governance, the judiciary relied on a similar methodology, this time with more orchestration by the Court president. The objectives here were also evident from the start. They included the creation of a real judicial career and the elimination of the reelection system, the development of a more practical system for judicial oversight both of the career and the administrative systems, further reorganization and rationalization of administrative offices, and the restructuring of the court system to effect a more rational workload. The results of the entire process were embodied in a new Judicial Organic Law (*Ley Orgánica del Poder Judicial*) that was approved in May, 1993, and went into effect in early 1994. One of the first steps was the creation of an internal council (*Consejo Superior del Poder Judicial*) to oversee the judicial career, including appointments of all personnel not specifically reserved to other bodies, and the general administration of the system. The council replaced the former system, in which the Supreme Court as a whole spent several days a week studying administrative and personnel decisions or delegated some matters to commissions composed of its members. Both arrangements, which are common to most Latin American Courts, were extremely time consuming and not regarded as very effective.

The council is a representative body, composed of three delegates from the various levels of the judiciary, one from the administrative employees, and one from the practicing bar. However, it is presided by the Court president, and it was widely held that he had manipulated the selection of its other members to ensure receptivity to his ideas. Given his management style, this was not unlikely, but it has produced few more specific complaints about subsequent operations. The one exception is the handling of the transition to a career system, especially as it involves existing judicial personnel. This was managed by a second new body, the Concejo de la Judicatura, created by a May, 1993, amendment to the law (No. 5155 of January 10, 1973) governing judicial service. As this council was named by the Court, there were similar suspicions as to the selection of its members. However, the principal problem was not external control, but rather the challenge of establishing objective standards. Candidates have complained that many of the selection criteria are unduly arbitrary, intrusive, or irrelevant. Examples include the use of psychological tests, medical standards that had little to do with judicial functions, and interviews with family members. The criticisms may stem from an exaggerated fear of the new system, but they are also indicative of a more general problem of translating abstract principles into concrete operations. Even the tests of legal knowledge that seem more relevant have been criticized as overemphasizing an ability to memorize laws and doctrine, as opposed to their appropriate application. After decades of proclaiming the superiority of merit-based appointments, Costa Rica is now finding, as others will as well, that they are not exactly sure how to define or identify merit. In the process they may be designing answers that are more complicated than necessary.

The additional changes in administrative offices and the distribution of judicial functions have been accomplished more gradually and with fewer setbacks. In the latter area the most important change are the addition of a new level of appellate courts that will also see *casación* for cases not reserved for the Supreme Court and the expansion of the corps of substitute functionaries (*actuarios* and *alcaldes supernumerarios*). This group had been created in 1969, but their limited number had encouraged a practice whereby positions were frequently filled "temporarily" by individuals whose real appointments were at a lower level. The practice had clear monetary advantages for the temporary employees, who received the higher salary. It was criticized by other members of the judiciary as an unnecessarily informal solution and one that encouraged patronage and favoritism.

As for the more strictly administrative reforms, there has been more reliance on external donors for funding and technical assistance. A small USAID project, which had earlier financed the expansion of the Judicial School, worked with the Court to develop pilot programs in court administration, decentralization, and automation. These became part of the Court's development program, the expansion of which was to be financed by a loan from the Inter-American Development Bank. Both the IDB and the USAID projects also promoted experiments in alternative dispute resolution, supported by the judiciary as a way of decongesting its own offices.

In connection with all these changes the Court, while acting on its own, has attempted to draw in a wider public, at least as an audience to their efforts. This has meant the opening and improvement of offices for attention to the public, and a series of public information campaigns. Automation has been important here as a means of providing information rapidly to parties concerned about individual cases. It has also been criticized as a sign that the judiciary is relying on computers to avoid resolving more fundamental problems. The Court has also developed more innovative, and less technologically enhanced means of reaching the public and further involving its own employees. Beginning in 1993, it initiated a program of annual regional and national consultations on administration of justice, opening them to the participation of anyone interested in the theme. While not many "outsiders" attended, the consultations did attract more attention to the judiciary's modernization program and also involved its entire membership in the formal validation of the development plan. Skeptics noted, as was apparent to any observer, that the validation involved a good deal of central orchestration, but it is still more than any other of the region's judiciaries has done to garner support with its own members.

In these first two areas, the judiciary was exercising its constitutional powers to effect its own internal reordering. Changes involving major restructurings, the new career and governance systems, procedural rules, or the acceptance of external assistance did require executive and legislative concurrence. This was never automatic, but it did not elicit much resistance or major modifications to the judiciary's proposals. Clearly had there been broader conflicts among the branches of government or the parties controlling them, the situation might have been different. Instead, relations were so tranquil that the legislature proved amenable to letting the judiciary carry over its unspent budgetary obligations into subsequent years.[67] One might have predicted more confrontational relations in the third area of reform, the proposed introduction of a radically new means for the Court's exercise of its judicial review function. Here the initial idea came from a group of constitutional lawyers, headed by the then Minister of Justice, Carlos José Gutiérrez. It responded to a concern, largely limited to this group, that the judiciary's exercise of these powers had been relatively weak. Influenced by long-standing debates among the international community of constitutionalists, the group identified the source of the problem as essentially structural, originating in the vesting of these powers with the Supreme Court as a whole. Their preference was for the establishment of a separate Constitutional Court or at least a Constitutional Chamber that would devote itself exclusively to protecting constitutionally guaranteed rights and deciding on the constitutionality of legislation. In this they opted for the European tradition of centralized protections as opposed to the American decentralized system. Prior to this Costa Rica had a mixed system, in which the Court decided on constitutionality and heard habeas corpus cases, whereas *amparos* (protections of other rights) could be seen by any judge. All judges were forbidden from applying unconstitutional legislation, but when questions arose, had to refer them to the Supreme Court.

With Gutiérrez's backing, the Ministry of Justice formed a special commission to study the proposal and draft legislation. Members included Gutiérrez himself, his son-in-law who was also a prominent constitutional scholar, and a member of the Supreme Court. The commission produced a first draft in October of 1983, within a year of its formation. Public discussions, the preparation of a second draft, and vetting by the Court led to the submission of a final draft to the Assembly in May, 1986. Further discussions by the Court and the Assembly finally brought the approval of the Law of Constitutional Jurisdiction in October of 1989.

Significantly, the proposal had outlived a change of administration, although not of party. The decision to opt for a Constitutional Chamber as opposed to a separate court was dictated by political expediency. It was expected to encounter less opposition than the creation of an entirely new body. Nonetheless, the new system, seemingly only a slight variation on its predecessor, was to have an impact even its proponents appeared not to anticipate.

Almost from its creation, which immediately followed the law's passage, the chamber was flooded with filings. By 1996[68] it had averaged about 7,000 filings a year, 40 percent of them *amparos*. Even more amazingly, it was able to keep abreast of its workload, although there were complaints that some cases lingered years without solution.[69] The initial complaints were minimal and the chamber enjoyed an enormous popularity with the broader public, which stemmed largely from its management of *amparos*. These could be filed fairly simply, without legal counsel. The chamber took it upon itself to do any required investigation, even as to the nature of the specific right violated. Once the chamber had effected an initial study of the demand, a decision to proceed with it brought an automatic injunction against the contested action. Thus, while the chamber did not award damages to the affected party, it could stop, temporarily or permanently, the action in question. Complaints against administrative actions might as well have been seen by the administrative courts and chamber. The public was quick to realize that the Constitutional Chamber or Fourth Chamber (*Sala Cuarta*) offered a much faster remedy. The law also extended its power to violation of rights by private parties.

In its handling of *amparos* the chamber perceived itself and was viewed by the public as the champion of the individual citizen against bureaucratic abuses and occasionally against those of private actors. Whether it actually made a dent in either or only represented a symbolic release for citizen frustrations is a subject for further study. It clearly was less popular with the publicly or privately powerful, who complained about its obstructing rational enterprise in the interests of an outmoded attachment to nineteenth century liberalism. Even if it eventually ruled against the requested *amparo*, the automatic injunction could hold up activities and impose real costs on those behind them. Thus, in some eyes, it encouraged nuisance litigation and provided a lever for those willing to threaten an *amparo* in hopes of forcing a private reconciliation.

If less frequently applied, the chamber's real power lay in its ability to declare laws unconstitutional, even before their passage. Here it has had numerous head-on confrontations with the executive over issues it has occasionally been accused of not fully understanding. Chamber members have noted that they have made decisions defending constitutional principles while unclear as to the concrete repercussions. One example is the case of extradition.[70] In addition to its firm stand against that of Costa Rican nationals for whatever reason and its invalidation of an Extradition Treaty with the United States, the chamber also became embroiled in a battle with the executive over the latter's unconsulted extradition of a group of Venezuelans accused of bank robbery. Here even popular opinion opposed the chamber, viewing the "criminals" as too dangerous to keep in the country. Another area where the chamber has held firm is on the Assembly's constitutional monopoly on law-making powers. Its view that many executive decisions were in fact laws led to its invalidation of the Transit Code (because it allowed the executive to determine the amount of fines) and a near decision, retracted at the last moment, to overrule the Central Bank's ability to set the exchange rate. In such rulings, the chamber has run against the opinion of the rest of the Court, which apparently would like see a little more flexibility.

Obviously any group of seven individuals who must jointly rule on 7,000 legal cases a year is bound to make some hasty and ill-considered decisions, as the members of the chamber themselves will agree. They have so far resisted the notion of simplifying their task by introducing filtering mechanisms, making access more difficult, or returning some parts of judicial review to lower instances. Their immediate remedy has been to increase their support staff and modernize their internal procedures, but neither resolves the underlying problem of the sheer quantity of their work. If the most problematic of Costa Rica's innovations, the chamber is also the most interesting, with effects that go beyond its immediate impact on the protection of constitutional rights. It is a curb on other institutions, including the rest of the judiciary, and in the latter sense operates much like a separate constitutional court.[71] Conceivably over the longer run, its activities may force the reconsideration of such basic constitutional issues as the distribution of powers among the branches of government and the limits of certain constitutionally guaranteed rights. Such repercussions were apparently not part of its proponents' program, but if the chamber, as one observer has suggested, is determined to "tak[e]...constitutionalism seriously,"[72] others will have to do so as well.

Costa Rica's current reform projects should keep its judiciary occupied for several more years. Continuity seems guaranteed in that the Court president, who has adopted this as his cause, was recently reelected for a second eight-year term. If his style is sometimes controversial, the positions he has promoted have successfully attracted a large following throughout the judiciary. His views conveniently lie somewhere between the complacent center and the more radical visions of some of his inner circle. Still, the judiciary may be facing immediate limits to its past tradition of expansive as well as expensive reforms. Some of these limits are political, and center, as discussed above, on its institutional independence in general and its judicial review powers in particular. Most recently, other actors have begun to weigh in on proposals to modify the courts' activities, no longer trusting in the judiciary's judgment.[73] If the trend continues, the next step may be to reexamine some past decisions especially as regards judicial control of other public sector institutions.

The other limits are more pedestrian, but no less serious. The IDB loan will finance new infrastructure and equipment, but the judiciary is finding it difficult to live on its budgetary earmark. In an era of public sector retrenchment it is unlikely to get further increases. Thus, it will have to substitute another strategy for its past pattern of expansion. A visit to any Costa Rican court suggests that there is substantial room for more efficient use of financial and human resources. However, encouraging greater efficiency may well be more difficult and more internally divisive than the adoption of a new code or computer technology, especially where the latter can rely on budgetary surpluses or external funding sources. Should such new strategies generate internal conflicts, it could strengthen the hand of external actors who have begun to question the institution's powers as a whole.

Colombia: Reform by Political Elites[74]

Colombia currently has the unfortunate distinction of being best known for its problems with drug trafficking and an almost endemic internal guerrilla movement. Despite seeming progress with the latter in the early 1990s, both constitute continuing threats to the country's stability and have proved equally resistant to attempts to eliminate them. Colombia's earlier history was also beset by periods of violence and disorder. During the 1940s and 1950s, these produced a near civil war, *la Violencia*, and 100,000 deaths. Order was only reestablished through recourse to the brief military dictatorship of General Rojas Pinilla and a pact between the dominant Liberal and Conservative parties. The pact created the National Front government in which the parties agreed to alternate control of the national presidency and share other political offices. The National Front officially ended in 1974, but the practice of shared office is partly honored to this day. Administrations controlled by one party frequently appoint members of the other to cabinet level and other important positions. The pact, which brought temporary peace to the country, has been criticized for entrenching the control of traditional elites and effectively, if nonviolently, obstructing the emergence of new political forces. Those not inclined to accept the arrangement have occasionally adopted more disruptive forms of expressing their discontent, including the formation of guerrilla movements.

Colombia's earlier development, like that of Costa Rica, was strongly influenced by a coffee economy based more on small and medium-sized holdings than on control by a few large landholders.[75] It also has been characterized by a dispersed population and intense regionalism. The nation's larger size made these traits a far greater obstacle to elites trying to create a national polity and economy. After the late nineteenth century, their struggle was for the most part conducted within a constitutional framework. The 1886 Constitution remained in effect, with few exceptions,[76] until 1991. Numerous revisions and modifications brought periodic shifts in the balance of powers among national institutions, and between them and subnational governments and elites. In this the judiciary has figured as an important element. Thus, efforts to reform it must be understood within this larger context. Many reforms did arise out of a concern with improving the sector's purely functional performance, but never without some attention to their broader political implications.

If El Salvador's reform was the most subject to external pressures, and Costa Rica's the most tranquil and least noticed, Colombia's has been characterized by the most extensive national debate. Here, technical and juridic principles were so tightly mixed with institutional and political interests as to make it difficult to determine where one began and the other ended. The sides of the debate reflected two separate institutional cultures, that of the traditional judiciary (*la Rama*[77]) and that of the political class, itself divided between its traditional members and newer, less conventional leadership. The traditional judicial and political elites are not that widely separated, and in fact include common members.[78] Still, their perspectives on the reasons for reform and the values and objectives that should guide it were not identical. Had it not been for their overriding interest in resolving the problem within a constitutional framework, the consequences might have been more disruptive. Instead, the result was a conflict so nuanced and so pervaded by technical detail that observers have difficulties determining who won. It is significant that they, thus, offer surprisingly diverse interpretations as to the implications of the 1991 Constitution and accompanying legal reforms, which represent the culmination of almost three decades of efforts to reshape the nation's justice system.[79]

Colombia's most recent reforms were also affected by external and broader domestic pressures. As regards the latter, it is the only one of the three countries where civil society played any kind of role. Nonetheless, they are predominantly the product of negotiations and disputes within and among these two groups, the judicial and political elites, and of their reaction to the justice system's inability to deal adequately with rising levels of domestic violence; armed political opposition; and the social, economic and political penetration of the drug cartels. However, the problems are both broader and of greater duration, relating to fundamental constitutional questions about the distribution of powers within the entire political system. As such, they are the source of a much longer process of transformation in the course of which the judiciary's relationship to the other governmental powers and political forces has undergone constant change.

Prelude to Reform

The roots of the current reforms can be traced to two events in 1945 and 1957 that substantially decreased the judiciary's traditional dependence on local political forces, and eventually on the national executive and legislature. The first of these was part of a more general effort to modernize the Colombian state via amendment of the 1886 Constitution and to make it more responsive to the demands of new social and economic conditions. Two principal themes were the strengthening of the executive vis-a-vis the Congress, and of the national government vis-a-vis subnational units.[80] In the case of the judiciary (at that time, including the courts and the Procuraduría General[81]), the latter theme was prioritized. Traditional practice and prior constitutional amendments had increased judicial susceptibility to local political pressures by allowing departmental and municipal councils to nominate or appoint lower level judges. This, like the Congress' role in the selection of the Court, had been opposed by national leadership. It was seen as still more damaging because of its greater effect on the standardization of judicial decisions. Thus, selection of the Supreme Court and the Procurador was left in the hands of the Congress, based on lists presented by the executive. The selection of the rest of the judiciary and the Procuraduría's *fiscales* reverted to the institutions themselves, eliminating the intervention of the various subnational assemblies.[82] Under the new system, the Court appointed appellate judges who in turn named the lower level judiciary. Similar mechanisms were adopted for the Procuraduría. The arrangement fell short of the reformers' goal of reducing or eliminating congressional intervention, but it represented a major step toward creating truly national institutions.

The second event, in 1957, also responded to broader national developments. In that year, leadership of the dominant Liberal and Conservative parties formed the National Front. Their immediate purpose was to de-escalate the intense partisan conflict that they blamed for the highly destructive internal war, *la Violencia* (1948-1953).[83] A plebescite held in 1957 approved a system whereby the Supreme Court would name its own members. The arrangement was extended to the Council of State, which in 1945 became the apex of a new system of separate administrative courts. Called *cooptación*, the mechanism gave the judiciary an autonomy unique in the region, although it was also accompanied by a tacit understanding that the Court would respect the partisan balance in its appointments.[84] In recent years, the bipartisan criteria were more honored in the breach, and have been more criticized by external observers than those within the system.[85] Although the resulting arrangement was also faulted for giving permanent tenure only to members of the Supreme Court and Council of State, the ordinary four-year appointments held by the appellate and administrative court judges and the two-year tenure for the lower level judiciary are not commonly regarded as encouraging exceptional abuses. The Supreme Court eased the situation with its informal ruling that judges with no charges against them would be automatically renamed. This practice became law with Decree No. 52 of 1987.

The Court was slow to respond to its new independence and to the remaining controls exercised by the executive. The 1886 Constitution and amendments introduced in 1910, 1936, and 1945[86] left the executive with three important sources of power vis-a-vis *la Rama*, which after 1945, included the administrative courts and until the late 1980s, the Procuraduría. These were his ability to declare a state of siege with its consequent waiver of constitutional guarantees (a situation in effect for almost the entire period following the 1948 *bogotazo*[87]); his ability, with congressional authorization, to legislate by extraordinary or legislative decree; and the continuing controls over the judiciary's administrative, budgetary and personnel systems exercised by the Ministry of Justice. In effect, much of the legislation shaping the judiciary and determining its procedures has been the product of these executive laws, most often elaborated by "litigating lawyers and law professors, and not by judges."[88] This in itself is not remarkable for the region. What is more unusual is *la Rama* and in particular the Supreme Court's gradual, if still far from effective, assertion of its right to a voice in the matter.

Beginning as early as the mid-1960s and with increasing incidence through the following decades, the Supreme Court came to contest some of these executive decrees both as they affected its own powers and those of other institutions. Among those found unconstitutional were a proposal in 1964 to transfer criminal instruction to the Procuraduría's *fiscales*, the constitutional reforms of 1976 and 1979 (the latter almost identical in its treatment of the judiciary to the 1991 reforms), a declaration of economic emergency (1987), a criminal procedures code (1981), a criminal procedures reform (1986), the extradition treaty with the United States (1986 and 1987), part of the judicial career law (1987), military courts' jurisdiction over civilians (1987), and the creation of a special court (1987). In some cases, the Court only objected to a situation after years of toleration. One example was the reversal of its 1984 decision allowing the military courts' jurisdiction over civilians. In others, it acquiesced in apparent response to political pressures and the force of public opinion. Its decision not to oppose the Constituent Assembly of 1990 is illustrative. However, its critics increasingly accused it of obstructionism in defense of principles that no longer mattered to anyone else. Among cases cited was its ruling against the 1964 reform, both as it regarded efforts to expand the role of the Procuraduría's *fiscales* and to reorganize the lower level courts and eliminate entirely the circuit courts. Here the Court stood on constitutional principle, arguing that courts mentioned in the constitution could not be eliminated by secondary law. The decision was technically correct. However, it was poorly received by the members of the Ministry of Justice who contended that their proposal, based on statistical studies of caseloads, would rationalize an archaic and inefficient territorial and functional division of labor.[89]

During this period, one of the Court's principal accomplishments was an extension of its independence through the termination of the Ministry of Justice's control of its administrative systems, including management of the judicial career. Following its disappearance at the end of the last century, the ministry had been recreated in 1945 for this purpose, assuming functions formerly exercised by a department within the Ministry of Government. With the passage of Extraordinary Decree 250 in 1970, the Court, Procuraduría, and Council of State had been given a formal voice in the ministry's decisions through their representation on its Superior Administrative Council (*Consejo Superior de Administración*). The practice was continued when Decree 52 of 1987 replaced the council with the Consejo Superior de la Administración de Justicia and its sectional councils. The Court eventually objected to this partial remedy and, in July, 1987, declared the ministry's participation in the national and local bodies unconstitutional. They were reformed with representatives from the Court, the Council of State and the Disciplinary Tribunal, and one delegate each from the lower level judges and administrative staff. The new councils' decisional powers were limited to management of the judicial career, since that was the basis of the Court's objection. Control of the judiciary's budget and other administrative affairs remained with the executive until 1989 when, by presidential decree, they were also turned over to the councils.[90] Both these transformations were further complicated by objections from lower levels of the judiciary and members of the Court itself. Some of the objections were matters of principle. They also arose because the new arrangement threatened traditional prerogatives enjoyed even with the ministry's control.[91]

Overview of the Sector

These debates about the management of the court system were conducted against a larger background of concern as to its efficacy and broader political role. The concern, as elsewhere, has for the most part been dealt with through the adoption of laws that frequently imitate practices of presumably more modern systems. In this regard, Colombia has surpassed any regional average, having, as one observer notes, "the best legislation in Latin America...or at least the most detailed, dogmatic and extensive."[92] It also has one of the largest and most complex judicial structures (*Rama Judicial*) in the region, the product not only of new legislation but of the retention of traditional organizational forms held over from the periods of greater political decentralization. By 1991, the nonadministrative court system was composed of three virtually independent jurisdictions. The first of these, the ordinary court system, with 20,000 employees, employed 5,000 judges divided among 3,600 courts.[93] These included a twenty-four member Supreme Court that, until 1991, exercised both appellate functions and powers of judicial review, twenty-seven appellate courts (*Tribunales Superiores de Distrito*), and seven different kinds of first-instance courts (district, circuit, territorial, municipal, criminal instruction, special and public order[94]). Technically, the ordinary system also included several special jurisdictions, most notably the customs and military courts. However, its oversight of these bodies was limited to the Supreme Court's appellate functions.

Colombia is also one of the few Latin American countries with an entirely separate system of administrative courts. Introduced in 1945, it is headed by its own supreme tribunal, the Council of State.[95] The courts exercise powers of judicial review over administrative actions, occasionally with a fairly broad interpretation as to what that includes.[96] A separate Disciplinary Tribunal, composed of four members selected by the Congress from lists presented by the executive, functioned between 1972 and 1991. It was responsible for disciplinary matters involving judges, justices, prosecutors, and the Procurador General; appeals of disciplinary processes against lawyers; and conflicts of competence among the various jurisdictions, including those between military and civilian courts. Other sectoral institutions included the Procuraduría General, a judicial police[97] and the Ministry of Justice, with the functions detailed above and control of the prison system. Of the three, only the Procuraduría was considered a part of *la Rama;* the 1991 Constitution places it outside as well.

Colombia's legal system, following regional trends, has gradually e-volved away from a pure civil code tradition. However, its 1987 Criminal Procedures Code was markedly inquisitorial, leaving criminal investigation to the judiciary. Efforts to transfer the function to the Procuraduría were frustrated by the Supreme Court's finding that they were unconstitutional. This resulted in the creation of a Direction of Criminal Investigation *(Dirección de Investigación Criminal)* within the ordinary court system. The right to defense, while implicit in the constitution and guaranteed by Supreme Court decision (May 1983),[98] was, like the prosecutorial role, underdeveloped. The Public Defense Law *(Ley de Defensa Pública de Oficio*, Decree No. 53 of 1987) established a small Public Defense Office in the Ministry of Justice. Most indigent defense continued to be provided by bench-appointed counsel.[99] Colombia was also one of the minority of Latin American nations to use juries for some trials; the practice was the subject of much criticism. The 1991 Constitution, while preserving the jury, changes it from a lay body to one composed of lawyers. The provision has not been implemented.

Given its complexity and size, it is not surprising that the Rama Judicial received an unusually large share of the national budget (2.9 percent in 1990 and 5.4 percent in 1995)[100] or that this amount still brought complaints of low salaries and inadequate installations and equipment, especially for the lower courts. Despite these complaints and the extraordinary pressures occasioned by the upsurge in internal violence and drug trafficking since the 1970s, criticisms of judicial performance were less directed at officials' honesty, competence, and dedication than at inefficiency, slowness, conservative bias in their decisions, and a tendency to be swayed by political pressures. As the Comisión Andina notes in an unusually sympathetic treatment, "in Colombia there is as much justice as society is capable of giving."[101] Also unusual for the region, many of these complaints were documented in studies conducted by universities and private foundations during the 1970s and after. These studies emphasize the judiciary's increasing inability to handle its workload, and the consequent aggravation of such more serious problems as impunity, overcrowded jails, and a high percentage (over 60 percent) of unsentenced prisoners.[102] Their authors also suggested that judicial ineffectiveness may have encouraged an increase in crime as well as a tendency for people to take justice into their own hands.

Although the situation was no better for civil jurisdictions,[103] domestic concern with crime, violence, and, if only for a minority, state repression encouraged more attention to the criminal courts. Here, a 1977 study found that of the 1,397,000 active cases, only 48,500 had entered the trial stage.[104] Furthermore, for those cases that were carried to completion, the average time elapsed was over twice the legal limits. Another study from the same source found that from 1970 to 1980, the criminal case backlog showed a slow but steady increase. As the percentage of cases retained remained fairly constant, this was mostly a function of the higher number of cases entering the system.[105] Findings from 1983 suggested that 58.8 percent of the criminal case backlog could be retired, either because the statute of limitations had run out or because there was little hope of advancing them further.[106] Interestingly, an analysis of the military courts, whose jurisdiction over civilians had been defended for reasons of greater efficiency, found little difference in the speed with which they dispatched cases. Taking into account the considerable difference in the respect they accorded due process, the analysts concluded that the argument was not valid.[107] Jumping ahead, a government sponsored analysis from 1996 found the situation to have changed only in its dimensions.[108] There were by then four million active cases in the entire common court system, one million of which remained in the criminal investigative state.

Colombia's growing rate of internal violence, impunity, corruption, and common crime have causes far beyond the justice system's failings. Nevertheless, the need for its further reform was one of the few points linking the many groups, inside the sector and the government and within the wider public, who sought a remedy for these problems. The priorities, specific objectives, and recommended measures of each group differed, depending upon whether their primary concern was the continuing and possibly increasing violations of human rights; the government's failure to deal with drug traffickers, the guerrillas, or common criminals; the inequitable, inefficient handling of cases; or the physical threats to and the poor working conditions of the judicial officials. There was also a concern, limited more to the political and judicial elites, with the increasing clashes between the executive and the judiciary, and what the former saw as the latter's blockage of valid reform projects. The judiciary, or more specifically the Court, of course, interpreted its role as one of holding the line against executive abuses of power. The proliferation of sector organizations and the increasingly unclear distribution of powers among them also seemed to have reached a point where some reordering was necessary. Here, attention was most often directed to the mass of courts at the lower level of the hierarchy and to the upmost levels, where three tribunals shared some aspect of the judicial review function. With a ratio of judges to population 1.5 times that of the United States,[109] a significant and increasing percentage of its budget going to the *Rama* and, by one count,[110] enough active cases to involve one of every ten Colombians in litigation, the traditions of partial reforms and disordered growth seemed to have reached illogical extremes.

The Consolidation of the 1991 Reforms

Once again, this criticism of the sector were only part of a more fundamental concern. By the 1980s, the political system seemed to have reached its own impasse, like the judiciary, a victim of continued tinkering and patching up, but never the subject of a substantial reordering. Here, many of the same problems figured, but on a larger scale—pervasive corruption; internal violence that between 1984 and 1991 had produced the deaths of thousands of political leaders, judges, union and peasant leaders, journalists and civilians in general; declining popular trust and involvement in traditional institutions, including the party system; and the nation's inability to deal with the growing power of the drug traffickers and their increasing penetration of the economy, society, and the political system. The latter was affecting international relations, especially, those with the United States, which periodically threatened to cut off economic assistance and take other punitive measures. In 1989 and 1990, the crisis reached a peak with the assassination of three presidential candidates and bombing attacks in Bogota and Medellin that produced thousands of civilian casualties. The government's response, in addition to stepping up both negotiations with and campaigns against the guerrilla and drug traffickers, was a proposed rewriting of the constitution. Such efforts had been made before. They had most often been blocked by the Court on the grounds that the constitution allowed only the Congress to conduct such a reform, a measure that the political leadership deemed impossible. Nonetheless, President Virgilio Barco (1986-1990) set constitutional reform as a main priority of his administration. He made two attempts to bypass the constitutional restraints, first calling for a referendum on the reform and then proposing a referendum on the convocation of a Constitutional Assembly. The first proposal was declared unconstitutional by the Council of State and the second was withdrawn by the government when it became linked to other referenda on negotiations with the guerrilla and the extradition treaty with the U.S.

Barco's third attempt at reform by "constitutional" means was more successful. The benefits were reaped by the following administration. By Decree 927, President Barco included a proposal on a Constituent Assembly in the up-coming presidential elections. The administration's hand was strengthened by a student movement following the assassination of the presidential candidate, Luis Carlos Galán, and calling for a Constituent Assembly. Observers are divided as to the impact of popular support on the administration's actions,[111] but it seems indisputable that it influenced the Supreme Court's decision (Ruling 54) to validate the move, despite the Procurador General's adverse response.[112] Backed by the popular vote, the newly elected president, César Gaviria, reached an agreement with the two sectors of the opposition Conservative Party and the M-19 ex-guerrilla group. On August 24, 1990, Gaviria issued Decree 1926 to convoke the election of a Constituent Assembly on December 9, 1990.

The exclusion of other parties from this agreement and the parameters it established for the process were already targets of criticism. A six-member advisory commission, selected by the president, was to draft the reform project, focusing on topics that included the Congress, the judiciary, the Public Ministry, public administration, human rights, political parties, departmental and municipal governments, states of emergency, participatory mechanisms, and economic issues.[113] The conspicuous absence of the presidency from the list was criticized by local analysts who, from the start, saw this as a maneuver to strengthen executive powers. Several former presidents from Gaviria's own Liberal Party also noted their opposition to what they viewed as a dubious means to achieve a new order. The Supreme Court's opinion on the decree was divided, with only fourteen justices voting to uphold it. However, both the press and the executive exerted strong pressures, noting that a negative decision would be going against public opinion.[114] On the basis of the Court's ruling, the Constituent Assembly declared that it would not be bound by any further judicial control, whether by the Court or the Council of State. This was in flat contradiction to the latter's informal opinion that the assembly was still subject to some restrictions. The assembly reiterated its position in Constituent Act 1 (May 9, 1990). Reactions among political leadership continued to be divided. This did not prevent an agreement by President Gaviria, the head of the Liberal party, and the Constituent Assembly's three joint presidents to close the Congress on adoption of the new constitution, convoke new congressional elections, and give extraordinary legislative powers to the president during the six-month gap. The president's actions were to be advised, but not controlled, by the *"congresito,"* a special thirty-six member commission.

The 1991 Reforms

The new constitution was promulgated on July 4, 1991. As noted, views vary on its implications, especially as regards the executive's powers vis-a-vis the other two branches of government. Americas Watch, while expressing concern about various provisions, contends that it is "a document of which Colombians can be proud," citing its human rights protections, limits on the president's emergency powers, creation of a Human Rights Ombudsman and Constitutional Court, and strengthening of accountability via the Procurador's ability to "dismiss public officials on serious disciplinary matters after a hearing."[115] Others see it as increasing democratic participation through electoral reforms, professionalization of the Congress, and the introduction of mechanisms for direct citizen initiation of, or vote on, legislation.[116] Domestic observers [117] tend to be more critical, finding the president's emergency powers strengthened, citing his permanent or provisional encroachment on various economic planning and policy making functions formerly exercised by the Congress, and interpreting some of the restraints placed on the legislature's activities as a means not of professionalizing the body, but rather of cutting its powers. The resolution of this debate is beyond the scope of this discussion and, in any case, as both sides admit, depends as much on how the relevant actors use their powers as on the content of the document.

What is more evident, and more relevant, are the changes the constitution introduces for the *Rama Judicial*'s organization and composition, its internal operations, and its relationship to the other branches of government. The constitution creates three new bodies, a Constitutional Court, a Judicial Council, and a Public Prosecutor's Office (*Fiscalía General*), eliminates others (the old Concejo Superior, the Disciplinary Tribunal, and the Direction of Criminal Investigation), and radically alters the functions of still a third set (e.g. the Procuraduría, now located outside the *Rama*, and housing a Human Rights Ombudsman and Public Defenders Office). The composition, tenure, and operating procedures of these institutions, when not set by the constitution, were the subject of an extensive package[118] of executive decrees issued during the transitional period. It is generally not true as some have argued,[119] that the result is more direct executive control of the *Rama*. The new arrangements did alter the balance of power within the sector, transferring to other entities functions formerly exercised by the judiciary, either directly or via its participation in the Concejo Superior.

The Constitutional Court assumed the Supreme Court's functions of judicial review, although not those exercised by the Council of State. Its seven members are selected by the Congress on the basis of lists submitted by the president, the Court, and the Council of State. They hold eight-year, nonrenewable terms. The Constitutional Court also exercises a review function over judicial decisions on the newly created *tutela*, protecting constitutional rights, as described below. An earlier proposal to have all such questions submitted to the Court for its prior decision was discarded as impractical.[120] As under the prior system, the division of judicial responsibilities remains a theme of occasional disputes. This is most evident as regards the Constitutional Court and the Council of State, and has been further complicated by the potentially overlapping competence of three other bodies, the Procuraduría, Judicial Council, and Supreme Court.

The Judicial Council in some respects resembles the old Consejo Superior. It differs from the latter in its institutional independence from the organizations (Constitutional Court, ordinary and administrative courts) whose personnel and administrative systems it now controls. The council's Administrative Chamber is composed of six justices, three selected by the Council of State, two by the Supreme Court, and one by the Constitutional Court. The members serve eight-year, nonrenewable terms. They have full-time appointments and, although representing the institutions, may not be selected from among their active members. The seven members of the Disciplinary Chamber also serve for eight-year terms, but are selected by the

Congress on the basis of lists presented by the executive. The chambers jointly prepare the sector's portion of the National Development Plan and its budget (coordinated with, but not including that of the Fiscalía),[121] decide on the territorial distribution of courts and their personnel structure, draft and present legislation affecting the sector, and prepare the lists from which the Supreme Court, Council of State, and their respective lower level bodies make judicial appointments. In all these tasks they are assisted by sectional councils created in each judicial district.

The Administrative Chamber is responsible for the more detailed management of the judicial career as well as that of the judiciary's administrative systems. The Disciplinary Chamber, which replaces the old Disciplinary Tribunal, hears questions of conflicts of jurisdiction and is a court of last appeal for disciplinary matters. It should be emphasized that although the Judicial Council prescreens candidates to the ordinary and administrative court systems, the Supreme Court and Council of State continue their practice of self-renewal (*cooptación*) and the final selection of the next lower level of judges. The latter in turn select the lowest instance. Permanent tenure (until retirement) is now extended to all judges in each jurisdiction.

The constitution introduced other important changes. Before discussing them, a few remarks are necessary. It should be emphasized that, however radical their combined effect, the changes discussed above and summarized below were hardly novelties. The reformers had been attempting to introduce them for over two decades, and had been frustrated at almost every turn by the judiciary's opposition. The new constitution both effected the reforms and, through its redistribution of institutional powers, reduced the traditional court system's ability to block any future changes. Whether the new arrangement would be any less obstructive was another question, but by dividing the judiciary's powers among a number of institutions, the reformers sought to reduce this risk. They further hedged their bets by ensuring that the Judicial Council and Constitutional Court did not have permanent tenure and were not self-perpetuating. If one set of incumbents proved difficult, there was always the hope that the next appointees would have a different perspective. Thus, past history and the nature of the reforms themselves discredit the notion that this was a recent executive scheme to increase its power over the judiciary. The reformers in fact had long argued that such changes would make the administration of justice in general and the judiciary in particular more effective and efficient. As we shall see, this has not been the immediate result.

A second major set of changes, which had also been in the offing for decades, radically altered the criminal justice process through the creation of a third new institution, the Office of Public Prosecution (*Fiscalía General*). While officially part of the *Rama*,[122] and headed by a Fiscal General selected by the Supreme Court on the basis of lists presented by the executive, the Fiscalía enjoys substantial independence. The Fiscal serves a four-year, nonrenewable term, and maintains responsibility for his institution's budget, administration, and selection of personnel. With the creation of an independent Fiscalía and the subsequent elaboration of its powers in the new Criminal Procedures Code (Decree 2700 of November 30, 1991), the Colombian criminal justice system advanced its formal transformation toward an accusatory model in which the responsibility for investigation of crimes (including supervision of the judicial police and any other administrative bodies performing their function), the bringing of criminal charges, and their argument in an oral hearing belong exclusively to the *fiscales*. There have been some fears expressed as to the powers attributed to the *fiscales* in the realization of their functions. Subject to most criticism are the weight given to confessions made in their presence, but not before a judge, and their ability to order detentions and conduct searches and seizures. More generally, the transfer of the investigative and prosecutorial roles from the judges to these specialized officials is regarded as an important advance. Furthermore, the decision to remove any criminal investigative duties from the Procuraduría General leaves the latter organization and its new Defensoría del Pueblo (Human Rights Ombudsman) free to conduct their protection of human rights, especially as it involves actions of the Fiscalía and judicial police. The reforms also expanded the Procuraduría's role to include oversight of administrative as well as judicial actions.

Based on the constitution's guarantee of a right to defense, the Criminal Procedures Code's provisions to the same effect, and the functions assigned to the newly created Defensoría del Pueblo, the latter now houses an Office of Public Defense to provide free services to those unable to pay for counsel. This replaces a department created within the Ministry of Justice in 1987 and is reputed to be more effective than the latter. Sadly, the improvement is still not great. This is the entity that has received least attention and the fewest budgetary resources under the new system. Its roughly 470 defenders, almost all of them contract employees, actually receive lower salaries than their predecessors.[123] Consequently, they are allowed to handle their own cases as well, a practice that would not seem to encourage attention to those for which they receive no fees. The office's current placement, within the Defensoría del Pueblo that itself is a part of the Procuraduría, is arguably a good part of the problem, hardly designed to attract the attention of either organization's policy and budget makers.

The constitution introduced several additional modifications to the sector's structure and operations. Its admirable listing of individual rights has been mentioned, but, in the protection of these rights, there are two further important innovations. The first was the strengthening of the provisions on habeas corpus, especially as regards its application to special and military courts and the requirement that petitions be ruled upon within thirty-six hours of their submission (Art. 30). The second was the introduction of a new protective measure, the *acción de tutela*, whereby citizens are granted an immediate temporary injunction against actions (or omissions) of a public official harming any of their other constitutional rights. The courts have ten days to rule on the claim. Appeals of their decisions are seen in the last instance by the Constitutional Court. Since *tutela* may also be used to contest judicial sentences, its potential as a "fast track" appeal[124] has, unfortunately, produced some immediate and so far unresolvable problems of court congestion. Another innovation, resolving a long-standing internal debate and overruling previous findings of the Supreme Court, was the recognition of the legal traditions of indigenous communities and of their members' right to use them to resolve internal conflicts so long as they do not violate the constitution or other national legislation.

In two other areas, the constitutional solutions have been less applauded by observers. The first of these is the question of civilian control of the military, especially, as regards military courts. The latter continue to have exclusive and final jurisdiction over crimes committed by officials during the course of active duty or during counterinsurgency operations. Furthermore their jurisdiction is extended to the police, as one source notes, giving legal recognition to a former de facto practice.[125] The second is in the perpetuation of the special and public order courts for handling drug and terrorist cases. These courts, with their "faceless judges," are now incorporated into one jurisdiction as "regional courts." Even their critics note that both the constitution and the new Criminal Procedures Code eliminated some of the most objectionable practices associated with these courts. They also provided additional due process guarantees formerly absent from their operations, for example clarifying that habeas corpus was in effect for them as well. Still, their maintenance remains highly controversial both inside and outside the country.

Finally, the constitution's prohibition of the extradition of Colombian citizens also deserves mention. This is a minor detail in the reform package, but a major source of friction between the Colombian and U.S. governments. In this and a few other details, many observers have claimed to see the influence of a very important "civil society group," Colombia's drug traffickers. The latter are rumored to have financed the campaigns of members of the Constituent Assembly and to have promoted the assembly itself as a means of rewriting the rules to favor their interests.[126] The truth of the matter may never be known. If it was their victory, the war is far from won. What is certain is that, while the grand outlines of the reform package followed proposals that had been around for decades, some last-minute compromises and the work of the smaller group drafting the enabling legislation introduced a number of unfortunate modifications. The final composition, placement, and powers of the Judicial Council are the most frequently cited example; that of the Public Defense Office; the retention of some fairly inquisitorial elements in the procedural code; or the inadequate implementation plans may be others. Paradoxically, criticism has centered both on the extensive and potentially repressive "judicial" powers given to the Fiscalía, and on what some consider to be impractically idealistic due process guarantees. The everpresent conspiracy theorists have gone so far as to suggest that some of this was intentional, a means of guaranteeing institutional gridlock. The more likely explanation is that the final decisions, and the enabling legislation in particular, were done too quickly and left to individuals lacking the wider vision of the reform's initial proponents.

It is too early to assess the impact of the reform package, and that, in any case, is not the purpose of this section. Nonetheless, a few observations are in order. First, the *Rama's* new governance system appears destined to produce conflicts among its members and obstruct progress on further reform implementation. The continuing lack of clarity as to the mutual, exclusive, or overlapping powers of the member institutions in handling their administrative and financial affairs is a constant source of friction. However, it is a mere nuisance compared to some more basic flaws in the overall design of the system. The National Judicial Council's impact on judicial operations is almost universally recognized as disastrous. There are, as many have noted,[127] several fundamental problems in its composition—the requirement that its members have the same qualifications as magistrates and so be eminent lawyers, but not necessarily administrators or managers; their full-time appointments; and the exclusion of active members of the institutions represented. In combination, these seem to have created a council of micromanaging amateurs, the least likely to help the judiciary respond to new challenges. As one observer noted,[128] asking them to run the judiciary is like asking a board of directors to serve full time running an enterprise.

Second, implementation of the new organizations and procedures has been partial, when not simply ineffectual. Poor design may be partly to blame. The major obstacle was a totally inadequate, in some cases nonexistent, transition plan. At the moment, the worst case is the Fiscalía. As Colombians like to say, it was created overnight; the Direction of Criminal Investigation's 1,100 instructional judges "went to bed as judges and woke up as fiscales." The Fiscalía, which now numbers 23,000 (including the 6,000 police investigators and administrative staff belonging to the CTI or Technical Investigative Corps[129]), accounts for roughly half of the *Rama's* budget. Nonetheless, it currently represents the major bottleneck in the criminal justice process, with over one million cases awaiting processing. Despite its success in prosecuting a number of high profile cases, public perceptions are that it is doing very little to combat ordinary crime.

The organization is gradually putting its house in order and has recently signed an agreement with the IDB for a loan project to reengineer its internal structures. This and extensive police and prosecutorial training financed by the U.S. government seem to be making a difference. However, once the Fiscalía assumes its new role more effectively, attention will rightfully turn to the courts, which have done little to change their own operations, the wholly inadequate public defense system, and the Procuraduría, the principle operations of which remain a mystery for most of the population. It is possible that those responsible for designing the new system opted for a kind of "catch-up" strategy, trusting that the organizations would grow into their new roles. It is more likely that they did not anticipate the difficulties, and that over the longer run, some of these roles will prove so impossible as to require further modifications.[130] As the reforms increased redundancies and costs, the modifications might also look to reversing these trends, which have arguably become problems and obstacles in their own right.

There is still a third problem relating to some of the unanticipated and still unresolved political consequences of the new arrangements. As noted, one set of problems involves the role and potentially excessive powers of the Fiscalía. Some critics have called into question the transition to a more accusatory system, holding that the more likely results are the worst inquisitorial nightmare, a criminal process working from a presumption of guilt. This is hardly inevitable, but the failure of the courts and defense to promote their own development increases the chances over the shorter run. Other problems are broader in their reach, if less immediately threatening. The existing situation, where any of four or five independent bodies may feel entitled to make definitive pronouncements on constitutional and legal issues, has not increased the sense of predictability or compliance with a single rule of law. Straightforward jurisdictional battles have so far been avoided by an apparent understanding that whichever organization first declares its competence is entitled to make the specific decision. The confusion arises when a related issue is submitted to a second entity, the decision of which may partially invalidate or at least alter the sense of the first one. This has raised judge-shopping to a whole new dimension, offering a choice among a Council of State, Constitutional Court, Judicial Council and even, occasionally, the Supreme Court or Procuraduría.

However, what was said of the constitution is also true of the sectoral reforms; their eventual impact will depend as much on how they are used as on the shape of or intent behind their present design. The Constitutional Court has provided an unpleasant surprise for any politicians who thought it would be less intrusive. In many of its decisions it has taken a very proactive stance on protecting individual rights, in this sense surpassing even its predecessor.[131] An important factor here was the Congress's last minute decision to select notable jurists, including some members of the former Supreme Court, as opposed to an initial list of more politicized appointees.[132] A new Constitutional Court will be elected in the year 2000 and some are already anticipating the selection of less independent members. Similar concerns have also been raised about the selection of a new Fiscal. Alfonso Valdivieso's willingness to pursue alleged corruption into the highest reaches of the government could easily provoke one of two reactions—an effort to choose a less proactive leader or one whose political agenda coincides more closely with that of other elites. For the judiciary, on the other hand, the potential for change remains unrealized. In its four years of existence, the Judicial Council has yet to produce a legal framework for the judicial career. A recent survey of new judges indicated that most believed contacts rather than merit had determined their appointment.[133] In short, things are hardly as they were before, but the situation remains very fluid and the political relationships and balance of power are still being defined. The complex division of responsibilities works against the system's capture by any single faction or interest, but the manipulations of a variety of actors and groups will complicate its operations and Colombian politics for some time to come.

Given the evident external and public pressures behind many of the reforms, it may seem surprising that they are not accorded more credit. While both strengthened the reformers' hand, the roots of reform and, especially, the specific proposals precede either. They originate, on the one hand, in the desire of local jurists (many of them the private lawyers and law professors who authored the revised codes and other legislation) to modernize their justice system in line with broader regional trends and, on the other, in their frustration and that of political elites as the Court increasingly used its powers of judicial review to block these and less sector-specific reforms. Their alliance was strengthened by the nature of the common external threats, few of which could be blamed on the sector, but all of which involved it. Had the Court been less independent, had the threats been less linked to crime and violence than to economic or social disaster, or had all parties felt less bound by constitutional norms, however broadly interpreted, it is likely that this alliance would not have formed. Change, at least on the justice side, would have been less comprehensive and more functional than political in its aims and impact. Instead judicial resistance was increasingly seen as obstructing efforts to resolve its own failings as well as the wider political and institutional crisis, and the two sets of problems and of objectives became inextricably linked. This development guaranteed sufficient political support to restructure the sector internally and to redefine once more its institutional and political relationships. If for different reasons, as in El Salvador, making the new system work will require additional elements. At the very least this means fully engaging the sector institutions and their broader membership and developing support for and thus understanding of the process among the general public or specialized groups within it.

Conclusions

A comparison of these three cases with the Peruvian experience allows some preliminary generalizations on the politics of justice sector reform and the ways in which they effect reform development and outcomes. While hardly a sufficient condition for real improvements, the kind of initial success experienced in the three cases is by definition a necessary one. Thus, a first question is how well the factors laid out in the introduction to this chapter explain that success and what other explanations should be added. Of course, there is always the possibility that even the "successful" programs are misdirected or contain the roots of their own subsequent failure. A part of that issue is reserved for the concluding chapters. So far as it relates to the political origins of reform, it receives some preliminary attention here.

A first point, which returns to themes raised in the introductory chapter, is that reform programs can be divided into two sets of objectives, one having to do with the functional (or technical) performance of the sector and the second with its broader political role. The two are interrelated so that efforts to address one often imply or require changes in the other. This is a relationship that proponents of reform often disregard, by intent or by oversight. Even when they are aware of it, an overwhelming concern with one set of objectives may cause them to underestimate or misjudge the other's role. This is an obvious source of some of the unintended consequences of reform programs, and also a potential cause of conflict within supporting alliances.

A second point also mentioned previously, but still more evident in the four cases, is that, however widespread the public or elite discontent with the sector, the traditional reform programs had much narrower roots. They arose within a small portion of the legal community, as much influenced by regional and international intellectual trends as by the level and content of domestic complaints. Absent the influence of this group, the public and elite response to discontent has usually been to delimit the powers of the objected institutions, replace their incumbents, or introduce alternative organizations. Contrary to these trends, the reformers have been more interested in changing the balance of power within the sector and between it and other branches of government, increasing judicial independence although not necessarily judicial powers, and altering internal procedures and operating principles. They have also promoted new institutions, but as complements to rather than substitutes for the existing ones. Thus, this group is distinguished by their efforts to define or redefine the problem and to introduce solutions unrelated to the principal public and elite dissatisfactions. Because of the uniqueness of their vision and the enormity of the proposed changes, they have been unable to act alone. The question, then, is how this narrow, but also very ambitious definition of reform, much of its transcending the concerns of potential allies, achieved broader support.

One part of the answer is that the allies themselves often accepted the package without fully understanding its implications. To be fair, many of the reformers may not have understood them either. This is arguably less the case of Costa Rica, with its judicially instigated reform, or even Colombia, where decades of frustrated reform efforts and broader institutional readjustments had involved its political elites in debates over just such details. However, certainly in El Salvador and, until very recently, in Peru, allies (including nongovernmental and external actors in the former case) seemed more willing to accept the proposals as progressive change without further inspection. Problems would arise once the reforms advanced far enough to force reappraisal and, in Peru, result in the government's withdrawal of active support and its substitution of a new reform strategy, based on a very different political vision. That reform survived in El Salvador is largely a consequence of its external supporters, who did not have to live with its unintended consequences and, in fact, could ignore them for the most part.

A second part of the answer lies in the identity and more specific interests of the broader reform alliance. Even Costa Rica's judicial leadership went beyond simple improved performance to include some political goals. In discussing the prerequisites for reform, critics have often focused on "political will,"[134] implying that its absence among political elites is the most common explanation of reform failure. They often go further, arguing that elites oppose sector reform because it will decrease their own political power. The concept and accompanying argument grossly oversimplify the situation. The sector is often more marginal to elite concerns than they suggest, the elite less monolithic, and the options for support far broader. Moreover, "political will" is a slippery concept. To the extent it is at all valid, it is likely to vary over time according to the perceived difficulties as well as the anticipated benefits of reform programs. Unfortunately, the costs may begin to outweigh the benefits as the programs evolve and as their more problematic aspects become visible. Here the temptation for political elites is to declare symbolic victory, withdraw further support, and depend on the usual solutions of expediency for any lingering complaints.

A final conclusion is that sectoral or external allies may be a more dependable source of support, the first because they are closer to the benefits that they may further shape to their liking, and the second because they are further removed from the difficulties. Yet, both are only as effective as the resources they bring to the task. For the traditional Latin American justice sectors, poor in financial, organizational, and human resources, this is a major impediment. It is also one for many external allies, capable of offering moral but not material support. Where this obstacle is overcome, and their political will is accompanied by material leverage, reform may be highly sustainable regardless of the will of the political elite. It may also be quite independent of "popular will" and, in the case of externally supported reforms, occasionally run against it. One significant aspect of the most recent Peruvian strategy is the effort to alter this conventional formula, with the political elite attempting to capture external resources while excluding or coopting sectoral interests. Whether access to resources will extend the politicians' usually short attention span, or whether they can forge a durable alliance with external groups will be important determinants of their success.

These initial conclusions lead to a last question: given the considerably similarity of the reform packages and the often arbitrary nature of their differences of detail, does it really make a difference who supports them so long as that support lasts? Here the answer depends not so much on who they are, but what objectives they are pursing and what kind of base these provide for an eventual expansion of the alliance. No matter how successful the initial reform, its complete trajectory will be lengthy and require, if not a broader alliance, at least different kinds of support. In the majority of cases reform does not originate within the sector or even include sectoral institutions among its early supporters. Without their eventual inclusion, however, the proposed changes are likely to be subverted or come to an untimely end. Political and external allies, while they may be highly motivated at the beginning, are usually pursuing shorter term goals. Once they believe those goals are achieved, or can declare victory, they may turn their attention to other problems. If they do not, the consequences can also be disruptive for sectoral development, which may increasingly respond to objectives that have little to do with the sector's overall functional performance. In either case, a reform that, for whatever reason, focuses on curbing institutional powers and removing unfriendly incumbents is not likely, at least in the current Latin American context, to provide much of a solution.

Where traditional institutions remain unresponsive, a preferable alternative may be the creation and empowerment of new ones. This requires political leadership willing to take risks and to cede some control. It also requires a familiarity with the sector and its institutional culture that external supporters and even local political elites may lack. It is here that the initial reform group, which is often sidelined as the reforms develop, could be usefully reintroduced, especially if they can be diverted from their preferred theoretical focus to the challenge of making their innovations work.

This can be best accomplished by convincing them to work within the target institutions, rather than allowing them to maintain their positions as disassociated critics. In some sense, Peru, Colombia, and El Salvador have all reached this stage, although only the Peruvian reformers appear to be pursuing the strategy consciously. Their problem, however, is the transparency of the ploy, their unwillingness to cede any real control, and their visibly mixed objectives. More generally, until a way is found to strengthen and improve sectoral leadership, the objectives of improved performance will be incompletely realized at best and the larger question of the sector's political future will remain unanswered.

The other potential source of support, conspicuous by its absence is all cases, is the public. Although the issues debated seem unlikely to attract broader interest, this is still surprising on two counts. First, the reform movement did derive momentum from the widespread public dissatisfaction with the sector's performance. Thus one might anticipate some interest in proposals to improve it. Second, if not for the mass public, then for more specialized groups and elites, the changes have more concrete implications. However, with the exception of a small number of human rights and legally oriented organizations, public participation in or even attention to the events has been minimal or at best sporadic. This may have ensured a continued prioritization of themes whose broader discussion might have brought other outcomes; the emphasis on human rights and legal protections are cases in point. It may also have prevented the subversion of efforts to serve the interests of powerful minorities. Still, whatever the advantages of the conscious or unintended exclusionary strategy, all four reforms have reached a point where it merits reexamination. Certainly some of the issues now being raised deserve wider discussion. In addition, the involvement of outside groups could reinject momentum into programs that, for one reason or another, are losing their dynamism. Obviously, public involvement is no more of a panacea than that of a greater variety of sectoral members, but without a wider support base and ideally one from both sources, the future direction and progress of the reforms may face more serious threats.

Notes

1. There is an extensive bibliography available for those interested in further information. In addition to the sources cited, more general works include those by Browning, 1971; Lindo, 1990; North, 1985; and Russell, 1984.

2. White, 1987, p. 95. See articles in Roseberry et al., 1995, for a detailed discussion of the Salvadoran coffee economy.

3. In the 1970s, the Gini coefficient for concentration of land ownership was the highest in Central America and "one of the five highest in the world" (Boyce et al., 1995, p. 10).

4. There is a conspicuous absence of recent research on economic concentration, but it appears to remain relatively high, dominated at the top by a small group of businessmen who through their links with government and control of financial and other critical services effectively manage the entrance of new competition.

5. The Ministry of War (*Ministerio de Guerra*) was in fact usually headed by a civilian, and the police belonged to the Ministry of Government.

6. Total economic (not military) assistance authorized by USAID over the period from 1980 to 1989 reached $2,675,000,000 (Boyce et al., 1995, p. 21).

7. See Boyce et al., 1995, passim, for a discussion of economic policies and a critical evaluation of their consequences.

8. CEPAL, 1993, cited in Boyce et al., 1995, pp, 24-25.

9. MIPLAN (*Ministerio de Planificación y Coordinación del Desarrollo Económico y Social*), as cited in Boyce et al., 1995, p. 39.

10. For a discussion of this situation and the role of the former death squads, see Joint Group, 1994.

11. See Lawyers Committee, 1993, for a discussion.

12. One important example is civilian control over police investigation of crimes. The 1991 amendments gave this to the Fiscalía and further stipulated the transfer of the highly controversial Division of Criminal Investigation (the former Special Investigative Unit) to the latter body. This did not occur and was reversed by a later constitutional amendment. The problem is complicated by a belief that the Fiscalía, in its current state, could not exercise effective control.

13. This was clearly the case of the new Family Code and Juvenile Offenders Law, the contents of which, once they went into effect, came as a shock to many legislators. Among the most surprised may have been the Arenista leaders who promoted the codes as part of their party's presidential campaign. The passage of the Sentencing Law in 1997 suggests little change. In a private communication, one observer commented that he doubted the legislators had read it carefully, especially as regards the provisions for improving prison conditions.

14. One principal target was the new Judicial Council because of its effect on powers held by the Supreme Court and its president. The Court's opposition prevented the formation of the council until 1989 and, even then, guaranteed its domination of the new body until further changes were introduced in 1991 and went into effect in 1993. See Lawyers Committee, 1993, for a discussion.

15. This was the new Family Code (and its accompanying Procedural Law), approved in March of 1994 and put into effect six months later. A number of local nongovernmental organizations (NGOs) had participated in the discussion of the code and were prepared to push for its effective implementation. However, public discussions of the laws taking place between its approval and passage into effect, made it quite apparent that most of the legal community had never paid much attention to its content.

16. As one of the foremost Salvadoran proponents of reform noted in his own case, "…it never crossed my mind to be a judge…because I had no ties with authorities or high ranking officials who might recommend me" (Oliva et al., 1991, p. 16; my translation).

17. Williams et al., 1991, p. 9.

18. Méndez, in Oliva et al., 1991, pp. 13-14.

19. Méndez, in Oliva et al., 1991, p. 32.

20. Méndez, in Oliva et al., 1991, p. 15.

21. The initial amendment did not include the justices of the peace in this system; in 1991, the council was also empowered to preselect them.

22. The initial legislation gave majority membership to members or representatives of the Court.

23. El Salvador is one of the few Latin American countries to use juries. The innovation was introduced in 1906 and continues to be used for a selected number of crimes (generally homicide and robbery). Interestingly, most Latin American reformers have opposed the adoption of a jury system, arguing that it is culturally inappropriate.

24. Mudge et al., 1988.

25. Current legislation actually facilitates this practice by allowing a judge to entrust evidence to a reliable person, a provision arguably justifiable given the lack of secure evidence rooms. Of course, there was never any intent that this be interpreted as a long-term loan for personal use.

26. Literally, "someone who gets things out" apparently both people and papers.

27. For a number of reasons, including the long delays to trial and the frequent intimidation of witnesses, the latter were usually not called to testify. Instead, depositions taking during the *instrucción* were read during the hearing.

28. A 1993 survey indicated a total of about 137,000 active cases in the entire judicial system, of which about 59,000 were criminal cases. Since the inventory was largely restricted to trial courts, the cases correspond to the 40 first-instance criminal and 70 first-instance mixed courts. Only 20 percent of the cases were less than a year old, and only 50 percent less than two years. Thus, the number of active criminal cases can be reduced by half, making an average of about 270 per judge (Proyecto de Reforma Judicial II, 1994, p. 8). The survey did not include prosecutors and *fiscales*, but less systematic studies suggest similar workloads. As late as 1995 public defenders handled from four to one hundred cases. Interviews, El Salvador.

29. Proyecto de Reforma Judicial II, 1994.

30. El Salvador's Public Ministry was created in the 1950s and included (under separate leadership) both the Fiscalía and the Procuraduría.

31. A press release issued by the Court in 1995 notes that the Constitutional Chamber had received 893 requests for habeas corpus and resolved 199 during the preceding year. For *amparos*, it had done somewhat better, resolving half of the 783 requests presented. It was by far the busiest chamber; the least occupied was the Administrative Chamber Its total caseload was about 120, including cases held over from prior years; the number resolved is not noted.

32. This was in some sense a mistake, the result of the hasty negotiation of these elements of the Peace Accords. The proponents used the Costa Rican judiciary as a model, but neglected to note that its budget also covered the public prosecutors, public defenders, and the investigative police.

33. In a rather pointed anecdote, one of El Salvador's more distinguished criminal lawyers noted the potential costs of complaining to higher authorities about the comportment of a judge. In his discussions with a former Court president, a per-

sonal friend, the two considered how they could get the judge to make a ruling he had delayed for months without incurring his anger and thus reprisals against the lawyer's client. The outcome was not quite as they planned. The judge dismissed the case, but ordered the detention of the suspect. Amazingly, there was no easy solution for the situation and, although the ex-defendant stayed free, so did the judge (Méndez, in Oliva et al., 1991, pp. 37-38).

34. The two most important elements in El Salvador were ICITAP's police training program and USAID's two judicial reform projects. These have been almost as closely watched as the Salvadoran reform itself. See Alvarez, 1992; Carothers, 1991, and WOLA, 1990, for general discussions of the USAID program, and Spence and Vickers, 1994, and Spence et al., 1995, for more specific discussions of its projects. Mudge et al., 1988, 1996, offer USAID-financed evaluations of its projects.

35. Alvarez, 1992, and Carothers, 1991, give some background on the U.S. programs; the reasons for the United Nations' involvement are more obvious, but their programs still merit further study.

36. As other observers note, the failure to include more Salvadoran lawyers, and especially those with doubts about the direction of the reform, may have contributed to the persistent opposition to the new legislation. In mid-1995, this opposition, taking advantage of popular concern over escalating crime, reemerged and threatened to prevent passage of the new legislation without substantial modifications. See Mudge et al., 1996, pp. 8-9.

37. See GAO, 1992; Spence and Vickers, 1994; Spence et al., 1995; and Lawyers Committee, 1989, 1993.

38. The program has been criticized for its slowness, but not its seriousness of intent. As of late 1995, approximately twelve judges had been removed from office and twenty more were acknowledged to be under investigation.

39. Significantly, while ARENA gave the Procuraduría's leadership to minority parties (traditionally the Christian Democrats), it has held onto the Fiscalía and, it is rumored, takes a strong interest in which cases the latter prosecutes. Intra-institutional interests are also at play, especially those involving the leadership's direct control of appointments. One informant who had worked closely with the Fiscalía reported a significant amount of internal corruption in the assignment of cases; some of these could be very lucrative for the official in charge.

40. Interviews, El Salvador, 1995. The parties of the Left insisted that certain proposed constitutional amendments be ratified before the codes were approved. Technically, this was not necessary, but observers saw it as a way of establishing ownership over a part of the reforms.

41. A proposed constitutional amendment designed to give two of the six percent to the Public Ministry (the Fiscalía, Procuraduría General, and Procuraduría de Derechos Humanos), has been roundly opposed by the Court. In franker private discussions, its members often admit that their current budget (still less than six percent) is more than they can spend.

42. In addition to the works cited here, see the bibliography in Edelman and Kenen, 1989.

43. Barker, 1991, p. 352.

44. Barker, 1991, p. 353.

45. See Stone, "Aspects of Power Distribution in Costa Rica," in Edelman and Kenen, 1989, p. 23, and Gudmundson, "Peasant, Farmer, Proletarian: Class Formation in a Smallholder Coffee Economy, 1850-1950," in Roseberry et al., 1995, pp. 112-150.

46. Pérez-Brignoli, 1989, p. 77, notes for example that the battles between Liberals and Conservatives "were much less marked" in Costa Rica.

47. As Edelman and Kenen, 1989, p. 52, note, aside from the problems of instability and concentration of power evident in other countries, maintenance of a large army also cut into the scarce supply of labor, needed for coffee cultivation.

48. See Barker, 1991, for a discussion of Costa Rica's long internal struggle over the placement of these powers.

49. Rico, 1988, p. 60.

50. Rico, 1988, p. 95.

51. See Llobet, 1993, pp. 13-24, on the drafting of the 1973 procedures code.

52. Rico, 1988, pp. 119-120.

53. This is sometimes a source of embarrassment for their members, as during the trial of an accused drug trafficker, Ricardo Alem, in the early 1990s. Mr. Alem was so grateful to his public defenders that he took out a full-page ad in a local paper thanking them, an acknowledgment they would just as soon have avoided. Interviews, Costa Rica, 1992.

54. The 1993 Judicial Organic Law now requires that those able to pay for their own defense will be charged a fee for the services of public defenders. Revenues accrue to the Public Defenders Office.

55. The agrarian legislation, for example, shows a bias for the small farmer that is said to be further emphasized in the formation of agrarian judges. Both it and the family code draw some of their doctrinal emphases from mid-century Spain.

56. For a discussion of the program and a fairly negative view of ILANUD's role, see GAO, 1993.

57. In the mid-1980s two justices resigned and one remained under investigation (although reelected by the Assembly with a bare margin) because of their suspected involvement in accepting bribes from drug traffickers.

58. Rico, 1988, p. 63.

59. Rico, 1988, p. 63.

60. These criticisms have been a phenomenon of recent years and still continue, especially in regard to the justices' entertainment allowances (bolsas de representación) and travel. An article in a local news magazine, Rumbo (San Jose, Costa Rica) November 12, 1991, pp. 11-17, detailed some of these expenses, lamenting that so little in turn (16.24 percent of the budget) was spent on the investigative police. Actually the amount spent on the justices was less than two percent of the total budget, but it was the nature of the expenses that was criticized.

61. "Reelection" of lower level judges was done by the Court. Reasons for a negative decision were never made public and there was no appeal.

62. In conjunction with a case involving the defendant mentioned in 53, above, an entire Superior Court was denied reelection. They applied a law the Constitutional Chamber had invalidated because they had not received official notice of the decision. Although their action was technically correct, the Court regarded their

failure to delay their ruling (so as to allow time for notice to arrive) as an act of insubordination.

63. For a discussion of Costa Rica's involvement here see articles in Chapters 6 and 7 in Edelman and Kenen, 1989.

64. See articles in Maier et al., 1993. Interviews in Costa Rica (July, 1996) suggested several explanations, the minimal one that blamed inadequate training, and a more global treatment that also mentioned inadequacies in the code itself and an utter lack of planning for its implementation.

65. Several members of the Costa Rican judiciary had collaborated with code reform efforts in El Salvador, Guatemala, and other countries. The experience also served to inform their own reform program back home.

66. His resignation was also motivated by his criticism of the Court's conflict with the executive over a notorious extradition case. The principal dispute was between the Constitutional Chamber and the high level executive officials who had allowed the extradition of five Venezuelans facing charges in their own country but also accused of bank robbery in Costa Rica. By the time it was resolved, the Court, the chamber, the Public Defenders Office, and the Public Ministry had all become involved.

67. See Costa Rica, Supreme Court, 1993, pp. 16-17.

68. Interviews, Costa Rica, July, 1996.

69. In early 1992, the press ran a series of articles claiming that the chamber was so saturated with work that its paralysis and that of the government was threatened. In response, the chamber began a modernization program, financed in part by an emergency grant from USAID, which successfully staved off both threats. One lingering problem involves the chamber's criteria for determining the priority of cases. For example, an issue involving the National Soccer Federation that threatened the postponement of an important match received immediate attention, whereas the Drug Law and Traffic Code remained in limbo for over a year.

70. In informal interviews following their decision against the treaty, chamber members expressed their uncertainty as to the likely impact on relations with the United States.

71. Because of its functional independence and its ability to set aside or mandate decisions from the other chambers, many observers consider it the equivalent of a separate court.

72. Barker, 1991.

73. Thus, in the passage of a the new Juvenile Justice Law in 1996, the legislature imposed last minute changes to come down harder on juvenile offenders, and forced its immediate entrance into effect, overriding the judiciary's preference for a year's delay in which to prepare the new courts and train personnel. The Assembly also never delivered the extraordinary budget it had promised to finance the code's implantation.

74. Works giving a broader overview of Colombian politics are Bagley et al., 1986; Dix, 1987; Hartlyn, 1988; and Kline, 1988.

75. See articles on Roseberry et al., 1995, for discussions.

76. For a discussion of the periods when the constitution was "invalidated" and attempts made to rewrite it, see Charria Angulo, 1988.

77. *La Rama* is the shortened name for *la Rama Judicial* or Judicial Branch. Those who consider themselves members are very selective about who else is included. Simply having served as a judge is not sufficient. Thus, Jaime Giraldo, one of the fathers of the current reform and a former judge and Minister of Justice, is, as one observer noted, not recognized as a member.

78. See note 77, above. While Giraldo in the end was critical of the 1991 reform package, it drew from many of his own proposals. See Giraldo, 1992, passim.

79. This is treated in the narrative. It is worth noting that even the usual critics like Americas Watch, while expressing reservations, found the reforms supportive of human rights and a more effective separation of powers, while many Colombians (including Giraldo) are concerned as to their enhancement of executive powers at the expense of the judiciary and Congress.

80. See Nemoga Soto, 1988, pp. 77-93, for a discussion of the background to these reforms, especially as they relate to the judiciary.

81. At the time this was all Colombia had of a Public Ministry, an entity responsible for overseeing (*fiscalizando*) judicial compliance with legal norms, and for representing the state in legal conflicts. Its role has since been expanded to include a Human Rights Ombudsman, legal defense, and oversight of administrative as well as judicial performance. The 1979 constitutional reform proposed to make it the home of the Fiscalía, which would handle the investigation and prosecution of criminal cases. However, the reform was declared unconstitutional by the Supreme Court.

82. See Nemoga Soto, 1988. Hinestrosa, 1987, pp. 20-26, summarizes the various appointment systems in effect from independence to 1987.

83. More sophisticated analysis of course finds other causes, including rural poverty, changing patterns of land holding, and the two-party system's failure to reflect the interests of the popular masses. See Dix, 1987; Kline, 1988; Hartlyn, 1988; and Bagley et al., 1986, for a discussion.

84. It is also commonly held that the military junta insisted on this arrangement, which would allow them to chose the first Court. Their immediate concern was preventing a more politically responsive entity (i.e. a Court chosen by the assembly) from turning around and investigating their past actions. See Gómez Albarello, 1996; Herrán, 1994; and articles in Leal Buitrago, 1996.

85. The National Front formally ended in 1974, although the bipartisan distribution of government positions continued afterwards. The Comisión Andina, 1988a, p. 73, while admitting it had lost its force in the lower level tribunals, still cites it as one of the impediments to judicial independence.

86. See Nemoga Soto, 1988, Chapter 3, for a discussion of the amendments and an analysis of the forces and motives behind them.

87. The *bogotazo* was the period of violence in the capital following the assassination of the presidential candidate, Jorge Gaitán. Its final products were the Rojas Pinilla dictatorship and the National Front.

88. Comisión Andina, 1988a, p. 72.

89. Nemoga Soto, 1988, pp. 97-100.

90. Only the judiciary's operational budget was transferred. Its investment budget remained in the hands of the ministry.

91. At issue was the reformed Concejo's intention to introduce a merit-based system requiring written examinations. This threatened the patronage formerly exercised by the appellate courts as well as the fate of those subject to examinations. The judicial employees' union called a strike to protest the measure, which was finally adopted when the Court announced that no appointments would be made without prior examination (Giraldo, 1992, p. 83).

92. Hernán Echavarría Olozaga, in introduction to Giraldo, 1992, p. xiv.

93. Comisión Andina, 1988a, pp. 59-60.

94. The special courts and public order courts use "faceless judges" to try suspected drug traffickers and guerrillas. Aside from the principles of due process violated by a "faceless" judge and anonymous witnesses, most complaints focused on the juridical shortcuts associated with these trials. See Americas Watch, 1992b, and Comisión Andina, 1988a, for discussions. Giraldo, 1992, also offers some observations on due process problems.

95. The Council of State predates the administrative court system it now heads.

96. Where its competence ended and that of the Supreme Court began, was occasionally a problem, which in turn could be submitted to the third body with powers of judicial review, the Disciplinary Tribunal. After 1991, the situation was further complicated by the extension of the Procuraduría's powers to the oversight of administrative actions. However, it operates more as an Inspector General than as an administrative court.

97. The situation of the judicial police is also complicated, as much a function, delegable to other bodies including the military, as an organization. In the latter form, it was under the control of the Procuraduría General until 1987. When it was transferred to the judiciary's *Dirección Nacional de Instrucción Criminal* in that year, a protest by the Procuraduría brought its initial return, which was overridden by the Supreme Court, leaving it with the Dirección (Comisión Andina, 1988a, pp. 86-94; Nemoga Soto, 1988, pp. 131-134).

98. In a May 10, 1983, decision, the Court found that the right to defense was included in the constitutional guarantees of due process.

99. Comisión Andina, 1988a, pp. 142-53.

100. Figures vary; those given here are from the government commission charged with studying sector financing. (See Columbia, Comisión, 1996, passim and p. 21.) The Comisión Andina 1988a, p. 86, estimated 7.7 percent for 1986 which it found inadequate, noting that this was lower than in prior years. By their calculation, the Rama received roughly 8 percent in 1994. Differences may be simple error or depend on definitions of the budget or the sector. However, 5.4 percent or even 2.9 is still high for the region, and the world.

101. Comisión Andina, 1988a, p. 21.

102. Giraldo, 1992, p. 27.

103. For example, a 1984 study found about the same number of civil cases (1,397,800) in judicial offices and an annual accumulation rate of 5.7 percent (Giraldo, 1992, p. 31).

104. Study from Instituto SER, cited in Giraldo, 1992, p. 20.

105. Study from Instituto SER, cited in Giraldo, 1992, p 60.

106. Giraldo, 1992, p. 21.

107. Cited in Giraldo, 1992, p. 22.

108. Colombia, Comisión, 1996, p. 11.

109. Giraldo, 1992, p. 10. More recent figures show 112 judicial employees per 100,000 population as opposed to 20 in the U.S. (*Miami Herald*, International Edition, August 4, 1997, p. 3A).

110. Then Minister of Justice, Enrique Low Murtra, as cited in Comisión Andina, 1988a, p. 85.

111. Ahumada, 1995, sees little impact; Americas Watch, 1992a, and Dugas, 1995, interpret it as key.

112. The Procurador General's opinion was based on the lack of connection between the executive decree and the state of siege declared in 1984. "What is presented as the supreme manifestation of participatory democracy may turn up to be a blank check for the next president and his advisors, twenty, thirty, or forty individuals who will be enabled to decide the way to convoke the Constitutional Assembly" (Alfonso Gómez Méndez, cited in Ahumada, 1995, note 4).

113. Ahumada, 1995, p. 5.

114. Ahumada, 1995, p. 6.

115. Americas Watch, 1992b, pp. 91-92.

116. Dugas, 1995, passim. Unlike Americas Watch, 1992b, he also is unreservedly approving of the accusatory system and the increased role for the Fiscalía.

117. See Ahumada, 1995, who shares this view and cites several local commentators to this effect.

118. See Colombia, Ministry of Justice, 1991, for a sample.

119. This is Ahumada's (1995) argument.

120. An earlier proposal to limit the council to the constitutionality of administrative actions of "general application" was discarded as impractical, Giraldo, 1992, pp. 163-164.

121. The extent to which this coordination includes some control is still a matter of dispute, regarding which the Council of State, the Supreme Court, the Procuraduría General, the Judicial Council, and the Fiscalía have all issued different opinions.

122. Initially, the Fiscalía was to be located in the executive branch. It was decided that this would increase its susceptibility to political control, leading to its placement within the judiciary. It was also argued that this made sense in that the *fiscales* had assumed some judicial functions, including their ability to decide on preventive detention and issue arrest and search warrants.

123. Defenders now receive one million pesos (about $1,000) a month as opposed to 1,800,000 under the former system. Official figures show them handling an average of ten cases for a possible total of thirty a year. Since many involve the special "abbreviated" process for minor offenses, productivity is quite low. Interviews, Bogota, October, 1996, and April, 1997.

124. Cappalli, 1990, notes a similar and longer term problem with the Chilean *queja*, the use of which as a fast track appeal has led to congestion at the Supreme Court level and driven out other more conventional forms of appeal. See also articles in Valenzuela et al., 1991.

125. Americas Watch, 1992b, pp. 93-94.

126. See Castillo, 1996, for one of the most dramatic arguments in this regard, where he "names names," and offers a detailed discussion of the treatment of extradition.

127. This is Giraldo's (1992) comment, both in his 1992 book and as cited by Ahumada, 1995. It was repeated by several other Colombians I interviewed.

128. Jaime Giraldo, personal interview, October, 1996.

129. The 2,000 CTI investigators represent only one quarter of the 8,000 investigative police. The rest belong to the National Police and the DAS, the Colombian equivalent of the FBI. The Fiscalía is responsible for coordinating the investigative actions of all of them, and of other police or military forces recruited for investigative tasks. The multiple organizations, organizational cultures, and different approaches to investigation have not made this easy despite the creation of a formal coordinating body.

130. It has been suggested that the Fiscalía be absolved over the short run from dealing with common crime, which could be handled by police and judges under a modified inquisitorial system. As noted, the current placement of Public Defense is also not optimal.

131. Gómez Albarello, 1996, is most optimistic about the new activism. However, he warns that it could cause the Congress to be much more careful when it chooses the new court in the year 2000.

132. Gómez Albarello, 1996, p. 46.

133. Colombia, Ministerio de Justicia, 1995, *El perfil de los jueces*, p 48. Cited in Gómez Albarello, 1996, p. 47.

134. This term is very popular with development agencies, who claim it as a precondition (most often violated in the breach) for the initiation of assistance projects. See Hansen and Blair, 1995.

8

Peru's Experience in Comparative Perspective: Prospects and Lessons for Reform

Despite its debt to the past, the Fujimori program constitutes a significant departure from justice reform trends elsewhere in Latin America. It deviates from the conventional model in its composition, political base, methods, and even the explicit vision of the reformed system it pursues. As for its implicit objectives or eventual impact, only time will tell. The new reformers' development of their program and their success in implanting it are consistent with the country's political *coyuntura* and, as a consequence, unlikely to be duplicated in less dirigiste systems. However, their efforts also respond to more widely shared conditions and could, over the longer run, provide a partial model for those frustrated with the failures, or even the successes, of more conventional reforms. In a number of other countries there are already indications of impatience with the slow advance, uneven impact, and unanticipated consequences of on-going programs. In the three case studies, where progress has been more notable, these developments are also visible. All three have substantially increased the budgets of their sectoral institutions and given the latter considerable leeway in determining their use. More recently, criticisms of the insufficient returns on these investments or of runaway institutional powers have begun to emerge. In a few countries just initiating their reforms, political leaders[1] have shown signs of interest in asserting more direct control. Lacking a Fujimori or Dellepiane, they have not advanced far, but neither have the factors motivating their attempts disappeared. In short, Peru's most recent departure from regional trends is of broader significance as a possible indication of where others may be heading. One crucial question is, thus, whether it is most responsive to a set of special circumstances or to factors and developments already present or likely to emerge elsewhere in the region.

As regards both the justice sector's shortcomings and the difficulties of overcoming them, Peru's longer history of reform efforts is hardly unique. The criticisms of performance detailed here would sound familiar to any informed observer in a majority of the region's countries. Many of them still strike a nerve among members of more advanced systems.² As illustrated in the shorter comparative case studies, there are important national variations, both in quantity and quality. Corruption and politicization are common complaints, but for some countries they are virtually the driving force behind the system's operations. Not surprisingly, high levels of both are usually associated with the most unprofessional or simply incompetent personnel. Sector officials could always use higher pay and better equipment, but in Costa Rica they are relatively, if not extraordinarily well reimbursed. Salaries of federal judges range from adequate to very comfortable in Mexico, Brazil, and Argentina, as do those of the ordinary judiciary in Chile and Uruguay. In other countries, it has been said that the government tolerates bribery as the only way to assure adequate "salaries."³ Costa Rica is also an exception in that for decades, it has maintained a reasonable salary level for all its sector professionals, not just high-ranking judges. Despite the regionwide adoption of more accusatory systems, El Salvador's practice of paying defenders and prosecutors substantially less than the ordinary judiciary is, unfortunately, still common.

Certain countries face additional obstacles because of their historical and social circumstances. Excessively concentrated control of the economy, exceptionally unequal income distribution, a long history of dictatorships and unconstitutional shifts of government, or particularly bitter partisan conflict are not propitious settings for the development of any kind of democratic institutions. These factors have evidently worsened Peru's situation, as they did that of El Salvador. In the latter country, a viable reform would still be unthinkable were it not for foreign pressures and assistance. As foreign attention turns elsewhere, there are already signs of a shift in the direction, if not the momentum of change. The subclass of societies with a large indigenous population also can anticipate additional challenges in shaping reforms to overcome the structural and attitudinal biases against those groups. However, this same kind of institutionalized marginalization affects the poor majority in general, whether ethnically distinctive or not. Throughout Latin America, Pásara's⁴ contention that justice has traditionally been for the middle classes is fairly accurate. Significantly, those countries where justice seems to work better (Costa Rica, Uruguay, and Chile) are also those where the middle class is proportionately and politically more important.⁵ Even in these less problematic cases, there has been a decline in satisfaction over the last few decades with sector performance, concerns about new kinds of corruption and politicization, and a growing sense of institutional irrelevance or inadequacy in the face of rapid socioeconomic change.

In most countries,⁶ public attention and that of would-be reformers first focused on criminal justice. The objective problems may be no greater there than in the civil courts and may, in fact, directly touch fewer people, but this is where such common vices as delay, formalism, failure to respect due process and basic rights, or simple inefficacy have their most dramatic effect on human lives. It may be true, as the saying goes, that you can steal more armed with a briefcase than with a gun, but violent crimes cause a more visceral public reaction. And, whether these crimes are perpetrated by state actors or by private citizens, the sector's failure to bring them to justice, or its complicity in their commission, causes more intense complaints than the periodic revelations of judges being paid off in civil cases or the more pedestrian observation that such cases, whether fairly resolved or not, are subject to interminable delays.

The specific focus of complaints has shifted over time, from human rights abuses, to crime control, to new kinds of political intervention both by the courts and in them, and to simple irregularities and inefficiencies in the handling of cases. The usual characterizations of the underlying causes are virtually identical. In the best cases, sector institutions and their individual members are described as governed by outmoded rules and procedures, and unresponsive to the new demands of society and social groups. In the worst, they are also depicted as corrupt, politicized, unprofessional, and increasingly irrelevant. While the situation is changing, most have been sorely underfinanced for decades. Their traditional status as the orphan branch of government has often created a vicious circle; lack of financing perpetuates poor performance and encourages corruption within sector institutions, which in turn decreases their value and, with it, the motivation to increase their budgets. Latin Americans have suffered for the past half-century from bad or, at best, inadequate justice, but this has also been cheap justice. One enormous extrasectoral obstacle to reform is reaching the understanding that any improvement will be more expensive. Costa Rica, a notable exception on both counts, provides a good argument for more generous financial support. It also suggests that higher budgets alone will have a slow and not entirely positive impact, a point that is further driven home by recent increases in funding for Argentina's federal courts.[7] In countries lacking Costa Rica's additional advantages or, like Colombia, simply facing more challenging environments, their impact could be still more mixed. For all the attention to Costa Rica's accomplishment, Colombia has in the last years spent a comparable proportion of its budget on its judiciary. This has not prevented complaints of inadequate funding, the irrational and inefficient proliferation of new courts and offices, or increasingly deficient performance.

The parallels in objective situations and public perceptions are no accident. Aside from the broader similarities in their historical and cultural backgrounds, the countries for the most part[8] inherited a common legal tradition. After independence they continued to be influenced, often nearly simultaneously, by many of the same extraregional trends, whether in the form of new codes, exposure to the same foreign jurists and doctrinal sources, or an increasing contact with Anglo-Saxon law. This has meant that their basic legal infrastructures look very much alike. This fact, combined with the sociohistorical commonalities, easily explains why current complaints are virtually interchangeable. The national justice systems can be said to share the same objective flaws and the same real or perceived lack of match with the national "realities." Thus, whether or not one accepts the inherent inferiority of the inquisitorial, written criminal process, its further development throughout the region encouraged the same type of vices. Confronted with a burgeoning workload, judges increasingly delegate to staff to do the written preparation of cases. The staff in turn are able to shape the preparatory documents to influence if not determine the outcome of judicial decisions and often accept or demand bribes to do just that. Time constraints and poor preparation in investigative techniques has also meant that "investigation" is increasingly confined to what can be done in the judicial offices, in effect the review of written police reports and the taking of depositions from witnesses. As the case studies also demonstrate, efforts to break this pattern with the introduction of an independent prosecutorial organization have encountered similar obstacles, ranging from judicial resistance and lack of police cooperation to inadequate financing and training for staff in the new institutions.

The situation of legal education provides another example. While its quality does vary from country to country, it universally stresses the limited interpretive powers of the judge and relies more on the memorization of legislation than its application to real cases. Because students usually pass directly from the equivalent of high school to law schools, and from there to judgeships, they are generally deficient in many potentially complementary areas of knowledge, no matter how well they may know the law. This has become more of a problem with the democratization of the profession. However selected, would-be lawyers and judges are now far less likely to have the kind of general educational and cultural preparation that was the privilege of their upper and upper middle class predecessors.[9]

Of the four countries studied, El Salvador is the worst off in this respect because of the combined impact of its educational "reforms" and its twelve years of civil war. Still, Colombia and Costa Rica's better trained judicial professionals show signs of an overly traditional education in the law that has ill prepared them to deal with more complex legal cases or with the challenges of institutional reform. The Costa Ricans' difficulties in designing a system for screening candidates to the judiciary and the Colombian Judicial Council's inability to assume its administrative duties are two examples of how such narrow education can distort the best intended reform measures. In all four countries, many of the newest codes are flawed by similar limitations as jurists attempt to treat contemporary social problems with doctrine drawn from the past century. The situation may be most apparent in areas like commercial law, but the family, agrarian and criminal codes often seem more grounded in nineteenth than twentieth or twenty-first century realities.[10]

Peruvian Reforms and Regional Trends

Latin America's justice systems share not only their afflictions, but also many proposed solutions. This, too, is more than coincidence or a mere consequence of objectively similar situations. It stems from the influence of the small number of the region's jurists who, since the 1960s, have been actively involved in efforts to reform what they perceived as the major failings of the systems. Although their initial focus was on revising and reforming basic codes, over time they have adopted a number of other common elements. Chief among them are measures to increase judicial independence by depoliticizing appointment systems; securing guaranteed budgets for judiciaries and increases for public ministries and other sector organizations; creating judicial councils and constitutional courts or chambers; and, generating interest in the adoption of modern information technologies. Contacts with European jurists and law schools, international agencies, and the various external assistance programs have fed this movement. In recent years it has also been influenced by direct contacts among the various national institutions. The formation of regional and subregional associations and work groups for judges, police, and other sector officials has been important, as has a still more recent tendency for countries with more advanced reforms to provide technical assistance to those just beginning. While at first such exchanges were financed by donor programs, more recently, the sectoral institutions have begun to arrange them directly.[11]

Peru's internal troubles since the early 1980s and, especially, after the *autogolpe* have diminished the country's active participation in the regional movement. Nevertheless, many of the changes suggested or adopted in Peru at the end of the 1970s and the continuing work on the new codes were clearly influenced by regional trends. Much of Peru's post-1995 emphasis on organizational and administrative reforms draws directly on experience with donor-sponsored programs and international contacts. Individuals who participated in these earlier activities are prominent as allies of the current reform and as its most important critics. Whatever the other effects of Peru's present programs, the adoption of new technologies and management techniques, if not the enormous investments, will be studied and possibly replicated by programs elsewhere in the region.

In the late 1970s and early 1980s Peru's reform efforts were at the forefront of the regional movement. Along with Venezuela, it was the first country to adopt a judicial council to depoliticize the appointment process. While the effort was not very successful in either case, that did not prevent a number of countries from imitating it. Peru's creation of a separate Public Ministry with responsibility for the prosecution, if not the investigation of crimes; its adoption of a guaranteed percentage of the national budget for the courts; and the establishment of a Constitutional Tribunal also put it among the first to attempt what have now become standard reform elements. In some areas, such as the creation of a separate agrarian jurisdiction with a built-in bias toward the small holder or *campesino*, it remains a regional model despite the partial dismantling of the system by subsequent administrations.

Although Peru's adoption, if not implementation of new codes did not stop with the Fujimori period, other countries have now taken the lead in the movement. The race to see who can develop the most "progressive" criminal legislation continues,[12] but attention finally seems to be shifting to making the laws work, with the concomitant realization that this is the far more difficult challenge. The same is true of such other innovations as constitutional courts, judicial councils, and judicial careers. By now a majority of countries have adopted some, if not all of these mechanisms. As even the most advanced examples demonstrate, however, they do not provide an automatic solution to the problems they address. Certainly, neither Peru nor the other three cases prove an exception to this rule. In each, partisan subversion or manipulation of the new processes and institutions is partly to blame. Their disappointing performance also originates in poor design and inadequately prepared personnel. These developments have not dampened the reformers' enthusiasm for the new mechanisms, nor have they led to a withdrawal of whatever additional domestic and external support had been attracted. In fact their implantation has often created new sources of support. Domestic groups, within and outside the sector, have begun to recognize that they provide alternative avenues for channeling their own interests. The actions of such opportunistic allies have not always been consistent with the reforms' official goals, especially when they involve the politicization of the new institutions. They have increased attention to reform and opened up the sector to a wider variety of influences.

The regionwide reform movement and its national variations have emphasized the sector's functional performance. They have also affected, if not always intentionally, its political role. So far, the effects have been limited to the institutional or constitutional level and, thus, to only a portion of their macropolitical potential. The issues raised by Peru's military government as to the sector's part in supporting the domination of traditional elites and its inherent bias against marginalized groups have not received much attention elsewhere, and have not been addressed by the main thrust of reform in Peru or in any other country.[13] The emphasis on human rights and institutional independence and neutrality presupposes equal treatment for all, but a traditionally neutral system, no matter how improved its functions, will still embody certain elite biases. These are evident both in the needs and values to which it responds and in its institutional style and culture. Efforts to increase legal services to the poor, provide interpreters for those not fluent in the official language, and enhance public knowledge of system workings can place the masses on a more equal footing, but they will not completely eliminate their inherent disadvantage in confronting a system shaped by and for the upper and middle classes. Because that disadvantage is a product of an entire socio-economic system, it is both impractical and illogical to expect the justice sector to adopt an active role in changing it. Short of calling for a revolutionary judiciary, there may, nonetheless, be additional measures that could be introduced to encourage services more in keeping with the needs and values of the broader public.

In this area, despite its impasse in advancing more traditional reforms, Peru has produced some novel programs, a few of which are included in its 1993 Constitution. Several of them represent complete innovations, in some instances contradicting the prevailing wisdom on reform. Most notable are the decision to elect justices of the peace and leave open the possibility for the election of first-instance judges and the recognition of customary law as a basis for judicial decisions. Both address problems of concern to other reformers. The first measure, in particular, is a radical departure from what is usually recommended and would seem to violate fundamental beliefs of even the most "progressive" members the legal community.[14] Its formal adoption by the current administration may be only another ploy to assert control over the court system, this time from below. Even so, it could open the way for more direct contact between the people and their judges, and significantly alter the manner in which the latter envision their role. As this potential effect runs counter to the new reformers' desire to decrease contact, it is no surprise that the status of Peru's justices of the peace is currently "under study." The second measure is equally novel, although its likely impact is slight. Still, of the several countries that have recognized traditional law, Peru is the first to permit its incorporation into the formal justice system rather than limiting it to indigenous communities.

The constitution's sections on the justice sector are also innovative and unconventional in what they eliminate or do not say, for example, the disappearance of a fixed percentage of the budget for the courts and the relative silence on judicial organization. These innovations also violate current juridical wisdom on reform,[15] but they represent improvements on its tendency to make independence synonymous with increased privilege and lesser accountability. Although present-day Peru provides no test for their effects, there are signs that reformers elsewhere are beginning to consider the convenience of similar changes. In an era where the rest of the public sector is suffering reductions in personnel and budgets, the contrary tendency in the justice institutions cannot be expected to continue uncriticized. If its members do not do their own belt-tightening, someone else may do it for them.[16]

Obstacles to Reform

With all these positive trends, it is logical to ask why Peru's results have been so disappointing and whether this is indicative of the future course of other reforms. In the light of post-1995 developments in Peru, the questions have still more ominous implications than was apparent three or four years before. The answer to the first question is found, in part, in the shortcomings shared with and, thus, threatening the entire regional movement. Peru's negative experience is useful as a warning of what to avoid. As to the common traits, Peru's conventional reform package—revised codes incorporating a move from written, inquisitorial systems to oral, adversarial ones; the creation of a separate prosecutorial function and a constitutional court; the introduction of a judicial council to depoliticize appointments; and the assignment of a fixed percentage of the national budget to the court—if undertaken somewhat earlier than in many other countries, encountered many of the problems now being experienced elsewhere and for many of the same reasons.

A first problem was the failure of Peru's reform movement to build on potential sources of support within the country. As one observer has noted, justice reforms in Latin America have traditionally been "guild" reforms,[17] mounted from within the legal establishment and often representing only a minority of its members. At best, broad popular interest in justice reform is a sporadic event, fed by occasional waves of scandal, crimes, or discoveries of corruption and human rights abuses. As compared to other things the public wants of its government, justice reform is a fairly low priority. However, it is relatively less expensive and difficult than many alternatives and, thus, can be carried along by a modest amount of support. Unfortunately, would-be reformers often seem more interested in the purity of their laws and proposals than in seeking wider backing. The absence of broader attention is not without advantages in that it reduces effective opposition. This means, however, that reform laws and plans often receive enough support for passage, but not enough for implementation.

This outcome is especially likely where, as in Peru, reform planning was kept to a small group and there was no effort or opportunity to draw in the Court, bar associations, or special interest groups. Peru's Judicial Organic Law was one exception, since it was developed in consultation with and clearly represented the interests of the judiciary, but it also suffered for lack of broader support. In this and other cases, the opposition was sometimes a little slow to mobilize. Once it did, however, it was able to obstruct or even reverse reform measures.[18] A more common problem has been a lack of interest and cooperation on the part of those needed to implement the reforms, that is, political and institutional elites and groups within the broader public. This can be contrasted with examples like Costa Rica, where the Court itself developed reform legislation and over time learned to involve the rest of the judiciary in its discussion; El Salvador, where international pressures and foreign assistance compensated for the lack of local interest; or Colombia, where concerned jurists and politicians combined efforts, albeit with more than judicial reform in mind.

A fourth example, not discussed in detail, is Uruguay. There, the new civil procedures code owes its success to its authorship by several distinguished local jurists and occasional members of the Court, and to the backing of local business groups. The involvement of the latter groups is unique to Uruguay. It emphasizes a point less evident in the other three cases. While the reformers always require broader support, its precise nature is defined by local political trends and the issues of the moment. In present-day Peru, it may be sufficient to attract the backing of the top levels of the elite, although this obviously presents other dilemmas. There is, in short, no universal formula. The allies available in one country at one point in time may never be available elsewhere or even in that same nation at some other historical moment. The more universal truth is that, as more groups are drawn into the discussion of a proposed reform, they are likely to demand changes in its content. As a result, the process is slowed and produces a less elegant and internally consistent package, but one, nevertheless, that will have a greater chance of surviving as more than a gleam in its authors' eye. Internal consistency may also be an overrated virtue, especially when, as often happens, it is the product of inattention to a majority of details. The effects are compounded when inattention in turn is caused by inexperience, ignorance, or a very narrow perspective. A comparison of any new code with its predecessor usually makes it evident, from what is altered and what is carried over, that its authors' radically new vision was considerably less global than promised.

It is also possible that the existence of a supporting alliance that agrees on the general goals of reform will prevent their subversion by groups who quickly perceive the ways to divert them to their own advantage. This has been a common problem with the establishment of judicial councils, created to decrease politicization, but often becoming even more effective channels for partisan intervention.[19] This development has frequently been a surprise to the promoters of the new mechanisms who, in their haste to get the measures approved, pay far too little attention to the details of their composition and operations. Earlier and broader discussion of the proposals might reduce the opportunity for such behind-the-scenes manipulations by adding more practical insights to the reformers' theoretical perspectives. Whether or not one agrees with the explicit goals of Dellepiane's reformers, the secrecy with which their strategy is being elaborated obviously increases the chances for its subversion to purely political ends.

Expanding the support for reforms also means that, of necessity, they must respond to more than a concern for ideological purity or to uniquely institutional interests. The jurists who have promoted the reforms were usually familiar with European trends and further influenced in criminal law by a strange mixture of German juridical theory, Dutch abolitionism, and the French deconstructionists.[20] Like any group of specialists, they tended toward arguments often intelligible only to themselves and increasingly out of touch with popular concerns. Many of the themes they emphasized—the curtailment of human rights abuses and arbitrary applications of the law and the elimination of unnecessary delay and the needless imprisonment of "innocent" suspects—were of potentially wider interest. However, the reformers made little or no effort to explain them in terms that any citizen, or even a fairly well educated one, might understand. Moreover, as the countries have moved out of an era of rampant and dramatic human rights abuses, the urgency that might have been felt by the ordinary public diminished, replaced by concerns with corruption, impunity of common criminals, or the apparent irrelevance of the ordinary legal processes. Thus, even where governments had passed legislation in a burst of enthusiasm for its progressive content, or because this was the only alternative to business as usual, the pressure to make it effective had disappeared. Few administrations have followed Fujimori's lead in promulgating additional and usually contradictory decrees as solutions of expediency for these emerging problems.[21] Many others have merely felt no need to make good on the legislated changes. That Colombia, Costa Rica, and El Salvador were able to go through with their reforms was the result of their fortuitous coincidence with additional interests of potential allies. These interests might not have sprung from the same ideological sources, but they did not explicitly contradict them.

This raises a second problem, the reformers' own lack of attention to implementation. The codes' authors frequently seem content with their passage alone, perhaps trusting that reality would eventually catch up, but not regarding that as their responsibility. When asked about implementation, their answer is often more laws to regulate the activities of the institutions that will carry out the reform. Where, as in Peru, the principal authors were outside the affected institutions, this is a realistic reaction, but it has a number of negative consequences for the overall feasibility of the proposals. The lack of interest in implementation often encourages the production of overly complex or impossible new requirements, innovations that even in the best of worlds would not work because they defy human and organizational capabilities.[22] It also means that reform proposals depend on new infrastructure or skills that will not be in place for some time, and without which, former practices will continue unchanged.[23] Finally, it fosters a neglect of whole areas where changes will be required if the new proposals are to work. Most of these areas do not require new legislation, but rather the development of programs for training, improved work methods, management information systems, oversight and disciplinary bodies, internal reorganizations and reassignment of personnel, and better administrative and planning systems. While the argument may be overstated, it has often been said that substantial improvement could be achieved, even under existing codes, with attention to some of these additional measures. Whether or not this is true, the changes dictated by the new codes will not be realized unless and until these complementary programs are introduced.

Fortunately, sector institutions and the external reform groups are beginning to understand this reality. Peru's new Judicial Organic Law's brief mention of such factors as technological change, training, and foreign assistance is a beginning. Dellepiane's almost exclusive focus on the first two elements, if arguably erring in the other extreme, was an evident reaction to their former neglect. Other countries have been more successful at integrating them into their existing reform programs. Costa Rica's judiciary has been exemplary in its use of training, development of administrative offices, and interest in modern management technologies. Foreign assistance programs have promoted their adoption in other countries. These are areas where donors believe they can provide support without becoming too "political."[24] However, lack of experience, including that of donor agencies, with such nonlegal matters continues to obstruct progress. A belief in the efficacy of training and modern technology does not guarantee their best use. There is a marked tendency to create false hopes of immediate improvement with the addition of a judicial school, a planning department, or a large computer purchase. Ironically, the traditional legal establishment's all-consuming fascination with the law may feed this tendency. Relative ignorance of other disciplines encourages the sense that they, unlike the law, have simple, clear-cut answers that, once supplied by the appropriate experts, can be accepted at face value. This makes the traditional legal profession undiscerning consumers of new technologies and methods. It does little to prepare them for the behavioral changes they will have to make to choose and utilize new techniques.[25] It may be just as well that most courts do not have the financial capability to carry these innovations to extremes. As with the new codes, there is a danger that initial disappointments will discourage further experiments.

A third, related area of problems involves the continuing emphasis of most reform proposals, especially new legislation, on the judiciary. Peru poses a partial exception in its earlier creation of a Public Ministry and a consequently slightly greater attention to the latter in its new codes. Yet, a reading of its reformed codes still indicates more concern with judicial processes and an implicit assumption that the actions of other entities will fall into place. Defense, as noted, is treated minimally; police and prisons are conspicuous[26] by their near absence; and the private bar also gets little attention. Presumably, all this was to be dealt with in complementary legislation. As in the case of the nonlegal aspects of implementation, one suspects that lack of attention signifies lack of importance. The reform process currently underway in Peru partially rectifies this situation with its simultaneous, if separate attention to the police and prisons. The Public Ministry and defense remain outside, as much for ideological and political as for strategic reasons. Both their absence and the lack of coordination among the other elements are bound to create further institutional conflicts.

This tendency is also evident in other countries, such as El Salvador, with its well-financed and increasingly powerful Court. The Court continues to absorb resources that might more logically be invested in other institutions, a trend that is hard to combat when the other institutions are so weak. That Costa Rica and Colombia have avoided the tendency, with Colombia possibly going to the other extreme in the case of the Fiscalía, is a result of very special circumstances unlikely to be duplicated elsewhere. The Colombian procedural code, in fact, devotes remarkably little space to the courts, the judges, or the trial, which may explain why the judiciary has been so slow to prepare for its new role. In this regard, the Colombians may be correct in arguing that their reform is unique, the product of the unusual circumstances surrounding its introduction. However, if the particular emphasis is atypical, the tendency to focus almost exclusively on one element unfortunately is not.

Panama is another atypical example. Since the 1940s, its criminal justice system has featured an unusually strong Public Ministry. As in Colombia, it exercises powers normally restricted to the judiciary.[27] In this situation, Panama's efforts to focus its recent reforms on the judiciary are reasonable, although they stem more from traditional biases than from an in-depth analysis of the sector's needs. It is surprising that more countries or their political leaders have not recognized the potential advantage in strengthening the prosecutor's office. Aside from the political pay-offs, a strengthened prosecution *and* defense could more effectively shake a complacent court into action than the usual strategies of increased budgets and independence. However, Colombia's recent experience with an independent and enthusiastic prosecutor may well discourage further experiments.[28] Mexico's strong, but unreformed Procuraduría is a negative example of another sort, a prosecutorial office that has been blamed for much of the corruption in the criminal justice system.[29]

The exaggerated focus on the judiciary is also evident in the frequent failure to hold broader consultations on legislation intended to reshape the sector and to limit the discussion to judicial leaders or reform-minded judges. Guatemala's new Criminal Procedures Code (1994) was written by a small group of jurists under the direction of the chief justice and was only made known to the rest of the judiciary, the Public Ministry, and the wider legal community after the final draft was completed. El Salvador's new code had yet to be formally discussed with the police three months before it was first scheduled to be approved (in April, 1995). Subsequent delays in its approval did not much improve the situation. Its Family Code (1994) was drafted without consultation with the Procuraduría General (in charge of legal assistance to the poor and "protection of the family"), a key institution in its implementation. In both Salvadoran examples, formal public presentations eventually gave these institutions and their members a chance to weigh in. Still, an earlier institutional view might have been more effective.[30] In the case of Colombia, as in many others, one problem is that the additional institutions barely existed when the legislation shaping them was being drafted. The logical question is with whom one would have consulted. Nonetheless, the lack of input from future institutional leaders or the officials who would be transferred to the new bodies led to unwelcome surprises when the legislation was enacted.

One critical factor in the successful implementation of all new criminal procedures will be the coordination between prosecutors and the police. All codes give the former control over the latter's investigations. What that means, operationally, remains a puzzle and a point of contention, even after new practices formally go into effect. If not evident to the reforms' authors, it is obvious to observers that the key to real change is less the different operations of the judiciary than it is of these two institutions and public defense. The issue is further complicated by its novelty and the consequent lack of successful models within the region. Any expectation that this might have encouraged more attention to the theme has not been met. A reading of most codes demonstrates greater emphasis on such traditional judicial functions as the appeals process, or judicial relations with the prosecution than it does on the latter's role vis-a-vis the police. One evident obstacle is that those writing the codes have never participated in an accusatory process and, so, base their descriptions of procedures on what they know best, even as they try to transcend it. This is true even of the one exception, Colombia, where the detailed discussions of prosecutorial and police actions remain visibly and extensively influenced by pre-existing practices.

The fourth and final problem is that of financing. Here, too, while the judiciary has suffered, it is the lack of increased budgets for these other institutions that has been most critical. If the problem is insufficient funding to do anything, the solution is admittedly more than larger budgets—and there are examples, if not many of them, to demonstrate just that.[31] Furthermore, budgetary needs should be divided into two types: one to cover operating expenditures and the other to finance reform itself. Generally, increases in both will be necessary to improve performance. Growing donor interest in sector reform or Peru's privatization windfall are a source of funds for one-time investments. Operating expenditures depend on the government budget and the national will to invest in better justice. Their contracted studies to the contrary, the Peruvian reformers' optimism about decreased operating expenditures seems excessive. Improved justice can be expected to cost more over the long haul. Donors have frequently tried to condition their assistance on increased domestic funding, but tight government finances and the fact that donors often make this a condition for all their programs (and not just those in justice) have reduced the efficacy of this leverage.

In addition, as more donors and other external assistance agencies become involved, this kind of conditionality is harder to maintain. Relationships among these actors are often as competitive as they are cooperative, a fact that beneficiary governments have increasingly used to their advantage.[32] High level meetings may promise cooperation, and it may in fact work in other sectors. In justice, the more usual rule at the moment of designing projects and signing agreements is every donor for itself. This competitive relationship has also discouraged the willingness of external assistance agencies to learn from or build on each other's experience, a particularly unfortunate development given the relative novelty of the area for all of them, the resources already wasted on redoing the same preparatory studies, and the occasional repetition of the same mistakes. The results have not been disastrous, but beyond the effects on attempted conditionality, they have encouraged overfinancing and redundancy in areas where everyone wants to work, and the funding of some activities that objectively represent fairly low priorities.[33] One can hope that this is a temporary phenomenon, and that as external agencies gain more experience, they will focus less on protecting their turf and more on working together. Since Peru, for better or worse, has remained beyond the pale for the last few years, its reforms have at least been spared the effects of inter-donor conflicts.

The Role of Elites and Vested Interests

Before proceeding to a discussion of Peru's special problems, more specific attention is due several factors with less impact on reform failures than is often supposed. These are the resistance presumably offered by political and economic elites and by sector leadership. The underlying argument in all cases is that these groups and individuals stand to benefit so much from the status quo that they will oppose change at every turn and have, thus, been the most important obstacles to reform. The mechanisms and the motivations attributed to the resistance are slightly different in the three cases and, thus, are best treated separately.

In the case of the political and economic elites, the usual contention is that these groups depend on the existing justice system to maintain their hegemony. In the extreme, the system's very dysfunctionalities are depicted as beneficial to them. In more moderate versions, they are portrayed as simply tolerating the inconvenience as the price for maintaining their power. Thus, the criminal justice system, the impact of which falls largely on the lower class (the majority of those arrested and imprisoned and the victims of human rights abuses), is seen as a mechanism for keeping the latter in their place. Rampant corruption here and in the civil justice system works to the benefit of elites who can buy their way out of trouble or pay for favorable decisions. Slow handling of cases benefits the wealthy who are best able to withstand delays. In short, the built-in biases of the system favor the elite and legitimate their position. Hence, they have no interest in reform and can be expected to oppose it across the board.

These arguments have attained some popularity among those critics of reform who believe it has not gone far enough. Within Latin America, they are associated with still another movement, "critical criminology" (*criminología crítica*), the members of which have often participated in the drafting and promotion of new codes. There is an apparent disjuncture between their depiction of the criminal justice system as a tool of the establishment and their reform proposals, which, while stressing due process principles, still do not call for its elimination.[34] Much of the literature arising out of Peru's New Law group anticipated these themes, although usually not this "abolitionist"[35] conclusion.

There are elements of truth in this analysis. Formal institutions will inevitably be shaped by and reflect the interests of dominant social groups. The latter also have the resources to bend those biases still further when necessary. However, it is a far cry from this to the discovery of a one-to-one correspondence between elite interests and system performance and the notion that every "dysfunctionality" is in the best interests of the elite. If the justice system did work this way fifty years ago, its calcification in the face of societal change and a diversification of elites and elite interests makes the continuation of that symbiotic relationship increasingly difficult to explain. The argument also fails to account for the increasing criticisms of sector performance and the passage of reform legislation, which one assumes any elite alliance would have squelched more effectively. Finally, if the system is holding the poor down, it is doing a poor job of it, and might better serve that end with a dramatic infusion of budgetary support for police, criminal courts, and prisons.

As has been suggested in earlier chapters, the real impediment is less elite opposition than the elite's lack of interest. The truly powerful still find other ways to resolve their conflicts, protect themselves, and punish their enemies. However, at some point the escalating decline in sectoral performance, the rampant corruption, unprofessionalism, and inefficiency, do become an embarrassment and an inconvenience. They make it harder to attract foreign investment and tourism, run a business, raise a family, or lead a normal life. In many countries they have also escaped the possibility of direct control. Whereas once a call to ones cousin, the judge, might have smoothed over any problems, sector officials are now less known and less predictable quantities.[36] Some take bribes, some succumb to political pressures, and some, inexplicably, stand on the little bit of power and authority they believe they hold. Hence, if elite notions of the goals of reform do not coincide with those of other social groups, the argument that they are a major *active* obstacle to change seems drastically overdrawn.

There is more room for this kind of argument in the case of political elites and justice system incumbents. Members of these groups do continue to draw direct benefits from the status quo, although not universally and not for the same reasons. For politicians, control of sector institutions, and especially of appointments, has traditionally been a consequence and means of access to power. The extent to which this control was exercised varied from country to country. Most entering administrations expected to pick a new Supreme Court or at least some of its members. Occasionally, they might replace a good many judges.[37] They often influenced transfers and promotions. As new institutions—judicial councils, special courts, prosecution and defense—emerged, the party in government usually maintained some role in their selection, although this has been limited when their introduction is already part of a reform movement. Throughout much of Central America, this same practice extended to the police, down to the very lowest levels. In Peru and elsewhere in South America, the "cop on the beat" was generally not a patronage appointee. Political appointees could generally be expected to recognize their political debt, on request, in their actions and decisions, but the primary purpose of controlling appointments was patronage, the ability to give jobs to supporters.

In recent times, under more competitive mass-based party systems, and with a heightened role for the judiciary as an arbiter of politically charged issues, control of appointments has become less an end in itself than a vehicle of partisan competition. This places a higher premium on partisan identification of the candidates and, it is argued, has produced a less distinguished and less professional judiciary. It has also brought partisan battles into many Courts, as fewer of them are chosen by a single party. The unintended effects on performance, legitimacy, and even the Court's (and thus any party's) ability to control the rest of the judiciary have usually been negative. In this context political elites face an interesting dilemma and one that makes them more open to reform proposals. While reluctant to lose a chance of controlling the judiciary and other sector institutions, they may find that what they really have is incomplete control of an increasingly illegitimate body and growing public complaints about ineffective and inefficient performance. Thus, if not for all parties, and not in all countries, justice sector reform becomes an interesting political platform. Politicians have, it is true, occasionally sabotaged reform measures through last minute changes designed to advance their partisan interests. This usually leaves the main portion of the reform untouched. The remaining impediment, as with the economic elites, has been a lack of sufficient interest to provide adequate funding, especially for such mundane items as salaries and operating budgets, or when they are provided, the expectation that this will automatically produce improvements.

In Colombia and Costa Rica, the decision to moderate partisan control over appointments preceded the broader interest in reform, coming as part of a systemic concern about the destabilizing impact of partisan competition. In both countries, the decision also led, if a bit later, to greater financial autonomy and larger budgets for the court system. The consequently more independent judiciaries have not been immune to other problems, including most recently, their entrance into conflicts with the executive. The earlier resolution of the first two issues may have eliminated any lingering elite ambivalence about reform. It also reduced its urgency. In Costa Rica, this left the judiciary to promote its own changes. In Colombia, it brought the more intense involvement of political elites only when the judiciary's shortcomings were again linked to a wider political crisis.

If economic and political elites receive indirect and decreasing benefits from dysfunctional justice sectors, the same is not true of some system incumbents. Undeniably, some lawyers, judges, police, and other functionaries, at all levels of private and public institutions, owe their livelihoods to what others perceive as system failures. Theirs are the vested interests most directly affected by reform measures, although it is easy to overestimate their numbers as well as the intensity and effectiveness of their opposition. It is also worth noting that, for all the disorder caused by threatened work stoppages, strikes, or more subtle forms of internal sabotage, opposition from the bottom is easily overridden by determined leadership. When institutional leaders refuse to cooperate or oppose reform, the prognosis is less positive and the outcomes more confrontational. The four case studies abound with examples. The conflict between the Colombian Court and executive over reform-related issues may be one of the best, especially given the Court's use of constitutional principles to defend its own powers.

Still it is naive to assume that the most direct way to overcome opposition is to replace the incumbents.[38] Peru, as one of the countries with the most dramatic experience with this tactic, provides ample evidence of its ineffectiveness. Politicians in Peru and elsewhere have proved adept at eliminating recalcitrant or overly independent leaders. They have either not wanted or have been unable to choose more capable substitutes. As for the main body of institutional members, a few, well-chosen dismissals can provide an object lesson to those who remain. Mass firings, absent other changes, in the end only make matters worse. The quality of system personnel is indeed a major obstacle to improvement, but more as passive than active resistance. None of the region's reforms has yet gone far enough to determine the severity of the problem or the extent to which it can be resolved with training, new incentive and control systems, and procedural and organizational change. Costa Rica, once again, is an exception, but of limited utility given the time it took the judiciary to professionalize itself from within. Dellepiane's efforts to effect the changes in years instead of decades will inevitably attract broader interest despite the high costs and dubious political agenda. However, the real test is not what can be imposed in three years time, but whether it can be maintained once external controls are reduced or removed.

Peru's Special Problems

Peru's lack of progress in effecting improvements can be blamed in part on obstacles found elsewhere. It also has suffered its own peculiar series of setbacks. To start, its socioeconomic and physical characteristics suggest a particularly difficult setting for this and many other kinds of reform. The country's size, difficulties of internal communication, vast differences in the living conditions of its populations and, accompanying cultural and educational differences, unequal distributions of wealth and income, and the presence of a large indigenous population subject to four centuries of exploitation combine some of the least favorable circumstances facing any country in the region. The concentration of wealth, services, and the educated and cultural elite in Lima, and the latter's traditional ties with European and later American cultural and economic influences are further negative elements. The historical tendency for Limeño elites to be more connected to events in international centers of influence than with their own national hinterland is changing. Still, an enormous gap remains, making it difficult to set truly national policies.[39] Compared with many of the region's countries, Peru has a relatively sophisticated and educated elite. While attuned to world trends, it has also been able to build its own distinctive local culture. Unfortunately, it is not shared by the mass of the national population. Thus, in justice reform, as in other areas, intellectual leaders may innovatively adapt the latest thinking, but in forms that remain out of touch with the larger national realities. Although the same can be said of several of its regional neighbors, the gap is especially wide in Peru.

One of the most dramatic demonstrations of this phenomenon is the Uchuruccay massacre of the early 1980s. Here a group of peasants purportedly stoned to death eight journalists who were investigating human rights abuses and the terrorist situation in a far removed area of Peru. Several of the peasants were eventually tried for the crime. The facts of the case were never satisfactorily clarified, and it became a cause celebre for many local political and ideological factions. To this day, many believe the incident was instigated by the military, who wished to remove inconvenient witnesses to their antiterrorist campaigns. Others claim that the journalists were the unfortunate victims of conflict between peasant groups or between the later and terrorist bands, or of peasant superstition.

Perhaps as significant is the controversy surrounding the trial and the earlier investigation of the incident by a group of social scientists and other intellectuals headed by the novelist and later presidential candidate, Mario Vargas Llosa. Vargas Llosa and his colleagues were accused of complicity in covering up government involvement, and of paternalism and prejudice in their treatment of the affair.[40] It was asked whether the *campesinos* could be charged with a crime they did not regard as such, and whether they ever truly understood why they had been arrested. Even if they could be considered guilty, others criticized their imprisonment as a kind of cultural crime by the state. Still others argued that these very considerations represented the worst kind of paternalism, one that treated indigenous citizens as little more than children. The confusion over the facts of the case combined with intellectual grappling over the theoretical issues never produced a satisfactory resolution. It, nonetheless, serves to illustrate the problems of defining and operationalizing justice in a country where the level of national integration is still far from complete.

In some sense these special obstacles have yet to be confronted; none of Peru's reforms have gone far enough to do more than indicate their presence. As suggested in the earlier discussion of Peru's new codes and of its current reform, these factors will reemerge and show their true dimensions as schemes designed in Lima are taken out to the hinterland, or just into the reality of Lima courts and police stations. There is another set of special problems that deserve mention as having already affected reform progress. It concerns the dramatic decline in the external prestige and internal morale of the judiciary over the last decades, a phenomenon felt throughout Latin America but compounded in Peru by the purges and other actions taken by recent administrations.

In an era where judicial prestige and morale is at an all time low in much of Latin America, Peru's situation may look no worse than that of many other countries. However, Peru's judges and other sector officials have taken an unusually hard public beating with several additional negative consequences for reform prospects. With the military's attacks in the early 1970s, Peru's judiciary was the first in the region to be the target of such extensive public criticism and may still hold the record as a victim of negative campaigns. The Belaúnde and García governments dropped the topic temporarily. Fujimori's justification for his *autogolpe* revived it. What his criticisms lacked in analytic depth they more than compensated with anecdotal evidence, with still more negative repercussions for the institution's public image. Peru's justice sector has also been the subject of an unusual amount of critical academic analysis. While this has less impact on public perceptions, it has certainly reached the eyes and ears of institutional incumbents and has further discredited them among political and intellectual leaders. Why Peru's judiciary and other sector institutions have been the subject of so much public and academic vilification remains unclear. It would be difficult to argue that they are objectively any worse than those in a number of other countries. They certainly have received far more negative attention.

Ironically, it was the two governments, the military and the Fujimori administration, which accorded least importance to the judiciary, that dealt them the hardest public blows. There may be a sort of perverse logic to this; the ideal scapegoat is one that can be sacrificed at least cost. Both regimes found ways to circumvent existing institutions or set up their own parallel systems to carry out their high priority programs. Once having delivered their diatribes and eliminated unfriendly judges, they shifted their attention elsewhere, a trend reversed by the present government only in the past two years. However, this lack of attention is also more generalized as witnessed by the low budgets assigned to the sector by all governments over the last twenty-five years. The country's economic problems of the 1980s were indeed shared by the entire public sector. The judiciary felt the dual injury of public contempt and some of the lowest salaries in the region. Salaries have finally risen in the last few years. Monies for equipment, construction, and new programs have only recently been increased, and their use and distribution, like the entire judicial budget, remain under external control.

The final legacy of the military, which did immeasurable damage to internal morale, was the system of special ratifications or purges of judges. For much of its recent history, Peru has been less affected than the rest of Latin America by the common practice of letting a new government form its own Court and occasionally replace a majority of judges. The Peruvian Court had always been exempt from the ratifications mandated in the 1920 and 1933 constitutions, and these in any case, were more honored in the breach for the rest of the bench. Governments routinely imposed their own candidates as vacancies emerged, but the Peruvian judiciary, if it could count on little else, enjoyed permanent tenure. While undoubtedly subject to pressures from local and national elites, judges were under no compunction to toe any particular ideological line or demonstrate any active partisan affiliation (aside from the one that got them their first appointment or any subsequent transfers). Hence, unlike many of their counterparts elsewhere, they could maintain some illusion of professional independence that, like their job stability, might compensate for low salaries, poor working conditions, and gradually eroding prestige.

All of this changed dramatically with the military's decision to summarily remove unfriendly judges and replace them with those with proper ideological credentials. Judges who did not lose their jobs, or new appointees, now found that a certain amount of revolutionary fervor, or an extraordinarily low profile, was a requirement for remaining on the bench. The purges and the new rules for appointments began to create unprecedented divisions within the legal community, between those seen as collaborators with the military and those who for whatever reason lost or did not receive positions. The situation was further complicated when the most progressive would-be reformers, the New Law group, decided to accept appointments as a means of carrying out their own reform programs. Their ideas, if carried into action, might have brought real improvements. Sadly, they arrived too late, and only succeeded in discrediting themselves and many of their proposals for change.

What was carried over into the next few governments was the practice of mass purges and the rancor behind it. Many of the reformers, distinguished jurists in their own right, permanently retired from the cause. Their recommendations and proposals remained buried in the judicial archives for over a decade. The divisions within the legal community allowed no effective resistance to the further politicization of the appointment process under Belaúnde and García, this time without even the pretext of ideological conviction behind it. The judiciary and Public Ministry still maintained a number of dedicated professionals within their ranks. Even they were tainted in popular perceptions and those of their colleagues at the bar as little more than lackeys of whatever group was in power. The continuing discussions of reform, which began to generate more interest in the later 1980s, rarely included seated judges, and still more rarely any members of the Court or Public Ministry. Then, just as a new reform movement finally reached agreement on substantive changes, Fujimori began the purges all over again.

There are few other countries in Latin America where governments have so effectively eroded the institutional integrity of the judiciary and probably none where it has been done so gratuitously. Fujimori and the military stacked the Court and then circumvented it. Political intervention in appointments is commonplace throughout the region. It generally is not accompanied by such vituperative attacks on the institution. Where it is established practice, it does not create the kind of internal divisions, nor has it tarnished incipient reform movements or their proponents to the extent it did in Peru. A quarter century of these policies has left the judiciary demoralized, discredited in the eyes of the public, and largely cut off from groups still interested in reform. The chance to revise the Judicial Organic Law and participate in the Constitutional Assembly's committee on the judiciary did attract some cooperation from would-be reformers. The government's continuing lack of active support for their programs soon ended this revival of interest. The stage may have been set by decades of judicial complaisance and inactivity, but in recent times one of the greatest obstacles to positive change was the government's own abandonment of the sector's core institutions, based on a perception of irrelevance that became a self-fulfilling prophecy.

Peru's Future Prospects for Reform

Peru's early start, abortive implementation, and subsequent stasis do offer some advantages. It now has in place much of the normative structure that could serve as the basis for reform. It also can benefit from the experience of those countries that have begun to enact similar reform packages. It has as well, for better or worse, a fairly docile judiciary and Public Ministry, whose members seem disinclined to engage in the more corrupt and scandalous practices of their predecessors. It is also possible that the Fujimori administration has imposed more order on the police and prisons, although probably not increasing the respect for human rights in either. Finally, with public finances now in better shape, the government has been able to move the sector institutions from abject to genteel poverty, dedicate its own funds to modernization programs, and again attract the interest of foreign donors. The latter would clearly feel more comfortable cooperating with a government with a stronger commitment to human rights and more transparent political objectives. That has not prevented their thinking about financing programs and entering into discussions with the administration.

On the negative side, the current program has again been captured by still another small band of insiders who once again are prepared to impose reform based on their own narrow vision. Their style corresponds to that of the current administration, which is also, conveniently, their principal source of support. This coincidence of interests has guaranteed rapid progress in introducing change. The greatest risk, as always, is that their departure will provoke the usual reaction, focusing first on purging the reformers and their collaborators and then on undoing as much of their program as possible. As in the past, most energies would be expended on punishing the guilty, creating still more hostilities and divisions within and outside the courts, and afterwards, attention would turn elsewhere. Fujimori's selections have undoubtedly produced an undistinguished judiciary, almost totally lacking in the kind of leadership needed to head a reform. However, if only out of fear, they may as a whole be more honest than their predecessors and, thus, conceivably more amenable to cooperating with a reform produced elsewhere.

If new purges and vindictive "reform" are the most dramatic risks, the eclipse of the old leadership and the issues they introduced is more disturbing. It was foreseeable before 1995 and accounts in good part for the lack of progress in the three years after the *autogolpe* when the old reformers enjoyed their last chance to push their program forward. The phenomenon has been aggravated by several subsequent developments, each with its own consequence for present and future actions. First, Peru's troubled 1980s and the post-*golpe* events turned attention elsewhere. Economic decline and recovery, privatization, terrorism, drug trafficking, and the emergence of new political forces all gave the population and political leaders other things to think about, both generally and in terms of their own survival strategies. The new constitution, while it promised changes for the justice sector, also created the basis for far more fundamental alterations of the country's political and economic structures. Working these out in practice would be a major task of the next decade, and one that made justice reform a far lower priority.

Second, the traditional reform package responded to interests and pressures that are no longer as strong as they were ten or fifteen years ago. The Fujimori administration's tendency to play fast and loose with human rights and due process has maintained some concern with these issues. However, its success in the war against terrorism has reduced wider public interest. For many, the success vindicated the tactics of expediency. Furthermore, the period of the worst violations appears to have ended. Ironically, the creation of a separate Human Rights Ombudsman may have isolated these themes from the issue of sectoral reform. Domestic and international human rights groups are already directing their attention and resources to the new organization, seeking to augment its role and influence its definition of its own policies and agenda. The latter will involve some instances of judicial or sectoral malfeasance, especially as they affect marginalized populations. However, the inevitable focus on specific cases and specialized issues will discourage a more systemic approach. It will inevitably leave the question of routine sector operations to Dellepiane and his reformers. Much the same may be true of the new Constitutional Tribunal, which by drawing attention to a small number of highly critical cases, and to the protection of the entity itself, will also divide the efforts of backers of comprehensive change.

Third, the government and the public's recourse to alternative mechanisms for doing the business of justice made the formal institutions look less important. Many of these alternative mechanisms (ranging from special courts to popular and elite vigilante groups) are unfortunate inventions. Others, like the Human Rights Ombudsman or private arbitration centers appear more positive, but still tend to divert public attention and that of potential reformers. To the extent they serve immediate needs, they remove pressure for more comprehensive solutions. Over the long run, the majority of informal and often illegal institutions represent a destabilizing, nondemocratic force. Over the shorter term, they, like the legal alternatives, may help hold things together, stave off impending crises, and reduce interest in the fate of the ordinary institutions they replace.

Finally, the administration's program to cut back the state's role in the economy, both by selling off its enterprises and liberalizing legal controls, has had a similar effect on the perceived importance of its formal justice institutions. Especially if combined with the development of arbitration or fast track treatment for large economic interests, it could divert several potential sources of support for change. This may not help the plight of the ordinary Peruvian caught up in the "normal" criminal or civil justice system, but the common citizen is likely to have other things on his mind, as higher priorities for any political activism. On the other hand, the judiciary and the rest of the sector maintain a potentially decisive influence, either as impediments or facilitators, on various government actions and policies. Thus, at present, the group with the major interest and the greatest role in setting the current reform agenda is the government itself. Whatever the other purposes, its actions constitute a sort of preemptive strike against the damages the sector could effect on the administration's program or its external image.

In short, Peru's traditional reformers lost their chance by setting their aims to broadly and their support too narrowly. Accidentally or intentionally, the Fujimori administration further undercut their appeal by co-opting, usurping, and dividing attention. If the broader issues raised by the traditional movement have a future in Peru, and most would accept that they should, they will require another raison d'être and another supporting alliance. This does not mean throwing out the old reform package or many of the ongoing efforts. It does recommend the addition of complementary actions aimed at tapping new sources of support and placing a different emphasis on the problems to be resolved. Human rights and due process are still necessary themes. A reform focused exclusively on their realization is too narrow and, furthermore, not likely to acquire sufficient momentum to guarantee even its own success. Modernization and technical proficiency are likewise important, but also not the only criteria for improvement. If Peru's justice system is to regain relevance and thus fulfill its role in helping to consolidate democratic development and national integration, it must change in a variety of ways. It must become more effective, efficient, intelligible and accessible and the justice it disperses must coincide more closely with social values. This does not imply the much feared "popularization of justice," wherein judges and other sector officials sacrifice their higher principles in favor of popular opinion. It does mean, however, that they are in touch with the latter and capable of justifying their principled decisions in terms that the wider public can understand. It also suggests that changes in substantive laws, procedures, and organizational practices take into account the concerns and complaints of the public, in short, that justice be perceived as a public good and not the exclusive property of sector professionals, be they jurists or administrators and planners.

The kinds of changes envisioned here will take much longer and should be done in less haste than had been expected by traditional or the new reformers. They will also require far more intra-institutional consultation and more open-ended experimentation than either reform package allows. Coordination among sector institutions is also essential and is conspicuously lacking, even in the current program. This is less critical in civil justice, but any criminal reform will founder if it is not encouraged. In all areas, the involvement of the bar and public interest and citizen groups is just as essential. Under current conditions, the forging of this larger alliance seems unlikely. The new reformers have been adept at coopting or neutralizing its potential leaders, but have been disinclined to accept them as equal partners in shaping their program. Their efforts to reduce inefficiency and corruption may produce some positive change, but certainly not in the areas of enhanced judicial independence, transparency, accountability, leadership, or an institutional ability to plot its own development and to respond to new demands emerging internally or externally.

A new government, perhaps spurred by the promise of external donor assistance, might take a more even-handed approach, assuming it can avoid the temptation of vindictive reform. Another possibility is a coalition of the old reformers, the Lima Bar Association or some similar professional group, a new Court (but one disposed to rise above past professional injustices), and other concerned nongovernmental organizations. It is anyone's guess where the movement might start. Especially with Peru's past history of opportunistic reforms, it seems particularly desirable that it grow to incorporate a wider selection of interests, motivated both by public concern and their own particular complaints about the status quo. Should Peruvians, or a significant number of them, not be able to agree on these objectives, then broad based reform will remain a dead issue for the foreseeable future. High visibility problems like crime, corruption, or delay will be attended by localized improvements (special courts, computerization, greater professionalization of the police, more, if not better, prisons), partial legislation, and continued direct government intervention in institutional affairs. Private lawyers will sharpen their skills and promote alternative mechanisms like arbitration. The poor will also receive their programs like the court tours, user-friendly guides, and simplified or alternative procedures. Those who are further removed from the main population centers will rely on their own informal justice or on special mechanisms (*rondas campesinas*, elected justices of the peace, and traditional law) sanctioned by the constitution or by government actions. Domestic and foreign human rights groups can work with the Human Rights Ombudsman and the Constitutional Court, offering general support and protection to both, publicizing their efforts, and helping the former in its specific investigations.

One evident danger, with fairly negative implications for further democratization, is the encouragement of a multitiered system, with differential treatment for different classes of citizens. Although one could argue that such a system will respond more adequately to their different needs, it hardly seems the appropriate basis for the sector or the country's further democratic integration. It will in essence perpetuate Peru's long-term tradition of noninclusive and, therefore, incomplete institutions whose lack of overarching authority must periodically be remedied by recourse to extraconstitutional mechanisms. Because this is a tradition, it is less worrisome than an entirely new trend. However, its further entrenchment in the justice sector will make future reform still more difficult. Over the shorter run, the Dellepiane reforms cannot reduce the sector's credibility much further. They will have a positive effect in removing obstacles to other kinds of socioeconomic reform. The sector's contribution to democratic institution building will be passive at best. By not creating additional problems, it can allow Peruvians to get on with the business of rebuilding a national society around it.

Peru's Lessons

Many of the obvious lessons to be drawn from the Peruvian case are fairly negative. This is not unexpected. Peru's reformers faced a set of exceptionally difficult challenges, even before the setbacks added by the military and the Fujimori governments. They also had the disadvantage of starting early and, so, lacked the benefits both of other examples and of participation in a growing community of jurists with experience in trying to put their ideas into practice. Today, anyone drafting a new code can consult not just with theorists, but with judges, prosecutors, and defenders who have lived the problems of the first model codes and who know where some of the pitfalls lie. If no country has yet developed a satisfactory model for the new prosecutors office, there are ongoing experiments to observe and variety of opinions as to how they might be improved. Countries like Costa Rica have developed defense, judicial training, and judicial administrative systems that are good enough to warrant imitation. The rebuilt police forces in El Salvador and Panama, if still far from ideal, nonetheless are a source of ideas for how to work improvements elsewhere. Colombia's disastrous overnight creation of its Fiscalía, like Guatemala's failure to prepare for its new code are dramatic arguments for planned and phased implementation. In short, if all the technical problems of reform implementation do not have solutions, the advances have still been substantial and there is a growing awareness that inattention to these details may be far more damaging than any error of doctrine.

This lesson has not fully penetrated. Not surprisingly, it was a Costa Rican justice who reminded his colleagues at a regional conference that until they developed an appreciation for other, nonlegal disciplines, they would not be able to implant effective reforms.[41] There were undoubtedly many present who did not understand what he meant and who went home to continue drafting codes as they always had. This relative enlightenment is still accompanied by the notion, apparently shared by Dellepiane's group, that reform is a one-time undertaking, and that improving sector performance is a question of a substantial investment of funds and a few years investment of time. International donors and lenders, with their own strict timetables, have contributed to the illusion. In particular, those who are investing large sums of money are under pressure to produce results, whether illusory or not. To admit that they are only helping to initiate a process that may never be finished, and that may reveal additional problems along the way, runs counter to their own incentive systems and internal politics. Domestic political and institutional elites face similar pressures. Once a reform has been announced, it must produce results and ideally in a reasonably short time. So long as those results are dramatic, the fact that they represent the exception rather than the rule, or are peripheral to real improvement is of secondary or negligible importance.

Because Peru's reforms never advanced that far, they have few lessons to convey here. However, there are some additional points to be extracted from its experience that still could serve other reformers. One of the most important is the limited positive impact of purely confrontational reforms, first because they undermine what little may remain of sectoral morale and integrity, and second because so few sectoral problems really begin with the sector. Where judges, police, and prosecutors are corrupt and incompetent, it is because the positions attract only this kind of candidate. If legal education is of poor quality, the alternatives may be no better. Peru's judges and prosecutors did not improve after the purges and conceivably became even worse. The other side to this argument is that to be successful, reform must focus on reactivating some kind of professional integrity and institutional identification among the sector's professionals. Despite the arguments that these groups usually oppose reform, Peru's experience with lay justices of the peace, agrarian courts, and the New Law activists suggests that this is not inevitable. Even should sectoral members not be reform leaders, little will be achieved if they are lagging as far behind as the Peruvian judges. The Fujimori administration's efforts to eliminate some of the more entrenched abuses of office (outside employment, hiring of relatives and irregular contacts between judges and attorneys) pose an interesting test of this argument. Imposed from outside over substantial if passive resistance from judicial employees, the measures may well curb the abuses. The impact on professional vocation is more dubious. Without that vocation, judicial performance will become more bureaucratized and formalistic.

To the extent the Fujimori government has a theory of judicial reform, it runs counter to conventional wisdom in positing that better performance comes out of lesser, not greater independence. It also contradicts the emerging consensus that isolation does not produce good judges. If the government continues with the experiment, the kind of judiciary, police, and prosecution it develops and the public reaction to whatever is produced will be interesting tests of both sets of hypotheses. The experiment may also be a warning to those elsewhere in the region of what can happen if they do not cooperate with less authoritarian reform programs. Peru's inventiveness does not end here. There are other innovations that bear watching should the government go forward with their implementation. Of particular interest are the two constitutional provisions that mandate the election of justices of the peace and recognize customary law as a part of the formal legal tradition. In as much as they run counter to the rest of Peru's current reform package, they may well remain dead letters. Should they not, they are among the most novel proposals to come out of the region's reform movement in the decade. On the positive side, they open up a new avenue of reform, removing some influence from the hands of intellectual and other elites, and giving the general public and its more marginalized members greater control over their judges and greater influence on the values shaping judicial decisions. On a less democratic note, they also raise concerns about the encouragement of multiple legal systems and second class justice for second class citizens.

Peru's contrariness goes beyond these two provisions. The elimination of the judiciary's budgetary earmark and of much of the usual constitutional description of how the judiciary will be organized and operate violate two common notions of how to augment judicial independence. Whatever the current administration's motivations, the potential consequences are not entirely negative. It is unfortunate that present circumstances do not allow a better test of how judicial independence is affected by these measures and how the results compare with the standard preference for earmarked budgets and less flexible, but also less manipulable organizational design.

In the more conventional reform areas, Peru's lessons may be largely superseded or simply duplicated by advances elsewhere. This later experience does not invalidate that of Peru. If anything, it has reemphasized and expanded some of the conclusions just beginning to be visible in the early Peruvian efforts. Fortunately some of the exceptionally negative lessons seem unlikely to be repeated in other reforms, owing to the special circumstances that produced them. Still, this is not impossible. Judicial purges remain a popular remedy, if one no other government has yet to incorporate in a reform program. Imposed, unconsulted reforms also have their proponents, whether out of sheer opportunism or simple frustration with judicial inertia. To date none of them has progressed far, lacking Dellepiane's blank check, but the variety of motives behind them are still very much in evidence. And while few governments have Peru's financial windfall to invest in modernization, the promise of external funding has kept alive the urge to promote new technology as the solution to judicial ills.

Whether Peru has fallen behind in the regional movement or charted a new course for others to imitate, its past failures and contemporary trends continue to pose some more basic questions about the value and significance of the effort as a whole. These questions are still more important today. The greater acceptance of justice reform has itself become an obstacle to success, encouraging a certain complacency about the promised benefits and the chances of their realization, and promoting routinization in program design. Reformers have become more sophisticated about the nature of their task, but their vision of its purpose and impact can still be characterized as both too broad and too narrow. Full success on their own terms will bring fewer of the promised benefits than proposed and a variety of unanticipated problems. Here, the unusual obstacles facing Peru's reforms, and many of the recent innovations deserve more reflection. They fall exactly into those murky areas the reformers have largely ignored. The next and concluding chapter, thus, takes a more speculative look at some of these issues and attempts to set justice reform within a wider context.

Notes

1. Minister of Justice René Blattman of Bolivia is one example. His sponsorship of constitutional and legislative reforms circumscribing the court's powers have been well received by many domestic and international observers, but nonetheless embody a top-down approach to sectoral development. The Dominican Republic's recent creation of an executive *Comisionado para la Reforma Judicial* is also relevant. Although the Comisionado's membership is multi-institutional, its head (a secretary of state without portfolio) shows strong indications of wanting to plan and implement reform with minimal participation. In both cases, the institutional aspects of sectoral reform have become linked to partisan conflict, as well as to the question of who will control the political resources forthcoming from external donors.

2. No one denies the relative isolation of the region's judiciaries as regards mass society, other sectoral actors, and the lower reaches of their own institutions. A

tendency to avoid political issues is also common and not without its advantages. Both in Costa Rica and Brazil (see Howell, 1995), Courts have pulled back from making foreseeably disastrous rulings on economic policy despite what they thought doctrine and national law dictated. Charges of corruption, politicization, or incompetence evoke more sensitivity. De Lima Lopes' (1997) or González Oropeza's (1996) contention that politicization and corruption are not problems in Brazil and Mexico, respectively, seems excessive and is contradicted by other evidence. Recent surveys of Brazilian judges (Bastos Arantes, 1997) indicate that they perceive political intervention as affecting performance.

3. Rospiglioli makes this argument for the entire public sector, but specifically mentions the corrosive effect on the judiciary, police, and armed forces. See Rospiglioli, 1991, p. 56.

4. Pásara, 1984, p. 206.

5. Observers also report that certain provincial systems in Argentina perform notably better. However, its federal systems is beset by many of the usual problems. There are also reportedly significant differences among Brazil's state systems.

6. Uruguay is the major exception. In Chile, Brazil, and Mexico criminal justice has also been deemphasized or ignored in favor of other reform elements.

7. See Verbitsky, 1993. Massive donor assistance projects and foreign loans have not always helped. While attempting to combat corruption, they also offer new incentives to engage in it.

8. Although all "Latin American" nations are considered members of the "Romanistic legal family," both by virtue of their colonial background (Spanish, Portuguese or French), and the post-independence impact of the continental (Napoleonic) tradition, they show varying exposure to other influences. Contact with the Anglo-Saxon legal system left its marks in the early adoption of juries and judicial review by a few countries. In more recent times, in both criminal and civil law, the influence of German, Italian and Spanish developments has been stronger. See Merryman, 1985, passim, and Zweigert and Kotz, 1987, pp. 119-120.

9. In its worst form, this results in lawyers and judges whose writing skills are deficient, who, as one law school dean noted, could not do legal research if they wanted to, and whose notion of an oral argument is long on histrionics and short on logic. Those who are adequately trained in these areas generally lack knowledge of economics, sociology, psychology, and other disciplines which they could presumably bring to bear on their understanding of cases.

10. In the criminal area, all codes have faced problems in dealing with modern crimes, especially those involving conspiracy, where efforts to give investigators access to private communications have run up against traditional views about the right to privacy. Here, two goals—the protection of an expanded list of human and legal rights and the system's efficacy in dealing with white collar or nonconventional crime—have come into conflict in a form for which traditional doctrine provides no easy answer.

11. For example, the authors of Uruguay's civil procedures code have frequently been invited to confer with jurists in other countries interested in adopting the code as a model. During the 1980s when Guatemala's Court president decided to sponsor the drafting of a new criminal procedures code, the Guatemalan Court hired its own

Argentine experts, preferring not to depend on the support of the U.S. government project operating in the country.

12. This is a curious aspect of the code reform movement. Those associated with new codes still make comparisons among them, usually claiming that their own is the most progressive, generally meaning more protective of due process and more purely accusatory.

13. Two exceptions are Nicaragua during the Sandinista period and Cuba, both with efforts to promote "popular justice." Currently, Nicaragua is undoing the Sandinista "reforms." One example is the replacement of the lay local judges with recently graduated law students. While the Sandinista judges were "popular," they were also highly partisan, a tendency that the present Court, including its Sandinista members, has rejected.

14. The decision to elect judges addresses the problem of partisan control of appointments by involving local communities. The more usual remedy is to try to depoliticize the central selection process.

15. The elimination of the Court's fixed percentage of the national budget is a less obvious improvement. Such percentages are usually determined arbitrarily and rarely delivered in their entirety. In other countries they often produce demands for further earmarking for other institutions that would not seem to be in the best interests of efficient budgeting of resources, either within the affected institutions or at the global level.

16. See Colombia, Comisión de Racionalización, 1996, with its recommendation that the judicial budget be held constant for three years to allow a rationalization and restructuring of its uses. The Costa Rican judiciary has found its six percent of the budget inadequate and, for the first time in forty years, is faced with the need to economize. Interviews, Costa Rica, July, 1996.

17. Pérez Perdomo, in IDB, 1993, p. 141.

18. Continued difficulties in passing new criminal codes in El Salvador and Ecuador, the delays in implementing Peru's criminal codes, and the conflictual handling of the new codes in Guatemala and Argentina are examples. In Argentina and Ecuador, the opposition was more personal and partisan than substantive.

19. See Pérez Perdomo, 1988, for a discussion of the overtly partisan motivations behind the creation of Venezuela's judicial council. Rico, 1993, covers a variety of Latin American and European examples.

20. See Zaffaroni, 1987, for an example of the results. The German influence is strongest and most universal, but Michel Foucault also has his followers. Fennell, 1995, includes a brief discussion of abolitionism.

21. One exception is El Salvador's "Emergency Law" passed in mid-1996. The law undermines many of the due process guarantees incorporated in recent legislation and even reverses some included in older codes. The law has been opposed by reform-oriented groups but is apparently supported by much of the public.

22. Thus, one Peruvian human rights advocate proposed a six-hour deadline for advising of a suspect's detention. When reminded that military detachments could be as much as a day away from radio contact with their bases, he suggested they fax their report. Arbitrary deadlines for completing investigations or trials, or the requirement that a suspect be provided counsel "immediately" are other examples.

23. In El Salvador, a new Juvenile Offenders Law advises judges to use alternatives to incarceration—probation, community service, and counseling—whenever possible. Unfortunately, the services do no yet exist. The provisions for interpreters and indigent defense in Peruvian legislation and most other new codes also seem likely to be honored in the breach.

24. For this reason, they, like investments in infrastructure, have become part of the World Bank and IDB programs. Training is interesting even for those not afraid of politics because it looks deceptively easy. Unfortunately, this often encourages a duplication of efforts.

25. One example is the fascination with "scientific evidence," essentially physical proof that relies on technical analysis (e.g. ballistics, fingerprints, blood typing, DNA analysis), and with expert witnesses. The notion that such " proof" is less than one hundred percent reliable and that its appreciation and use require an understanding of its limitations has been slow to penetrate the region's legal community.

26. The two criminal codes, like those approved or under study in other countries, make reference to various aspects of prison conditions, including humane treatment, and the goal of reeducation. However, in Peru as elsewhere, intrasectoral competition for budgetary funds generally means a lack of collective interest in promoting higher budgets for prisons.

27. The Panamanian prosecutor, as in post-1991 Colombia, is able to order detentions and searches and seizures without judicial orders. In both countries, unless the *fiscal's* actions are protested, the judge does not have knowledge of a criminal case until an indictment is filed.

28. It has been remarked that President Samper may regret his decision to extend the Attorney General's term, given the latter's investigations of campaign financing. Following Valdivieso's resignation to run for the national presidency, the investigations tapered off.

29. See González Oropeza, 1996, for a discussion.

30. In the case of the Family Code this might have avoided the Procuraduría's total lack of preparation and its consequent role as a major bottleneck in implementation.

31. The Salvadoran Court's use of its budgetary earmark to finance infrastructure and equipment may over the long run, in conjunction with the current reform program, produce real improvements. However, increasing judges' salaries, and giving them better working conditions did not bring noticeable changes in their performance or their handling of legal principles. This required other measures that were introduced later.

32. Haiti's announcement in mid-1996 that it would close its courts, dismiss all judges, and select and train replacements would apparently invalidate ongoing donor assistance. The Haitian government seemed to be counting on donors (e.g. the French), whose prior investment has been minimal, to support the new policy. In 1995, the Salvadoran Court, with a twenty-three million dollar IDB loan in the offing, pressed the U.S. government to accelerate the remaining disbursements in its grant program and to finance activities the latter had not considered high priority. The nearly explicit threat was that the Court would terminate the program early, and sacrifice the few million dollars remaining, if this were not done.

33. Training and automation are two areas that attract everyone. They are perceived (not entirely correctly) as easy, less likely to incur political opposition, and relatively showy. Although the resource demand in both areas is enormous, uncoordinated planning runs the risk of incompatible or contradictory projects. On the other hand, administrative reorganizations tend to be neglected since they are technical and not very exciting. Some of the worst examples of redundant activities are near misses, where saner heads prevailed before monies were spent. During the early 1990s, they included two separate proposals to finance Nicaragua's writing of a new Criminal Procedures Code, a seeming plethora of state-of-the-art forensics laboratories for Guatemala, and a plan to construct a single regional training center for all Central American judges. The latter would have made donor funding of a series of national judicial schools completely superfluous.

34. For an example, see Zaffaroni, 1987.

35. Critical criminology has also been influenced by the European abolitionist movement, which called for the abolition of the criminal justice system. See Fennell, 1995, for a discussion of the movement's lingering influence in the Netherlands.

36. Interviews in the Dominican Republic (December, 1996) indicated that private economic actors and members of large law firms became interested in judicial reform when they began losing cases they had formerly won with a little political pressure or a bribe. Private economic groups have thus provided financing for a local NGO, FINJUS, which has been at the forefront of the movement for reform.

37. Most de facto governments are slower to do this, perhaps because they expect that the judiciary will toe the line. However, any sign of noncompliance has usually brought a hasty decision to replace individuals or entire Courts.

38. Pérez Perdomo argued that efforts to work improvements by replacing the current judges presuppose that better ones will be found. He suggests this is not likely. See Pérez Perdomo in IDB, 1993, p. 148.

39. For example, one of the problems confronting the military's agrarian reforms during the 1970s was their incomplete understanding of the peasant farmers they sought to benefit. An insistence on the imposition of communal forms of land holding was based on the military advisors' romanticized version of *campesino* tradition. Still more basic was a faulty appreciation of how much land there was to go around, and what constituted viable holdings.

40. For his own account of the events, see Vargas Llosa, 1990, pp. 85-226. See also *Quehacer* (Lima), 32, 1984, pp. 10-17.

41. This was a member of the Costa Rican Constitutional Chamber in the 1991 International Meeting on Justice Reform in Latin America, sponsored by the Inter-American Development Bank.

9

Justice Reform in the Region: Some Concluding Observations and a Look Ahead

This more speculative chapter looks beyond the case studies to address some issues they raise, if often indirectly, but without providing sufficient evidence for any resolution. Various shortcomings of the attempted reforms, in Peru and elsewhere, have been noted in the foregoing discussion. For the most part the logic of the reforms has been accepted and criticism has been phrased in terms of the reforms' failure to meet their own goals. Less sympathetic critics have not stopped here. They have characterized the movement and its purported goals as intentionally or unintentionally misguided, an unconvincing attempt to resolve the wrong problems or an inadequate attack on the right ones, but in either case of dubious value.[1]

So as not to raise expectations as to a sudden change of heart, I will note that I do not share that conclusion. This final discussion remains sympathetic to the reforms and convinced that they do address problems worthy of resolution. Still, aside from their possible failure on their own terms because of poor design and implementation, it does argue that they suffer from two further limitations, which can be summarized as the reformers' excessive optimism about their ability to effect changes that make a tangible difference in people's lives, and their shortsighted analysis of their proposals' political implications. Neither observation detracts from the value of their objectives or from the chances that they will realize some of them. They do, however, indicate the desirability of further reflection, modifications, and possibly additional courses of action to address situations that the conventional reforms will not affect or may worsen.

A Schematic Approach to Reform Strategies

In the opening chapter, the question as to why bother with the justice sector was answered with an argument on its two contributions to democratic development: its provision of a basic public service as a means of ensuring social and political stability, and its embodiment of certain values critical to a functioning democracy. In more general terms, these can be summarized as the technical or functional and the political goals of justice reform, the first attempting to improve the sector's performance of its conventional role and the second altering that role's political content and orientation. "Political" is here used in the macro rather than micro sense, relating to the values and identifications shaping institutional actions, not just partisanship. Of course, both sets of goals in the end are political, but only the second represents an explicit attempt to change the political base for the sector's actions. It is worth mentioning that such attempts need not be limited to making it more democratic. The concerns raised about Peru's post-1995 reform reflect just such a consideration.

A distinction has also been made between reform measures that act on the internal workings of the sector and those that target its external relationships. Despite the apparent duplication, the objectives of reform should be separated from the targets of change. There is no simple one-to-one correspondence between them. The incorporation of democratic values is a change in internal procedures, albeit with political objectives, whereas a modification in external relationships, and thus in interinstitutional politics (e.g. a change in who makes judicial appointments) may aim only at improving technical performance. By combining the two dimensions, goals and targets of change, the result is a four-cell table (table 9.1) depicting four reform strategies. Within each cell, the activities most often adopted

TABLE 9.1:   Conventional Reform Strategies and Activities

Targets of Change	*Objectives*	
	Technical	*Political*
Internal procedures	Administrative systems	Substantive codes
	Procedural codes	
	Automation	Ethnics codes
	Disciplinary systems	
	Training	
	Merit appointments	Prison reforms
	Reorganizations	
External linkages	Judicial career	Civilian police
	Internal appointments	Prosecutors Office
	Judicial councils	Defenders Office
	Higher budgets	Judicial review
		Constitutional Courts

in conjunction with the strategy are displayed. Where activities occupy more than one cell, it is because they may be used for more than one purpose. This illustrates a first analytic conclusion. In effect there are far fewer things one can do to effect changes than there are reasons for doing them. Thus, to understand what is being attempted, one must look beyond the type of activity to its specific aims and content.

Starting in the upper left-hand quadrant, the first strategy pursues functional goals (i.e. improved performance) through the modification of internal procedures. It is where most reform measures have focused and where the lessons learned are most obvious. As noted, even purely technical change will affect the larger political system. An emphasis on efficacy and efficiency is itself a change in values; like the overall goal of strengthening system performance it has obvious macropolitical implications. However, here the impact is indirect and less threatening to the status quo than that of strategies seeking to alter the relative power of individual or institutional actors or the values and perspectives informing their actions. It is for this reason that improvements in the sector's public service function can be stabilizing for any regime type and why radical critics often oppose conventional reforms as disincentives to more fundamental change. This conclusion is strengthened by their portrayal of these reforms as augmenting social control. Even absent that effect, a more efficient performance of the sector's other functions can be expected to decrease at least some forms of social discontent. Although a majority of reform *activities* may operate in the first quadrant, most reform *programs* have not been limited to this strategy. They may introduce additional types of actions or adapt or tailor these basic activities to further political aims. Thus, the criticisms of reform's inherently conservative bias may be overstated, overlooking the potentially multiple objectives pursued through a single type of activity and the consequent need to analyze content as well as form in predicting impact.

It is the consequences of the other three types of strategies that are of more interest, since it is reform's alleged neglect or mismanaged treatment of political objectives and intersectoral relationships that has earned it the most criticism. These are also the areas where the reform programs themselves seem least clear as to their own objectives or the means for achieving them. Some confusion is produced by the fact that most reforms mix strategies. However, it also has other sources, as well. Before addressing them, the other strategies are briefly reviewed. To make the discussion less complicated, it focuses on changes in the direction most frequently dictated by reforms. However, it should be recognized that these strategies are not unidirectional. "Reform" could conceivably aim at lesser rather than greater independence from external actors, or introduce more elitist or authoritarian rather than democratic values. Again, the current Peruvian efforts are illustrative on the first count, and in the eyes of many critics, on both.

Preceding clockwise from the upper left, the second quadrant combines changes in internal procedures with an insertion of new political objectives, and is best typified by the democratic values argument. The goal is to change the political content of intrasectoral operations by modifying the values on which they are based. Common activities are revised codes embodying different principles (most frequently, an emphasis on human rights and due process, but they might also extend to biases toward or against certain social groups—as in the Peruvian agrarian courts), modified recruitment policies, training of sector personnel, and the introduction of incentive and evaluation systems to reinforce their new perspectives. Most prison reforms have also emphasized new values, including a more humanistic treatment of inmates or rehabilitation as opposed to punishment. Many of the activities utilized here may also be used for purely technical ends. Thus, an analysis of their likely impact must consider their more specific focus and content. For institutions already enjoying a good deal of independence, the introduction of new values may be sufficient to effect change. Where extra-institutional linkages allow considerable external control or where current institutional leadership does not endorse the reforms, a formal adoption of new values will be insufficient to guarantee their impact.

The lower right-hand quadrant combines political goals with extra-institutional change, introducing new values and new linkages with the wider political system. This strategy may combine activities from quadrants two and four (e.g. new procedural and substantive norms and new appointment systems). It is best exemplified by the introduction or redistribution of functions and powers among sectoral and extrasectoral institutions, for example in amplifying judicial review or the prosecutor or courts' role in investigating official malfeasance. Here, it removes the additional political obstacles to the revised internal operating principles and simultaneously alters the institutions' extrasectoral political role. Where that alteration increases independence, even without the explicit addition of new functions, it is also the most difficult strategy to implement, the hardest to control, and the most likely to provoke unanticipated consequences and adverse reactions. This is where most reforms eventually aimed, combining more explicit, somewhat reoriented definitions of functional roles and operating principles with a variety of measures to protect their performance against external intervention. However, there is a tendency for them to slip back into one of the other quadrants. These is usually because of external resistance to the often unanticipated consequences of the new independence or as a result of the institutions' incomplete absorption of the new values.

Where external resistance is strong, the political changes may be reversed and expanded functions discouraged or removed. The movement returns to the first quadrant, technical measures to produce technical improvements, a program by now acceptable to most political elites. The recent elimination of the Colombian Court's judicial review functions is an example, and one which may well be repeated elsewhere. Since in Colombia, the reversal has not affected the other institutions created in the reform, their future development may keep part of the strategy in the third quadrant or shift it to the fourth. The Fujimori government's more radical assertion of control over its judiciary and subsequent attention to judicial inefficiency and corruption is another, if far more drastic case. Where resistance comes from within the sector, the movement may be to the fourth quadrant, a change in extra-institutional linkages combined with technical change but no effective alteration in operational values. The Salvadoran reform currently occupies this quadrant. Efforts to change values and procedures, embodying some of them in new institutions, have lagged far behind the empowerment of a Court whose assumption of the new operating principles is far from complete. Strategies located in the third and fourth quadrants alter the institutions' influence as political actors. Only in the former can they be expected to operate externally (and internally) on the basis of new values and a consequent reinterpretation of their purpose.

In real life, the measures included in any single reform program often reflect a mix of these strategies, frequently utilizing the same activities to further both technical and political ends. This may be part of their initial design. More often it is the consequence of reform politics and of alliances among groups pursing different goals. Furthermore, even allies jointly pursing political or technical change often differ as to the specific ends and interests they are advancing. One may seek to impose values encouraging judicial neutrality, the other judicial activism. A change in external linkages may seek to eliminate external control or work to alter the identity of those exercising it. A certain amount of such confusion is essential to holding the reform alliance together. Where interests are in conflict, the longer run outcome will either serve one of them or reach an impasse, thus furthering none.

The Colombian Fiscalía is an interesting example of such mixed motives at work. It initial backer, the Conservative politician, Alvaro Gómez Hurtado, proposed it a means of combating crime and strengthening the state's social control function. However, the drafting of the Criminal Procedures Code and the legislation creating the Fiscalía was also influenced by the due process doctrine instrumental in shaping such laws elsewhere. Last minute efforts to incorporate contributions from both camps produced an exceptionally strong prosecutorial function that nonetheless is inhibited by certain procedural details, some of which seem to serve neither interest very well. The Fiscalía's placement within the *Rama*, but with semi-autonomous status and joint executive-Court participation in the selection of its head was another consequence of conflicting pressures. It brought its own problems and interinstitutional tensions, unanticipated by either party. It is not evident that the drafters realized they were making compromises, or when they did, what the consequences were likely to be.[2]

Apropos of such confusion, it is worth repeating that the common criticism that conventional reforms are "overly technical"[3] is based on a failure to separate mechanisms from their goals, or to recognize that a single reform activity may encompass both technical and political ends. This is reflected in the diagram by the placement of some activities between two or more quadrants. One of the best examples is training, which is used to improve technical performance but which can also inculcate new values. Procedural codes likewise can operate on both a technical and political level. If to a lesser extent, they may also modify external linkages by redefining and redistributing powers and functions. Nicaragua's draft Organic Law for the Judiciary attempts to do both, in effect incorporating an entire fourth quadrant reform strategy. Although it remained unapproved through early 1997, its unusually ambitious thrust apparently had not been noticed by the Assembly and was not a factor in the delays.[4]

On the other hand, measures to reduce external intervention or increase institutional independence may have virtually no impact on the political values shaping performance. Thus, the formal inclusion of multiple objectives or of activities usually associated with them does not guarantee that they all will be realized. As shown in the foregoing discussion, real impact is less a question of initial intent than of the appropriateness of design, the level of resistance encountered, and the political skills and resources of different members of the reform alliance. This lesson has long been apparent in other types of reform. If justice reformers have been slow to absorb it, their inexperience and the novelty of the issues are equally to blame. The situation is visibly changing as actors become aware of the potential for manipulating activities to alternative ends and of the danger of assuming automatic outcomes. Over the next few years this should make the politics of justice reform more conflictual and may alter the identity of those seeking to shape it.

The Limits of Conventional Reform Strategies and Some Possible New Directions

The most problematic aspect of these strategies has been their political impact, whether as the values they promote (quadrant two), the constitutional issues they raise (quadrant three), or the sector's broader sociopolitical relationships (quadrant four). While conventional reforms have touched on all of them, their treatment has been fairly superficial and often unintended. In all three issue areas, a principal problem has been the rather narrow perspective from which they are defined—either that of expert jurists, political elites, institutional leaders, or their foreign allies. The four perspectives are usually not identical. Even in combination they represent only a portion of the potential answers or interests they might incorporate. This in itself is not an obstacle to reform. Given the importance of the issues involved, it does raise questions as to the real significance of the improvements being sought and the further consequences of their being realized.

Reform Values and Their Public Impact

The question of values has been most overtly addressed and in a form that is consistent with the argument as to the sector's role in enhancing democracy. The emphasis on due process, human rights, and judicial neutrality has been a constant from the beginning. Even the deviations of expediency have been presented as just that—temporary measures justified by the crisis of the moment, but not intended to eclipse the longer term goals. The paradox of course is the apparent public acceptance of these deviations for the furtherance of such other values and objectives as increased social control, public safety, and the elimination of corruption. The underlying dilemma transcends the sectoral issues to more fundamental debates on the essence of democracy—and whether this lies in certain universal values and procedures (usually equated with the liberal democratic model) or in a more intimate connection to popular will (the participatory or communitarian model). This is not a debate that the reformers or the present work is likely to resolve. However, it has some corollary and more concrete aspects that do deserve attention because they are susceptible to more immediate remedial actions.

The first of these lies in a recognition that popular will is often not democratic, either in the values it endorses or its approach to procedural legitimacy. This is an obvious point, but one that many reform groups have chosen to ignore. In doing so, they have too often seen the main obstacle to their efforts in the opposition of the powerful, rather than in the disinterest or resistance of the broader public. As has been argued, overcoming elite opposition is often easier than attracting elite support or more to the point, that of the nonelites. The support required extends beyond that needed for the reforms' passage to eventual cooperation with the reformed procedures. Increased public education in reform principles would help; it is unlikely to resolve the entire problem. What little information exists on public attitudes toward the justice system does not indicate a rejection of the most general reform values. It does suggest a different ranking of priorities. Thus, two surveys conducted in Chile in the 1990s found that what the poor most wanted was more police.[5] If this is the case in Chile, one might imagine the results in El Salvador or Colombia. Similarly, in many countries, fears about public security have fed citizen interest in imposing heavier penalties on individuals convicted of crimes, and have clearly decreased the general concern with rehabilitative measures or the safeguarding of defendants' rights.[6]

Short of ceding to popular opinion and pursuing less democratic values, or deciding to pursue a democratic reform nondemocratically, there are additional alternatives and three areas where the issue of reform values merits more examination. The three have to do with the ways the more abstract principles have been elaborated and more specifically: the extent to which their elaboration and application may distance reform from popular understandings and practices; the potential conflict among the reformers' own goals; and the influence of strictly institutional interests. It is in these three areas that the reformers' own perspectives and their isolation from popular interests may actually broaden the cultural gap, to a large extent, unnecessarily.

It has been suggested, for example, that the reformers' definition of due process encourages a needlessly conflictual approach to dispute resolution,[7] one which sacrifices satisfactory solutions for compliance with formalistic requirements, and an exaggerated emphasis on confrontation between the parties. Excessive formalism was a common criticism of traditional systems. It is not evident that the normal run of procedural change has transcended this complaint. Substituting one set of unintelligible procedures for another will not heighten public acceptance. While reformers have talked about making justice more accessible, immediate, and transparent, the short term advances are not very convincing. This is obviously a place for further procedural simplification and more public education and information campaigns. The Chilean survey noted above also indicated the public's desire for more information on system workings. Respondents blamed a part of their dissatisfaction with outcomes on their own ignorance and consequent inability to press for results. The demand does not appear unique to Chile and suggests a tolerance for a certain level of procedural formality so long as it does not constitute an insurmountable obstacle to access. Beyond this, some experiments with conciliation, application of traditional substantive and procedural norms to intracommunity conflicts, and Peru's constitutional recognition of customary law as a source of jurisprudence are potentially interesting. Still, a caveat should be introduced here. These measures have often been endorsed and adopted because of their intellectual appeal with little basis for knowing what they will mean in practice.

The rediscovery of conciliation is a good example. It has been recommended as more compatible with popular norms and as a more democratic means of resolving conflict. Both claims can and should be more carefully examined. Whether or not conciliation is more popularly acceptable, there is no guarantee that the mechanisms actually adopted are any more congruent with popular practices than the formal procedures they replace.

There is also no guarantee that either variation is particularly democratic, except in the sense of imposing conventional notions as to who should prevail in a conflict.[8] Experience in Latin America and elsewhere has produced mixed results in terms of the democratizing impact of such popular mechanisms as conciliation, consensual decision making, or application of community norms. Whether conducted by judges or by community notables, they may reinforce existing authoritarian practices and prejudices. Like many of the other due process principles, they are probably best judged not against some ideal standard (which is bound to be controversial in any case) but against the most likely alternatives. If conciliation produces more satisfactory decisions, reduces conflict, and is regarded as legitimate by participants, then it is worth adopting. The test, however, is in the results, not in its theoretical benefits.

As unpopular as it may be with the legal profession, the elimination of the requirement that all cases be handled by a lawyer is also interesting. This means for facilitating access is in large part the reason for the popularity of Costa Rica's Constitutional Chamber. As the justices note with pride, they will receive and consider any complaint, no matter how it is presented. If additional investigation is required, the chamber sees that it is done. The chamber has not waived any of its internal formalism or otherwise "popularized" its application of constitutional principles. The fact that the public knows it will be heard and receive a rapid decision seems to outweigh any lingering dissatisfaction with the form or content of the ultimate rulings. This is not to suggest the imitation of the Costa Rican model, which in larger countries would be a disaster. Moreover, even in Costa Rica, there are concerns about the unnecessary constitutionalization of many complaints. However, allowing *pro se* representation in local courts or other equally accessible, decentralized fora is an alternative worth exploring.

Training of community members in dispute resolution or as paralegals are other measures worthy of serious consideration. Such programs have rarely figured in the conventional reform agenda and have often been opposed by the legal community as popularizing justice and violating due process rights. More recently, some of this opposition seems to be dissipating, although a lack of more positive attention remains. In short, the problem is not that the public does not value due process or procedural legitimacy, but rather that its notion of what it entails may be different from what is introduced. It is also possible that the differences are not that great. Still, without a better understanding of how the public or the various publics handle disputes and believe they should be handled, placing a more precise definition on the abstract notion of due process is fairly risky. The procedural reforms introduced on this basis may not be viewed as more legitimate and may needlessly detract from satisfaction with their impact.

As regards substantive values, especially the definition of basic legal and human rights, there appears to be a similar cultural gap; the resolution may be still more difficult. Although elite culture in Latin America symbolically accepts the "universal" liberal democratic standards, neither elites nor the public have always adhered to them. Where levels of national integration remain low, there may be a variety of real standards and a large amount of intolerance for differences. Under these circumstances, attempting to derive new values from popular consensus is probably impossible over the short run. This has not prevented the proliferation of new rights within the re-formed codes and constitutions, nor the further elaboration of their content. Realistically, many of these will remain as little more than a symbolic con-cession to their promoters' sentiments or interests,[9] although one with mix-ed implications for the enhancement of the rule of law.

There is a far more practical issue involving the conflicts among those official reform values that have received more than symbolic attention. Until such values became a part of real legal practice, the conflicts went largely unnoticed. As courts begin to apply them in their decisions, they have become extremely visible. The list of examples is not unusual and coincides with those faced by any justice system attempting to work to more democratic principles—conflicts, for example, between the right to infor-mation and the right to privacy, especially of those suspected or accused of crimes; between the right against self-incrimination or to be considered innocent and the public's belief that it has a right to protection from "crim-inals;" between the right of children and minors to special protection and the emphasis on reducing impunity; or between the individual's right to engage in activities not specifically prohibited by law[10] and the community's desire to be protected from unpleasant or potentially dangerous actions or to have certain lifestyles and cultural preferences reenforced. The difference is that the Latin American reformers have taken a particularly broad view of the activities covered by these guarantees that appears to place them far ahead of national public sentiment. They have also taken that view at a time when changing conditions have begun to force its reconsideration and occasional compromise elsewhere. This phenomenon was to be expected. After years of rights existing only in the abstract, jurists lack practice in their real application and will require time to make the adjustment.

Whatever the reason, the prevailing outlook has produced some extreme-ly unpopular legal interpretations and decisions. In El Salvador, an article in the draft criminal procedures code seeking to protect both the right to privacy and the presumption of innocence met so much popular protest that it had to be removed. The article prohibited the release of information on a criminal case before sentencing. It critics charged that it violated both the freedom of the press and the public's right to information. The Costa Rican Constitutional Chamber has challenged a law making flight from the site of a traffic accident a criminal offense, finding it in conflict with the right against self-incrimination. Ecuador's new juvenile code prohibits using handcuffs on minors as a violation of their right to protective treatment. El Salvador is still deciding whether this same right implies a similar prohibition. Since violent juvenile crime is not the problem in Ecuador that it has become in El Salvador, national realities might dictate different answers. El Salvador's code also sets the maximum sentence a juvenile may serve for any crime as seven years, a very unpopular provision given the upsurge in gang violence. The traditional prohibition of wire tapping and interception of private correspondence even under judicial orders has been maintained in some new legislation to protect the right to privacy. This produces some obvious difficulties for the reforms' simultaneous emphasis on controlling organized and "modern" criminality. As noted, Costa Rica's Constitutional Chamber came close to removing the Central Bank's ability to set the exchange rate, which it interpreted as an unconstitutional usurpation of the Assembly's exclusive legislative powers. All of these decisions may be justifiable, especially given that the violation of the rights and principles involved often exceeds the instances of their extreme application. However, popular reaction has not been positive and could undermine the broader goal of expanding constitutional guarantees.

To the extent any immediate solution exists, it lies in part in the wider discussion of these rights and in the reformers' own recognition that extremely broad interpretations of all of them will inevitably produce conflicts, sometimes among the rights themselves and, more often, with public sentiments. The position that a minor cannot commit a crime or that the criminal process itself violates the presumption of innocence,[11] while intellectually intriguing, is not terribly compatible with popular wisdom or with national realities. In some cases, the rights emphasis poses conflicts with the larger reforms of which they are a part. Restrictions[12] on information maintained on juveniles, even in closed files (right to privacy and special protection for the minor), make it difficult to combat juvenile "crime." They also hinder the effective application of the treatment programs and alternative sentences incorporated in new juvenile codes. If the police, judge, prosecutor, and defender do not know whether a juvenile has been arrested previously, they cannot use his record against him. However, lacking such knowledge, they cannot "individualize" treatment, as the law requires, and they might be tempted to take a hard line just in case. Rather than creating a new right, and probably encouraging its immediate violation through the maintenance of illegal files, the better solution and that most consistent with the purpose of the legislation, would appear to be allowing closed files and controlling their use.

Most of the illustrations, as might be expected, lie in the criminal justice area and stem from the usual public concern that the criminals get all the rights. They are not the only examples. The Costa Rican Constitutional Chamber's restrictive interpretation on the law-making function is applicable to all areas of administrative and executive activity. Defining that function very broadly and limiting its exercise to the Assembly may have been appropriate when the state did very little. Under current conditions, however, it could bring government to a halt. Efforts to introduce constitutional provisions or secondary legislation protective of the rights of groups believed to need special attention have sometimes been opposed by the groups themselves. One of the reasons for the dismantling of Peru's agrarian jurisdiction was its legislative bias toward communal holdings and the prohibitions on sale of community lands. Even before the Fujimori administrations's free market emphasis, this had been protested by some of the presumed beneficiaries, who saw this as a violation rather than a protection of their interests. Similarly protective legislation in Costa Rica, setting minimum limits on the duration of agrarian contracts, was also criticized by tenant farmers, who themselves wanted the possibility of shorter term agreements.[13] Another frequent area of debate is that of family legislation where juridical values or jurists' notions of popular culture may not coincide with reality. It is hard to say whether Salvadoran public opinion supports the recognition of common law marriages, the criminalization of familial violence, or the state's provision of legal assistance to those seeking divorce.[14] However, the heated discussions of these issues and the form they were finally given in the new family legislation only theorized about public preferences. No one ever thought to ask the public to define them.

The introduction and interpretation of the norms that will guide sectoral behavior involve a series of essentially political decisions. These begin with the selection of the abstract principles and extend to their application to concrete cases and to the details of secondary legislation. "Democratizing" the system's operations may inevitably require the imposition of some unpopular values. The most that can be wished is that this be recognized when it occurs. Pretending that these are the choices the public wants or seeking justification in legal doctrine is ultimately a much weaker means of legitimization. However, where these values are in conflict (as most are at some point) or where the decisions of detail require second guessing popular preferences or reactions, the juridical perspective is often too limited, resulting in arbitrary choices for want of better information. It also frequently fails to recognize the implicit conflicts with the simultaneous goal of improving the functional performance of judicial and other governmental institutions. An executive branch that cannot determine such legal details as the exchange rate or the fine for speeding, a legal assistance office that cannot provide counsel to women seeking divorce or men accused of child abuse, or a prosecutor unduly restricted in his investigatory role[15] are organizations that cannot perform their newly mandated functions. In countries with more participatory cultures, wrong guesses may be quickly noticed and challenged, or they may be headed off by a more thorough preliminary discussion. In most of Latin America with more restricted participation and a tradition of not taking rights seriously, the more likely result is a greater gap between legal theory and real practice and a further erosion of the rule of law.

Constitutional Issues

The issue of reform values cannot be separated from the two other areas: the constitutional impacts and their sociopolitical bases. All three are linked by the question of whose interests are represented. There are more central constitutional themes, which are also treated, but the reforms' tendency to prioritize certain institutional interests deserve first mention. In a number of the cases discussed above, the choice of values is as much motivated by institutional perspectives as it is by abstract principle. Two examples involve the emphasis on privacy and on judicial independence. Reformers and reformist courts have frequently argued against the release of information on criminal cases prior to a final sentencing. Their reasoning is that this violates the assumption of innocence and the defendant's right to his good name.[16] To avoid the most obvious conflict, the principle of public justice is sometimes more narrowly interpreted as the defendant's right to a public hearing, not the public's right to knowledge of the case. Given the frequent practice of judges informing the press on the progress of their investigations and even their tentative conclusions,[17] the argument has merit. It also has a self-serving side. Whether or not judges release information prematurely, they generally do not want to be subject to uncontrolled public pressure or scrutiny or to have to make difficult decisions while in the limelight. Thus, the question is whose privacy is really being protected, that of the defendant or that of the judge.

The self-serving aspect of judicial independence requires no further explanation. A judiciary that is absolutely independent is also absolutely unaccountable for its actions. Even when they were more politically dependent, Latin American judiciaries were frequently accused of operating in splendid isolation. The more independent Costa Rican judges have been described as a closed caste with an oligarchic outlook. Complaints have been targeted not only at their functional independence but also at the use of the judicial budget to finance trips, representational allowances, and other special privileges.[18] Here too, the pursuit of an abstract principle is hard to separate from the furtherance of strictly institutional interests that the public may have good reason not to support. This also becomes a problem, as it did in both Costa Rica and Colombia, when independence is used to advance less widely shared values, or when it results in conflicts with the normal operation of other institutions. This last theme transcends the problem of particularistic interests and introduces a second set of constitutional issues relating to the reforms' effects on the balance of power within the political system as a whole.

The emphasis on judicial independence has most often treated this as the elimination of external interference. With the increasing interest in expanding the powers of judicial review it has added the judiciary's role in checking the abuses of other institutions. To a lesser extent, other sector institutions, including some new creations, have also been given certain countervailing powers, either within the sector or vis-a-vis extrasectoral actors. When combined with an emphasis on different operating principles, constitutional rights, and rule of law as opposed to partisan and personal loyalties, the intent or at least the effect is to introduce very fundamental political change. These implications escaped the attention of some political elites who either believed the new powers would be used to their benefit or who did not foresee the full consequences of the proposals. Objectively, the development can be termed positive, providing a check on executive powers the traditionally weaker legislatures were usually unable to offer. However, there are several caveats as regards its further evolution.

The first of these regards the values and interests being promoted. This has been amply treated above and needs no further comment. Second, while the arrangement has increased interinstitutional conflict, it is not clear that it has added to the interests represented, rather than simply redistributing political resources among them. True, the issues of constitutionalism have traditionally focused more on avoiding or eliminating concentrations of power than expanding access. Still, in societies where access is already extremely restricted, their democratizing impact is also fairly limited. Curbing executive abuses is important. However, where the participants to · these conflicts have more in common with each other than they do with the majority of citizens, the battles may be waged over increasingly narrow issues. Costa Rican citizens may really not care who sets traffic fines any more than Colombians worried about the maintenance of the traditional circuit courts. Constitutionalism does matter, but in these societies where the power being redistributed is still held by a small class, the number of fundamental problems it will affect may not be very large. Thus, the benefits it brings, at least in its current form, may well be exaggerated.

Third, when it does affect issues of greater concern, it may do so in ways that obstruct activities appearing to have broader backing. As discussed, the Colombian Court only withdrew its objections to a Constituent Assembly in the face of intense pressure, some of it from the public. It also held up a much needed sector reform for years on the basis of constitutional principles and institutional interests. The Costa Rican Constitutional Chamber recognized popular values in making a rapid decision on a case involving the Soccer Federation. It kept the country without a traffic code, or imported private vehicles for considerably longer. The Brazilian Supreme Federal Tribunal backed off from nullifying President Collor's economic plan and further prevented lower courts from issuing injunctions in favor of individuals seeking access to their frozen bank accounts. Here it was not immediate popular pressure, but rather a fear of being blamed for an economic disaster that caused it to uphold a clearly unconstitutional action.[19] In most countries, judicial review functions could be exercised much more actively before raising such problems. Still, there is an emerging concern that the model of separation and distribution of powers on which they are based may not be appropriate to contemporary citizen or governmental needs.

This is particularly true of the accompanying tendency to send every suspected violation of rights to the constitutional courts or chambers. Not only in Costa Rica, but also in Colombia and Chile,[20] the result had been an overwhelming caseload for the constitutional and ordinary jurisdictions, bypassing completely the administrative courts that might more appropriately handle much of it. This development stems from the well-founded expectation that cases so handled will receive more prompt attention. If the trend continues, the expectation will be less frequently met. It can also be asked whether justices trained in constitutional law are the most appropriate to handle violations of normal legal rights or arbitrary administrative actions. Not only may they be less familiar with the issues, their participation will up the stakes, escalating individual and institutional conflicts that could be resolved more consensually. One alternative solution would be to develop the existing administrative courts. Either as a separate jurisdiction or as part of the ordinary court system, these bodies exist in most countries; however, they are universally underutilized and generally misunderstood or unknown by the ordinary citizen. Another remedy might turn to the omnipresent but often ineffectual ombudsman's office.[21] Contrary to prevailing trends to maintain their focus on human rights issues, the ombudsmen could specialize in purely administrative complaints, leaving the transcendental constitutional ones and the protection of basic human rights to the constitutional chambers. Of course, if as in Brazil, the entity (in this case the Public Ministry) handles this as a constitutional issue, the alternative mechanism will not have a different impact. Even with the current trend to cut back on governmental services, the recognition of administrative abuses as they affect individual citizens is only likely to increase. As the more basic human rights situation improves, administrative abuses may replace them as a primary cause of concern. Given this development it is none to early to reconsider the dominant constitutional model, and that incorporated in reform programs, and to seek modifications to update it for contemporary demands.

The Sociopolitical Impact of Conventional Reforms

A final set of questions, and one that has brought the most heated criticism, relates to the sociopolitical impact and foundations of reform. Even the second and third strategies, with their emphasis on new values, have addressed this concern rather tangentially through their focus on universalizing judicial treatment and eliminating state abuses of power. However, as the critics are quick to argue, universal standards are of limited help in addressing the injustices of a highly inegalitarian society. Realistically and contrary to some of the critics' recommendations, eliminating those injustices exceeds the possibilities of sectoral reform. This does not preclude the potential use of reform to open up the sector to a broader variety of interests. The most effective way of doing this may be less through a direct attempt to rework sectoral values than through shifts in the sector's external linkages.

The tendency of current reforms is to redefine these linkages to decrease the control exercised by the executive, legislature and political parties in favor of judicial councils and/or the institutions themselves. The objective has been to enhance judicial independence by making control of personnel, budgets and legislation shaping the sector the responsibility of sectoral actors or of more neutral organizations. This reduces extraneous political and institutional pressures. It may also further distance sector institutions from the populations they presumably serve. Eliminating external controls or shifting them to another elite body may exacerbate the development of a judiciary increasingly out of touch with broader national reality or encourage the formation of a self-perpetuating judicial caste.

If the judiciary's isolation is reflected in the values it pursues, it originates in its internal composition and how it is determined. Here the more radical critics have often supported the measures advocated by conventional reforms. For once their examination of the implications has not gone far enough. In endorsing these solutions, they are apparently forgetting their own complaints that the traditional judiciary was formed by and for members of the middle and upper class. Transferring control of its operations to the judiciary itself or to external judicial councils composed of judge-like members reduces partisan intervention. It is less likely to alter the class identifications of judicial actors or the tendency for the institution's public service functions and democratizing impact to be oriented toward these same groups. It also will not decrease whatever sense of irrelevance or alienation the prevailing institutional culture produces in its nonelite clientele.

The solution is probably not to call for the election of judges or their selection only from the popular classes. On the other hand, where the judiciary has most contact with the masses, at the level of the local judge or justice of the peace, there may be room for modifications. These could take the form of Peru's decision to involve communities in their selection, or, as in present-day Nicaragua, to make local-level service or work in legal clinics or public defense a requirement for entrance to the bar or to the judiciary.[22] Admittedly, similar programs are already in place in many countries and just as often abused. Participants either buy their way out of service, or use it to collect illegal fees from their clients. However, adequately organized and supervised, and reenforced with the introduction of user evaluations, they could both increase access for marginalized groups and change institutional outlooks. Such linkages could also be enforced by creating offices for citizen complaints about the police, introducing judicial or police ombudsmen, strengthening bar associations' disciplinary powers over their members, or promoting institutional outreach programs. The latter take judges, police, defenders, and prosecutors into the communities to explain their roles and to elicit community support. The goal is to improve relations and communication, and involve the community in everything from public security to the establishment of educational and work programs for minors.

Not surprisingly, these measures are often far more difficult to introduce and implement than any new code or program of constitutional guarantees. They are much more labor intensive, harder to supervise, and, most importantly, they run squarely up against institutional interests, culture, and the self-image not only of the judiciary but of most other sector actors. Discussions of judicial outreach programs with Salvadoran judges or of similar programs with the Salvadoran police predictably met complaints that there was no time for them. The judges further objected that they just would not work.[23] The resistance, like the failure to incorporate this type of program, are important indications of the self-imposed limits even of the most ambitious reforms. However, if justice reform is to reach the entire population and not just the minority the sector has traditionally served, ways will have to be found to expand its relevance for and contact with more than this small group.

The comments and suggestions offered above could be incorporated into a revised or expanded reform program, one that both redirects existing activities and adds several new ones. In table 9.2, below, the changes are most evident in the addition of activities in quadrants three and four. Although the first two quadrants remain much the same, both the technical and political objectives of their activities would also be modified. The former would involve greater simplification of procedures, more public information campaigns and the addition of conciliation and other non-traditional procedural reforms. In the second quadrant, the change is hardest to diagram, since it entails shifts in the value content of the activities. Training, for example, would include more than legal education, em-

TABLE 9.2:   Modified Reform Strategies and Activities

	Objectives	
Targets of Change	Technical	Political
Internal procedures	Administrative systems	Substantive codes
	Procedural codes	
	Automation	Ethnics codes
	Disciplinary systems	
	Training	
	Merit appointments	Prison reforms
	Reorganizations	Traditional law
	Procedural simplification	
	Public information campaigns	
	Conciliation—court annexed	
External linkages	Judicial career	Civilian police
	Internal appointments	Prosecutors Office
	Judicial councils	Defenders Office
	Higher budgets	Judicial review
	Community selection/evaluation	Constitutional
	of local judges	Courts
	Outreach program	Judicial Ombudsman
	Citizen complaints office	Paralegals
	Service internship for law	Alternative dispute
	students	resolution
		Police Ombudsman

phasizing courses on socioeconomic conditions, and internships in offices serving marginalized groups. Entrance examinations would also emphasize this kind of knowledge, and public service activities would be included in the assessment of candidates' credentials. The modification is not a radical one, in most cases constituting the addition rather than the substitution of goals and mechanisms and, thus, in the way they shape activities.

The final question is who would promote this revised program. Its modified aims are potentially less compatible with those of sector actors than are those on the conventional list. Since many of the indigenous NGOs are staffed by legal professionals, they themselves participate in the traditional legal culture and may be just as adverse to this form of popularization.[24] Political elites might derive a benefit from supporting the cause, but only if there is public demand. External donors and lending agencies might help develop wider interest through a very selective financing of experimental governmental and private programs. However, in light of the difficulties still confronting conventional reforms, the adoption of a modified agenda may have to wait until they have made further advances. It may be to much to expect that they assume additional objectives before they have advanced the existing ones further. Nonetheless, there is room for pilot programs and the support of groups and individuals interested in pursing some of these nonconventional approaches. Given the large amount of external funding about to be invested in the sector, much of it in infrastructure and automation, a part of it could be directed to these additional questions and to the problems that conventional reforms have not been prepared to address.

There is another reason for seeking these modifications which should be of more direct interest to the traditional reform groups and their closest allies. Until now, even when justice reform attracted hidden agendas, they tended to be fairly innocuous—a political leader who saw this as a popular and noncontroversial platform, a Court president with aspirations to higher office, or a middle class professional seeking alternative employment by founding an NGO. However, a few years experience have made it apparent that the resources and the issues at stake are worth more attention, and worth the attention of more important actors. If economic and even many political elites have been willing to let others define the issues and their solutions, their self-marginalization is coming to an end. The new concern is not that reform will go nowhere, but rather that it will go in directions its authors may never have intended or imagined. If current programs do not take steps to forge the sector's links with and relevance to a wider variety of social forces, there are signs that a smaller, less representative, but more powerful group of forces may preempt those efforts by cementing their own links first. In Peru, the die may already have been cast.

Conclusions

Despite the negative precedent set by Peru's earlier efforts, the attempt to reform Latin American justice systems has made some significant progress over the past decade. Few of the improvements promised by the reformers have been achieved, but the negative lessons, including those from Peru's experience, have been absorbed and the reforms underway today seem more likely to produce concrete results. While their ambitions and promises have been much grander, it appears that most of the results will lie in the direction of reshaping the systems in line with the new codes. This time there is a chance that they will actually reorient organizational structures and performance. Justice, and especially criminal justice, will follow new procedures and, in many cases, more effectively and more consistently with the legal norms. The use of sector organizations as repositories for otherwise undistinguished party loyalists will decline, judicial careers will be established, and appointment systems will for once focus on the relevant abilities and credentials of candidates. Courts and other sector institutions will have higher budgets and be able to pay their members a living salary. Administrative systems will be rationalized and the use of the budgets put under more professional control. Judicial review will be introduced or expanded and used to protect an increasing number of legal and basic human rights. Its use as a broader check on government operations and policies will probably be subject to some measure of judicial restraint, if only because most courts will not want responsibility for potential disasters. Most countries will also offer some kind of free legal defense and make it more widely available to indigent clients.

These changes will come, but in most cases very slowly and always lagging far behind the introduction of the new legislation dictating their realization. Inadequate legal education, poorly prepared system incumbents, and the force of traditional practices and perspectives will continue to inhibit more rapid change, as will the vast inequalities and maldistribution of resources and power within the surrounding societies. The problems of the moment, including high crime rates, social disorder, and economic crises, will provide their own source of setbacks. Continued lack of intrasectoral coordination and the different rates of development of its member institutions will pose additional obstacles. Funding provided by donors will continue to be invested according to the latter's policies, which frequently will not coincide with objective needs. No one wants to finance assistance to prisons; everyone wants to sponsor courses in human rights or donate computers, especially where that creates a commercial opening.

Considering the past and present condition of most of the region's justice systems, it would be hard to object to the changes promoted by the reform movement. They may not be everyone's choice of priorities, but they do represent improvements. For all the difficulties these programs will face, they may be more realistic than anything else that might be devised. Furthermore, although most of the changes are "technical" in the sense of focusing on improving the performance of the sector's overt functions, they also imply political transformations. Over the shorter run these come through the new values and new institutional relations they introduce; over the longer run, normalizing their performance will make institutions less susceptible to external influence for irregular ends. External pressures will always be exercised and, when great enough, will produce irregular decisions and actions. However, in the vast majority of cases they will eventually become the exception rather than the operative rule.

The ultimate question is whether this more methodical, bureaucratized administration of justice is the most appropriate for societies in need of so many other kinds of fundamental change. Although certainly an improvement over what it replaces, it could further insulate the sector from the more dynamic social forces, enshrining values and relationships increasingly irrelevant to the shifting needs of the surrounding societies. Perhaps in this sense, the likelihood that reforms will proceed slowly is an advantage, leaving space for modifications in the medium and longer term. The uneven pace of reform offers similar benefits. The imbalance of powers among institutions, the unequal attention to new values, and the inevitable conflicts they encourage will provide an incentive to question the logic behind them, and perhaps to discard a part of it.

Reformulating the foregoing discussion, there are three areas where this reexamination is desirable. The first is the match between the reformers' values and those of the larger society. The reforms have imposed a number of political decisions, most often presented as doctrinal truth. In concrete detail many of them pose conflicts among themselves and with social preferences. As these conflicts evolve, some of these decisions will have to be reconsidered. If they are not, the larger interest in furthering the rule of law will be eroded. The second is still more practical and empirical and relates to the reformers' assumptions about the consequences of their recommendations and innovations. Some of these—for example the political neutrality of new appointment systems, the greater financial and temporal economy of accusatory systems, or the direct, positive relationship between judicial budgets and the quality of judicial performance[25]—have already been shown to be in error. There are any number of others deserving of much more scrutiny. These include several mechanisms adopted based on a fleeting acquaintance with some practice assumed to work better somewhere else. Often the success of these practices is greatly exaggerated; if not, it is usually produced by a special set of circumstances the adopting country does not share.[26] Fortunately, as societies begin to have more experience with the real-life application of these arbitrary inventions, they may come to distinguish real impact from wishful thinking and be somewhat more cautious about what they adopt as a guaranteed improvement.

Finally, there is the question as to the adequacy of the larger juridical models, especially in the constitutional jurisdiction, but also in family, criminal and other areas that the reformers have promoted. It can be argued that all of these are partially based on an outmoded notion of the problems and challenges facing contemporary societies and an oversimplification of the available remedies. The criminal codes often seem to derive from a nineteenth century notion of conventional crime—the hungry father stealing a loaf of bread for his family—rather than the white collar criminal or drug lord. In their procedural form, they seek to choose between or mix elements from the inquisitorial and accusatory traditions, both of which are under fire in their countries of origin[27]. The family codes, while accepting the reality of common law unions and single mothers, still seem dedicated to protecting a familial ideal that may never have existed. The model agrarian codes are informed by Spanish and Italian legislation from the 1930s and also look to the examples of the Mexican *ejido* and Peru's failed experiments with communal holdings.[28] The constitutional jurisdiction, based on liberal democratic models and a great concern for individual freedom and the separation of functions and powers may not be in tune with the realities of a necessarily more interrelated and interdependent society, where no one makes a move without affecting someone else and someone else's rights. They may also be dedicated to protecting citizens against abuses that fortunately seem on the decline, while overlooking those that are likely to proliferate in the future.

Reform, like war, is inevitability shaped more by the last battle than by the present one. Unfortunately, the consequences are less immediately visible and themselves subject to varying interpretations. Should the reformers declare victory, their claims may be uncontested, however pyrrhic the results. Hence, the recommended strategy is more attention to their efforts and a more discerning appraisal of their implications. Justice reform does not belong to the reformers any more than justice belongs to the judges. Overcoming that cultural prejudice is the most difficult, but also the most important challenge on the road to making reform work.

Notes

1. Although not going to this extreme, WOLA, 1990; Youngers, 1992; Popkin, 1994; Spence et al., 1993, 1994; and the Lawyers Committee, 1989, 1993, express some of these concerns. They are also raised, more surprisingly, in GAO, 1992, 1993, and some of USAID's internal documents. See Hansen and Blair, 1995.

2. See Giraldo et al., 1997; Fernández León, 1996; and Orozco Abad, 1996, for discussions of these contradictions and compromises.

3. While the criticism is most often heard from more radically oriented groups, it is also endorsed by a surprising variety of other sources. Critics of USAID's programs on this basis range from nongovernmental organizations to AID's Inspector General's office and the Government Accounting Office. See WOLA, 1990, and GAO, 1993.

4. The law creates a Constitutional and an Administrative Chamber within the Court, to the apparent end of increasing judicial powers in both areas. It earmarks a portion of the national budget for the judiciary, changes the judiciary's governance and appointment systems, and suggests further alternations of the criminal justice process. Even if it is approved, it seems doubtful that it will be implemented as written.

5. Ulloa González and Vargas, 1995.

6. This is most evident in public support for the death penalty, the elimination of which is a principal aim of much of the new legislation. In Guatemala, in July of 1996, opinion polls conducted regarding a particularly grisly rape and murder of a young child indicated that 80 percent of the population favored the execution of the convicted assailants. No public authority, not even the human rights ombudsman or Church officials, was willing to intercede against public opinion.

7. De Lima Lopes, 1997, offers this argument as regards the Brazilian Supreme Federal Tribunal's treatment of social rights litigation and public action law suits. It is also offered by many proponents of alternative dispute resolution.

8. This issue has been raised in regard to the conciliation of family disputes. The fear is that either the conciliator or the couple themselves may automatically assume certain male rights that are anything but egalitarian.

9. El Salvador's new Family Code was supported by numerous advocacy groups, each of which was insistent on the inclusion of rights essential to its own political agenda. Most of them are so vaguely stated (e.g. the child or the third generation's "right to respect") as to have no foreseeable concrete impact. Most of the conflict over the law's content focused on a smaller number of provisions and rights perceived as having a more immediate effect on family relations. Brazil so far seems to be the only country where there has been much effort to claim these broader social rights; its Public Ministry's assertive role in this regard is also interesting. See Howell, 1995; de Lima Lopes, 1997; Bastos Arantes, 1997; and Fuks, 1995, for discussions of the advances and difficulties.

10. Whether this right is explicitly recognized or not, the strong streak of individualism in Latin American culture means that it often is evoked by those believing that legislation violates their right "to do what they want with their own property." Whatever its conflicts with a tradition of state intervention that many trace to the colonial period, this individualism also permeates the thinking of many of the region's constitutional lawyers in their interpretation of various constitutional guarantees. While certainly expressed in a more sophisticated form, it can be seen in their interpretations of the right to privacy or against self-incrimination, both of which are fairly restrictive of state powers.

11. Llobet Rodríguez, 1993, discusses this, although admitting that investigations, trials, and some restrictions on the defendant's actions are practical necessities.

12. These are incorporated in many recent juvenile codes. The underlying principle is that only a minimum of information in any form should be retained, and then, only for juveniles who have been charged and tried. The reason is to protect the juvenile's "image." It represents a valid fear that, if records are maintained, they might be used against the juvenile at some later date.

13. Interviews, Costa Rica.

14. The head of the Legal Assistance Office (*Procuraduría General*) believed there was a conflict between his institution's mandate to protect the family and the provision of free counsel to women seeking divorce. This position came as a surprise to women who sought just such assistance, which they believed was promised under the new Family Code.

15. The restrictions on the prosecution or a simple failure to understand its operations are frequent criticisms of the new criminal legislation. Given past abuses (more by police and judges), some restrictions are obviously in order. However, it is also evident that the drafters of the code had little familiarity with the prosecutorial function and were so concerned with fending off abuses that they neglected to consider what was needed for the institution to operate.

16. This position is taken by the Costa Rican Court and, under its influence, the court of El Salvador. Both constitutions speak of a right to ones *propio imagen*, a term

difficult to translate and not always consistently interpreted by jurists in either country. At one point, the Salvadorans suggested it extended to ones photograph (a very literal interpretation) and, thus, that a defendant's picture, even after conviction, could not be used by the press without permission.

17. In late 1995, even as the press "gag law," was being debated in the Salvadoran Assembly, judges continued to make public statements about their progress in investigating cases and the weight of the evidence against the suspects. Fortunately, an earlier practice, whereby police posed detainees with confiscated weapons for press photos, had been largely stopped, as had the press' habit of referring to the suspects as the perpetrators.

18. In 1995 the Costa Rican press did an expose on the use of the Court's funds to give scholarships, at full salary, to justices. No one was opposed to the justices doing further study, even in Europe, but it was suggested that as students, they should live on student budgets and that the lower level judiciary might benefit more from such opportunities.

19. Howell, 1995, passim.

20. See Brumm, 1992, for his discussion of the use of the *queja* appeal and what he calls the constitutionalization of legal rights.

21. The introduction of ombudsman's offices throughout Latin America follows on the efficacy of a few of them in investigating human rights abuses. As has been noted by others, their success in this effort may eliminate much of the reason for their existence. Furthermore, in some countries (e.g. Costa Rica), there is a question as to whether the extent of such abuses merits the office's introduction. Here, as in other countries, they currently seem to be searching for a mandate, often settling on issues like the protection of women's or children's rights (El Salvador) or the monitoring of judicial performance (Costa Rica). Although these are valid causes, the broader area of administrative abuses may be a more worthy challenge and one that will keep them busy for years. This does, however, raise the question as to their relationship to the administrative courts.

22. Unfortunately, Nicaragua's new draft Judicial Organic Law may reverse this practice by making admission to the bar and prior experience a prerequisite for appointment, even to the lowest levels of the judiciary. The draft law is said to have been based on the law in effect in the Netherlands and, as such, may be still another example of misguided imitation.

23. These were undertaken in 1995 as an informal effort to expand sectoral and public understanding of the new Juvenile Offenders Law.

24. An anonymously authored document on Peruvian legal services supported by NGOs raises some of these issues, suggesting a certain reluctance to empower their clients as opposed to leading them. See Anonymous, 1988.

25. For all the emphasis on earmarked percentages of the national budget, a review of the proportion spent on justice in more developed countries indicates that many Latin American nations already spend relatively more, with far poorer results. Of course, the base is much smaller, but the notion that Latin American nations must spend six to eight percent or more on their justice sectors seems exaggerated. See Dakolias, 1995, p. 192.

26. In the criminal justice area, reformers have shown a fascination with boot

camps and victims' rights, not realizing that both are very controversial and hardly to be described as undebatable successes.

27. See Damaska, 1997, for a discussion of current thinking in both Europe and the United States on the inadequacy of both criminal and civil justice procedures.

28. One of the recognized regional experts in agrarian law, the Costa Rican justice, Ricardo Zeledón, has acknowledged the impact of the Cuban, Mexican, and Peruvian agrarian reforms on his thinking. While all three share similar ideals, they have arguably been superseded by more recent economic developments.

Acronyms and Abbreviations

AOJ	Administration of Justice
AP	Popular Action (Peru)
APRA	American Popular Revolutionary Alliance (Peru)
ARENA	National Republican Alliance (El Salvador)
Art.	Article
CAL	Lima Bar Association
CEPAL	Economic Commission for Latin America (also ECLA, ECLAC)
COPEI	Committee of Independent Political Electoral Organization, Social Christian Party (Venezuela)
CORELESAL	Revisory Commission for Salvadoran Legislation
CTI	Technical Investigative Corps (Colombia)
DEA	U.S. Drug Enforcement Agency
DINCOTE	Antiterrorist Division (Peru)
DIRCOTE	Antiterrorist Direction (Peru)
D.L.	Decree Law
DOJ	Department of Justice
EAP	Economically active population
FMNL	Farabundo Martí National Liberation Front (El Salvador)
GAO	U.S. Government Accounting Office
ICITAP	International Criminal Investigative Training Assistance Program
IDB	Inter-American Development Bank
IFI	International financial institution
ILANUD	United Nations Institute for Crime Prevention and Treatment of the Delinquent
IMF	International Monetary Fund
INL	Bureau of International Narcotics and Law Enforcement
INPE	National Prison Institute (Peru)
JP	Justice of the peace
JRP I, II	Judicial Reform Project I, II (El Salvador)
LDC	Less developed country
MOJ	Ministry of Justice
MRTA	Túpac Amaru Revolutionary Movement (Peru)
NGO	Nongovernmental organization
OCIPJ	Office for Internal Control for the Judicial Power (Peru)

OIJ	Office of Judicial Investigation (Costa Rica)
ONUSAL	United Nations Mission in El Salvador
OPDAT	Office of Professional Development and Training
PDC	Christian Democratic Party (El Salvador)
PCN	Party of National Conciliation (El Salvador)
PIP	Peruvian Investigative Police
PPC	Popular Christian Party (Peru)
PRI	Institutional Revolution Party (Mexico)
SUNAT	National Tax Administration Superintendency (Peru)
TGC	Tribunal of Constitutional Guarantees (Peru)
UNDP	United Nations Development Program
USAID	United States Agency for International Development
USIA	United States Information Agency
USIS	United States Information Service
WOLA	Washington Office on Latin America

References

Abad Y., Samuel. 1990. *Selección de jurisprudencia constitucional*. Lima: Comisión Andina de Juristas.

Aguilar Bulgarelli, Oscar. 1986. *La Constitución de 1949*. San Jose: Editorial Costa Rica.

Ahumada, Consuelo. 1995. "The Constituent Assembly and the New Constitutionalism in Colombia." Paper presented at the 1995 meetings of the Latin American Studies Association.

Albán Gómez, Ernesto, Santigo Andrade Ubidia, César Coronel Jones, Jorge Egas Peña, Fabían Guido Flores, Galo García Feraud, Miguel Macías Hurtado, Carlos Pérez Padiño, José Troya Jaramillo, and Jorge Zavala Egas. 1994. *La Casación: Estudios sobre la Ley No. 27*. Quito: Corporación Editora Nacional.

Alvarez, José E. 1992. "Promoting the 'Rule of Law' in Latin America: Problems and Prospects." *The George Washington Journal of International Law and Economics* 25: 2, pp 281-331.

Ambos, Kai. 1989. *Terrorismo y ley*. Lima: Comisión Andina de Juristas.

Americas Watch. 1992a. *Peru: Civil Society and Democracy Under Fire*. New York: Human Rights Watch.

Americas Watch. 1992b. *Political Murder and Reforms in Colombia*. New York: Human Rights Watch.

Ames, Rolando, Carlos Chipoco, César Delgado, Raúl Ferrero, Felipe MacGregor, Benjamín Madueño, Carlos Montoya, Roberto Ramírez del Villar, Luis Roy Freyre, Marcial Rubio, and Felipe Villavicencio. 1988. *Violencia y estado democrático de derecho*. Lima: CODEPP.

Amnesty International. 1991. *Peru: Human Rights in a Climate of Terror*. London.

Amnesty International. 1992. *Peru: Human Rights and the Government of President Alberto Fujimori*. New York.

Anderson, T. 1971. *Matanza: El Salvador's Communist Revolt of 1932*. Lincoln, Nebraska: University of Nebraska Press.

Anonymous. c. 1988. "Los grupos "innovadores" de servicios legales en el Perú." Report prepared for various donors, Lima, Peru.

Asheshov, Nicholas. 1988. "The 1987 Peruvian Bank Job." *The Andean Report* Lima. October, pp. 233-277.

Astiz, Carlos A. 1969. *Pressure Groups and Power Elites in Peruvian Politics*. Ithaca: Cornell University Press.

Ayala, Enrique, Rodrigo de la Cruz, Ariruma Kowii, Luis Maldonado, Gónzalo Ortíz, José Quimbo, Galo Ramón, José Sánchez-Parga, Julio César Trujillo, and Alberto Wray. 1992. *Pueblos indios, estado y derecho*. Quito: Corporación Editorial Nacional.

Bagley, Bruce, ed. 1986. *State and Society in Contemporary Colombia: Beyond the National Front*. Boulder, Colorado: Westview.

326

Barker, Robert. 1986. "Constitutional Adjudication in Costa Rica," *University of Miami Inter-American Law Review*.17:2, pp. 15-48.

Barker, Robert. 1991. "Taking Constitutionalism Seriously: Costa Rica's Sala Cuarta." *Florida Journal of International Law*, 6:3, pp. 349-397.

Barrig, Maruja. 1980. *La ley es la ley: la justicia en la literatura peruana*. Lima: CEDYS.

Bartra Cavero, José. 1990. *Procedimiento administrativo*. Lima: Editorial Ital Perú.

Bastos Arantes, Rogério. 1997. "Direito e Política: instituições judiciais e conflitos coletivos." Paper presented at the Latin American Studies Association meeting.

Bell, John. 1992. *French Constitutional Law*. Oxford: Clarendon.

Bernales Ballesteros, Enrique. 1996. *La Constitución de 1993: Análisis comparado*. Lima: CIEDLA.

Bernales Ballesteros, Enrique, ed. 1993. *Del golpe de estado a la nueva Constitución*. Lima: Comisión Andina de Juristas.

Bipartisan National Commission on Central America. 1984. *Report*. New York: Wiley.

Bonilla, Heraclio, ed. 1991. *Los Andes en la encrucijada: Indios, comunidades y estado en el siglo XIX*. Quito: Libri Mundi.

Bourricaud, François. 1969. *Power and Society in Contemporary Peru*. New York: Praeger.

Boyce, James K., Carlos Acevedo, Deborah Barry, Michael Conroy, Manuel Pastor, Jr., Eva Paus, Hermán Rosa, Alexander Segovia, and Elisabeth Wood. 1995. *Adjustment toward Peace: Economic Policy and Post-war Reconstruction in El Salvador*. San Salvador: United Nations Development Program.

Brandt, Hans-Jurgen. 1987. *Justicia popular*. Lima: Friedrich Naumann Foundation.

Brandt, Hans-Jurgen. 1990. *En nombre de la paz coumunal*. Lima: Friedrich Naumann Foundation.

Browning, D. 1971. *El Salvador: Landscape and Society*. London: Oxford University Press.

Brumm, Nicholas D.S. 1992. "Divergent Models of Public Law in Latin America: A Historical and Prescriptive Analysis." *University of Miami Inter-American Law Review*, 24:1, pp 1-35.

Buscaglia, Edgardo and Pilar Domingo Villegas. 1995. "Impediments to Judicial Reform in Latin America." Paper presented at the Latin American Studies Association meeting.

Caballero, José María. 1981. *Economía agraria de la sierra peruana*. Lima: Instituto de Estudios Peruanos.

Caballero, José María. 1988. *Decentralización y democracia*. 2nd Edition. Lima: CEDYS.

Cappalli, Richard. 1990. "Comparative South American Civil Procedures: The Chilean Perspective." *University of Miami Inter-American Law Review*, 21:2, pp. 239-310.

Caravedo, Baltazar. 1993. *El problema del descentralismo*. Lima: Universidad del Pacífico.

Carothers, Thomas. 1991. *In the Name of Democracy*. Berkeley: University of California Press.

Carranza, Elías, Mario Houed, Luis Paulino Mora, and Eugenio Raúl Zaffaroni. 1983. *El preso sin condena en América Latina*. San Jose, Costa Rica: ILANUD.

Castillo, Fabio. 1996. *Los nuevos jinetes de la cocaína*. Bogota: Oveja Negra.

Catacora González, Manuel. c. 1990. "La reforma del Código de Procedimientos Penales." Unpublished manuscript. Lima.

Catacora González, Manuel, Javier de Belaúnde López de Romaña, Octavio Linares Alencastre, and Hugo Manchego Adrián. 1988. *Nueva estructura del poder judicial.* Lima: EDIMSSA.

Chaplin, David. 1976. *Peruvian Nationalism: A Corporatist Revolution.* New Brunswick: Transaction Books.

Charria Angulo, Alfonso. 1988. *Plebiscito, referéndum, o dictadura?* Bogota: Impresores Interamericanos.

Chetwynd, Eric, John Hatch, Linn Hammergren, Ronald Johnson, Dennis Rondinelli, and Patricia Salinas. 1985. "Integrated Regional Development." Unpublished evaluation prepared for USAID/Lima, June.

Chunga Lamonja, Fermín G. 1986. *La justicia de paz en el Perú.* Lima: Friedrich Naumann Foundation.

Cleaves, Peter and Martin Scurrah. 1980. *Agriculture, Bureaucracy, and Military Government in Peru.* Ithaca: Cornell University Press.

Colombia, Comisión de Racionalización del Gasto y de las Finanzas Públicas. 1996. "El sistema judicial y el gasto público." Santafe de Bogota, October 10.

Colombia, Ministry of Justice. 1991. *La revolución pacífica de la justicia.* Santafe de Bogota.

Comisión Andina de Juristas. 1988a. *Colombia: el derecho a la justicia.* Lima.

Comisión Andina de Juristas. 1988b. *Perú y Chile: Poder judicial y derechos humanos.* Lima

Constable, Pamela and Arturo Valenzuela. 1991. *A Nation of Enemies.* New York: W. W. Norton.

Cooper, H. H. 1968. "A Short History of Peruvian Criminal Procedures and Institutions." *Revista de Derecho y Ciencias Políticas,* 32, pp. 215-267

Cooper, H. H. 1971. "Habeas Corpus in Peru: Myth and Reality." *Cleveland State Law Journal,* 20, pp. 603-616.

Costa Rica, Supreme Court. 1993. *Informe de labores del Presidente de la Corte Suprema de Justicia.* San Jose.

Crabtree, John. 1992. *Peru Under García.* University of Pittsburgh.

Dakolias, Maria. 1995. "A Strategy for Judicial Reform: The Experience in Latin America." *Virginia Journal of International Law,* 36:1, pp. 167-231.

Damaska, Mirjan. 1997. *Evidence Law Adrift.* New Haven: Yale University Press.

de Belaúnde López de Romaña, Javier, ed. 1984. *La administración de justicia en América Latina.* Lima: Consejo Latino Americano de Derecho y Desarrollo

de Belaúnde López de Romaña, Javier, José Dellepiane, Francisco Eguiguren, Carlos Ernesto Giusti, Carlos Montoya Anguerri, Vladimir Paz de la Barra, and Lorenzo Zolezzi. 1996. *Desafíos de la Justicia en el Perú.* Lima: Instituto de Defensa Legal.

de Lima Lopes, José Reinaldo. 1997. "Brazilian Courts and Social Rights: A Case Study." Paper presented at the 1997 meetings of the Latin American Studies Association.

de Soto, Hernando. 1986. *El otro sendero.* Lima: Instituto Libertad y Democracia.

Díaz Rodríguez, Francisco. 1993. "Diez años de Constitución: un balance y una perspectiva. Organo Judicial." San Salvador: CESPAD.

Dix, Robert H. 1987. *The Politics of Colombia.* New York: Praeger.

Domingo, Pilar. 1995. "Democratization without Separation of Powers? The Case of the Mexican Supreme Court." Paper presented at the 1995 meetings of the Latin American Studies Association.

Domingo, Pilar. 1997. "Judicial Independence: The Politics of Supreme Court Judges in Mexico." Paper presented at the 1997 meetings of the Latin American Studies Association.

Drzewieniecki, Joanna. 1995. "Indigenous People, Law, and Politics in Peru." Paper presented at the 1995 meetings of the Latin American Studies Association.

Dugas, John C. 1995. "Structural Theory and Democratization in Colombia: The Role of Social Classes, Civil Society, and the State in the 1991 Constitutional Reform." Paper presented at the 1995 meetings of the Latin American Studies Association.

Eastman, Jorge Mario. 1988. *La reforma constitucional de 1979*. Bogota: Oveja Negra.

Edelman, Marc and Joanne Kenen, ed. 1989. *The Costa Rica Reader*. New York: Grove Weidenfeld.

Eguiguren, P. Francisco, ed. 1987. *La constitución peruana de 1979*. Lima: Editorial Cuzco.

Eguiguren, P. Francisco, Walter Albár, and Samuel Abad. 1991. *Violencia estructural en el Perú: Derecho*. Lima: Asociación Peruana de Estudios e Investigación para la Paz.

Fennell, Phil, Christopher Harding, Nico Jörg, and Bert Swart, eds. 1995. *Criminal Justice in Europe*. Oxford Press.

Fernández León, Whanda. 1996. *Fiscalía: Juez y parte*. Bogota: Librería Profesional.

Ferrandino Tacsan, Alvaro. 1993. "La defensa de oficio en el Perú." Unpublished report for USAID/Peru.

Finkel, Jodi. 1997. "The Politics of Mexico's 1994 Judicial Reform." Paper presented at the Latin American Studies Association meeting.

Flores Polo, P. 1984. *Ministerio Público y Defensor del Pueblo*. Lima: Cultural Cuzco.

Florida International University (FIU). 1987. "La administración de justicia en Honduras." Unpublished study for USAID.

Fruhling, Hugo E. 1993. "Human Rights in Constitutional Order and in Political Practice in Latin America." In *Constitutionalism and Democracy: Transitions in the Contemporary World*, ed. Douglas Greenberg, Stanley N. Katz, Melanie Beth Oliviero, and Steven C. Wheatley, pp. 85-104. London: Oxford University Press.

Fuks, Mario. 1995. "Environment-Related Litigation in Rio de Janeiro: Shaping Frames for a New Social Problem." Paper presented at the 1995 meetings of the Latin American Studies Association.

Galleguillos, Nibaldo H. 1997. "Checks and Balances in New Democracies: The Role of the Judiciary in the Chilean and Mexican Transitions: A Comparative Analysis." Paper presented at 1997 Latin American Studies Association meetings.

Gamarra, Eduardo. 1989. *The System of Justice in Bolivia*. Miami: Center for Administration of Justice, Florida International University.

García Belaúnde, Domingo. 1979. *El habeas corpus en el Perú*. Lima: Universidad Nacional Mayor de San Marcos.

García Rada, Domingo. 1963. "El Poder Judicial en el siglo XX." In *Visión del Perú en el siglo XX*. Lima: Librería Studium.

García Rada, Domingo. 1978. *Memorias de un juez*. Lima: Editorial Andina.

García-Sayán, Diego, ed. 1987. *Derechos humanos y servicios legales en el campo.* Lima: Comisión Andina de Juristas.

García-Sayán, Diego, ed. 1990. *Narcotráfico: Realidades y alternativas.* Lima: Comisión Andina de Juristas.

Gardner, James. 1980. *Legal Imperialism: American Lawyers and Foreign Aid in Latin America.* Madison: University of Wisconsin.

Giraldo Angel, Jaime. 1987a. *Jueces y justicia en Colombia.* Bogota: Instituto SER

Giraldo Angel, Jaime. 1987b. *Reforma de la justicia en Colombia.* Bogota: Instituto SER.

Giraldo Angel, Jaime. 1992. *Reforma constitucional de la justicia.* Bogota: Librería Profesional.

Giraldo, Jaime, Iván Orozco, and Rodrigo Uprimny. 1997. *Justicia y sistema político.* Bogota: Instituto de Estudios Políticos y Relaciones Internacionales, Universidad Nacional.

Gómez Albarello, Juan Gabriel. 1996. "Justicia y democracia en Colombia: en entredicho?" *Análisis Político,* 28, pp. 42-64.

González, Daniel and Ana Garita. 1990. *La multa en los códigos penales latino-americanos.* Buenos Aires: Depalma.

González Oropeza, Manuel. 1996. "The Administration of Justice and the Rule of Law in Mexico." In *Rebuilding the State: Mexico After Salinas,* edited by M. Serrano and V. Bulmer-Thomas, pp. 59-78. London: The Institute of Latin American Studies.

Gootenberg, Paul. 1991. "Population and Ethnicity in Early Republican Peru: Some Revisions." *Latin American Research Review,* 26:3, pp. 109-58.

Gorriti, Gustavo and Sarah Kerr. 1992. "Fujimori's Plot." *New York Review of Books, 39:12,* June 25, pp. 18-22.

Graham, Carol. 1992. *Peru's APRA.* Boulder: Lynn Reiner.

Grynszpan, Mario. 1997. "Democratização e acesso diferencial à Justiça no Brasil." Paper presented at the 1997 Latin American Studies Association meeting.

Gutiérrez, Carlos José. 1979. *El funcionamiento del sistema jurídico.* San Jose, Costa Rica: Juricentro.

Hammergren, Linn. 1983. *Development and the Politics of Administrative Reform.* Boulder: Westview.

Hansen, Gary and Harry Blair. 1995. *Weighing in on the Scales of Justice.* USAID, Center for Information, Documentation and Evaluation.

Hartlyn, Jonathan. 1988. *The Politics of Coalition Rule in Colombia.* New York: Cambridge University Press.

Herrán, María Teresa. 1994. *El Fiscal: la dualidad de la imagen.* Bogota: Tercer Mundo.

Hilbink, Lisa. 1995. "What is the Role of the Judiciary in a Democracy? The Judicial Reform Debate in Chile and Proposals for Future Research." Paper presented at the 1995 Latin American Studies Association meeting.

Hinestrosa, Fernando. 1987. *La administración de justicia en Colombia.* Bogota: Universidad Externado de Colombia.

Howell, Katarina. 1995. "Politicized Justice? Judicial Review in Democratizing Brazil." Paper presented at the 1995 meetings of the Latin American Studies Association.

Hurtado Pozo, José. 1979. *La ley importada.* Lima: CEDYS.

Hurtado Pozo, José. 1980. *La nueva constitución y el derecho penal.* Lima.

Hurtado Pozo, José. 1984. *El Ministerio Público.* Lima: EDDLI.
Inter-American Development Bank. 1993. *Justicia y desarrollo en América Latina y el Caribe.* Washington D.C.
Israel Olivera, Raúl and Manuel Israel Olivera. 1985. *Corrupción en el Poder Judicial y el Ministerio Público.* Lima: Editorial San Marcos.
Jacob, Herbert, Erhard Blankenburg, Herbert M. Kritzer, Doris Marie Provine, and Joseph Sanders. 1996. *Courts, Law, and Politics in Comparative Perspective.* New Haven: Yale University.
Joint Group for the Investigation of Illegal Armed Groups with Political Motivation in El Salvador. 1994. *Report.* San Salvador.
Kline, Harvey F. 1988. "Colombia: Modified Two-Party and Elitist Politics." In *Latin American Politics and Development,* 2nd edition, edited by Howard Wiarda and Harvey Kline, pp 249-269. Boulder, Colorado: Westview.
Lawyers Committee for Human Rights. 1989. *Underwriting Injustice: AID and El Salvador's Judicial Reform Program.* New York.
Lawyers Committee for Human Rights. 1993. *El Salvador's Negotiated Revolution: Prospects for Legal Reform.* New York.
Leal Buitrago, Francisco, ed. 1996. *Tras la huellas de la crisis política.* Bogota: Tercer Mundo.
Lindo, H. 1990. *Weak Foundations: The Economy of El Salvador in the Nineteenth Century.* Berkeley: University of California Press.
Llobet Rodríguez, Javier. 1993. *La reforma procesal penal.* San Jose, Costa Rica: Corte Suprema de Justicia, Escuela Judicial.
Long, Norman and Bryan Roberts, ed. 1978. *Peasant Cooperation and Capitalist Expansion in Central Peru.* Austin: University of Texas Press.
López Maya, Margarita. 1995. "Por qué no avanza la reforma constitucional en Venezuela?" Paper presented at the Latin American Studies Association meeting.
Lowenthal, Abraham, ed. 1975. *The Peruvian Experiment: Continuity and Change under Military Rule.* Princeton University Press.
Mackinson, Gladys and Mabel Goldstein. 1993. *La magistratura de Buenos Aires.* Buenos Aires: Literaria Jurídica.
Maier, Julio, Luis Torello, Raúl Tavolar, William Davis, Cristián Riego, Alberto Binder, and Olmán Arguedas. 1993. *Reformas procesales en América Latina: la oralidad en los procesos.* Santiago: Corporación de Promoción Universitaria.
Marchego Adrián, Hugo, ed. 1989. *Problemas de la justicia agraria en el Perú.* Lima: Editorial Cuzco.
Marchena Gómez, Manuel. 1992. *El Ministerio Fiscal: su pasado y su futuro.* Madrid: Marcial Pons.
Martín Pallín, José Antonio. 1989. *Perú: La Independencia del Poder Judicial.* Geneva: Centro para la Independencia de Jueces y Abogados.
Mauceri, Philip. 1989. "Violence and State Response in Peru." Paper presented at the 1989 meetings of the Latin American Studies Assocation.
Maxfield, Sylvia. 1992. "The International Political Economy of Bank Nationalization: Mexico in Comparative Perspective." *Latin American Research Review,* 27:1, pp. 75-104.
McClintock, Cynthia. 1981. *Peasant Cooperatives and Political Change in Peru.* Princeton University Press.

McClintock, Cynthia. 1984. "Why Peasants Rebel: The Case of Peru's Sendero Luminoso," *World Politics*, 27:1, pp. 48-84.

McClintock, Cynthia and Abraham Lowenthal. 1983. *The Peruvian Experiment Reconsidered*. Princeton University Press.

McConnell, Shelley. 1995. "Democracy in Balance: Evolving Relationships Between the Branches of State in Nicaragua since 1990." Paper presented at the 1995 meetings of the Latin American Studies Association.

Mejía Mori, Beatriz, ed. 1987. *La justicia de paz en el pueblo*. Lima: Friedrich Naumann Foundation.

Merryman, John Henry. 1985. *The Civil Law Tradition: An Introduction to the Legal Systems of Western Europe and Latin America*, 2nd Edition. Stanford: Stanford University Press.

Merryman, John Henry and David S. Clark. 1973. *Comparative Law: Western European and Latin American Systems*. New York: Bobbs-Merrill.

Mixán Mass, Florencia. 1986. *Juicio oral*. Lima: Marsol.

Monroy Gálvez, Juan. 1967. *Temas de proceso civil*. Lima: Studium.

Mudge, Arthur, Steve Flanders, Miguel Sánchez, Adolfo Saenz, and Gilberto Trujillo. 1988. "Evaluation of the Judicial Reform Project, No. 519-0296." Unpublished study for USAID/El Salvador.

Mudge, Arthur, Robert Ewigleben, and Robert Page. 1993. "Evaluación del proyecto de administración de justicia en el Perú." Unpublished study for USAID/Peru, Checchi and Company, Washington D.C.

Mudge, Arthur, Tirza Rivera, Mary Said, and Luis Alonso Roa. 1996. "Judicial Reform II Evaluation." Final draft of study prepared for USAID/El Salvador, Management Systems International.

Murray, Daniel E. 1987. "A Comparative Study of Peruvian Criminal Procedure." *University of Miami Law Review*, 21, pp. 607-649.

Nader, Laura. 1990. *Harmony Ideology: Justice and Control in a Zapotec Mountain Village*. Stanford University Press.

National Center for State Courts (NCSC). 1993. "An Assessment of the Office of the Public Defender in El Salvador." Unpublished study for USAID/El Salvador.

Navarro, Sonia, ed. 1992. *La justicia constitucional: una promesa de democracia*. San Jose, Costa Rica: ILANUD.

Nemoga Soto, Gabriel Ricardo. 1988. *El estado y la administración de justicia en Colombia*. Bogota: Ministry of Justice.

Nijboer, J. F. 1993. "Common Law Tradition in Evidence Scholarship Observed from a Continental Perspective." *The American Journal of Comparative Law*, 41:2, pp. 299-338.

North, L. 1985. *Bitter Grounds: The Roots of Revolt in El Salvador*. Westport, Connecticut: Lawrence Hill.

Núñez Palomino, Pedro Germán. 1996. *Derecho y comunidades campesinas en el Perú, 1969-1988*. Lima: Centro de Estudios Regionales Andinos.

Nyrop, Richard F., ed. 1981. *Peru: a Country Study*. Washington: American University.

Oliva, Roberto, José María Méndez, and Mario Antonio Solano. 1991. *Reformas constitucionales del órgano judicial*. San Salvador: CENITEC.

Olivera Díaz, Guillermo. 1986. *El proceso penal peruano*. Lima.

332

Orozco Abad, Iván. 1995. "Política de seguridad y política criminal en la administración Gaviria." *Política Criminal* Bogota. 5, pp 55-86.
Orrego Moreno, Alfonso. c. 1985a. *La prueba en el proceso penal.* Lima: Cultural Cuzco.
Orrego Moreno, Alfonso. c. 1985b. *Elementos de derecho procesal penal.* Lima: Ediciones Jurídicas Sociales.
Palmer, David Scott. 1986. "Rebellion in Rural Peru: The Origins and Evolution of Sendero Luminoso." *Comparative Politics*, 18:2, pp. 127-46.
Palmer, David Scott. 1991. "Research on Drug Trafficking in Peru." Unpublished paper for State of Art Conference on Drug Trafficking Research, University of Miami, March 11-14.
Palmer, David Scott, ed. 1992. *Shining Path of Peru.* New York: St. Martin's Press.
Pareja Pflucker, Piedad. 1989. *Justicia y Constitución.* Lima: Centro de Estudios Peruanos.
Pásara, Luis. 1978. *Reforma agraria: Derecho y conflicto.* Lima: Instituto de Estudios Peruanos.
Pásara, Luis. 1982. *Jueces, justicia y poder en el Perú.* Lima: CEDYS.
Pásara, Luis. 1988. *Derecho y sociedad en el Perú.* Lima: Virrey.
Pásara, Luis and Jorge Parodi, ed. 1988. *Democracia, sociedad y gobierno en el Perú.* Lima: CEDYS.
Pastor, Manuel J. and Carol Wise. 1992. "Peruvian Economic Policy in the 1980s: From Orthodoxy to Heterodoxy and Back." *Latin American Research Review*, 27:2, pp. 83-118.
Patrón Faura, Pedro and Pedro Patrón Bedoya. 1985. *Nuevo derecho administrativo en el Perú.* Lima: Studium.
Peña Cabrera, Raúl. 1991. *Nuevo Código Penal y leyes complementarias.* Lima: A.F.A. Editores Importadores.
Pérez-Brignoli, Héctor. 1989. *A Brief History of Central America*, translated by Ricardo B. Sawrey and Susana Stettri de Sawrey. Berkeley, Calif.: University of California Press.
Pérez Perdomo, Rogelio. 1988. "La administración de justicia en Venezuela: Evaluación y alternativas." Unpublished paper, reproduced by ILANUD, Costa Rica.
Peru, Ministry of Justice. 1981. *Esquema para política penitenciaria.* Unpublished document.
Peru, Ministry of Interior. 1985. *Estudio de la criminalidad en Lima Metropolitana y Callao: Primeras soluciones*, 1983-4. Unpublished document.
Peru, Senate, Comisión Especial Sobre las Causas de la Violencia y Alternativas de Pacificación en el Perú. 1989. *Violencia y pacificación.* Lima: DESCO.
Popkin, Margaret. 1994. *Justice Delayed: The Slow Pace of Judicial Reform in El Salvador.* Cambridge, Mass.: Hemispheric Initiatives.
Prado Saldarrieaga, Víctor. 1989. *El tráfico de drogas en el Perú.* Lima: Cultural Cuzco.
Prado Saldarrieaga, Víctor. 1990. *Derecho penal y política.* Lima: EDDILI.
Proyecto Reforma Judicial II. 1994. *La realidad de la justicia salvadoreña.* San Salvador: Checchi and Company.
Quiroga León, Anibal, ed. 1990. *Sobre la jurisdicción constitucional.* Lima: Pontífica Universidad Católica.
Ramírez, Ramón. 1985. *Justicia y política.* Lima: Instituto de Estudios Jurídicos.

Ramírez, Ramón. 1991.*Código de Procedimientos Penales.* Lima: Empresa Editorial Latina.

Reid, Michael. 1985. *Peru: Paths to Poverty.* London: Latin American Bureau.

Revilla, Ana Teresa and Jorge Price. 1991. *La Administración de la justicia informal.* Lima: Fundación M. J. Bustamante de la Fuente.

Rico, Jose María. 1993. "Los concejos de la magistratura: análisis crítico y perspectivas para América Latina." Florida International University, Center for Administration of Justice.

Rico, Jose María and Luis Salas, ed. n.d. "Latin American Codes of Criminal Procedures." Florida International University, Center for the Administration of Justice.

Rico, Jose María, Luis Salas, Enrique Gutiérrez, and Carlos Cruz. 1988. *La justicia penal en Costa Rica.* San Jose, Costa Rica: EDUCA.

Roseberry, William, Lowell Gudmundson, and Mario Samper Kutschbach. 1995. *Coffee, Society, and Power in Latin America.* Baltimore: Johns Hopkins University.

Rosenn, Keith S. 1986. "Civil Procedure in Brazil." *The American Journal of Comparative Law,* 34:3, pp. 487-525.

Rosenn, Keith S. 1987. "The Protection of Judicial Independence in Latin America." *University of Miami Inter-American Law Review,* 19:1, pp. 1-35.

Rosenn, Keith S. 1995. "Federalism in the Americas in Comparative Perspective." *University of Miami Inter-American Law Review,* 26:1, pp. 1-50.

Rospiglioli, Fernando. 1989. "Perspectivas del proceso democrático peruano." Unpublished paper for the 1989 meetings of the Latin American Studies Association.

Rospiglioli, Fernando. 1991. "Perú: El peligro de la desintegración." In *Crísis y transición en los países andinos,* Diego Cardono, ed. Bogota: Fondo Editorial CEREC.

Rubio, Marcial and Enrique Bernales. 1988. *Constitución y sociedad política.* Lima: Mesa Redonda.

Ruiz-Eldredge, Alberto. 1980. *La constitución comentada.* Lima: Atlántida.

Russell, P. 1984. *El Salvador in Crisis.* Texas: Colorado River Press.

Sagasteguí Urteaga, Pedro. 1996. *Teoría general del proceso judicial.* Lima: Editorial San Marcos.

Salas, Luis and José María Rico. 1989a. *La justicia penal en Guatemala.* San Jose, Costa Rica: EDUCA.

Salas, Luis and José María Rico. 1989b. *La justicia penal en Honduras.* San Jose, Costa Rica: EDUCA.

Salas, Luis and José María Rico. 1993. "Administration of Justice in Latin America." Florida International University.

Salgado, Hernán, ed. 1988. *La reforma de la Constitución.* Quito: Jurispuce.

Santana, Roberto. 1995. *Ciudadanos en la etnicidad: Los indios en la política o la política de los indios.* Quito: Biblioteca Abya-Yala.

Schmidt, Gregory D. 1992. "Understanding the Fujimori Tsunami: Partisan Competition and Electoral Rules in the 1990 Peruvian General Election." Paper presented at the 1992 meetings of the Latin American Studies Association.

Schwank Durán, John and M. Guisela Mayén. 1992. "Investigación básica sobre derecho consuetudinario en tres comunidades mayahablantes de Guatemala." Guatemala: Asociación de Investigación y Estudios Sociales ASIES.

Seligmann, Linda. 1995. *Between Reform and Revolution: Political Struggles in the Peruvian Andes, 1969-1991.* Stanford University Press.

Sequeiros Vargas, Iván. 1996. *Análisis y comentarios a la Ley Orgánica del Poder Judicial*. Lima: Grijley.

Serrano, Monica and Victor Bulmer-Thomas, eds. 1996. *Rebuilding the State: Mexico After Salinas*. London: Institute of Latin American Studies.

Sheahan, John. 1989. "Reducing Poverty in Latin America: Markets, Democracy and Social Choice." Paper presented at the 1989 meetings of the Latin American Studies Association.

Shodt, David. 1991. "Ecuador Justice Sector Assessment: Social Soundness Analysis." Florida International University.

Sierra, María Teresa. 1995. "Indian Rights and Customary Law in Mexico: a Study of the Najas in the Sierra de Puebla." *Law and Society*, 29:2, pp. 227-254.

Smith, Gordon. 1996. *Reforming the Russian Legal System*. Cambridge: Cambridge University Press.

Smith, Jennifer. 1992. "U.S. Peruvian Drug Relations." Paper for State of Art Conference on Drug Trafficking, University of Miami, March 11-14.

Smith, Ralph, Roderico Segura, Edgardo Derbes, Guillermo Díaz, Francisco Dúeñas, Juan Alberto Martínez, Sharon Philips, and Gabriel Píloña. 1990. "Analysis of the Public Ministry of Guatemala." Unpublished study for USAID/Guatemala, Checchi and Company, Washington D.C.

Sojo Picado, Guillermo. n.d. *El recurso de casación penal por violación de la ley*. San Jose, Costa Rica: Investigaciones Jurídicas.

Solís Luis G. and Richard Wilson. 1991. *Political Transition and the Administration of Justice in Nicaragua*. Miami: Center for the Administration of Justice, Florida International University.

Spence, Jack and George Vickers. 1994. "A Negotiated Revolution? A Two Year Progress Report on the Salvadoran Peace Accords." Cambridge, Mass: Hemispheric Initiatives.

Spence, Jack, George Vickers, and David Dye. 1995. "The Salvadoran Peace Accords and Democratization: A Three Year Progress Report and Recommendations." Cambridge, Mass: Hemispheric Initiatives.

Squella, Agustín. 1992. *La cultura jurídica chilena*. Santiago, Chile: Corporación de Promoción Universitaria.

Starn, Orin. 1992. "New Literature on Peru's Sendero Luminoso." *Latin American Research Review*, 27: , pp. 212-226.

Stavenhagen, Rodolfo and Diego Iturralde, ed. 1990. *Entre la ley y la costumbre: el derecho consuetudinario indígena en América Latina*. Mexico: Instituto Indigenista Interamericano.

Stokes, Susan C. 1995. "Economic Reform and Public Opinion in Peru, 1990-95." Paper presented at the 1995 meetings of the Latin American Studies Association.

Stotzky, Irwin P., ed. 1993. *Transition to Democracy in Latin America: The Role of the Judiciary*. Boulder: Westview.

Strier, Franklin. 1994. *Reconstructing Justice*. Chicago: University of Chicago Press.

Tarzona-Sevillano, Gabriela. 1990. *Sendero Luminoso and the Threat of Naroterrorism*. Washington: Center for Strategic and International Studies.

Tate, C. Neal and Torbjörn Vallinder, eds. 1995. *The Global Expansion of Judicial Power*. New York: New York University.

Thome, Joseph. 1993. "Administration of Justice in Latin America: A Survey of AID Funded Programs in Argentina and Uruguay." Development Associates, Inc.: Arlington, Virginia.

Thorp, Rosemary and Geoffrey Bertram. 1978. *Peru 1890-1977: Growth and Policy in an Open Economy*: New York: Macmillan.

Ulloa González, Mirtha and Macarena Vargas. 1995. "Políticas públicas y necesidades de justicia de los sectores pobres." *Estudios Sociales* Chile. 83:1, pp. 51-98.

Universidad Católica del Perú and Escuela de Administración de Negocios (ESAN). 1991. "Evaluación del sistema judicial peruana." Unpublished report presented to USAID/Peru, September.

United Nations Latin American Institute for Crime Prevention and the Protection of the Delinquent (ILANUD). 1991. *Necesidades de capacitación de los jueces penales en Ecuador*. San Jose, Costa Rica.

United States General Accounting Office (GAO). 1992. "Foreign Assistance: Police Training and Assistance." GAO/NSIAD-92-118.

United States General Accounting Office (GAO). 1993. "Foreign Assistance: Promoting Judicial Reform to Strengthen Democracies." GAO/NSIAD-93-194.

Urban, Greg and Joel Sherzer. 1991. *Nation-States and Indians in Latin America*. Austin: University of Texas Press.

Valdivia Pezo, Ernesto. c. 1986. *Enseñanza de la práctica de derecho y realidad social*. Lima: Editorial Cuzco.

Valenzuela, Eugenio, ed. 1991. *Proposiciones para la reforma judicial*. Santiago: Centro de Estudios Públicos.

Vargas Llosa, Mario. 1990. *Contra viento y marea*. Barcelona: Seix Barral.

Vargas Llosa, Mario. 1993. *El pez en el agua*. Barcelona: Seix Barral.

Vega Torres, José Martín. 1990. *Fuerzas policiales, sociedad y constitución*. Lima: Instituto de Defensa Legal.

Verbitsky, Horacio. 1993. *Hacer la Corte*. Buenos Aires: Planeta.

Vescovi, Enrique and María del Carmen Rueco. 1991. "Los primeros resultados de la reforma de la justicia en Uruguay: un balance a los dieciocho meses de la entrada en vigencia del Código General del Proceso." Montevideo: Editorial IDEA.

Villaba, Enriqueta Davis. n.d. "Situación actual del sistema de administración de justicia en Panamá 1990-1991." Unpublished study for USAID/Panama.

Washington Office on Latin America (WOLA). 1990. "The Administration of Justice Program in Latin America."

Weaver, Frederick Sturton. 1994. *Inside the Volcano*. San Francisco: Westview.

Webb, Richard. 1977. *Government Policy and the Distribution of Income in Peru, 1963-1973*. Harvard University Press.

Webb, Richard and Graciela Fernández Baca. 1991. *Perú en números 1991*. Lima: Cuanto S.A.

White, Alistair. 1987. *El Salvador*. San Salvador: UCA.

Wiener, Raul A. 1996. *Fujimori: el elegido del pueblo*. Lima: Graphos 100.

Williams, Jaime, Leopoldo Schiffin, and Marco Sarmiento. 1991. "Estrategia Proyecto de Reforma Judicial." Unpublished report for USAID/El Salvador, Checchi and Company, Washington D.C.

Wilson, Richard. 1993. "Report and Recommendations on the Operation of the Instituto de Defensoría de Oficio." Unpublished report for USAID/Panama.
Woy-Hazleton, Sandra and William A. Hazleton. 1989. "Political Violence and the Future of Peruvian Democracy." Paper presented at the 1989 meeting of the Latin American Studies Association.
Youngers, Colette. 1992. "Peru Under Scrutiny: Human Rights and U.S. Drug Policy." WOLA Briefing Series: Issues in International Drug Policy, #5, January.
Zaffaroni, Eugenio Raúl. 1987. *Manual de Derecho Penal*. Buenos Aires: EDIAR.
Zeledón, Ricardo. 1982. *Proceso agrario comparado en América Latina*. San Jose, Costa Rica: Universidad de Costa Rica.
Zeledón, Ricardo. 1987. *Código Civil y realidad*. San Jose, Costa Rica: Alma Mater.
Zolezzi Ibarcena, Lorenzo. n.d. "Relevancia social del juez civil, modernización del proceso y capacitación judicial." Unpublished manuscript.
Zweigert, K. and H. Kotz. 1987. *An Introduction to Comparative Law*. 2nd revised edition. Oxford: Clarendon Press.

Legislation

[Note: date given for legislation corresponds to its initial promulgation. No attempt has been made to document the often substantial amendments, nor has an effort been made to cite all of the decree laws mentioned in the text]

Colombia, Constitución Política. 1991.
Colombia, Código de Procedimiento Penal. 1991.
Colombia, Decreto No. 2067, September 4, 1991, Régimen procedimental de la Corte Constitucional.
Colombia, Decreto No. 2653 November 25, 1991, Concejo de la Judicatura.
Colombia, Decreto No. 2699, November 30, 1991, Estatuto Orgánica de la Fiscalía General de la Nación.
Costa Rica, Constitución Política. 1949.
Costa Rica, Código Penal. 1970.
Costa Rica, Código de Procedimientos Penales. 1974 and 1996.
Costa Rica, Ley de la Jurisdicción Constitucional. 1989.
Costa Rica, Ley Orgánica del Poder Judicial. 1993.
El Salvador, Código de Familia. 1994.
El Salvador, Constitución Política. 1983.
El Salvador, Ley del Menor Infractor. 1994.
El Salvador, Ley Orgánica Judicial. 1984.
El Salvador, Ley Procesal de Familia. 1994.
El Salvador, Proyecto del Código Penal. 1994.
El Salvador, Proyecto del Código Procesal Penal. 1995.
Peru, Código Penal. 1924 and 1990.
Peru, Código de Procedimientos Penales 1939 and 1991.
Peru, Constitución Política del Perú 1979 and 1993.
Peru, Ley Orgánica del Ministerio Publico 1981.
Peru, Ley Orgánica del Poder Judicial 1963 and 1991.
Peru, Proyecto del Código de Procedimientos Penales. c. 1995.

Index

Formalism (*see* legal formalism)
Fujimori, Alberto
  criticism of judiciary, 3, 60, 282
  compared to military government, 3,
    175, 197–198, 282–284
  economic policies, 8–9, 41, 59–60
  neglect of justice sector, 165, 176–178
  judicial reform strategy, 290
  origins of *autogolpe*, 59–60
  origins of post–1994 reforms, 180–182
  police and prison reform, 284
  reelection, 61

Galán, Luis Carlos, 240
García, Alán, 58, 69, 73–74, 85, 98,
  99, 150–151, 154–155, 282–283
Gaviria, César, 240–241
Gómez Hurtado, Alvaro, 301
Guatemala, 7, 22, 26, 84, 119, 275,
  289
Gutiérrez, Carlos José, 229–230
Guzmán, Abimael, 60–61, 154

Habeas corpus, 95, 139, 148, 150, 214,
  230, 244–245
Haiti, 191
Haye de la Torre, Victor, 58
Honduras, 4, 14, 22, 128
Human Rights Ombudsman
  general, 6, 12, 311
  Colombia, 244
  El Salvador, 207, 208, 215
  Peru, 184, 193, 285–286, 288

ILANUD (United Nations Institute for
  Crime Prevention and Treatment of
  the Delinquent), 224
Informal justice institutions, 11, 44, 71,
  140, 286
Inquisitorial procedures, 15–17, 21, 72,
  266
Instrucción, 85–86, 118–125, 214
Inter–American Development Bank
  (IDB), 181–184, 218–228, 232, 247

Judicial activism, 29, 31, 164
Judicial appointments

general, 298 (table), 314 (table), 317
  Costa Rica, 27–28, 137, 223, 228
  Colombia, 27–28, 234, 235, 279
  El Salvador, 210, 213, 217
  Peru, 70–71, 80–81, 93–94, 97–98,
    137, 138, 149–150, 282–283
  politicization of, 17–19, 28, 149–150,
    212, 267, 278–279
Judicial budgets
  Colombia, 236, 238, 265
  general, 22, 28, 77, 222, 232, 265,
    275–276, 298 (table), 314 (table), 317
  Peru, 104, 145, 147–148, 186, 269,
    290
Judicial career
  Costa Rica, 227
  general, 18, 74, 138, 187–188, 268,
    298 (table), 314 (table)
Judicial councils, 12–14, 22, 30–31, 94,
  268, 298 (table), 314 (table)
Judicial independence, 9, 18–19, 28,
  84, 136–137, 154, 194, 196–197, 235,
  267, 269, 290, 299, 309–310, 312–313
Judicial Organic Law
  definition, 116
  history of 1991 law in Peru, 161–162
Judicial outreach, 313, 314 (table)
Judicial ratifications, Peru, 49, 76, 79,
  138, 144, 147–150, 179, 282–283
Judicial restraint, 139
Judicial review
  Colombia, 247
  Costa Rica, 222, 225, 229–232
  general, 6, 22, 27–28, 242, 298
    (table), 300–301, 314 (table)
  See also Constitutional courts
Juez de ejecución, 155
Juez de instrucción, 85–87, 119–123, 213
Justice system
  definition, 11–12

Land
  litigation over, 51, 140–141
  reform in Peru, 54, 55, 140–141, 317
Latin American model code, 226
Law and development, 157–161, 224
Law determination, 9, 10